LIBRARY OF HEBREW BIBLE/ OLD TESTAMENT STUDIES

708

Formerly Journal for the Study of the Old Testament Supplement Series

Editors
Claudia V. Camp, Texas Christian University, USA
Andrew Mein, Durham University, UK

Founding Editors
David J. A. Clines, Philip R. Davies and David M. Gunn

Editorial Board
Alan Cooper, Steed Davidson, Susan Gillingham, John Goldingay,
Norman K. Gottwald, James E. Harding, John Jarick, Tracy Lemos,
Carol Meyers, Daniel L. Smith-Christopher, Francesca Stavrakopoulou,
James W. Watts

THE BOOK OF KINGS AND EXILIC IDENTITY

1 and 2 Kings as a Work of Political Historiography

Nathan Lovell

LONDON • NEW YORK • OXFORD • NEW DELHI • SYDNEY

T&T CLARK
Bloomsbury Publishing Plc
50 Bedford Square, London, WC1B 3DP, UK
1385 Broadway, New York, NY 10018, USA
29 Earlsfort Terrace, Dublin 2, Ireland

BLOOMSBURY, T&T CLARK and the T&T Clark logo
are trademarks of Bloomsbury Publishing Plc

First published in Great Britain 2021
This paperback edition published in 2022

Copyright © Nathan Lovell, 2021

Nathan Lovell has asserted his right under the Copyright, Designs and Patents Act, 1988, to be identified as Author of this work.

Cover design: Charlotte James

For legal purposes the Acknowledgements on p. ix constitute an extension of this copyright page.

All rights reserved. No part of this publication may be reproduced or transmitted in any form or by any means, electronic or mechanical, including photocopying, recording, or any information storage or retrieval system, without prior permission in writing from the publishers.

Bloomsbury Publishing Plc does not have any control over, or responsibility for, any third-party websites referred to or in this book. All internet addresses given in this book were correct at the time of going to press. The author and publisher regret any inconvenience caused if addresses have changed or sites have ceased to exist, but can accept no responsibility for any such changes.

A catalogue record for this book is available from the British Library.

Library of Congress Control Number: 2020949132

ISBN: HB: 978-0-5676-9532-1
PB: 978-0-5676-9856-8
ePDF: 978-0-5676-9533-8

Series: Library of Hebrew Bible/Old Testament Studies, ISSN 2513-8758, volume 708

Typeset by: Trans.form.ed SAS

To find out more about our authors and books visit www.bloomsbury.com and sign up for our newsletters.

לשירי אביגיל
My song and my joy

וליצחק
My laughter

Contents

List of Figures and Tables	xi
List of Abbreviations	xiii
Preface	xvii

Chapter 1
KINGS AS POLITICAL HISTORIOGRAPHY 1
  1.1. Introduction 1
  1.2. Method and Previous Work 9
  1.3. Challenges to Reading Kings as Political Historiography 17
      1.3.1. The Literary Context of Kings and DtrH 18
      1.3.2. The Historical Context of Kings 28
      1.3.3. Summary and Synopsis of the Present Work 38

Chapter 2
THE NARRATIVE STRATEGY OF KINGS 40
  2.1. The Challenge of Structuring Kings 40
  2.2. Juxtaposition and Meaning: The Aborted Attack on Moab 43
  2.3. The Literary Structure of Kings 48
      2.3.1. Narrative Arcs in Kings: The Word of God and Its Fulfilment   48
      2.3.2. Kings as Narrative Intercalation 50
      2.3.3. The Plot: Inner and Outer Kings 59
      2.3.4. Supporting Evidence 64
  2.4. Conclusions: The Narrative Strategy of Kings 71

Chapter 3
COVENANT: WHAT IS ISRAEL? 74
  3.1. The Mosaic Covenant in Kings 74
  3.2. The Covenant as Destiny: A Framework for Political Identity 75
      3.2.1. Deuteronomy and Political Identity 75
      3.2.2. David within the Covenant 78
      3.2.3. The Covenant and Repentance: Josiah's Reforms 85
      3.2.4. Covenant, Grace, and Destiny 87
  3.3. The Covenant within the Historiography of Kings:
      Political Redefinition 88
      3.3.1. Conquest: Solomon's Golden Age 91

3.3.2. Conflict: Elijah's Struggle for the Soul of Israel	98
3.3.3. Crisis: The Assyrian Dark Ages	103
3.3.4. Why the Exile? Manasseh as Culmination	111
3.4. Conclusions	114

Chapter 4

NATIONHOOD: WHO IS ISRAEL?

	116
4.1. Nationhood: The Name 'Israel'	116
4.1.1. The United Monarchy	118
4.1.2. Judah	119
4.1.3. Both Peoples, but Neither Kingdom	124
4.2. Israelite Boundary Markers and the Nations: The Resettlement of 2 Kings 17	128
4.3. Israel-Incipient: The Preservation of a Remnant	133
4.3.1. The Ahab Cycle: From Baal to Jeroboam's Yahwism	137
4.3.2. The Jeroboam Cycle: From Israel to Judah	145
4.3.3. From Judah to Exile	153
4.4. Conclusions	157

Chapter 5

LAND: WHERE IS ISRAEL?

	159
5.1. The Political Significance of the Promised Land	159
5.2. Centralisation of Worship in the Book of Kings	162
5.2.1. Name Theology, Sacrifice, and Prayer	164
5.2.2. The Shrine (תומב) Theme: Yahweh or Apostasy	167
2.3. Centralisation of Worship: Summary	170
5.3. Israel's Relationship to the Land: The Status of the Land during the Exile	171
5.3.1. The 'Empty Land' Motif and Land Ideology	171
5.3.2. Land, City, and Temple: 2 Kings 24–25	176
5.3.3. The Empty Land in Kings	179
5.4. Yahweh's Relationship to the Land	180
5.4.1. Yahweh Uncontainable: God Over Every Land	182
5.4.2. Yahweh Locatable: Found in a Place	188
5.5. Conclusions	198

Chapter 6

RULE: THE KING AFTER EXILE

	201
6.1. Royal Ideology and the Book of Kings	201
6.2. The Deuteronomic Ideal for Kingship	207
6.2.1. The Exemplary Role of David	207
6.2.2. The Paradigmatic Virtues of the Incomparable Kings	212
6.2.3. Democratisation of Monarchy: Rehoboam and the Role of the 'People of the Land'	220

6.3. The Deuteronomic Moderation of Zion Kingship	224
6.3.1. Solomon's Zion and the ANE Royal Ideal	227
6.3.2. Zion and Ancient Near Eastern Shepherd Kings	232
6.4. The Future of the Monarchy	236
6.4.1. Prophetic and Royal Power: Elisha and the Aramaean Wars	237
6.4.2. The Question of a Messiah	243
6.4.3. Conclusions	247

Chapter 7
CONCLUSIONS:
ISRAEL AMONG THE NATIONS   249
   7.1. The Political Vision of Outer Kings   250
   7.2. The Political Vision of Inner Kings   254

APPENDIX:
PROMISE AND FULFILMENT NARRATIVE ARCS IN KINGS   258

Bibliography   262
Index of References   288
Index of Authors   301
Index of Names and Places   306

Figures and Tables

Figures

2.1	The Narrative Arcs in Kings	52
2.2	Regnal Formulae in Kings	54
2.3	Regnal Formulae, Inner and Outer Kings	57
2.4	Narrative Arcs, Inner and Outer Kings	58
4.1	The Ahab Remnant Cycle	138
4.2	The Jeroboam Remnant Cycle	146
4.3	The Judah to Exile Remnant Cycle	154
5.1	Land in Kings	178
5.2	Land and Yahweh's Domain in Kings	199

Table

1.1	Parallels between 3 Kgdms 2:35*a-o* and MT 1 Kings	36
2.1	The Narrative Pace of Kings	56
2.2	The Pattern of Alternation in Outer Kings	66
2.3	The Pattern of Alternation in Inner Kings	68
3.1	The Intertextuality between Manasseh's Sin and the Sins Ascribed to Various Other Kings of Judah and Israel, as well as the Narrative Précis of 2 Kgs 17.6-20	113
4.1	The Title 'Israel' in Kings	117
4.2	The Three Judgment Cycles in Kings, Leading to the Remnant Theology of the Book	136
4.3	Allusions to Israel's Various Historical Eras in the Narrative Précis of 2 Kgs 17.7-20	149
5.1	The Two-Stage Exile of 2 Kings 24–25	176
5.2	Inner Kings' Narrative Settings Outside of Israel	181
5.3	Intertextuality between 2 Kings 19, 1 Kings 8 and Deuteronomy 4	187
5.4	The Function of the Temple in Solomon's Prayer	192
5.5	The (Non-Military) Miracles Performed by Elisha	195
6.1	Interactions between a Prophet and the King in Inner Kings	237

ABBREVIATIONS

Primary Sources

α	Aquila
𝔊*	The 'original' text of the Septuagint
𝔊°	The Old Greek translation
𝔊ᴸ	The Lucianic tradition of the LXX
𝔏	Vetus Latina
LXX / 𝔊	Septuagint
MT	Masoretic Text
σ	Symmachus
𝔖	Peshitta translation, in Syriac
θ	Theodotion
𝔗	Targum

Journals, Reference Works, and Series

AB	Anchor Bible
ABR	*Australian Biblical Review*
AIL	Ancient Israel and its Literature
AJBI	*Annual of the Japanese Bible Institute*
AOTC	Abingdon Old Testament Commentaries
ATD	Das Alte Testament Deutsch
AUSS	*Andrews University Seminary Studies*
AYBD	*Anchor Yale Bible Dictionary*. Edited by David N. Freedman. New Haven, CT: Yale University Press, 1992.
BA	*Biblical Archaeologist*
BASOR	*Bulletin of the American Schools of Oriental Research*
BBB	*Bulletin de bibliographie biblique*
BETL	Bibliotheca ephemeridum theologicarum lovaniensium
BHS	*Biblia Hebraica Stuttgartensia*
Bib	*Biblica*
BibInt	*Biblical Interpretation*
BSac	*Bibliotheca Sacra*
BTCB	Brazos Theological Commentary on the Bible
CBQ	*Catholic Biblical Quarterly*
CBQMS	Catholic Biblical Quarterly Monograph Series

CBR	*Currents in Biblical Research*
ConB	Coniectanea biblica
COS	*The Context of Scripture: Canonical Compositions, Monumental Inscriptions, and Archival Documents from the Biblical World.* Edited by William W. Hallo and K. Lawson Younger Jr. 3 vols. Leiden: Brill, 1997–2002.
DBI	*Dictionary of Biblical Imagery.* Edited by Leland Ryken et al. Downers Grove, IL: IVP, 1998.
DOTH	*Dictionary of the Old Testament: Historical Books.* Edited by Bill T. Arnold and H. G. M. Williamson. Downers Grove, IL: IVP, 2005.
DOTP	*Dictionary of the Old Testament: Prophets.* Edited by Mark J. Boda and J. Gordon McConville. Downers Grove, IL: IVP Academic, 2012.
ETL	*Ephemerides theologicae lovanienses*
FAT	Forschungen zum Alten Testament
FOTL	Forms of the Old Testament Literature
FRLANT	Forschungen zur Religion und Literatur des Alten und Neuen Testaments
HALOT	*The Hebrew and Aramaic Lexicon of the Old Testament.* Edited by Ludwig Köhler, Walter Baumgartner and Johann J. Stamm. Leiden: Brill, 1994.
HBAI	*Hebrew Bible and Ancient Israel*
HSM	Harvard Semitic Monographs
HTR	*Harvard Theological Review*
HUCA	*Hebrew Union College Annual*
ICC	International Critical Commentary
Int	*Interpretation*
JAJS	Journal of Ancient Judaism, Supplements
JAOS	*Journal of the American Oriental Society*
JAR	*Journal of Anthropological Research*
JBL	*Journal of Biblical Literature*
JBQ	*Jewish Bible Quarterly*
JCS	*Journal of Cuneiform Studies*
JESOT	*Journal for the Evangelical Study of the Old Testament*
JETS	*Journal of the Evangelical Theological Society*
JHebS	*Journal of Hebrew Scriptures*
JNSL	*Journal of Northwest Semitic Languages*
JQR	*Jewish Quarterly Review*
JR	*Journal of Religion*
JRS	*Journal of Religion and Society*
JSJ	*Journal for the Study of Judaism*
JSOT	*Journal for the Study of the Old Testament*
JSOTSup	Journal for the Study of the Old Testament, Supplement Series
JTI	*Journal of Theological Interpretation*
JTS	*Journal of Theological Studies*
LASBF	*Liber Annuus Studii Biblici Franciscani*

NICOT	New International Commentary on the Old Testament
NIDOTTE	*New International Dictionary of Old Testament Theology & Exegesis*. Edited by Willem A. van Gemeren. Grand Rapids, MI: Zondervan, 1997.
NTS	*New Testament Studies*
OBT	Overtures to Biblical Theology
OTE	*Old Testament Essays*
OTL	Old Testament Library
PRSt	*Perspectives in Religious Studies*
SBL	Society of Biblical Literature
SBLDS	Society of Biblical Literature Dissertation Series
SBLSCS	Society of Biblical Literature Septuagint and Cognate Studies
SBT	Studies in Biblical Theology
SBTS	Sources for Biblical and Theological Study
SemeiaSt	Semeia Studies
SHANE	Studies in the History of the Ancient Near East
STDJ	Studies on the Texts of the Desert of Judah
SubBi	Subsidia Biblica
Them	*Themelios*
TSK	*Theologische Studein und Kritiken*
TynB	*Tyndale Bulletin*
VE	*Vox Evangelica*
VT	*Vetus Testamentum*
VTSup	Vetus Testamentum, Supplements
WAWSup	Writings from the Ancient World, Supplement Series
WBC	Word Biblical Commentary
WMANT	Wissenschaftliche Monographien zum Alten und Neuen Testament
WTJ	*Westminster Theological Journal*
ZA	*Zeitschrift für Althebräistik*
ZAW	*Zeitschrift für die alttestamentliche Wissenschaft*
ZDPV	*Zeitschrift des deutschen Palästina-Vereins*

Preface

I once read some excellent advice; that if I were ever to write a book, I should write the book I most wanted to read. That book, I admit, may still be to come. I hope, at least, that I have written something that I would have found useful when I started this project.

As someone embarking on a research project focussing on the book of Kings, I was bewildered. One expects a certain amount of disagreement in the literature. But it seemed that for every explanation of every passage I could find a published counter-example. I sat one day with a virtual pile of about 500 journal articles on my computer desktop, and categorised them by the section of the book they addressed. Was Solomon a hero or a villain? Was the Deuteronomist pro- or anti-monarchic? What should we make of Josiah's untimely death in battle after Hulda's prophecy that they would bury him in peace? Were the Elijah narratives inserted after the book was finished, or did they predate the Deuteronomist? Was there one or two invasions of Judah by the Assyrian forces in Hezekiah's time? Has history judged Jezebel, Ahab, and Jeroboam, the villains of Kings, unfairly? The debates are endless.

But neither was I inclined to accept that what I had before me in my Bible was a mish-mash collection of material that was haphazardly assembled into a history. If being an undergraduate taught me anything about writing, it's that haphazard, mish-mashes don't get marks. They certainly don't evoke the volume of secondary literature that Kings still does, the better part of 3,000 years after it was penned. If it had been truly a mish-mash, Kings would have faded into oblivion long ago.

I came to biblical studies after half a career in Artificial Intelligence. I used to program robots to understand what they were seeing. And so I spent my time perfecting the art of looking at large volumes of computer code and seeing how the different parts, written over time by many people, all come together to play a role in the completed programme. In that field they call it 'systems analysis'. In biblical studies we talk about interpreting the parts by the whole. It's the same thing, really. Computer code has thousands of pieces, hundreds of redactions, and tens of authors.

But in the end it works. It was my strong conviction that Kings does too. And I wanted to understand how.

I hope that this book will help people reading Kings to understand where some of the disputes come from, and why they don't ultimately impact the coherence and logic of what is, I believe, a finely crafted, well thought-out, piece of history writing. I've tried to address many of the scholarly disputes along the way. But it's the big-picture I'm most concerned to communicate. From the moment Nathan engineers Solomon's ascension, till the demise of the kingdom several centuries later, with all the strange intricacies of floating axe-heads and bones that resurrect the dead along the way, Kings works. This book is about how. Kings works as historiography. I believe it works as Scripture too, but that would be a different book.

I owe a special thanks to my family. This is the sixth year in which my wife, Diane, and two children, Shiri and Isaac, have had to endure this project. Shiri is now seven, and Isaac now five, so those who have young families will know how valuable and necessary Diane's support and endless love has been to me. Thank you, Lovell family, for never wavering.

This book began as a PhD project, and I owe a great debt to my two supervisors, Andrew Shead at Moore Theological College in Sydney, and Ian Young at the University of Sydney. I also owe special thanks to Rachelle Gilmour, now at Trinity College in Melbourne, who offered many very helpful suggestions at that stage of the project. I feel keenly how much they have each enriched my work in different ways. There are many others to thank as well – too many to mention by name. So: to those who reviewed or marked my work; and to those who proof-read chapters; to those who listened to my conference presentations and offered erudite suggestions; and to those who sat in my classes prodding me with questions; to those who have endured my sermons; and to my colleagues and friends at George Whitefield College in South Africa – thank you all.

Finally, to my friends in churches, seminaries, and universities around the world, and to the members of the Church Missionary Society of Australia who commissioned me to work in Cape Town and who have supported my family financially, thank you. If I have learned anything from the book of Kings, it is that God is sovereign over history and that he is able to fulfil his promise to build his kingdom, in spite of – and often through – the weaknesses and failures of his servants. Like you, my prayer is that God's kingdom would take root below, richly and deeply in African soil, and bear fruit above. We trust that the zeal of Yahweh of Hosts will accomplish this.

1

Kings as Political Historiography

1.1. *Introduction*

This study is an exploration of the ideology of the book of Kings when it is read as a work of political historiography. In the course of scholarship on the book there have been many proposals about what Kings is and how it should be read. For some it has been regarded as an anthology of material or a record of God's actions in history.[1] For others it has been regarded as an explanation for the downfall of the Israelite nation.[2] In Marvin Sweeney's words, the book is 'a highly theologized account of Israel and Judah's history [that] attempts to explain why Judah and Israel – or more properly, the Davidic monarchy – came to an end'.[3]

Most have recognised that the exilic compiler of the material probably had an agenda that moved beyond archiving Israel's history and explaining their current plight of exile.[4] When Martin Noth claimed that the Deuteronomistic History (DtrH) provided an explanation for the exile, Gerhard von Rad agreed, but countered that it also provided hope for the

---

1. See, e.g., the summaries in Richard S. Hess, 'Introduction: Foundations for a History of Israel', in *Ancient Israel's History: An Introduction to Issues and Sources*, ed. Bill T. Arnold and Richard S. Hess (Grand Rapids, MI: Baker Academic, 2014), 1–22.

2. E.g. Martin Noth, *The Deuteronomistic History*, trans. David J. A. Clines, 2nd ed., JSOTSup 15 (Sheffield: JSOT, 1981), 97–9. For the many proposals that have adjusted the position see my literature review in Nathan H. Lovell, 'The Shape of Hope in the Book of Kings: The Resolution of Davidic Blessing and Mosaic Curse', *JESOT* 3 (2014): 2–3.

3. Marvin A. Sweeney, *I & II Kings*, OTL (Louisville, KY: Westminster John Knox, 2007), 5.

4. I argue below for an exilic date for the book.

restoration of the Judean monarchy.⁵ Implicitly, then, even though it is an account of history, the book also looks forward. As Sweeney continues, it is not only an explanation of the downfall of the monarchy but also demonstrates 'how this lesson might influence any attempt to restore Israelite or Judean life in the land'.⁶ By looking backwards to the past, the book is able to shape the community for the future.

For many, then, Kings has been understood as a theological account of Israel's history that attempts to teach its readers theological lessons. And this is true. However, overlapping with this theological agenda is a political one. Indeed, since Israel understood themselves as a community in relation to God, the two cannot be separated.

Adrian Hastings has said, 'Nationalism is not the awakening of nations to self-consciousness: it invents nations where they do not exist'.⁷ This is what the book of Kings does. It is an attempt to invent a nation, but not *ex novo*. From the context of the exile, much of what gave Israel a cultural and national identity had been stripped away: the Davidic throne, the temple, the promised land.⁸ Looking backward, as we shall see, the book of Kings gives its readers a sense of continuity with those pre-existing traditions. Looking forward, it provokes hope that what was lost might be recovered. However, for the exilic readers, its primary task was to construct an authentically Israelite expression of identity that could cope with the temporary absence of those national symbols.

Anthony Smith suggested that exile 'is the nursery of nationalism'.⁹ This is because the felt needs of the community are so great and so many. Perhaps the book of Kings resulted from the need to demarcate and preserve Hebrew identity and culture within a Babylonian milieu.¹⁰ Or perhaps it was the continuation and redefinition of orthodox Yahwism

---

5. Gerhard von Rad, *Old Testament Theology*, vol. 1, trans. David M. G. Stalker (New York: Harper & Row, 1962), 341–3.

6. Sweeney, *I & II Kings*, 5.

7. Adrian Hastings, *The Construction of Nationhood: Ethnicity, Religion and Nationalism* (Cambridge: Cambridge University Press, 1997), 9.

8. See, e.g., J. Gordon McConville, *God and Earthly Power: An Old Testament Political Theology, Genesis–Kings* (London: T&T Clark, 2008), 156.

9. Anthony D. Smith, *Chosen Peoples: Sacred Sources of National Identity* (Oxford: Oxford University Press, 2003), 19.

10. E.g. E. Theodore Mullen, *Narrative History and Ethnic Boundaries: The Deuteronomistic Historian and the Creation of Israelite National Identity* (Atlanta, GA: Scholars Press, 1993), 9–10. See also James R. Linville, *Israel in the Book of Kings: The Past as a Project of Social Identity* (Sheffield: Sheffield Academic, 1998), 18–25, though he proposes a Persian context.

in the new context.¹¹ Maybe it was done to create a sense of hope for a restored polity,¹² and to provide instruction concerning what went wrong the first time.¹³ The project might have been transformative, either to create a new way of thinking about Israel,¹⁴ or to call them to covenant repentance and renewal.¹⁵ It may have simply been to encourage good order and quell social dissatisfaction.¹⁶ Or the history may have served the exilic interest against those who remained in the land.¹⁷ We will investigate all of these possibilities throughout this study.

This is the role of political historiography in general, which recounts the past for a specific reason.¹⁸ The book of Kings is an invitation to the

---

11. E.g. Hillel I. Millgram, *The Elijah Enigma: The Prophet, King Ahab and the Rebirth of Monotheism in the Book of Kings* (Jefferson, MO: McFarland, 2014), 18–20.

12. Classically, von Rad, *Old Testament Theology*, 341–3. See also Iain W. Provan, *1 & 2 Kings*, NIBC (Grand Rapids, MI: Baker Academic, 1995), 87–93; Provan, 'The Messiah in the Book of Kings', in *The Lord's Anointed: Interpretation of Old Testament Messianic Texts*, ed. Philip E. Satterthwaite, Richard S. Hess, and Gordon J. Wenham (Eugene, OR: Wipf & Stock, 2012), 76–81; and Thomas R. Hobbs, *2 Kings*, WBC 13 (Waco, TX: Word, 1985), 268–9.

13. E.g. David Janzen, 'The Sins of Josiah and Hezekiah: A Synchronic Reading of the Final Chapters of Kings', *JSOT* 37 (2013): 351–2; Janzen, 'An Ambiguous Ending: Dynastic Punishment in Kings and the Fate of the Davidides in 2 Kings 25.27-30', *JSOT* 33 (2008): 57; Yairah Amit, *History and Ideology: Introduction to Historiography in the Hebrew Bible* (Sheffield: Sheffield Academic, 1999), 64; and J. Gordon McConville, 'Narrative and Meaning in the Books of Kings', *Bib* 70 (1989): 48.

14. E.g. Richard D. Nelson, 'The Anatomy of the Book of Kings', *JSOT* 40 (1988): 40.

15. Hans W. Wolff, 'The Kerygma of the Deuteronomic Historical Work', in *The Vitality of Old Testament Traditions*, 2nd ed. (Atlanta, GA: John Knox, 1982), 93–7. See also Donald F. Murray, 'Of All the Years the Hopes – or Fears? Jehoiachin in Babylon (2 Kings 25:27-30)', *JBL* 120 (2001): 263–5; and Peter R. Ackroyd, *Exile and Restoration: A Study of Hebrew Thought of the Sixth Century BC* (Louisville, KY: Westminster John Knox, 1968), 79–81.

16. Peter I. Kaufman, *Redeeming Politics* (Princeton, NJ: Princeton University Press, 1992), 4.

17. Christoph Levin, 'The Empty Land in Kings', in *The Concept of Exile in Ancient Israel and its Historical Contexts*, ed. Ehud Ben Zvi and Christoph Levin (New York: de Gruyter, 2010), 62, 89.

18. John Coakley, 'Mobilizing the Past: Nationalist Images of History', *Nationalism and Ethnic Politics* 10 (2004): 531–4; and Edward W. Said, *Culture and Imperialism* (New York: Random House, 1993), 3. See also the essays in Amit, *History and Ideology: Introduction to Historiography in the Hebrew Bible*; and Ehud

exilic community to make *this* way of telling history *their* way of telling history. And through that appropriation, the book becomes a statement of political identity. This study is not concerned with whether it was successful, only in analysing the attempt. It is through this mechanism of social appropriation that literature takes on political significance. Almost any genre is suitable,[19] among them myths, legal codes, epic fiction, heroic fable, and poetry.[20] The modern context might add science fiction, for example, which portrays utopian or dystopian futures, warning all the while of current challenges or embracing modern trends. Different genres work in various ways, some by becoming an agreed narrative of origins or destiny, some by the portrayal of virtue which shapes values and ideals.[21] When authors write with a community in mind, it becomes political: to 'effect a transformation of belief, [and] a re-evaluation of [collective] identity'.[22]

The classification of the genre of Kings as historiography requires elaboration because the term is not used consistently by scholarship.[23] By it, I indicate my focus on the literary means by which the text describes the past and impacts its readers, as opposed to the study of what actually happened.[24] Norman Gottwald's study on *The Politics of Ancient Israel*

Ben Zvi, 'Prophetic Memories in the Deuteronomistic Historical and the Prophetic Collections of Books', in *Israelite Prophecy and the Deuteronomistic History: Portrait, Reality, and the Formation of a History*, ed. Mignon R. Jacobs and Raymond F. Person Jr. (Atlanta, GA: SBL, 2013), 75–81.

19. Coakley, 'Mobilizing the Past'.

20. For an examples from ancient Mesopotamia see Peter Machinist, 'Literature as Politics: The Tukulti-Ninurta Epic and the Bible', *CBQ* 38 (1976): 455–82; and Mark W. Hamilton, *A Kingdom for a Stage: Political and Theological Reflection in the Hebrew Bible*, FAT 116 (Tübingen: Mohr Siebeck, 2018), 68–75.

21. Coakley, 'Mobilizing the Past', 532, 542–5.

22. Nelson, 'The Anatomy of the Book of Kings', 40.

23. See, e.g., Robert Alter, 'Imagining History in the Bible', in *History and...: Histories within the Human Sciences*, ed. Ralph Cohen and Michael S. Roth (Charlottesville, VA: University Press of Virginia, 1995), 53–72; Alison L. Joseph, *Portrait of the Kings: The Davidic Prototype in Deuteronomistic Poetics* (Minneapolis: Fortress, 2015), 1–6; Amit, *History and Ideology*, 11–19; Rachelle Gilmour, *Representing the Past: A Literary Analysis of Narrative Historiography in the Book of Samuel*, VTSup 143 (Leiden: Brill, 2011), 7–26; and John Van Seters, *In Search of History: Historiography in the Ancient World and the Origins of Bible History* (New Haven, CT: Yale University Press, 1983), 1–5.

24. The history must have at least seemed plausible to its original audience, or it would not have functioned as intended. I take it, then, that exilic readers shared none of the modern historical reservations concerning resurrections, angelic armies, and fire from heaven. See Hamilton, *A Kingdom for a Stage*, 55.

is an example of the latter type.²⁵ It shares with mine an interest in the ideological framework in which ancient Israelite politics operated.²⁶ However, his interest moves behind the text to reconstruct Israel's pre-exilic frameworks of political thought. His method uses source and historical criticism to strip away the ideological biases of the text, and then to complement those results with archaeological and other data to reconstruct the history.²⁷ By contrast, my interest in the exilic historiography of the book means that I wish to analyse precisely those perspectives and biases that his method seeks to move beyond.²⁸ By *historical context*, therefore, I mean the context of its original author and readers, that is, the exilic context, and not that of the events reported by the narrative.

I will use Smith's ethnosymbolic approach to the analysis of national identity.²⁹ It is a particularly suitable approach for several reasons. First, even though nationalism is strictly a modern phenomenon,³⁰ Smith recognises that modern national identity has a much more ancient prototype in the construction that underlies ethnic identities.³¹ At no point was Ancient Israel a nation in the modern sense, but in Smith's framework it bore all the marks of possessing a national identity, as we shall see. Second, Smith's approach foregrounds the role that history, myth, and religion play

---

25. Norman K. Gottwald, *The Politics of Ancient Israel* (Louisville, KY: Westminster John Knox, 2001).

26. Gottwald, *The Politics of Ancient Israel*, 1–6.

27. In his *The Politics of Ancient Israel*, Gottwald discusses his method on pp. 32–5 and gives examples of implementation on pp. 37–112.

28. Attention has been given recently to the same task with respect to Assyrian ideology and the biblical response, especially in Isaiah. On Assyrian imperial ideology see Mario Liverani, *Assyria: The Imperial Mission* (Winona Lake, IN: Eisenbrauns, 2017); and Wilfred G. Lambert, 'The God Assur', *Iraq* 45 (1983): 82–6. For a concise review of the development of the field see Mark W. Hamilton, 'The Past as Destiny: Historical Visions in Sam'al and Judah under Assyrian Hegemony', *HTR* 91 (1998): 217–21. On Isaiah's subversive response see Shawn Z. Aster, *Reflections of Empire in Isaiah 1–39: Responses to Assyrian Ideology* (Atlanta, GA: SBL, 2017); Baruch A. Levine, 'Assyrian Ideology and Israelite Monotheism', *Iraq* 67 (2005): 411–27. The seminal study is Peter Machinist, 'Assyria and its Image in the First Isaiah', *JAOS* 103 (1983): 719–37. We will revisit some of this material below when we come to 2 Kgs 18–20, which is shared with Isaiah.

29. Primarily Smith, *Chosen Peoples*; but see also Anthony D. Smith, *The Ethnic Origins of Nations* (Hoboken, NJ: Blackwell, 1986). Smith's corpus builds on a conceptual framework supplied by John Anderson in *Nations Before Nationalism* (Chapel Hill, VA: University of North Carolina Press, 1982).

30. Benedict Anderson, *Imagined Communities: Reflections on the Origin and Spread of Nationalism*, 2nd ed. (London: Verso, 1991), 39–48.

31. Smith, *The Ethnic Origins of Nations*, 6–19.

in the formation of national identities. Smith defines a nation as 'a named human population occupying a historic territory and sharing common myths and memories, a public culture, and common laws and customs for all members'.[32] From this, he can propose a working definition of national identity:

> National identity [is] the maintenance and continual reinterpretation of the pattern of values, symbols, memories, myths and traditions that form the distinctive heritage of the nation, and the identification of individuals with that heritage and its pattern.[33]

This pattern is like a national fingerprint, a unique composition that makes each nation what it is.[34] For the purposes of analysis, Smith chooses to study it through the categories of *community, territory, history*, and *destiny*,[35] but these are not definitive. Oliver O'Donovan, a political theologian, uses *salvation, possession*, and *judgment*, by which he refers (abstractly) to national composition: what has been gained by the nation (salvation), how it is kept (possession), and by what structures it is ruled (judgment).[36] Within the field of biblical theology,[37] E. Theodore Mullen uses *land, leader*, and *locus*,[38] and Graeme Goldsworthy selects *people, place*, and *rule*,[39] each to analyse the political identity of Israel.

For the purpose of this study, I have selected four categories to analyse the political ideology of the book of Kings: *covenant, nationhood, land*, and *rule*. Other categories may have proved equally profitable. However,

---

32. Smith, *Chosen Peoples*, 24. See also Anderson's definition (*Imagined Communities*, 5), a nation is 'an imagined political community…both inherently limited and sovereign'.

33. Smith, *Chosen Peoples*, 24–5.

34. Smith's (*Chosen Peoples*, 3–8) wider agenda is to explain the critical role that religion plays in the formation of this pattern.

35. Smith, *Chosen Peoples*, 31–2.

36. From this triangle O'Donovan (*The Desire of the Nations: Rediscovering the Roots of Political Theology* [Cambridge, MA: Cambridge University Press, 1996], 49–66) can derive a second, by which he can analyse political power: *judicial authority* (the salvation that ensures possession), *executive authority* (the exercise of salvation in judgment), and *legislative authority* (the judgment that ensures possession).

37. O'Donovan (*The Desire of the Nations*, 21) credits the resurgence of interest in political theology generally to a renewed interest in biblical theology.

38. Mullen, *Narrative History and Ethnic Boundaries*, 9.

39. Graeme Goldsworthy, *The Goldsworthy Trilogy* (Exeter: Paternoster, 2000), 54.

my concern was to avoid imposing categories foreign to the text by selecting ones that emerged naturally from my reading of the book.[40] These categories arise because the historiography of Kings directly addresses Israel's continuity with what had been lost in exile: the covenant had been broken, the nation dismantled, the land lost, and the king imprisoned.

1. *Covenant:* Smith's definition of *nationhood* includes 'a public culture', and 'common laws and customs'. This comes close to the way the book of Kings draws on the Mosaic covenant, in particular as it is expressed in the deuteronomic tradition.[41] The book of Kings, I will argue, draws on Israel's covenant as the primary reference point of identity. However, on its own the covenant only imagines what might have been. It is the dialectic that Kings creates between the covenant and the Davidic promise that moves the ideology of the book beyond a statement of what Israel had lost, to imagine a destiny – a hoped for future – they might embrace.[42]

2. *Nationhood:* Smith argues that it is more important that members of a nation identify with each other around a shared heritage than it is that they share an actual ethnicity.[43] For this reason nations must be 'named human populations'.[44] Israel are, therefore, those who have a rightful claim to the name, and this is a subject that the book of Kings reflects on at some length. It remembers the political crisis that saw the division of Israel into two 'Israels', it recalls the dissolution of the one that kept the name 'Israel'. Who, then, is Israel? Common with other exilic thought, Kings also begins to wrestle with whether and to what extent an outsider such as Naaman (2 Kgs 5) or the Samarian population (2 Kgs 17:24-41) can ever be called Israelite.

---

40. A tempting category was *power*, as several recent, similar works demonstrate (e.g., McConville, *God and Earthly Power*; Keith Bodner, *Jeroboam's Royal Drama* [Oxford: Oxford University Press, 2012]; and Moshe Halbertal and Stephen Holmes, *The Beginning of Politics: Power in the Biblical Book of Samuel* [Princeton, NJ: Princeton University Press, 2017]). However, the emphasis on rule in Kings seems to revolve around the characters of the leaders, rather than exercise of power. Because of this, I have subsumed this discussion within the larger framework of *rule*.

41. See S. Dean McBride, 'Polity of the Covenant People: The Book of Deuteronomy', *Int* 41 (1987): 233–4.

42. On *destiny* as a political category see Smith, *Chosen Peoples*, 216–17.

43. In Smith's language (*Chosen Peoples*, 24; *The Ethnic Origins of Nations*, 13–15) this is the distinction between an *ethnie* (group with shared culture) and an *ethnicity* (group with shared genetic heritage).

44. Smith, *Chosen Peoples*, 24.

3. *Land:* The connection between people and territory is intrinsic to human culture.[45] Contrary to Western intuition, the nationalistic ideology that saw boundaries placed on cartographically accurate world maps is only one modern expression of this reality.[46] In truth, human rootedness in a place is linked to our economic, judicial and cultural realities. Land is more than where we live; it is the territory we will defend; it defines the jurisdiction of our laws; and it is the ultimate source of all wealth. Within Ancient Near Eastern (ANE) polytheistic societies, land also sometimes defined the boundaries of a deity's influence, giving it a religious significance.[47] This is true of Israel also, who centralised worship of Yahweh at the temple. The book of Kings shares the view of the Old Testament more generally that Israel's land was inherited as part of the covenant.[48] To what extent, then, could Israel be Israel from Babylon?

4. *Rule:* Since anarchy is not a viable political arrangement, human societies cannot exist without some form of authority. They require some institution with power to decide 'who gets to do what with what'.[49] However, what form such government might take is an ongoing experiment as it was also for Israel. Where 1 and 2 Samuel recount the transition from a decentralised, tribal or clan-based organisation to a centralised monarchy,[50] the book of Kings recounts how God's promise to David for a dynastic kingdom (2 Sam. 7.12-16) plays out in subsequent history.[51] The exilic situation brings

---

45. See Smith, *Chosen Peoples*, 131–8, 139–65; Jonathan Leeman, *Political Church: The Local Assembly as Embassy of Christ's Rule* (Grand Rapids, MI: IVP Academic, 2016), 117–18; Coakley, 'Mobilizing the Past', 552–3, and Craig G. Bartholomew, *Where Mortals Dwell* (Grand Rapids, MI: Baker Academic, 2011), 167–242.

46. See Anderson, *Imagined Communities*, 174–81.

47. Daniel I. Block, *The Gods of the Nations: Studies in Ancient Near Eastern National Theology* (Grand Rapids, MI: Baker Academic, 2000), 19–20.

48. For works that attempt to analyse the overall land ideology in the Old Testament, see Norman C. Habel, *The Land Is Mine: Six Biblical Land Ideologies*, OBT (Minneapolis, MN: Fortress, 1995); and David Frankel, *The Land of Canaan and the Destiny of Israel: Theologies of Territory in the Hebrew Bible* (Winona Lake, IN: Eisenbrauns, 2011).

49. Leeman, *Political Church*, 55–6.

50. Older models of pre-monarchic Israel's polity were based on an analogy to Greek tribal amphictyonies. Newer research tends to emphasise the primacy of local, familial or clan-based units. See, e.g., Gottwald, *The Politics of Ancient Israel*, 35–52.

51. Bradley J. Parker ('The Construction and Performance of Kingship in the Neo-Assyrian Empire', *Journal of Anthropological Research* 67 [2011]: 366) explores the way Assyrian historiography legitimises their royal ideology.

obvious challenges to a nation accustomed to self-rule. The book of Kings constructs an ideology of rule compatible with the covenant traditions. It does this for two reasons. First, by comparison with an idealised covenant-shaped king, the narrative can explore what went wrong, apportioning the majority of blame to the rulers themselves. And second, the creation of a political ideal contributes to Israel's hope about what royal authority might look like when the promise to David would be realised.

This study explores the way that the narrative of Kings, read as an integrated and coherent narrative, might have shaped the identity of its exilic audience with respect to these categories.

1.2. *Method and Previous Work*

The approach I take in this study has elements of both older redaction-critical methods and newer literary ones. The former approach shares with mine a concern to identify the ideological position of the text, which has been one cornerstone of critical scholarship on DtrH. Usually, however, scholarship has used this technique to discern ideological tensions within the history in order to distinguish redactional layers.[52] By contrast, my concern is to explore the ideology of the entire narrative, taken as a whole. I will argue below that this is not the same thing as an analysis of the ideologies of any of the various Dtr redactors. The existence of redactional layers raises questions for my approach, but these are better dealt with in their own section below. It suffices here to note that my interest both overlaps and diverges from traditional redaction-critical scholarship.

My interest in the overarching narrative of Kings also invites comparison with newer literary approaches that examine the final form of the text.[53] Many studies have purely literary objectives, such as understanding characterisation, or plot, but my approach follows those who move

---

52. Classically, e.g., Frank Moore Cross, *Canaanite Myth and Hebrew Epic: Essays in the History of the Religion of Israel*, OTL (Cambridge, MA: Harvard University Press, 1973), 274–8. See my literature review and discussion in the section on DtrH below.

53. For the purposes of this study, I have drawn from: Robert Alter, *The Art of Biblical Narrative* (New York: Basic, 1981), 3–22; Brevard S. Childs, *Old Testament Theology in a Canonical Context* (Philadelphia, PA: Fortress, 1989), 1–19; Adele Berlin, *Poetics and Interpretation of Biblical Narrative* (Sheffield: Almond, 1983), 13–21; Meir Sternberg, *Poetics of Biblical Narrative: Ideological Literature and the Drama of Reading* (Bloomington, IN: Indiana University Press, 1987), 1–83; and Shimeon Bar-Efrat, *Narrative Art in the Bible* (London: T&T Clark, 2004), 9–11.

beyond this goal. By taking the literary shape of the text as an indicator of intent or purpose, it is possible to derive theological, philosophical, or ideological results through literary analysis.[54] Such studies can be

54. In order of appearance, works include: Michael Walzer, *Exodus and Revolution* (New York: Basic, 1986); Mullen, *Narrative History and Ethnic Boundaries*; Daniel Elazar, *Covenant and Polity in Biblical Israel* (New Brunswick, NJ: Transaction, 1995); Thomas L. Pangle, 'The Hebrew Bible's Challenge to Political Philosophy: Some Reflections', in *Political Philosophy and the Human Soul: Essays in Memory of Allan Bloom*, ed. Michael Palmer and Thomas L. Pangle (Lanham, MD: Roman & Littlefield, 1995), 67–82; Jan Joosten, *People and Land in the Holiness Code: An Exegetical Study of the Ideational Framework of the Law in Leviticus 17–26*, VTSup 67 (Leiden: Brill, 1996); O'Donovan, *The Desire of the Nations*; Sara Japhet, *The Ideology of the Book of Chronicles and its Place in Biblical Thought*, BEATAJ (Frankfurt: Lang, 1997); Bernard M. Levinson, 'The Reconceptualisation of Kingship in Deuteronomy and the Deuteronomistic History's Transformation of Torah', *VT* 51 (2001): 511–34; Steven Elliott Grosby, *Biblical Ideas of Nationality: Ancient and Modern* (Winona Lake, IN: Eisenbrauns, 2002); Aaron Wildavsky, *Moses as Political Leader* (Jerusalem: Shalem, 2005); David Van Drunen, *A Biblical Case for Natural Law* (Grand Rapids, MI: Acton Institute, 2006); Jerome T. Walsh, *Ahab: The Construction of a King*, Interfaces (New York: Liturgical Press, 2006); McConville, *God and Earthly Power*; Joshua Berman, *Created Equal: How the Bible Broke with Ancient Political Thought* (Oxford: Oxford University Press, 2008); Daniel Berrigan, *The Kings and their Gods: The Pathology of Power* (Grand Rapids, MI: Eerdmans, 2008); Mira Morgenstern, *Conceiving a Nation: The Development of Political Discourse in the Hebrew Bible* (University Park, PA: Pennsylvania State University Press, 2009); David J. Reimer, 'Isaiah and Politics', in *Interpreting Isaiah*, ed. David G. Firth and H. G. M. Williamson (Grand Rapids, MI: IVP Academic, 2009), 84–103; Wes Howard-Brook, *Come Out My People! God's Call Out of Empire in the Bible and Beyond* (Maryknoll, NY: Orbis, 2010); Louis C. Jonker, *Historiography and Identity (Re)formulation in Second Temple Historiographical Literature* (New York: T&T Clark, 2010); Bartholomew, *Where Mortals Dwell*; Robert Karl Gnuse, *No Tolerance for Tyrants: The Biblical Assault on Kings and Kingship* (Collegeville, MN: Liturgical Press, 2011); Gilmour, *Representing the Past*; Michael Walzer, *In God's Shadow: Politics in the Hebrew Bible* (New Haven, CT: Yale University Press, 2012); Yoram Hazony, *The Philosophy of Hebrew Scripture* (Cambridge, MA: Cambridge University Press, 2012); Joseph Blenkinsopp, *David Remembered: Kingship and National Identity in Ancient Israel* (Grand Rapids, MI: Eerdmans, 2013); Matthew B. Schwartz and Kalman J. Kaplan, *Politics in the Hebrew Bible: God, Man, and Government* (Lanham, MD: Jason Aronson, 2013); Halbertal and Holmes, *The Beginning of Politics*; Jeremiah Unterman, *Justice for All: How the Jewish Bible Revolutionized Ethics*, JPS Essential Judaism (Lincoln, NE: University of Nebraska Press, 2017). With reference to Kings in particular, other than Linville's treatment which I review below: on Jeroboam see Bodner, *Jeroboam's Royal Drama*; on Elijah

sub-divided into two groups. One approach is to treat the texts as self-contained works that use the narrative genre to reflect on abstract ideas.[55] This hermeneutic is literary because it understands the genre of the text itself as instructional narrative. In the words of Leon Kass, the Bible teaches us 'not what happened, but what always happens'.[56] Keith Bodner's work on Jeroboam (1 Kgs 11–14) is an example from the book of Kings.[57] He finds that through the characterisation of Jeroboam, his interactions with other characters, and the narrative critique concerning him, 'the reader accesses a sophisticated meditation on power'.[58] There is value in reading Kings in this way, as many of the works I cited above demonstrate, but this will not be my approach.

The alternative is to treat the texts as examples of literature written for a particular purpose within a specific historical context, and this will be my approach.[59] This method finds its roots in John Van Seters's 1983

and Elisha see Walter A. Brueggemann and Davis Hankins, 'The Affirmation of Prophetic Power and Deconstruction of Royal Authority in the Elisha Narratives', *CBQ* 76 (2014): 58–76. Jehu has been a popular choice. See Patricia Dutcher-Walls, *Jezebel: Portraits of a Queen* (Collegeville, MN: Liturgical Press, 2004); Nkikho Mtshiselwa, 'A Re-Reading of 1 Kings 21:1-29 and Jehu's Revolution in Dialogue with Farisani and Nzimande: Negotiating Socio-economic Redress in South Africa', *OTE* 27 (2014): 205–30; and Mtshiselwa, 'Reconstructing a Deuteronomistic Athaliah in the (South) African Context: A Critique of the Patriarchal Perception of Women', *VE* 36 (2015): 1–8.

55. E.g. Hazony, *The Philosophy of Hebrew Scripture*, 79.

56. Leon R. Kass, *The Beginning of Wisdom: Reading Genesis* (Chicago, IL: University of Chicago Press, 2006), 10, 54. For a developed explanation of how texts, considered apart from their original context, continue to carry ideology, see Sternberg, *Poetics of Biblical Narrative*, 84–128. Some narratives in the ancient world were written in this way, as a general instruction for wisdom. Examples include the Egyptian 'Tale of Sinuhe' or the 'Tale of the Two Brothers'. See *COS*, I.38, I.40.

57. Bodner, *Jeroboam's Royal Drama*. Halbertal (*The Beginning of Politics*) has also recently taken this approach to the entire book of Samuel, reading it as a consistent meditation on the nature of power. Bodner's work on Elisha is similar at places (e.g., *Elisha's Profile in the Book of Kings: The Double Agent* [Oxford: Oxford University Press, 2013], 127) and Walter Brueggemann's various reflections are also typical of this category (e.g., 'The Affirmation of Prophetic Power').

58. Bodner, *Jeroboam's Royal Drama*, 15, see also pp. 150–1.

59. My focus on the role the history played within its context invites comparison with some similar social-scientific approaches. See Philip F. Esler and Anselm C. Hagedorn, 'Social-Scientific Analysis of the Old Testament: A Brief History and Overview', in *Ancient Israel: The Old Testament in its Social Context*, ed. Philip F. Esler (Minneapolis, MN: Fortress, 2006), 32.

study, *In Search of History*. This book was an important development in scholarly understanding of how and why ancient societies wrote accounts of their history. Van Seters began by defining the genre of 'history' in a way that excludes a great deal of historical material. For Van Seters, history had to be more than political propaganda, and more than the accidental or anthologised accumulation of material.[60] Rather, he argues, history is 'the intellectual form in which a civilisation renders account to itself of its past'.[61] That is, history writing is concerned with the role that the retelling of past events plays in the present context of the author. These roles are numerous:

> The functions of tradition – the uses of the past – are so varied and many that no simple formula can cover them all. The tendency of many biblical scholars to confine the role of tradition in ancient Israelite society to the religious realm and to see all narrative texts about the past as cult functional is far too restrictive. Tradition can be used to fortify belief, explain or give meaning to the way things are, invest persons and institutions with authority, legitimate practices, regulate behavior, give a sense of personal and corporate identity, and communicate skills and knowledge. The forms that the verbal tradition may take – whether poetry or prose, whether sung, spoken, or written – are almost endless. Many traditional forms – laws, proverbs, genealogies – have specific functions. But some are more complex and their function more embracing: such is the genre of history, which may contain within it many kinds of traditional material. But a history is not the sum of its parts, and to analyze a history by taking it apart to discern the original function of the various elements will never yield the meaning of the whole.[62]

Van Seters, then, identified the following characteristics of true history writing:[63] (1) it moves beyond reporting past events to consider the reason for recalling them, and the attribution of significance to the author's contemporaries; (2) it examines the causes of present conditions and circumstances as a function of the outworking of past events, though this need not be according to a modern conception of causation: recourse to divine agency, for example, might perform this function; (3) it is national

---

60. E.g. Van Seters (*In Search of History*, 100–126) argues that Hittite 'history' and Babylonian chronography (pp. 55–99) are not true history writing.

61. Van Seters (*In Search of History*, 1) is drawing on Johan Huizinga ('A Definition of the Concept of History', in *Philosophy and History: Essays Presented to Ernst Cassierrer*, ed. Raymond Klibansky and Herbert James Paton [New York: Harper & Row, 1963], 9).

62. Van Seters, *In Search of History*, 3.

63. Van Seters, *In Search of History*, 4–5.

and corporate, not focused on the deeds or events of an individual except as they play a part in national history; and (4) it is part of a literary tradition and plays a role in the corporate tradition of a people.[64]

Although Van Seters's work focused on how and when this genre of history writing emerged in the ancient world, the basic observation that ANE history writing functioned ideologically has since been developed by others. Baruch Halpern, for example, has argued that the historical intention of the author must be examined when assessing ancient history writing.[65] It was, he claims, the ancient author's intention to 'lead the reader to believe that the work is a valid representation of the past'.[66] And so as 'readers today, it is our task to get back into the mental state of the historian's ideal audience, the sophisticates who shared the historian's assumptions, and who therefore stood open to be persuaded by his logic'.[67] Even though some have questioned his insistence on authorial intent,[68] Halpern has succeeded in highlighting the role that the selection and arrangement of material plays in shaping the argument of the historical account.[69] Marc Brettler has also reached a similar conclusion, showing the way the Chronicler adapted and composed his earlier sources (Samuel and Kings) to create an ideological 'narrative that presents a past'.[70]

---

64. This definition of 'history' will be useful for some purposes and not for others. What matters for the historian in this model is not the accuracy of the events, but their plausibility to his audience, and so may be almost entirely fictive, as Van Seters thought was the case. However, one need not accept the sceptical position, as Baruch Halpern demonstrates: *The First Historians: The Hebrew Bible and History* (New York: Harper & Row, 1988), 30–2.

65. Halpern, *The First Historians*.

66. Halpern, *The First Historians*, xxii.

67. Halpern, *The First Historians*, 276.

68. E.g. Marc Brettler (*The Creation of History in Ancient Israel* [London: Routledge, 1995], 11–12). Joseph (*Portrait of the Kings*, 12–13) responds to this scepticism by noting that exhaustive knowledge of the author is not necessary to discern intent, and that it has been the dominant position of scholarship to assume intent was available. See also Robert D. Bergen, 'Text as a Guide to Authorial Intention: An Introduction to Discourse Criticism', *JETS* 30 (1987): 327–36; and William K. Wimsatt and Monroe C. Beardsley, 'The Intentional Fallacy', in *The Verbal Icon: Studies in the Meaning of Poetry*, ed. William K. Wimsatt (Lexington, KY: University of Kentucky Press, 1954), 3–18.

69. See, e.g., Halpern's discussion on the arrangement of Judges (*The First Historians*, 138–40).

70. Brettler, *The Creation of History in Ancient Israel*, 12. See also H. G. M. Williamson's prior analysis of Chronicles: *Israel in the Book of Chronicles* (Cambridge: Cambridge University Press, 1977).

Mullen applied the general logic of history writing developed by Van Seters and others to a particular analysis of DtrH in his 1993 study, *Narrative History and Ethnic Boundaries*.[71] He showed that DtrH could be understood as a statement of communal identity, intended to protect exilic Israel from cultural assimilation:[72]

> The recognition of the importance of narrative in the social construction of reality, especially as it applies to such ideas as national and ethnic self-consciousness, provides the basis for the application of this new approach to various materials within the Hebrew Bible. This method of interpretation concentrates on the [way that narratives] define and bound a particular people as a separate and identifiable ethnic group…[such that] they may become public symbols that provide the basis for the continued redefinition and self-understanding of that group.[73]

More than any other, my own work has been influenced by James Linville's *Israel and the Book of Kings*, which advances Mullen's thesis in several directions. Most notably, Linville examines Kings as a coherent whole, as 'literature of attribution',[74] which is his term for identity politics. For Linville, Kings is a retelling of Israel's history that was intended to help post-exilic Israel to construct and express a communal identity in light of their new political existence.[75] Linville seeks to avoid what he labels the 'piecemeal' approach of historical criticism that divides the book into its source material, as well as the critical approach that tries to reconstruct the literary history of the book at the expense of its wider ideological argument:[76]

> Hardly any of the [source and historical-critical studies] attempt to address the present text of the deuteronomistic history as it might have functioned with respect to the formation of the community whose identity as an ethnic

---

71. Mullen, *Narrative History and Ethnic Boundaries*. See Linville, *Israel in the Book of Kings*, 83.
72. Mullen, *Narrative History and Ethnic Boundaries*, 9–10.
73. Mullen, *Narrative History and Ethnic Boundaries*, 15.
74. Linville, *Israel in the Book of Kings*, 16–37.
75. Linville (*Israel in the Book of Kings*, 18–37, 69–73) follows Philip Davies's reconstruction of the history of Ancient Israel (*In Search of Ancient Israel: A Study in Biblical Origins*, JSOTSup 148 [Sheffield: Sheffield Academic, 1992], 90–107), which ascribes the composition of the book of Kings to the post-exilic period. I discuss my view below.
76. Linville, *Israel in the Book of Kings*, 18–25, 38–49.

group was threatened by the exile with complete assimilation and ethnic dissolution. It is from this position that the present attempt to develop a new model for the interpretation of Hebrew narrative begins. Additionally, none of the major studies of the deuteronomistic history attempts to address the essential religious character of the text or the mythological dimensions that permeate both its contents and its design.[77]

Linville claims the book of Kings was not a simple record of events, but rather part of a process of community re-definition. By retelling her history, Israel gave to herself a narrative not only about what happened, but about who she currently was, and what it meant to be Israelite:

> In my understanding, every society is engaged in a continual process of reformulating its sense(s) of its own being. Such processes, however, are marked by specific projects, such as the writing of books, which may be deliberately intended to address the current state of the process as it appears to specific individuals.[78]

Thus Linville uses literary observations, for example, characterisation, plot, and structure, to analyse the ideological intention and argument of the book.[79] He therefore seeks 'to combine with the [historical] interests… some appreciation of how this "construction" of "Israel" is a product of story-teller's art'.[80] The relationship between historical, diachronic methods, and literary, synchronic ones has not always been easy,[81] but Linville applies the latter to the former by taking the literary features as indicative of authorial intent within a historical context:[82]

---

77. Linville, *Israel in the Book of Kings*, 5.
78. Linville, *Israel in the Book of Kings*, 97.
79. Linville (*Israel in the Book of Kings*, 19 n. 9) cites a number of literary studies that have been formative on his work, some of which I review in Chapter 2.
80. Linville, *Israel in the Book of Kings*, 20.
81. E.g., contrast comments made by H. W. Frei (*The Eclipse of Biblical Narrative: A Study in Eighteenth and Nineteenth Century Hermeneutics* [New Haven, CT: Yale University Press, 1974], 134–6, 151–4) and Alter (*The Art of Biblical Narrative*, 12–14) with Halpern (*The First Historians*, 4–6).
82. The most thorough analysis on the method is perhaps Sternberg, *Poetics of Biblical Narrative*, 84–98; but see also comments in Bergen, 'Text as a Guide to Authorial Intention', 327–36; Berlin, *Poetics and Interpretation of Biblical Narrative*, 13–20; and J. P. Fokkelman, *Reading Biblical Narrative: An Introductory Guide* (Louisville, KY: Westminster John Knox, 1999), 20–45.

[My approach is...] in some aspects, rather conservative. It is not fundamentally opposed to the approach taken by Williamson in his study of Chronicles, in which the book's selection of events and the wording employed is taken as indicative of the Chronicler's views on the integrity of Israel, an analysis informed by reference to what might be known of the book's historical context.[83]

Studies more recent than Linville's have advanced these ideas. One such study published in 2015, by Alison Joseph, moves beyond the literary analysis of individual narratives to comment on the way the compiler of the material has selected and arranged the narratives themselves. Her study of the literary portrait of David in the book analyses what she calls the 'Historiographical Poetics' of Dtr.[84] She draws together the historical conclusions of Halpern and Brettler, with the narrative observations of literary theorists Meir Sternberg, Robert Alter and others:[85]

Bringing into play the method of the newer literary critics of the Bible, I consider the process of historiography, not just for its presentation of the past, but also for the ways in which the historian crafts his history in order to present the past, evaluating and cataloguing the literary style and techniques that he uses to make his history successful... [I also] build on the redaction scholarship, demonstrating the various selectional techniques [the Deuteronomist] uses to make choices of what to include of the record of the past in his historical narrative and how to include it. Previous scholarship has tended not to consider the ways in which earlier traditions are integrated into the text as well as why a specific Deuteronomist makes the choices he does. These two impulses make up the historiographical poetics.[86]

Thus Joseph can combine the outcomes of redaction-critical and literary-critical study.[87] The redaction history of the book conveys something of

---

83. Linville, *Israel in the Book of Kings*, 20; referring to Williamson, *Israel in the Book of Chronicles*.
84. Joseph, *Portrait of the Kings*, 37.
85. Joseph, *Portrait of the Kings*, 10–18.
86. Joseph, *Portrait of the Kings*, 31.
87. Joseph's analysis (*Portrait of the Kings*, 38–58) proceeds along two independent axes, of 'selection' and 'composition'. With respect to the former she claims that the Deuteronomist: (1) was committed to his sources, even if they did not make precisely the point he wanted to make, (2) was loyal to the prophetic tradition that provides a prophecy–fulfilment framework, and (3) ordered his material with an eye to both chronology and thematic juxtaposition. With respect to the second axis, Joseph comments that the Deuteronomist creatively manipulated his sources towards two ends: (1) to promote the Deuteronomistic programme, and (2) the composition of a historical account that attributes events to theological causes.

the selection and presentation of the material in the final form.[88] This in turn signals the author's intentions. Significant advances have also been made by Rachelle Gilmour and others,[89] in understanding the logic of narrative arrangement in a book like Kings, and I will review this literature in Chapter 2 in the context of my own discussion of the literary structure of the book.

Gordon McConville's 2008 study, *God and Earthly Power*, has also been influential on my own, both as an example of a text-oriented engagement with political theology,[90] and also for his discussion of the way the biblical literature relates to its ANE milieu. Where earlier studies, such as that of Van Seters's, focused on the similarities of form between Israel's historical literature and other ANE examples,[91] McConville shows that the ideology within the text is sometimes constructed polemically against its culture.[92] For example, McConville reads the Primary History as a demonstration that Israel's Yahwism 'never takes the form of the domination of the weak…[but] is advocated in political weakness…in the face of [Assyrian] power'.[93] So the extent to which the text confronts the dominant ideologies of its cultural milieu is an important factor.

1.3. Challenges to Reading Kings as Political Historiography

My method should now be clear. In treating Kings as a work of political historiography I intend to read it as a coherent piece of literature, in the form of a narrative that recounts Israel's history. It was produced with an explicit purpose to shape the political identity of the exilic community, and so embodies a consistent national ideology.

---

88. Hamilton, *A Kingdom for a Stage*, is another example of a work that shares this basic approach, though broader in scope. Hamilton brings different parts of the Old Testament into political dialogue with each other.

89. See Rachelle Gilmour, *Juxtaposition and the Elisha Cycle* (London: T&T Clark, 2014), 5–68.

90. This work is a book-length development of an essay that was originally a response to O'Donovan's exegetical political theology in *The Desire of the Nations*. The original response is: J. Gordon McConville, 'Law and Monarchy in the Old Testament', in *A Royal Priesthood? The Use of the Bible Ethically and Politically: A Dialogue with Oliver O'Donovan*, ed. Craig G. Bartholomew (Grand Rapids, MI: Paternoster, 2002), 69–88.

91. E.g. Van Seters, *In Search of History*, 31–52.

92. McConville, *God and Earthly Power*, 12–29.

93. McConville, *God and Earthly Power*, 29.

There are several assumptions that underlie this statement which may raise objections from those who are accustomed to reading the book as part of DtrH. It is necessary therefore to set my approach within the context of the wider discussion. Since my approach involves both literary and historical elements, I have divided my discussion here along those lines as well. The issues are interrelated; my classification is for organisational purposes. First, I place the book into a literary context by addressing questions concerning DtrH and the feasibility of reading Kings on its own. In this section I also address questions of redactional and ideological fragmentation. Second, I have placed the book into an exilic historical milieu, which is a decision that also requires further discussion. In this section I also address the issue of other versions of the text, including the LXX, and the question of post-exilic textual fluidity.

1.3.1. *The Literary Context of Kings and DtrH*

i. *The Literary Coherence of Kings and DtrH*

Is there such a thing as 'The Book of Kings'?[94] Standard critical discussion has posed two challenges, the first concerning whether Kings can be isolated from DtrH, and the second concerning the literary coherence of the narrative. I take the second of these challenges first, which is the problem of fragmentation implied by the existence of multiple redactors.

Robert Wilson's treatment of unity and diversity within Kings identifies several features of the book which show the redactional diversity of the narrative.[95] He categorises these under three headings: linguistic, structural, and thematic. Linguistic evidence he finds to be the least compelling, relying on a claim that different editors prefer different words or phrases,[96] and linguistic arguments are not common in scholarship on Kings because, as Noth observed, linguistic consistency is one of the primary indicators of Deuteronomistic editing.[97] The second feature is structural.[98] Wilson notes that the regnal formulae are very consistent

---

94. Only in the traditional Jewish counting is it reckoned a single work. In the Masoretic tradition it is two: 1 Kings and 2 Kings. I take it that this division is arbitrary, since it is impossible to read either book on its own. Within the Greek tradition, the book of Kings does not stand alone either. It takes its place as the second pair of volumes within 1–4 Kingdoms, the first pair being 1 and 2 Samuel.

95. Robert R. Wilson, 'Unity and Diversity in the Book of Kings', in *A Wise and Discerning Mind: Essays in Honor of Burke O. Long*, ed. Saul M. Olyan and Robert C. Culley (Providence, RI: Brown University Press, 2000), 303–8.

96. Wilson, 'Unity and Diversity in the Book of Kings', 303.

97. See Moshe Weinfeld's catalogue of Dtr phraseology: *Deuteronomy and the Deuteronomic School* (Ann Arbor, MI: Clarendon, 1972), 320–65.

98. I discuss the structural features of the book in Chapter 2.

throughout the narrative until Josiah and not so afterwards. He also notes that this is the point at which the book's interest in David also changes. Along with others,[99] Wilson observes that this evidence suggests a version of the book that concluded at that point, with 2 Kings 24–25 being a later revision. Even if we grant this, it does not follow that the book we have is incoherent in its present form, as Wilson also notes,[100] and as I show in Chapter 2.

The more serious objection to literary coherence has been Wilson's third category of thematic evidence. Wilson notes several themes such as the reason for the fall of Jerusalem, which is not always consistent, or whether repentance can reverse judgment. I return to both of these in Chapter 3. The theme that concerns us here is the attitude of DtrH towards the monarchy.[101] At times DtrH seems to be positive towards the idea of kingship, promising David an eternal kingdom, for example (2 Sam. 7.1-17). At other times DtrH seems negative, warning the reader of the consequences of appointing a king (1 Sam. 8.1-22) or setting laws that curtail his power (Deut. 17.14-20). This tension exists within Kings also, which adds obedience as a condition to the unconditional promise of 2 Samuel 7 (e.g., 1 Kgs 2.4), while seeming to reaffirm the Davidic promise (e.g., 1 Kgs 11.36). Given that I expect to produce a statement on the royal ideology of Kings as an outcome of this study,[102] it will be necessary to review some proposed solutions.[103] If the book fractures along ideological lines and contains two different royal ideologies, then this may raise *a priori* questions as to our ability to offer a coherent ideological reading of the text.

Reactions to the tension between royal ideologies have developed in two directions.[104] In 1973, Frank Moore Cross argued that a single redaction was unlikely to explain DtrH in the form it now exists. He proposed an initial pre-exilic redaction of the material (by Dtr_1) followed by a second,

---

99. E.g. Iain W. Provan, *Hezekiah and the Books of Kings: A Contribution to the Debate About the Composition of the Deuteronomistic History* (New York: de Gruyter, 1988); and Baruch Halpern and David S. Vanderhooft, 'The Editions of Kings in the 7th–6th Centuries BCE', *HUCA* 62 (1991): 179–244.

100. Wilson, 'Unity and Diversity in the Book of Kings', 307–8.

101. Wilson, 'Unity and Diversity in the Book of Kings', 306.

102. Note that Linville's *Israel in the Book of Kings* avoids this problem because it does not produce a statement of royal ideology (e.g., pp. 61–9). This allows Linville to be more indifferent to the objections posed by DtrH than I am.

103. The following survey is focused particularly on this question of royal ideology, and so not a complete survey of the literature on DtrH.

104. Juha Tanska, 'Changing Paradigms in Biblical Criticism: 2 Kings 22:1–23:30 in the Flux of Discourses' (PhD diss., University of Helsinki, 2011), 123–9.

exilic edition that updated the history and produced minor emendation to several passages within it (Dtr$_2$).[105] Dtr$_1$ wrote a pro-monarchic version of Israel's history as an *apologia* for Josiah's reforms in the seventh century. Dtr$_2$ redacted the material from exile, from an anti-monarchic point of view. He blamed Israel's current situation on the failure of Israel's kings to keep the covenant. Cross's proposal has been followed by North American scholarship, the so-called Harvard School. Notable proponents of this school for our focus on Kings include Richard Nelson,[106] Gary Knoppers,[107] Marvin Sweeney,[108] and Steven McKenzie.[109] Although each of these scholars, and others, have modified Cross's proposal in various ways, this school holds in common Cross's basic assertion of at least one pre-exilic, pro-monarchic redaction, followed by at least one exilic, anti-monarchic redaction.[110]

The so-called Göttingen School approached the problem from a different perspective.[111] In 1971, Rudolf Smend proposed several redactional layers in the book, all of them exilic or early post-exilic, that could be discerned by the genre of the material (historical, prophetic, etc.).[112]

---

105. Cross, *Canaanite Myth and Hebrew Epic*.

106. Richard D. Nelson, *The Double Redaction of the Deuteronomistic History*, JSOTSup 18 (Sheffield: Sheffield Academic, 1981).

107. Gary N. Knoppers, 'Theories of the Redaction(s) of Kings', in *The Books of Kings: Sources, Composition, Historiography and Reception*, ed. Baruch Halpern and André Lemaire, VTSup 129 (Leiden: Brill, 2010), 69–88.

108. Marvin A. Sweeney, *King Josiah of Judah: The Last Messiah of Israel* (Oxford: Oxford University Press, 2001), 8–12.

109. Steven L. McKenzie, *The Trouble with Kings: The Composition of the Book of Kings in the Deuteronomistic History* (Leiden: Brill, 1991).

110. Provan (*Hezekiah and the Books of Kings*, 90) and Halpern ('The Editions of Kings', 179–244) also agree with the conclusion, though for structural reasons. Therefore, the Harvard School has reached the same conclusion of one or more pre-exilic redactions from two different lines of evidence, the one ideological and the other structural.

111. For an overview of this line of scholarship see Reinhard G. Kratz, *The Composition of the Narrative Books of the Old Testament* (London: T&T Clark, 2005), 184–5.

112. Rudolf Smend, 'Das Gesetz und die Völker. Ein Beitrag zur deuteronomistischen Redaktionsgeschichte', in *Probleme biblischer Theologie: Festschrift Gerhard von Rad*, ed. Hans W. Wolff (Munich: Kaiser, 1971), 494–509; English translation: 'The Law and the Nations. A Contribution to Deuteronomistic Tradition History', in *Reconsidering Israel and Judah: Recent Studies on the Deuteronomistic History*, ed. Gary N. Knoppers and J. Gordon McConville, SBTS (Winona Lake, IN: Eisenbrauns, 2000), 95–110. Smend understood the second redaction (Dtr$_N$) as early post-exilic, but his followers tended to assert the completion of the entire history within the

Smend focused on Joshua and Judges, but the approach has since been expanded to the rest of DtrH. Relevant for this study are Walter Dietrich, who focused on the book of Kings,[113] and Timo Veijola, who worked on the royal ideology of DtrH.[114] In this schema, the initial redaction was by a writer concerned to record Israel's history (Dtr$_G$ for *Geschichte*), followed by a writer who added a prophetic perspective (Dtr$_P$), and finally a nomistic redactor (Dtr$_N$). Veijola argued that Dtr$_G$ was pro-David, Dtr$_P$ was anti-monarchic, and Dtr$_N$ was anti-monarchic but pro-David.[115]

A second problem of fragmentation does not appear to be related to royal ideology, but is. Not all the sections of the book appear at first to be Deuteronomistic. For example, much of the Elijah and Elisha material from 1 Kings 17 to 2 Kings 13 does not use deuteronomic language, and neither does it often employ the theological ideologies which mark Dtr.[116] At some places, the theology appears anti-Deuteronomistic.[117] What should be done with these sections?[118]

---

exilic period (by 560 BCE). No agreement exists, and today scholars of this school hypothesise redactional layers in the post-exilic period. See my discussion below, and Thomas C. Römer, 'The Current Discussion on the So-Called Deuteronomistic History: Literary Criticism and Theological Consequences', *Christianity and Culture* 46 (2015): 48–9; Sandra L. Richter, 'Deuteronomistic History', *DOTH*, 219–30.

113. Walter Dietrich, *Prophetie und Geschichte: Ein Redaktionsgeschichtliche Untersuchung zum deuteronomistischen Geschichtswerk*, FRLANT (Göttingen: Vandenhoeck & Ruprecht, 1972); Walter Dietrich, 'Martin Noth and the Future of the Deuteronomistic History', in *The History of Israel's Traditions: The Heritage of Martin Noth*, ed. Steven L. McKenzie and M. Patrick Graham, JSOTSup 182 (Sheffield: Sheffield Academic, 1994), 153–75; and for a summary in English see Provan, *Hezekiah and the Books of Kings*, 18–19.

114. Timo Veijola, *Die ewige Dynastie: David und die Entstehung seiner Dynastie nach der deuteronomistischen Historiographie*, Annales Academiæ Scientiarum Fennicae, Series B (Helsinki: Suomalainen Akatemia, 1975); and Timo Veijola, *Das Königtum in der Beurteilung der deuteronomistischen Historiographie: Eine redaktionsgeschichtliche Untersuchung*, Annales Academiæ Scientiarum Fennicae, Series B (Helsinki: Suomalainen Akatemia, 1977). For a summary in English see Richter, 'Deuteronomistic History', 219–30; or Provan, *Hezekiah and the Books of Kings*, 19–20.

115. Veijola, *Die ewige Dynastie*, 68, 79, 126, 42; cited by Richter, 'Deuteronomistic History', 219–30.

116. From these chapters, only 1 Kgs 20–22 and 2 Kgs 8–11 are commonly thought to be Deuteronomistic.

117. For example, Elijah's sacrifice on Mt. Carmel (1 Kgs 18.31-38) is illegal by the standards of Deut. 12. I return to examine this in Chapter 5.

118. For an overview of the problem including bibliography see McKenzie, *The Trouble with Kings*, 81–100.

Some commentators pass over this material, explaining it as non-Dtr, preserved only because of Dtr's fidelity to his source material.[119] Knoppers, for example, published two volumes on *The Deuteronomistic History of the Dual Monarchies*, from Solomon to the exile, with nearly no analysis of the Elijah–Elisha material.[120] Sweeney does something similar in his substantial contribution to the role of Josiah in Kings.[121] Sweeney regards the northern kings as 'foils for the presentation of the Davidic kings who dominate the work from beginning to end',[122] but this seems unreasonable given the volume of narrative they occupy. Omitting material in these kinds of studies is understandable for scholars who are examining the theology of Dtr, since non-Dtr material is not relevant. However, studies like these show that, depending on how one understands the task, a theology of the book of Kings is something different from a theology of DtrH. So we cannot take this path.

Dietrich dealt with the problem of the Elijah–Elisha material differently. Dietrich's thesis assigned this material along with other prophetic voices in the history to Dtr_p, who included the material because of a

---

119. See Noth, *The Deuteronomistic History*, 24–6. Rarely is the material thought post-Dtr because it appears northern in origin and it is difficult to understand why pre-exilic material from the Northern Kingdom came to be included in a southern, post-exilic book. For examples of scholars who take it to be post-Dtr see: McKenzie, *The Trouble with Kings*, 98–100; Antony F. Campbell, *Of Prophets and Kings: A Late Ninth-Century Document (1 Samuel 1–2 Kings 10)*, CBQMS (Washington: Catholic Bible Association, 1986), 111–24; and Susanne Otto, 'The Composition of the Elijah–Elisha Stories and the Deuteronomistic History', *JSOT* 27 (2003): 487–508. On the northern nature of the material see Gary A. Rendsburg, *Israelian Hebrew in the Book of Kings* (Winona Lake, IN: Eisenbrauns, 2002), 148–9.

120. Gary N. Knoppers, *Two Nations Under God: The Deuteronomistic History of Solomon and the Dual Monarchies: The Reign of Solomon and the Rise of Jeroboam*, HSM 52 (Atlanta, GA: Scholars Press, 1993); and Gary N. Knoppers, *Two Nations Under God: The Deuteronomistic History of Solomon and the Dual Monarchies. The Reign of Jeroboam, the Fall of Israel, and the Reign of Josiah*, HSM 53 (Atlanta, GA: Scholars Press, 1994). Volume 1 examines the role of Solomon, and Volume 2 moves directly from the reign of Jeroboam to the fall of Israel.

121. Marvin Sweeney (*King Josiah of Judah*) is interested in the figure of Josiah in the Old Testament, not the book of Kings, and so he considers only the initial Dtr1 redaction in his investigation. Sweeney's investigation of DtrH moves backwards through the history, passing directly from 2 Kgs 17 to Jeroboam without devoting substantial attention to anything in between. The relevant chapter is titled 'The Presentation of the Northern Kingdom of Israel in 1 Kings 12–2 Kings 17' (pp. 77–92) but focuses almost exclusively on 1 Kgs 12 and 2 Kgs 17.

122. Sweeney, *I & II Kings*, 6.

particular interest to add the prophecy–fulfilment schema to the basic historical outline provided by Dtr$_G$.[123] By doing so Dtr$_P$ gave a reason for the exile in terms of the fulfilment of the word of God that came through the prophets (see, e.g., 2 Kgs 17.13-14). The Elijah and Elisha narratives fit this schema much better than the proposed Josianic redaction of the Harvard school because centralisation of worship is only an issue in a pre- or post-exilic context. The Elijah and Elisha material, on the other hand, gives a concrete example of a prophetic call to repentance that was not heeded, ending in exile (e.g., 1 Kgs 19.17-18).

However, now the issue returns to the ideology of kingship we have been discussing. One trouble with the Göttingen proposal is that, since Dtr$_P$ explains the exile, it is anti-monarchic. So how does one account for 2 Samuel 7, which is prophetic in genre but positive concerning kingship? Veijola's solution was to fragment 2 Samuel 7 into Dtr$_P$ and Dtr$_N$, but this is unconvincing because it breaks his own genre-based schema.[124]

Both models then, Harvard and Göttingen, have struggled to account for the retention or creation of pro-monarchic material within a redaction whose primary purpose is anti-monarchic. In my judgment the most likely explanation is that, whatever the textual history, the final text embraces a more complex perspective.[125] Neither the existence of this tension, nor the existence of a redactional history, implies that the book of Kings, taken in its final form, is incoherent.[126] The discussion just clarifies the challenge, which I take up again in Chapter 6.

ii. *The Literary Independence of Kings within DtrH*

A second challenge posed by the theory of DtrH to reading the book of Kings as a unified work is whether it makes sense to understand the book as independent of the rest of the history. If Kings is a subsection of a larger history, then does it make any more sense to read 'Kings' than it does to isolate say, the Solomon narratives (1 Kgs 3–10)?

---

123. Dietrich, *Prophetie und Geschichte*. Note that DtrP did not exist for Smend, who was focused on Joshua and Judges. Only those scholars working with Samuel and Kings, particularly Dietrich, found it necessary to propose this layer of redaction in order to deal with the tension in royal ideology.

124. See Provan, *Hezekiah and the Books of Kings*, 24–9; and Gary N. Knoppers, 'There Was None Like Him: Incomparability in the Books of Kings', *CBQ* 54 (1992): 38–42.

125. Veijola already ascribed a pro-Davidic, anti-monarchic position to DtrN. I shall examine what this may be in Chapter 6.

126. Michael Avioz, *Nathan's Oracle (2 Samuel 7) and its Interpreters*, Bible in History (Bern: Peter Lang, 2005), 9–10.

The theory that the entire history was the product of one or more Dtr(s), or a Dtr school, no longer enjoys the hegemony amongst critical scholars it once did. As Knoppers comments, 'one can no longer assume a widespread scholarly consensus on the existence of a Deuteronomistic history'.[127] The concept of Dtr editing still commands a wide consensus as the best theory we have to account for the common unifying linguistic and theological features across Deuteronomy to 2 Kings.[128] However, it does not follow from this that the same editorial activity created the entire history in its present shape. Some modern proposals understand the books as having literary histories that are independent of, though related to, each other. At some point in their development they have all undergone a Dtr revision, but this need not be at either the point of their origin, or the point of their final formation.[129]

127. Gary N. Knoppers, 'Is There a Future for the Deuteronomistic History?', in *The Future of the Deuteronomistic History*, ed. Thomas Römer, BETL 147 (Leuven: Leuven University Press, 2000), 120. For a brief review of alternative theories and challenges see Knoppers, 'Theories of the Redaction(s) of Kings', 84–7; and Thomas C. Römer, *So-Called Deuteronomistic History: A Sociological, Historical and Literary Introduction* (London: T&T Clark, 2007), 38–41. See also Ernst Axel Knauf, 'Does a "Deuteronomistic Historiography" (DtrH) Exist?', in *Israel Constructs its History: Deuteronomistic Historiography in Recent Research*, ed. A. de Pury, Thomas Römer, and J. D. Macchi, JSOTSup 306 (London: T&T Clark, 2000), 388–98.

128. Römer, *The So-Called Deuteronomistic History*, 40. For this reason the terms 'Deuteronomistic', and 'Deuteronomist' are still used by scholars who focus entirely on a synchronic analysis of the material. E.g., Robert M. Polzin, *Moses and the Deuteronomist: A Literary Study of the Deuteronomic History, Part One: Deuteronomy, Joshua, Judges* (New York: Seabury, 1980).

129. Römer argues that the books originated in the pre-exilic period as separate scrolls, evidenced by the fact that they are separate genres: a vassal treaty, a conquest account, and a chronicle. See Raymond F. Person, 'In Conversation with Thomas Römer, The So-Called Deuteronomistic History: A Sociological, Historical and Literary Introduction', *JHebS* 9 (2009): 7. Knauf has demonstrated that Kings and Samuel have distinct literary histories that are unrelated to each other. See Knoppers, 'Theories of the Redaction(s) of Kings', 85. A. Graeme Auld (*Kings Without Privilege: David and Moses in the Story of the Bible's Kings* [Edinburgh: T&T Clark, 1994], 171–2) envisages a rolling corpus model that begins with the composition of Kings alongside Chronicles as two alternative histories, post-exilic in origin, drawing from a common (non-Dtr) source. Helga Weippert ('Die "deuteronomistischen" Beurteilungen der Könige von Israel und Juda und das Problem der Redaktion der Königsbücher', *Biblia* 53 [1972]: 301–39) understands the history to be comprised of blocks of material that have grown independently, but these blocks do not correspond to the books that are now present in the Hebrew Bible. Wissmann argues for a post-exilic composition of Samuel–Kings that was initially non-Deuteronomistic. See Christoph Levin, 'On the Cohesion and Separation of Books within the Enneateuch', in *Pentateuch, Hexateuch,*

Claus Westermann and Gordon McConville have both proposed that it may be preferable to understand the Primary History as a series of distinct works edited in conversation with one another.[130] There are several lines of evidence. Westermann's argument is diachronic: he finds source-critical evidence for a series of pre-DtrH narratives that begin with the exodus and grow over time into the books we now find in the primary history.[131] Much of the source material is pre-monarchic, though it does not reach its final form until the post-exilic era.[132] Westermann proposes that Dtr editing represents only one redactional layer of these books. Dtr does not create Israel's history, but adds only a thin interpretive theological framework to the existing series of books. This interpretive framework is what we now call Dtr theology. McConville reaches a similar conclusion from a synchronic perspective, by noticing that recent scholarship focusing on literary readings of the various individual books has been very successful.[133] He cites Barry Webb's study of Judges:

> This is perhaps clearest in [Webb's] treatment of the final part of the book, Judges 17–21, which is often thought to be a separate strand within it. Here, though he calls it a 'Coda', it finds a place in the development of the theme of Judges, and constitutes the end of this particular story. In the search for 'blocks', therefore, Webb's work suggests that the story of the judges closes at the end of the book called Judges, and not, as others have thought, with the narratives of Saul and Samuel.[134]

or Enneateuch? Identifying Literary Works in Genesis through Kings, ed. Thomas B. Dozeman, Thomas Römer, and Konrad Schmid, AIL (Atlanta, GA: SBL, 2011), 254–7. See also James R. Linville, 'Rethinking the "Exilic" Book of Kings', *JSOT* 22 (1997): 21–42; and Linville, *Israel in the Book of Kings*, 69–73.

130. See also Kurt L. Noll, 'Deuteronomistic History or Deuteronomic Debate? (A Thought Experiment)', *JSOT* 31 (2007): 311–45.

131. Claus Westermann, *Die Geschichtsbücher des Alten Testaments: Gab es ein deuteronomistisches Geschichtswerk?*, Theologische Bücherei Altes Testament (Gütersloh: Kaiser, 1994), 13–39. See also Richter, 'Deuteronomistic History', 219–30; and Knoppers, 'Is There a Future for the Deuteronomistic History?', 120–4. Cf. Noth (*The Deuteronomistic History*, 76): '…[DtrH] is not a matter of a "Deuteronomistic redaction" of a historical narrative that was already more or less complete'.

132. See also A. Graeme Auld, *Life in Kings: Reshaping the Royal Story in the Hebrew Bible* (Atlanta, GA: SBL, 2017), 89–102, who proposes that Kings and Chronicles both draw on a pre-exilic 'synoptic' narrative.

133. J. Gordon McConville, 'The Old Testament Historical Books in Modern Scholarship', *Them* 22 (1997): 3–13. See also McConville, *God and Earthly Power*, 8–10.

134. McConville, 'The Old Testament Historical Books in Modern Scholarship', 9, discussing Barry Webb, *The Book of Judges: An Integrated Reading*, JSOTSup 46 (Sheffield: JSOT, 1987).

Literary studies of the other books in DtrH show similar conclusions.[135] If there does not exist a 'book' called Judges, or Samuel, for example, then why do the 'appendices' of Judges and Samuel function so well as conclusions to those sections? Why do these books have such strong internal structural and thematic coherence, and closure?[136] My own explorations of literary structure in Chapter 2 will show this internal coherence to be true of Kings also.[137]

Even though there is no scholarly consensus on the relationship of the book of Kings to DtrH, one advantage of removing it from the literary context of DtrH, and reading it as an independent book, is that it can re-open observations of both theology and context that had been closed.[138]

We have already noted in the section above that a theology of Kings is not identical to a theology of the Deuteronomist. We might add to that an observation concerning its intertextuality.[139] As with the other books in DtrH, Kings depends heavily on the traditions and texts located outside of DtrH. There are many traditions in Exodus, for example, that Kings assumes the reader knows, not all of which are replicated in Deuteronomy.[140] Kings assumes knowledge of the 'covenant with Abraham, Isaac and Jacob' (2 Kgs 13.2; Exod. 2.24) a phrase which

---

135. E.g. Gillian Keys's critique (*The Wages of Sin: A Reappraisal of the 'Succession Narrative'*, JSOTSup 221 (Sheffield: JSOT, 1996], 213–17) of the succession narrative concludes that 1 and 2 Samuel were incorporated into DtrH as a single block.

136. E.g. Robert P. Gordon, *1&2 Samuel* (London: Paternoster, 1986), 21; and Robert M. Polzin, *David and the Deuteronomist: A Literary Study of the Deuteronomic History, Part 3: 2 Samuel* (Bloomington, IN: Indiana University Press, 1993), 202.

137. Christoph Levin ('On the Cohesion and Separation of Books within the Enneateuch', 132–3, 152–4) explains this phenomenon by a process of literary growth, where the Enneateuch was initially conceived as a single work, but forced into separate books by the requirement of scroll length. Each book then grew separately, but in continued dialogue with all the others.

138. See, e.g., Avioz, *Nathan's Oracle*, 9–10.

139. On the problem of intertextuality and redaction-criticism see Thomas Römer, 'How Many Books (teuchs): Pentateuch, Hexateuch, Deuteronomistic History, or Enneateuch?', in Dozeman, Römer, and Schmid, eds., *Pentateuch, Hexateuch, or Enneatuech?*, 40.

140. The argument below does not suggest that the author of Kings had access to the completed versions of these other books. The literary history of all of the books was probably co-dependent, so that they reached their final form in conversation with one another. See, e.g., Christoph Berner, 'Literary Connections Between Exodus 1–15 and 1 Kings 1–12?', in Dozeman, Römer, and Schmid, eds., *Pentateuch, Hexateuch, or Enneatuech?*, 211–40.

only occurs in Exodus.[141] It also knows the contents of the main exodus tradition (e.g., 2 Kgs 17.7-8), the ark traditions (1 Kgs 8.4-11), the golden calves (1 Kgs 12.28; Exod. 12.28), Pharaoh's 'hard labour' (1 Kgs 12.4; Exod. 1.14), and the details surrounding the tabernacle which the temple replaces. The intertextuality between Kings and Exodus is as extensive as that of the books in DtrH,[142] except Deuteronomy itself.[143] There are relationships between Kings and other books that also deserve mention, the latter prophets for example, but to do so would take us too far from our present course.[144] All of this suggests that there is value in considering Kings as an independent book, read within the literary context suggested by its own inter-textual allusions.

iii. *Dtr and Nomenclature of Authorship*

A note on nomenclature is now in order. I have elected, where possible, to avoid language associated with the Deuteronomistic hypothesis. This has not always been possible where I engage with others who use a version of the theory. In the place of 'deuteronomist(s)' I prefer 'author', and in the place of 'Deuteronomistic History' I prefer 'Primary History'. I have tried to avoid the adjective 'deuteronomistic' altogether, and I use the variant 'deuteronomic' to refer only to that which pertains to the book of Deuteronomy.[145]

---

141. The only other occurrence of this phrase is Exod. 2.24, though see Lev. 26.42 which also mentions all of the patriarchs together.

142. From the traditions found in Joshua the book knows at least of the capture of Jericho (1 Kgs 16.34, though, relocated to Josiah in 𝔊ᴸ) and, as I show in Chapter 5, the traditions surrounding crossing the Jordan. From Judges, Kings knows the cycle of apostasy and salvation, as I show in Chapter 4; and from Samuel, other than the obvious and repeated allusion to 2 Sam. 7, it knows the story of Uriah the Hittite (1 Kgs 15.5), and the words of Sheba the son of Bichri (1 Kgs 12.16).

143. Within Deuteronomy, Kings assumes knowledge particularly of the first two commandments (Deut. 5.6-10), the so-called altar laws (Deut. 12), the laws against intermarriage (Deut. 7.3-4), the covenant blessings and curses (Deut. 27–28), the punishment of exile for apostasy (Deut. 4.25-28), the law of the king (Deut. 17.14-20), the Passover (Deut. 16.1-8), the law concerning punishment of children for the sin of the fathers (Deut. 24.16), and makes many other textual allusions and references besides these.

144. E.g. the mention of Jonah in 2 Kgs 14.25; or the literary dependence (one way or another) of 2 Kgs 18–20 on Isa. 36–39 and 2 Kgs 25 on Jer. 39 and 52.

145. This may cause some confusion, since for some this term is synonymous with 'Deuteronomistic'. See, e.g., Raymond F. Person, *The Deuteronomic School: History, Social Setting, and Literature*, Studies in Biblical Literature (Atlanta, GA: SBL, 2002), 7.

The reader should not misunderstand my intention. As I discussed above, the theory of DtrH remains the most plausible way to explain the commonalities of language across the books. However, as we have seen, the relationship of this editorial work to the final version of the book is unclear, and the theology of Kings is only coterminous with Dtr theology in some versions of the theory. By avoiding the language, I hope to avoid ambiguity on the one hand, since there are now so many versions of the theory, and prejudgment on the other. To speak of the Dtr theology involves a predetermination of what it means for a text to be classified as Deuteronomistic, which is a route I am eager to avoid.

By using the term 'author', I also am not trying to indicate that I believe the entire book is the product of a single hand all at once. I am persuaded that the book originates in some form in the pre-exilic period, but whether this pre-exilic text should be regarded as a version of Kings in its own right, or as the source material used by a later author, is a separate question. I am inclined towards the latter. Nevertheless, even if it exists, it is not the theology of the pre-exilic text that interests us. At some point, the book of Kings reached something close to the form we now have it.[146] It is at that point that the book is 'authored' and that is what I mean by 'author'.

1.3.2. *The Historical Context of Kings*

i. *Kings as Exilic Literature*

I have located the book of Kings within a Babylonian milieu, written in response to the national crisis of the exile, and intended to ground the Israelite identity in their pre-exilic history. Until recently, this claim would not have been controversial in scholarship.[147] *Prima facie* the history seems exilic because it concludes with the release of Jehoiachin in 562 BCE and knows nothing of the Persians, or of Cyrus's decree. The book has much in common with Israel's other crisis literature, particularly Jeremiah,[148] in its focus on issues of covenant and judgment, restoration, and the relationship between the word of God and historical events.

---

146. I return in the next section to a discussion of the final form of Kings.

147. Noth's theory (*The Deuteronomistic History*, 79–83) centred on the idea that the history was written to explain the exile. The debate immediately following concerned to what extent the book offered hope to the exiles. See my review in Lovell, 'The Shape of Hope', 4–5. Until the turn of the century, both Harvard and Göttingen schools continued to assume an exilic finalisation of composition. See, e.g., Richter, 'Deuteronomistic History', 219–30.

148. The theological and textual relationship between Kings and Jeremiah is well explored in the literature, from historical-critical, text-critical, and theological perspectives. So similar are the books that Jeremiah has sometimes been thought to

Challenges to this position have come from several places. The first is that advanced by Linville, who places the composition of Kings in the late Persian or early Hellenistic periods.[149] He does this because he follows Philip Davies's reconstruction of the canonical process, which understands the composition of all the biblical history within that period.[150] Linville claims the book uses the exile as a symbol to assure the diaspora communities now in Egypt and Mesopotamia that they too belonged to Israel.[151] Despite this, Linville acknowledges that Kings has exilic appearance:

> If Kings strikes the reader as a product of an exile, then one has made clearer observation of the attitude of its producers towards their world, rather than of the narrowly defined range of dates in which these writers laboured.[152]

However, Linville's argument relies on a historical reconstruction which is itself speculative, and so must overcome through special pleading the objection that Kings appears exilic.[153] It is true that the book *could* be the product of a post-exilic milieu. But I hope to demonstrate in this study how well Kings works, and makes sense, when read as what it appears to be.

---

be the author of Kings. For a recent overview see Gershon Galil, 'The Message of the Book of Kings in Relation to Deuteronomy and Jeremiah', *BSac* 158 (2001): 406. See also Person, *The Deuteronomic School*, 9–13.

149. Linville, 'Rethinking the "Exilic" Book of Kings', 21–42; *Israel in the Book of Kings*, 70–3; and 'On the Authority of Dead Kings', in *Deuteronomy–Kings as Emerging Authoritative Books: A Conversation*, ed. Diana V. Edelman, Ancient Near East Monographs (Atlanta, GA: SBL, 2014), 203–22.

150. Davies, *In Search of Ancient Israel*, 99–120; Linville, *Israel in the Book of Kings*, 25–7. For a range of more moderate positions with respect to the history of Israel, see the essays in H. Shanks et al., eds., *The Rise of Ancient Israel: Symposium at the Smithsonian Institution, October 26, 1991* (Washington: Biblical Archeology Society, 1992). For conservative scholarship consult B. T. Arnold and R. S. Hess, eds., *Ancient Israel's History: An Introduction to Issues and Sources* (Grand Rapids, MI: Baker Academic, 2014). I deal specifically with the question of composition below.

151. Linville, 'Rethinking the 'Exilic' Book of Kings', 38–42.

152. Linville, *Israel in the Book of Kings*, 71.

153. Rendsburg goes further, noting the improbability of a theory that post-exilic Judahite scribes used a pre-exilic northern dialect of Hebrew to fabricate their narratives concerning the north: Rendsburg, *Of Prophets and Kings*, 149. See Chapter 2 of this study for my discussion.

Recent work within the Göttingen school has often taken position similar to Linville's that, while Kings may originate in an exilic context, it has substantial post-exilic redactions. Blanco Wissmann, for example, argues for a redactional layer as late as the Persian era, because it was not till then that 'in the ancient Near East in general the concept of "law" gained importance'.[154] Similarly, Thomas Römer has argued for a Persian-era Deuteronomistic redaction of DtrH.[155] However, the date of Dtr_N varies amongst proponents of the position,[156] and also relies on historical speculation about the implausibility of pre-exilic law-code traditions.[157] There is no external evidence of a Dtr_N redaction, or that it is necessarily post-exilic if it exists. And perhaps the most pervasive critique of the Göttingen school has been the theory's inability to suggest a plausible post-exilic context for Dtr_N.[158]

---

154. Felipe Blanco Wissmann, '"He Did What Was Right": Criteria of Judgment and Deuteronomism in the Books of Kings', in Dozeman, Römer, and Schmid, eds., *Pentateuch, Hexateuch, or Enneateuch?*, 255. Wissmann's larger argument relies on parallels between the judgment formula in Kings with neo-Babylonian literature, in an attempt to show that there was no pre-exilic (Assyrian) version of Kings.

155. Römer, *The So-Called Deuteronomistic History*, 165–84; and 'The Case of the Book of Kings', in Edelman, ed., *Deuteronomy–Kings as Emerging Authoritative Books*, 187–202. Within the Göttingen School, DtrN was sometimes thought to be post-exilic. E.g. on DtrN in 1 Kgs 8, see Ernst Würthwein, *Die Bücher der Könige: 1 Könige 1–16*, ATD 11/1 (Göttingen: Vandenhoeck & Ruprecht, 1977), 95–6; Dietrich, *Prophetie und Geschichte*, 74; and see also D. F. O'Kennedy, 'The Prayer of Solomon (1 Ki 8:22-53): Paradigm for the Understanding of Forgiveness in the Old Testament', *OTE* 13 (2000): 75–6. Scholars date DtrN widely depending on how they reconstruct the literary history of Deuteronomy. For an example of a late DtrN see Kratz, *The Composition of the Narrative Books of the Old Testament*, 159–86.

156. In earlier German works, all of the redactional layers were thought to be exilic or near-exilic. Later work tends to understand DtrG as exilic, with varying dates for subsequent layers. See Römer, 'The Current Discussion on the So-Called Deuteronomistic History', 48–9; or Richter, 'Deuteronomistic History', 219–30.

157. For a conservative opinion based on critical scholarship see Christopher B. Ansburry and Jerry Hwang, 'No Covenant Before the Exile? The Deuteronomic Torah and Israel's Covenant Theology', in *Evangelical Faith and the Challenge of Historical Criticism*, ed. Christopher M. Hays and Christopher B. Ansburry (London: SPCK, 2013), 74–94.

158. E.g. Knoppers, *Two Nations Under God 1*, 38–42; Provan, *Hezekiah and the Books of Kings*, 22–31. Dever ('Archeology and the Question of Sources in Kings', in Halpern and Lemaire, eds., *The Books of Kings*, 538) also notes that there is archaeological evidence for at least one pre-exilic (i.e. seventh century BCE) redaction.

A more common challenge is based on manuscript evidence. Does the textual evidence show an ongoing process of composition in the post-exilic period?[159] What is the relationship between the MT version (or some other 'final form' text) and the exilic text?[160]

It is no longer feasible to assume that an exilic text is recoverable through text-critical means.[161] This results from discoveries at Qumran which show that the text of the various books in the Old Testament was in some measure fluid throughout the Persian period.[162] Neither is it simple to draw a fixed boundary between composition and transmission, nor between redaction-criticism and text-criticism.[163] Raymond Person Jnr.,

---

159. For an overview and discussion of the textual evidence that exists for the book of Kings see Emanuel Tov, *Textual Criticism of the Hebrew Bible*, 3rd ed. (Philadelphia, PA: Fortress, 2011), 306–11. Most of our textual data come from the versions of the book (MT, LXX, Targums, Syriac, or Latin). Only three fragments of Kings have been found at Qumran, and preserve only about 50 verses between them, all quite similar to the MT. See Julio C. Trebolle Barrera, 'Qumran Fragments of the Books of Kings', in Halpern and Lemaire, eds., *The Books of Kings*, 19–27; Mordechai Cogan, *1 Kings: A New Translation with Introduction and Commentary*, AB 10 (New Haven, CT: Yale University Press, 2008), 85. There is also pertinent textual data preserved in fragments that contain the parallel passages within Isaiah and Jeremiah, though the relationship of these parallels is debated.

160. The difficulty of this question means that final form readings are often employed even by scholarship that is interested in questions of textual history, e.g., Cogan, *1 Kings*, 85–6.

161. Cogan, *1 Kings*, 85–6.

162. Moshe Greenberg, *Studies in the Bible and Jewish Thought* (Philadelphia, PA: Jewish Publication Society, 1995), 191–208. There is less particular evidence at Qumran concerning Kings than other books, but there is little doubt that the general result holds. However, the nature of the fluidity is a matter of ongoing discussion. Many advocate a model of stability alongside fluidity. See Arie van der Kooij, 'Standardization or Preservation? Some Comments on the Textual History of the Hebrew Bible in the Light of Josephus and Rabbinic Literature', in *The Text of the Hebrew Bible: From the Rabbis to the Masoretes*, ed. Elvira Martín-Contreras and Lorena Miralles-Maciá, JAJS 13 (Göttingen: Vandenhoeck & Ruprecht, 2014), 63–78; Tov, *Textual Criticism of the Hebrew Bible*, 29–31; or Emanuel Tov, 'Some Thoughts about the Diffusion of Biblical Manuscripts in Antiquity', in *The Dead Sea Scrolls: Transmission of Traditions and Production of Texts*, ed. Sarianna Metso, Hindy Najman, and Eileen Schuller, STDJ 92 (Leiden: Brill, 2010), 151–69.

163. The literature demonstrating this result is substantial. Studies on passages within Kings in particular include: Trebolle Barrera, 'Qumran Fragments of the Books of Kings', 3–19; Person, *The Deuteronomic School*; Adrian Schenker, 'Jeroboam and the Division of the Kingdom in the Ancient Septuagint: LXX 3 Kingdoms 12:24a–z,

for example, has used text-critical observations to argue for the continued activity of the Deuteronomistic school into the post-exilic era.¹⁶⁴

Our question, however, is not whether the text has post-exilic changes, but against which historical background we should read it. The mere fact of changes does not address this question; we must assess their nature. Do the post-exilic changes reflect intentional authorial activity, whereby the book has been modified to address the particular concerns of a post-exilic audience? Is there, for example, a P redaction? Only 1 Kings 8 is sometimes argued to show evidence of P due to the appearance of the cloud and other supposedly late theophanic elements, and I return to the discussion in Chapter 5.¹⁶⁵ Mostly, the changes we observe are those we would expect to see in the normal process of updating, preservation and transmission.¹⁶⁶

MT 1 Kings 11–12; 14 and the Deuteronomistic History', in Pury, Römer, and Macchi, eds., *Israel Constructs its History*, 214–57; Julio C. Trebolle Barrera, 'Redaction, Recension, and Midrash in the Books of Kings', in Knoppers and McConville, eds., *Reconsidering Israel and Judah*, 475–92; Trebolle Barrera, 'Old Latin, Old Greek, and Old Hebrew in the Books of Kings (1 Ki 18:25 and 2 Ki 20:11)', *Text* 13 (1986): 85–94; Trebolle Barrera, 'The Text-Critical Use of the Septuagint in the Books of Kings', in *VII Congress of the International Organisation for Septuagint and Cognate Studies, Leuven 1989*, ed. C. E. Cox, SBLSCS (Atlanta, GA: Scholars Press, 1991), 285–99. For a more substantial bibliography on the result in general, including works by Auld, Tov, and Rofé, see Person, *The Deuteronomic School*, 21–2 n. 12.

164. Person, *The Deuteronomic School*, 21–9.

165. See also Gary N. Knoppers, 'Prayer and Propaganda: Solomon's Dedication of the Temple and the Deuteronomist's Program', *CBQ* 57 (1995): 233–9. Knoppers argues that the P sections are integral to the purposes of Dtr₂, and Kings must therefore be drawing on prior traditions that would later be characteristic of P.

166. Certain modifications to the text would be expected in, e.g., David Carr's model of textual transmission (*The Formation of the Hebrew Bible: A New Reconstruction* [New York: Oxford University Press, 2011]), e.g., errors of memory that do not drastically modify the overall shape or themes of the work. Carr's model is particularly relevant for what he calls 'long-duration literature': those texts 'deemed by a certain group to be a heritage to be transmitted from one generation to another by performance and memory'. This would include the book of Kings (pp. 34–5). Carr's model of transmission involves rehearsal and transmission of texts from memory in a communal setting, but with a recourse to a written work to settle disputes. In this setting, several kinds of changes would be expected (pp. 60–2): variation in word order; shifts between semantic equivalents; shifts in designations of figures (e.g., אלהים for יהוה or מלך ישראל for אחאב); shifts in prepositions with similar force; additions or omissions of minor particles (such as כל); updating of language after diachronic shifts; and the reduplication of similar ideas or language from other places in a way that does not significantly impact the discourse. In this latter category we can include instances of repetition or translation of Deuteronomic language, as scribes

As McKenzie astutely commented, 'a later addition does not a redaction make'.¹⁶⁷

Person's book, *The Deuteronomic School: History, Social Setting and Literature*, provides an interesting case-study. His argument for post-exilic Dtr activity relies on text-critical observations. Assuming the priority of the LXX,¹⁶⁸ he notices several differences between the LXX and MT that must be post-exilic and that appear to be Deuteronomistic in nature:

> The text-critical studies summarized above have suggested that each of these passages contain post-LXX additions to the MT, most of which appear to be postexilic... Therefore, the text-critical evidence alone suggests a postexilic setting for some redactional activity of the deuteronomic school in the Deuteronomic History.¹⁶⁹

How can Person know that the changes are *Deuteronomistic*? His argument relies on the same commonalities of language and theology that have always characterised the school.¹⁷⁰ For this reason, Person observes that these changes are impossible to detect by redaction-critical means alone:

> These postexilic additions in the final Deuteronomic redaction...have been incorrectly treated by many as originating in the exilic period at the hand of Deuteronomic redactors. These additions have been so treated because the themes and language therein are so similar to the material in the earlier redactions...that these scholars could not discern a thematic or phraseological difference between what the text-critical evidence suggests came from different stages of the redaction of the Deuteronomic History. In other words, for the study of the Deuteronomic History, the stylistic and thematic criteria for redaction-criticism have proven insufficient in discerning different redactional layers evident from text-criticism. This insufficiency of the stylistic and thematic criteria can be explained by noting that the language and themes of the different redactional layers are so similar that the application of these criteria could not separate out the different layers.¹⁷¹

who are familiar with the style and idiosyncratic phrases import them into places that they did not exist already. In other words, this kind of preservation and transmission is not especially suited to letter-accurate duplication of texts, but it is well suited to the preservation of literary shape, meaning, and theology.

167. Steven L. McKenzie, 'The Books of Kings in the Deuteronomistic History', in McKenzie and Graham, eds., *The History of Israel's Traditions*, 299.
168. See my comments in the next section.
169. Person, *The Deuteronomic School*, 48.
170. Person, *The Deuteronomic School*, 4–7.
171. Person, *The Deuteronomic School*, 49–50.

In other words, Person argues post-exilic additions exist in the text, but there are no thematic, stylistic, or theological criteria by which we might discern them. He suggests several texts from DtrH that may have been post-exilic including 2 Samuel 7, but his historical reconstruction comes with the following disclaimer:

> My criticism of the above interpretations does not suggest that they require, rather than an exilic setting, a post-exilic setting…it may be that further research will show that some of the above passages were produced in the exilic period, while others were produced in the post-exilic period.[172]

On closer inspection, this is true of many claims of post-exilic insertions. Römer's list of proposed post-exilic changes is often cited, but they are in fact minimal in Kings.[173] He lists a heavier emphasis on monotheism in Solomon's prayer of dedication, and the acceptance of a diaspora situation in the ending of 2 Kings.[174] However, monotheism is recognised in literature regarded as exilic (e.g., Isa. 44.6), and the ending of the book is explained by an exilic context more easily than a Persian one.

Even though there may be post-exilic fluidity in the text, there are no passages that conclusively demonstrate a post-exilic interest. It is therefore reasonable to conclude that post-exilic textual fluidity was not of the kind that reflected a distinctive ideology or generated theological modifications. There is still the question of the LXX, to which I return below, but the result here is that the most feasible historical context against which to read the book remains exilic.[175]

ii. *Which Text of Kings? The Question of the Septuagint*

At the least, Kings circulated in two recensions in the post-exilic era: there was some *Vorlage* of the LXX,[176] and the text that stabilised to the

---

172. Person, *The Deuteronomic School*, 55–6.
173. He suggests several other changes within DtrH, and particularly within Deuteronomy.
174. Römer, *The So-Called Deuteronomistic History*, 174–6.
175. In a result similar to my own, Ben Zvi ('Prophetic Memories', 100) argues that it would have been impossible for the prophetic corpus to take its present shape in a community where the historical narrative of DtrH (or something similar) was not already known. The final form of DtrH may have evolved, but the basic narrative must have been established.
176. In the LXX, 1 Kings and 2 Kings are labelled 3 Kingdoms and 4 Kingdoms respectively (following 1 and 2 Kingdoms, which are 1 and 2 Samuel in MT). This is a convenient distinction which I retain.

MT.[177] The text of the two versions is very similar between 2 Kings and 4 Kingdoms, but there are several larger differences between 1 Kings and 3 Kingdoms.[178] Notably, 3 Kingdoms includes a long alternative version of the Jeroboam story (3 Kgdms 12.24*a-z*), and several transpositions and repetitions within Solomon's narratives. There are also chronological differences in the regnal formula throughout 1–2 Kings / 3–4 Kingdoms.[179]

As we noted above, these alternative versions do not represent an alternate theological or ideological version of the book. Take for example the summary of Solomon's wisdom in 3 Kgdms 2.35*a-o*,[180] which mostly represents a different arrangement of the material in MT:

---

177. The relationship between these two texts is a matter of ongoing discussion. The traditional view reads the LXX as a rewritten version of the MT. See, e.g., Andrzej S. Turkanik, *Of Kings and Reigns: A Study in the Translation Technique in the Gamma/Gamma Section of 3 Reigns (1 Kings)*, FAT 2/30 (Tübingen: Mohr Siebeck, 2008); Marvin A. Sweeney, 'A Reassessment of the Masoretic and Septuagint Versions of the Jeroboam Narratives in 1 Kings/3 Kingdoms 11–14', *JSJ* 38 (2007): 165–95; Tov, *Textual Criticism of the Hebrew Bible*, 306–8. Others challenge this. E.g. Schenker ('The Septuagint in the Text History of 1–2 Kings', in Halpern and Lemaire, eds., *The Books of Kings*, 3–17) and Trebolle Barrera ('Textual Criticism and the Literary Structure and Composition of 1–2 Kings/3–4 Kingdoms: The Different Sequence of Literary Units in MT and LXX', *Septuaginta* [2012]: 55–78) argue that 𝔊^L, the *Vetus Latina*, and Josephus together preserve a pre-Kaige layer, closer to 𝔊*, and represent a different textual tradition than the MT text. (See the next footnote.) A complete literature review of both positions can be found in Sweeney, 'A Reassessment of the Masoretic and Septuagint Versions', 165–9.

178. The outer sections of the book, 2 Kgdms 10.1–3 Kgdms 2.22 (βγ) and 3 Kgdms 22.1–4 Kgdms 25.30 (γδ), appear to be based on a different Greek base text than the middle section, 3 Kgdms 2.23–21.43. These outer sections show signs of a Kaige revision, which stands behind the major LXX recensions (𝔊^O, θ, α, and σ). The middle section, comprising most of 3 Kingdoms, does not, and is closer to 𝔊^L. This has led scholars to conclude that 3 Kgdms 3.1–21.43 may preserve something of 𝔊* which likely represents a different textual tradition than what is found in the MT or LXX. See Ernst Würthwein and Alexander A. Fischer, *The Text of the Old Testament: An Introduction to the Biblia Hebraica*, trans. Errol F. Rhodes, 3rd ed. (Grand Rapids, MI: Eerdmans, 2014), 122–4.

179. Tov, *Textual Criticism of the Hebrew Bible*, 306–8.

180. All of the substantial variant readings come from the non-Kaige sections of Kings (i.e. 3 Kgdms 2.23–21.43), which is to be expected.

Table 1.1. *Parallels between 3 Kgdms 2:35a-o and MT 1 Kings*

(Sections that are not paralleled are translated.)

LXX 3 Kingdoms 2:35a-o[181]	**MT 1 Kings**
35a-b	4.29-30
35c	3.1
35d	5.15
35e	7.23
35f(α), 'And he built the citadel and its defenses, and he cut through the city of Dauid'	
35f(β)-g	9.24-25
35h(α)	9.23
35h(β)	5.16
35i-k, 'And he built Assour and Magdo and Gazer and Upper Baithoron and Baalath; only after he built the house of the Lord and the wall of Ierousalem round about, after these he built these cities'	
35l-o	2.8-9

The information present in 3 Kgdms 2.35a-o that is not in 1 Kings is of historical interest, but nothing in this material causes us to evaluate Solomon differently. Such is the case with many of the substantial variants. The exception is the alternative version of the story of Jeroboam in 3 Kgdms 12.24a-z. In part, this story is also a different arrangement of material otherwise known from 1 Kings 11, 12, and 14. There are, however, enough substantial differences between the MT and LXX versions of this story that it probably represents an alternative version of the incident.[182]

Between the two versions, Jeroboam is portrayed more negatively in the LXX. 3 Kingdoms 12.24*b* notes that his mother is a prostitute where she is a widow in 1 Kgs 11.26,[183] and the LXX has him explicitly 'aspiring to the kingdom' (v. 24*b*), where MT attributes a fear to Solomon based only on Jeroboam's capability and Ahijah's prediction (1 Kgs 11.25-26, 40). In the LXX Jeroboam marries the daughter of Pharaoh, Ano (v. 24*e*), which is not mentioned in MT but may be read as a further sign of his

---

181. All English translations in this table are from the New English Translation of the Septuagint. Available online: http://ccat.sas.upenn.edu/nets/edition/.

182. The story has generated substantial scholarly interest. See, e.g., Schenker, 'Jeroboam and the Division of the Kingdom', 214–57; Zipora Talshir, *The Alternative Story of the Division of the Kingdom: 3 Kingdoms 12:24a-z* (Jerusalem: Simor, 1993); and Sweeney, 'A Reassessment of the Masoretic and Septuagint Versions', 165–95.

183. However, this verse is also present in 3 Kgdms 11.26, where she is also a widow.

threat to Rehoboam after Solomon's death.[184] And there are numerous differences in the details of story of Jeroboam's sick child (3 Kgdms 12.24g-n/1 Kgs 14.1-18).

However, the location of the narrative in the LXX has more significant consequences than any of the details. By placing the narrative into the context of the Shechem assembly, the LXX has a prophetic condemnation of Jeroboam and his offspring before either the golden calves, or the creation of the Northern Kingdom. It uses a formula normally reserved for the prophetic denouncement of a dynasty:

> I will utterly destroy from Ieroboam one that urinates against a wall [i.e. all the male offspring] and the dead of Ieroboam will be in the city; the dogs will devour them, and the birds of the air will devour the one who has died in the field. (3 Kgdms 12.24m, NETS)

In 1 Kings 14, the story follows after the golden calves, and Yahweh's condemnation of Jeroboam is explicitly in response to the calves (1 Kgs 14.9). In 3 Kingdoms 12, the story follows the return of Jeroboam from Egypt, and we can only infer (though it is not stated) that he is being condemned simply for aspiring to Solomon's kingdom (v. 24b).

From this, we do end up with a different assessment of Jeroboam's characterisation in Kings than Kingdoms. However, the theology of the division of the kingdoms remains the same because Ahijah's prophecy to Jeroboam is still given before the assembly in both versions (1 Kgs/ 3 Kgdms 11.29-39),[185] and 3 Kingdoms reminds us of this prophecy at Shechem (3 Kgdms 12.24o). In both versions the division of the kingdom results from Solomon's sin and the prophetically announced initiative of Yahweh (3 Kgdms 12.24y).

In the next chapter, I develop a structural and thematic overview of the book of Kings. This overview attempts to encapsulate all the things that make the book of Kings work as literature: its plot, thematic development, and its literary structure. My analysis in that chapter applies equally well to either version of the book. As I demonstrated here, they also have little significance for my ideological argument. This accords well with the result above, that any post-exilic fluidity in the text of Kings is not significant for the presentation of the book's ideology and theology. Given this, my study will use a final-form reading of the MT.[186]

---

184. Has Jeroboam's alliance with Egypt now superseded the late-Solomon's, which was formed the same way (3 Kgdms 2.35c)?
185. LXX omits v. 39, but this is repeated information in any case.
186. The LXX would have worked just as well, but most scholarship deals with the MT and it is more familiar as the base text of the major English translations.

1.3.3. *Summary and Synopsis of the Present Work*

In summary, then, this study explores the way that the narrative of Kings, read as an integrated narrative, might have shaped the national identity of its exilic audience. I propose that the book of Kings constructs, through the narration of a national history, an expression of Israelite identity. I shall argue that this provided the exiles with a sense of continuity with the past, hope for the future, and an expression of identity that could cope with the immediate problem, which was the loss of the land, the temple, and the Davidic monarch.

The first task of the study, then, is to develop an approach to reading Kings that integrates the book into a coherent whole. In Chapter 2 I discern an overarching narrative structure within the book, to provide a big picture against which all the smaller parts can be interpreted. I propose in this chapter that Kings can be described as a literary intercalation of two stories, which I label Inner and Outer Kings. Inner Kings (1 Kgs 16.23–2 Kgs 15.38) focuses on the story of the Omrides and Yahweh's purpose to destroy Ahab's dynasty, announced to Elijah, and fulfilled through Elisha, Jehu, and Hazael. Outer Kings tells the story of the two kingdoms in relation to Yahweh's promise to David for an eternal kingdom. The two stories, I claim, are mutually interpretive.

Having established this, it will be possible to move to an analysis of the ideology of the book using the categories I have outlined above. In Chapters 3 through 6, I analyse the roles of the *covenant, nationhood, place,* and *rule* in the book, and attempt to discern the way these concepts should shape the (exilic) community's self-understanding.

Chapter 3 examines the role that the covenant plays within Israel's social politics as it is narrated in Kings. I argue that the covenant is used in the narrative in several ways. First, it gives shape to what it means to be Israel, and second it defines who Israel is in dialectic with the surrounding nations. As Israel abandons the covenant, they become politically less like Israel and more like the nations, until they are finally assimilated. The covenant is also integrated with the Davidic promise such that the fulfilment of that promise can only occur by means of Israel's faithfulness to the covenant. The unconditional nature of the promise therefore gives hope that one day a covenantally faithful Israel will emerge, and this is the basis of hope for the future of Israel in the book.

Chapter 4 focuses on issues of nationhood by examining the way the concept of Israel is given definition in the narrative in the wake of their two political crises: first the division of the kingdoms, and second the exile. I claim that neither of these events fundamentally changes what it means to be an Israelite. On the one hand the division of the kingdoms does not create two versions of 'Israel', it creates a schism within one people. On the other, through the exile, a remnant of Israel is preserved. The remnant is, in the metaphor of Kings, a seed – Israel in embryonic form – from which a new Israel can be grown.

Chapter 5 analyses the role of the land in the narrative of Kings as it relates to the theme of Yahweh's presence. I show that, in the thought of the book, Yahweh is not contained within Israel's territory, but he makes himself available there. The temple represents Yahweh's purpose to be found amongst his people, but the narrative of Kings shows that Yahweh is not restricted by it, and so this is not the only place that Yahweh can be found. Because of this, it relativises the role of the land in relation to the political identity of Yahweh's people. The possibility is opened of forming a genuine worshipping community that is centred on prophetic activity rather than cultic structures.

In Chapter 6 I examine the royal ideology presented in the book. I claim that the book of Kings is positive towards the institution of kingship, but within this general approval presents an *apologia* for a particular kind of rule, set within the ANE ideologies of kingship. The book of Kings presents an argument that Israel's kings should be characterised by servanthood in the manner of the shepherd-king ideal of Mesopotamian culture. Kings does not look to Solomon as an ideal ruler of a golden age past and engenders no hope for a return to that kind of kingdom. I argue that the combination of the Davidic expectation in the narrative with a clear ideology of rule creates hope for an ideal future ruler of a different kind.

Finally, Chapter 7 integrates the various ideological findings, to produce a statement of the ideology that underlies the narrative of kings, and a statement of the rhetorical strategy used by the author to influence the identity of its exilic readers.

2

The Narrative Strategy of Kings

2.1. *The Challenge of Structuring Kings*

Our task in this chapter is to develop a way of reading the book of Kings as a coherent narrative. This is the first step in our wider programme, which is to assess the ideology presented by that narrative. If a reading of Kings as political historiography is to be achieved, then a way of understanding the individual narratives in relation to the wider shape of the book is required, so that Kings can be understood as a single, intelligible whole. However, this task is not straightforward.

Much of the groundwork for modern approaches to the structure of the book of Kings was laid by Charles Burney in his 1903 *Notes on the Hebrew Text of the Books of Kings*.[1] Four decades before Noth proposed DtrH,[2] and seven before Cross proposed his theory of double redaction,[3] Burney had already observed within the books of Kings the textual elements that would lead to both theories: (1) that the books are a collation of pre-existing narrative and archive material, (2) that they have been structured by the insertion of regnal formulae which provide a chronology to an otherwise juxtaposed series of pericopes,[4] and (3) that there are signs that this editorial activity took place both prior to and after Israel's exile by the hand of a (Dtr) theologian.[5] These observations have led scholars in two main directions when investigating the structure of the book.

---

1. Charles F. Burney, *Notes on the Hebrew Text of the Books of Kings* (Oxford: Clarendon, 1903).
2. Noth, *The Deuteronomistic History*, 134.
3. Cross, *Canaanite Myth and Hebrew Epic*, 274–8.
4. Burney, *Notes*, ix–x. John Van Seters (*In Search of History*, 35) shows that this compositional strategy exists more broadly in ANE literature.
5. Burney (*Notes*, ix, xiii–xv) identifies the redactions as 'deuteronomic', following Wellhausen's (pre-Noth) schema (p. ix).

2. The Narrative Strategy of Kings

The road most frequently travelled has been to examine the structure of the book created by the Dtr(s).[6] The Dtr frame comprises those parts of the narrative voiced by the narrator and considered original to the hand of the Dtr(s), as opposed to the source material which they have selected and arranged. Because of this, the Dtr frame material is also usually regarded to be the clearest indicator of the purpose of the book as a whole.[7] The regnal formulae are one obvious structuring device,[8] giving dates for the reigns of each king as well as organising the source material to oscillate between northern and southern accounts. These formulae provide a temporal frame for the wider narrative,[9] and the reader may use a rough chronology to relate any small part of the narrative to the wider book.[10] Although not all voiced by the narrator, the several speeches that Noth identified as deuteronomistic perform a similar function (e.g., 1 Kgs 8.12-53; 11.1-13, 29-39; and 2 Kgs 17.7-23).[11] These are also considered original to the hand of the Dtr(s), and so also form part of the Dtr frame.

Attentiveness to the Dtr frame structure often yields a linear, sequential approach to the book.[12] In these approaches the narratives tend to be

---

6. E.g. Sweeney (*I & II Kings*, 81–811) understands Kings as a series of 38 accounts structured around the regnal formulae.

7. E.g. McConville ('1 Kings VIII 46-53 and the Deuteronomic Hope', *VT* 42 [1992]: 67–79) understands Solomon's dedication (1 Kgs 8) as programmatic of the purpose of Dtr, and Sweeney (*I & II Kings*, 8–10) proposes two exilic redactions based on the relationship between the Dtr speeches in 2 Kgs 17 and 1 Kgs 11–13.

8. I include the theological evaluations of each king within these formulae. On the pattern of regnal formula see Robert L. Cohn, 'The Literary Structure of Kings', in Halpern and Lemaire, eds., *The Books of Kings*, 112–15; and Burke O. Long, *1 Kings: With an Introduction to Historical Literature*, FOTL (Grand Rapids, MI: Eerdmans, 1984), 159–64. The regnal formulae are considered as the core component of the Dtr(s) framework: Cross, *Canaanite Myth and Hebrew Epic*, 274–89; and Provan, *Hezekiah and the Books of Kings*, 33–56, 90, 134–43.

9. Cohn, 'The Literary Structure of Kings', 108–9.

10. Note, however, that the chronology provided is not absolute. See below.

11. Noth, *The Deuteronomistic History*, 18–20. Apart from the formulae, only 2 Kgs 17.7-23 is voiced by the narrator in Kings. Other speeches, occurring on the lips of characters, are assessed as deuteronomic based on style. On this, see my discussion in Chapter 1.

12. Examples include Terence E. Fretheim, *First and Second Kings* (Louisville, KY: Westminster John Knox, 1999), 8–14; and Walter A. Brueggemann, *1 & 2 Kings*, SHBC (Macon, GA: Smyth & Helwys, 2000), 4–5. This approach also lends itself to character-focused treatments, which tend to move in chronological sequence, e.g., Jerome T. Walsh, *1 Kings*, Berit Olam: Studies in Hebrew Narrative & Poetry

understood as arranged roughly according to chronology and selected because they are illustrative of Dtr theology.

A second, more recently furrowed track has suggested that Kings may have a concentric structure overlaid on its chronological arrangement. This is partly required by the selection of the source material, which recounts a history that moves from one kingdom to two and then back again. So Jerome Walsh, for example, proposes the following:[13]

    A. Solomon and the United Monarchy (1 Kgs 1–11)
        B. Jeroboam and the Division of the Kingdom (1 Kgs 12)
            C. Kings of Israel and Judah (1 Kgs 13–16)
                D. The Omride Dynasty (1 Kgs 17–2 Kgs 11)
            C'. Kings of Israel and Judah (2 Kgs 12–16)
        B'. Fall of the Northern Kingdom (2 Kgs 17)
    A'. Kingdom of Judah (2 Kgs 18–25)

These concentric structures provide an alternate way of relating smaller units to the wider purpose of the book,[14] sometimes foregrounding what strictly linear structures have relegated to the background. For example, the northern narratives of Section D are often sidelined in Dtr analysis, but become central to the book in a concentric structure. However, unlike the Dtr frame approach, structures that focus on the arrangement of material have no implicit theology, which means that meaning must be sought by a close attention to the literary features and the arrangement itself.[15]

(Collegeville, MA: Liturgical Press, 1996), v–vi; and Robert L. Cohn, *2 Kings*, Berit Olam: Studies in Hebrew Narrative & Poetry (Collegeville, MA: Liturgical, 2000), xv.

    13. Walsh, *1 Kings*, 373–4. There is some variation between commentators, who see either 5 or 7 sections. E.g. Cohn, 'The Literary Structure of Kings', 110–11; and George Savran, '1 & 2 Kings', in *The Literary Guide to the Bible*, ed. Robert Alter and Frank Kermode (Cambridge, MA: Belknap, 1990), 148. Cohn ('The Literary Structure of Kings', 116–17) attempts a theological integration between the concentric and linear structures that result from the redactor's theology of history.

    14. E.g. Peter Leithart ('Counterfeit Davids: Davidic Restoration and the Architecture of 1–2 Kings', *TynB* 56 [2005]: 32–3) connects the concentric structure to the Davidic motif of the book suggesting each concentric ring is shaped by analogy to David.

    15. Existing studies tend to focus on Solomon (1 Kgs 1–11), or Elijah and Elisha (1 Kgs 17–2 Kgs 13). On Solomon see, e.g., Bezalel Porten, 'The Structure and Theme of the Solomon Narrative (I Kings 3–11)', *HUCA* 1 (1967): 93–128; Kim I. Parker, 'Repetition as a Structuring Device in 1 Kings 1–11', *JSOT* 42 (1988):

2.2. *Juxtaposition and Meaning: The Aborted Attack on Moab*

How then might we analyse the overall literary structure of Kings? One more puzzle piece is necessary before we can proceed, which is the way that the juxtaposition of individual narrative units creates meaning. This point is best demonstrated by an example. The series of incidents following Elijah's ascension (2 Kgs 2–3) have proven difficult for interpreters, not because they are unclear in themselves, but because their relationship to the wider purpose and theology of the book is not immediately obvious. One need only examine the range of interpretive opinions that exist for the incident where Israel attacks Moab,[16] only to be seemingly thwarted by a child sacrifice at the last moment (2 Kgs 3.26-27).[17] If the narrative had turned up on some archaeological relic, it would have been interpreted as the defeat of Yahweh's army through a sacrifice to Moab's god, but its presence in Kings is vexing. How should such passages be treated?

19–27; Amos Frisch, 'Structure and its Significance: The Narrative of Solomon's Reign (1 Kings 1–12:24)', *JSOT* 51 (1991): 3–14; Marc Z. Brettler, 'The Structure of 1 Kings 1–11', *JSOT* 49 (1991): 87–97; Richard S. Hess, 'The Form and Structure of the Solomonic District List in 1 Kings 4:7–19', in *Crossing Boundaries and Linking Horizons: Studies in Honour of Michael C. Astour on His 80th Birthday*, ed. G. D. Young, Mark W. Chavalas, and R. E. Averbeck (Bethesda, MD: CDL, 1997), 279–92; David S. Williams, 'Once Again: The Structure of the Narrative of Solomon's Reign', *JSOT* 86 (1999): 49–66; John W. Olley, 'Pharaoh's Daughter, Solomon's Palace, and the Temple: Another Look at the Structure of 1 Kings 1–11', *JSOT* 27 (2003): 355–69. On Elijah and Elisha see, e.g., Robert L. Cohn, 'The Literary Logic of 1 Kings 17–19', *JBL* 101 (1982): 333–50; Otto, 'The Composition of the Elijah–Elisha Stories', 487–508; Philip E. Satterthwaite, 'The Elisha Narratives and the Coherence of 2 Kgs 2–8', *TynB* 49 (1998): 1–28; John W. Olley, '2 Kings 13: A Cluster of Hope in God', *JSOT* 36 (2011): 199–218; Zipora Talshir, 'Towards the Structure of the Book of Kings: Formulaic Synchronism and Story Synchronism (1 Kings 12–2 Kings 17)', in *Texts, Temples, and Traditions: A Tribute to Menahem Haran*, ed. Michael V. Fox et al. (Winona Lake, IN: Eisenbrauns, 1996), 73–88; Jerome T. Walsh, 'The Organization of 2 Kings 3–11', *CBQ* 72 (2010): 238–54. See also Gilmour, *Juxtaposition and the Elisha Cycle*, which I discuss below.

16. The equally difficult story concerning Elisha and the bears (2 Kgs 2.23-25) evidences a similar bewildering array of interpretations. See Sweeney, *I & II Kings*, 275; or Bodner, *Elisha's Profile in the Book of Kings*, 1–5.

17. There is no need to list the various interpretive approaches here. For a literature review see Helen Paynter, *Reduced Laughter: Seriocomic Features and their Functions in the Book of Kings*, Biblical Interpretation Series (Leiden: Brill, 2016), 17–21. For a typical example see Burke O. Long, *2 Kings*, FOTL (Grand Rapids, MI: Eerdmans, 1991), 44–8.

On the one hand, approaching them through a Dtr lens is possible but often yields results that either fragment the narrative, or feel imposed upon it. What interest do the Dtr(s) have in recounting the Moab incident? One possibility is that they wished to explore the logic of prophetic fulfilment, but no clear result has emerged.[18] Perhaps the incident comments on the limitations of royal power.[19] However, would the Dtr(s) really have questioned divine sovereignty to do it?[20] Only Noth's explanation of textual inconveniences such as this has found widespread acceptance: that it is simply preserved out of Dtr(s) begrudging faithfulness to his sources.[21]

On the other hand, the concentric approach has not proved immediately helpful either, because it is difficult to see how the episode contributes to its literary context, which is Section D in Walsh's schema above. How does this strange episode contribute to an exploration of the Omride dynasty, except that it happens to involve an Omride king?

In order to make sense of the narrative, the reader is forced to look for literary hints that relate this narrative to its surrounding material. Gilmour has formalised the process by examining the way that immediate literary context creates meaning through the juxtaposition of narrative units:

> Biblical authors and editors deliberately used juxtaposition to shape the meaning of their narrative and…there are many indicators in the text for how they intended the interpretation to be affected. Furthermore…juxtaposed narrative units are important to the interpretation of every episode and story in the biblical narrative.[22]

Gilmour's work not only demonstrates that juxtaposition creates meaning[23] but also begins to analyse how.[24] In her view, it is the literary

---

18. See, e.g., the debate between Raymond Westbrook, 'Elisha's True Prophecy in 2 Kings 3', *JBL* 124 (2005): 530–2; and Jesse C. Long, 'Elisha's Deceptive Prophecy in 2 Kings 3: A Response to Raymond Westbrook', *JBL* 126 (2007): 168–71.

19. E.g. Brueggemann and Hankins, 'The Affirmation of Prophetic Power', 60–2.

20. Brueggemann and Hankins, 'The Affirmation of Prophetic Power', 62.

21. Noth, *The Deuteronomistic History*, 24–6.

22. Gilmour, *Juxtaposition and the Elisha Cycle*, 3–4. See also Van Seters, *In Search of History*, 37.

23. The idea that juxtaposition creates meaning in Hebrew thought is well studied with respect to parallelism and other poetic devices, and may be best understood to be a characteristic of Hebrew thought more generally. See, e.g., Bernd Janowski, *Arguing with God: A Theological Anthropology of the Psalms* (Louisville, KY: Westminster John Knox, 2013), 14–21.

24. Gilmour (*Juxtaposition and the Elisha Cycle*, 23–32) builds on a dialogical hermeneutic pioneered with respect to DtrH by Robert Polzin, who sees the different

mechanics of the text that encourage the reader to see connections between narratives:[25]

1. Repetition: key words, phrases, or sentences, *Leitwörter*, word pairs, puns, and other word play.
2. Parallelism: of plot with different or similar characters, narrative analogy, plot reversal, and repetition of plot.
3. Embeddedness: *mise-en-abyme*,[26] and other embedded material (e.g., poetry).

---

tensions and episodes in the narrative as a conversation between voices. Drawing on Russian literary theorist Mikhail Bakhtin, Polzin developed and outlined his approach in *Biblical Structuralism: Method and Subjectivity in the Study of Ancient Texts* (Philadelphia, PA: Fortress, 1977); and 'Literary Unity in Old Testament Narrative: A Response', *Semeia* 15 (1979): 45–50. See also R. M. Polzin and E. Rothman, eds., *The Biblical Mosaic: Changing Perspective* (Atlanta, GA: SBL, 1982). His application to DtrH follows in *Moses and the Deuteronomist*, *Samuel and the Deuteronomist: A Literary Study of the Deuteronomic History Part Two: 1 Samuel* (San Francisco, CA: Harper & Row, 1989), and *David and the Deuteronomist*. His volume(s) on Kings are still forthcoming, though now seem unlikely to appear. On Bakhtinian approaches, see Mikhail Bakhtin, *Problems of Dostoevsky's Poetics*, trans. Caryl Emerson (Minneapolis, MN: University of Minnesota Press, 1984). For overviews of the application to biblical literature see Barbara Green, *Mikhail Bakhtin and Biblical Scholarship: An Introduction* (Atlanta, GA: SBL, 2000); Walter L. Reed, *Dialogues of the Word: The Bible as Literature According to Bakhtin* (Oxford: Oxford University Press, 1993); and Carol A. Newsom, 'Bakhtin, the Bible, and Dialogic Truth', *JR* 76 (1996): 290–306. Examples of application to the book of Kings include Paul S. Evans, 'The Hezekiah–Sennacherib Narrative as Polyphonic Text', *JSOT* 33 (2009): 335–8; Alice Wells Hunt, 'Bringing Dialogue from Cacophony: Can Bakhtin Speak to Biblical Historiography?', *PRSt* 32 (2005): 325–7; Dennis T. Olson, 'Biblical Theology as Provisional Monologization: A Dialogue with Childs, Brueggemann and Bakhtin', *BibInt* 6 (1998): 162–80; and Paynter, *Reduced Laughter*, 32–40. Like other purely literary methods we discussed in Chapter 1, the interest of these studies often diverges from my own in that they are not interested in the original historical context, at times denying that it is possible for the narrative to make an ideological point of the type I am proposing. E.g. Newsom, 'Bakhtin, the Bible, and Dialogic Truth', 292–4.

25. Gilmour, *Juxtaposition and the Elisha Cycle*, 33–45.

26. *Mise-en-abyme* refers to an embedded narrative that retells or is analogous to the wider story. It is possible to understand 1 Kings 13 as an example of this. See, e.g., David A. Bosworth, 'Revisiting Karl Barth's Exegesis of 1 Kings 13', *BibInt* 10 (2002): 360–83.

Having observed a literary connection, the reader must then pause to reflect on what kind of relationship is being encouraged, which Gilmour groups into two broad categories:[27]

    A.   Chronological: causal, consequence, and hindsight.

    B.   Dialogical: contradiction, corroboration, and question and answer.

Several interpreters have approached 2 Kings 3 by attempting to relate it to its surrounding material in this or similar ways, producing largely complementary results. Keith Bodner, for example, analyses the sequence of narratives and finds 2 Kings 3 to comment on royal and prophetic succession:

> What needs to be taken into account, and has not been adequately considered by interpreters, is the significance of this final verse [of 2 Kgs 3] within the larger theme of succession that has been witnessed in 2 Kings 1–3. When Mesha sacrifices his first-born son and heir to the throne, it forms a bitter contrast to Elisha's prophetic succession [in 2 Kgs 2]. Consequently, Elisha's succession to the prophetic office is bracketed by flawed succession narratives of both Israelite [2 Kgs 1] and Moabite [2 Kgs 3] royalty… Far from any charge of false prophecy at the end of 2 Kings 3, there is a vindication of prophetic succession and a corresponding eclipse of kingship.[28]

Similarly, Philip Satterthwaite detects a series of 'linked themes' that this section of Kings explores, each contributing to the broader purpose of defining faithful Israel: the destruction of Ahab's line, the war against Baal, the war against Aram, and the miracle accounts.[29] Yael Shemesh also finds something similar: a polemic against Baal worship, an exaltation of the institution of prophecy, and religious and social satire against the royal house.[30]

My own approach to 2 Kings 3 begins by noticing the various elements of repetition between it and 1 Kings 22. In both narratives a son of Ahab begins to reign in Jehoshaphat's time (1 Kgs 22.51 [22.52, Heb.] and

---

    27. Gilmour, *Juxtaposition and the Elisha Cycle*, 19–32.
    28. Bodner, *Elisha's Profile in the Book of Kings*, 71–2. Bodner also utilises the repetition of uncommon words. He connects, e.g., 2 Kgs 1 to 1 Kgs 18, by contrasting what occurs in the upper room (עליה): death in the first case, life in the second.
    29. Satterthwaite, 'The Elisha Narratives', 3–9.
    30. Yael Shemesh, 'The Elisha Stories as Saints' Legends', *JHebS* 8 (2008): 5.

2 Kgs 3.1 are nearly identical). In both cases the northern king approaches Jehoshaphat for help and receives an identical reply: 'I am as you are, my people as your people, my horses as your horses' (כמוני כמוך כעמי כעמך בסוסי כסוסיך, 1 Kgs 22.5; 2 Kgs 3.7). And in both narratives Jehoshaphat also asks, 'Is there not another prophet of Yahweh here?' (האין פה נביא ליהוה עוד, 1 Kgs 22.7; 2 Kgs 3.11). The repeated plot is striking. What is its function?

A chronological connection is likely. In this middle part of the book Israel and Judah are allied. The alliance begins in 1 Kings 22, and re-emerges in 2 Kings 3, and then climaxes in 2 Kgs 8.18 and 2 Kings 11 with a marriage that will eventually place the Omride queen Athaliah on the Judean throne. The chronology therefore highlights a causal sequence, of which 2 Kings 3 is one step, that results in the most serious threat to the Davidic monarchy recorded in the book (note also 2 Kgs 3.14). Thus 2 Kings 3 contributes to the wider plot of the book.

Each of these readings, including my own, has in common an attempt to ground the meaning of the story in its literary context by discerning textual clues which link 2 Kings 3 to its surrounding material. Through attentiveness to this juxtapositional logic, then, we can refine the Dtr frame and concentric approaches we examined earlier. The observations provide interpretive options that move beyond what is available from the isolated story, and free the interpreter from having to discern a single point, moral, or lesson in each narrative. 2 Kings 3 may still illustrate Dtr theology (or not!), but this would not exhaust the meaning of the narrative. Its contribution to the theology of prophetic and royal power is significant, as is its place in the wider narrative. In this case, each reading has drawn a similar conclusion:[31] that the power dynamics between king and prophet are being explored, and that the narrative contributes to the wider plots concerning Ahab and Aram.[32] These conclusions are unavailable to those focused narrowly on either the Dtr frame or concentric structures.

---

31. The broad agreement demonstrates that, while subjectivity is inevitable, the method provides a degree of objectivity to the interpretation and perhaps avoids some of the interpretive excess of Bakhtinian analysis. This is because many of the cues Gilmour describes can be grounded in syntactic observations.

32. See, e.g., Brueggemann and Hankins, 'The Affirmation of Prophetic Power', 60–2.

2.3. *The Literary Structure of Kings*

In the remainder of this chapter I develop a structure for the book based on the literary approach we have been discussing above. My structure is an attempt to provide a framework that utilises the literary mechanics of the book itself, primarily the plot and the various intertextual connections Gilmour has enumerated.[33] This will become clear as we progress.

The claim that the book is a narrative implies a genre agreement between the reader and the author that the overall shape of the book will follow a larger pattern.[34] Narratives begin with a *contract*: a description of the characters and the setting, and the establishment of expectations within the mind of the reader. These expectations can then be met, modified or thwarted as tension mounts throughout the *plot*. Finally, narratives end with *closure*: a resolution to all the expectations and tensions in the reader's mind. These elements, then, define narrative shape – a *narrative arc* – and must be present if Kings is to be considered a narrative: *contract*, *plot*, and *closure*.

2.3.1. *Narrative Arcs in Kings: The Word of God and Its Fulfilment*

There are various narrative arcs in Kings. The narrative arcs that operate entirely within their own pericope do not concern us here. Arcs that straddle textual units, and especially those that bridge the divisions created by regnal formulae, bring a wider coherence to the book. In these cases readers detect a story that transitions across the reigns of individual kings and dynasties.

In Kings, this is often done through a prophecy-fulfilment motif that permeates the narrative, and acts as a kind of causation within the historical logic of the book.[35] Von Rad observed that fulfilment of prophecy is one of the standard features of DtrH (e.g., Josh. 21.45; 23.14).[36] He

---

33. I am also indebted to Yairah Amit (*Reading Biblical Narratives: Literary Criticism and the Hebrew Bible* [Minneapolis, MN: Fortress, 2001], 46–9) for many of the literary categories I use in this chapter.

34. Amos Oz, *The Story Begins: Essays on Literature*, trans. M. Bar-Tura (New York: Harcourt Brace, 1996), 7–8, cited in Amit, *Reading Biblical Narratives*, 38–41, 48–9.

35. E.g., Cohn, 'The Literary Structure of Kings', 114–16; Fretheim, *First and Second Kings*, 10–14; and Gina Hens-Piazza, *1–2 Kings*, AOTC (Nashville, TN: Abingdon, 2006), 7–9.

36. Gerhard von Rad, 'The Deuteronomic Theology of History in 1 and 2 Kings', in *From Genesis to Chronicles: Explorations in Old Testament Theology* (Minneapolis, MN: Fortress, 2005), 156.

tabulated the prophecies given in the book, matching them to their fulfilment, and noted that every prophecy that is given is eventually fulfilled,[37] often explicitly 'according to the word of Yahweh' (כדבר יהוה).[38] Von Rad's list is not comprehensive,[39] so I have provided my own tabulation in an appendix to this volume.

Because of this, the reader of Kings comes to the book already aware of the expectation that Yahweh's word will not fail. This is reaffirmed early in Kings (1 Kgs 8.56), but the Solomon narrative adds to it a repeated theme of explicit fulfilment (מלא) of individual promises (e.g., 1 Kgs 2.27; 8.15, 24).[40] The vexing story of the two prophets in 1 Kings 13 also explores this issue directly. With many other commentators, I judge that story to comment on the certainty of the fulfilment of the word of God to Jeroboam.[41] It introduces two important prophetic motifs, both already known from other parts of the history: the motif that often announces a prophecy ('the word of Yahweh came to…', …ויהי דבר יהוה היה אל, 1 Kgs 13.20; 16.1; 17.2, 8; 18.1, 31; 21.17, 28; 2 Kgs 20.4);[42] and the motif that flags its fulfilment ('according to the word of Yahweh', כדבר יהוה,

---

37. Von Rad, 'The Deuteronomic Theology of History in 1 and 2 Kings', 157–9. Note that some prophecies are fulfilled in surprising ways. The most serious challenge is Huldah's prophecy (2 Kgs 22.15-20), which predicts that Josiah would be buried 'in peace'. He is eventually killed by an Egyptian in battle (2 Kgs 23.29). In my judgment the inconsistency is one of appearance more than substance. See Michael Pietsch, 'Prophetess of Doom: Hermeneutical Reflections on the Huldah Oracle (2 Kings 22)', in *Soundings in Kings: Perspectives and Methods in Contemporary Scholarship*, ed. Mark Leuchter and Klaus-Peter Adam (Minneapolis: Fortress, 2010), 77–8.

38. Von Rad, 'The Deuteronomic Theology of History in 1 and 2 Kings', 159.

39. See also Wray Beal's list, which sorts the fulfilments by what kind of character announces them: *The Deuteronomist's Prophet: Narrative Control of Approval and Disapproval in the Story of Jehu (2 Kings 9 and 10)* (New York: T&T Clark International, 2007), 184–5.

40. There are other prophetic fulfilments that are not made explicit. E.g. 1 Kgs 4.20-21 (4.20–5.1, Heb.) indicates the fulfilment of Gen. 15.18 and 22.17.

41. E.g. James K. Mead, 'Kings and Prophets, Donkeys and Lions: Dramatic Shape and Deuteronomistic Rhetoric in 1 Kings XIII', *VT* 49 (1999): 205; D. W. Van Winkle, '1 Kings XII 25–XIII 34: Jeroboam's Cultic Innovations and the Man of God from Judah', *VT* 46 (1996): 105–7; Mark O'Brien, 'Prophetic Stories Making a Story of Prophecy', in Jacobs and Person Jr., eds., *Israelite Prophecy and the Deuteronomistic History*, 175; and Jerome T. Walsh, 'The Contexts of 1 Kings 13', *VT* 39 (1989): 368–9.

42. See also 1 Sam. 15.10; 2 Sam. 7.4; 24.11. Note that we have already seen this formula in 1 Kgs 6.11.

1 Kgs 13.26; 14.18; 15.29; 16.12, 34; 17.5, 16; 22.38; 2 Kgs 1.17; 4.44; 7.16; 9.26; 10.17; 14.25; 23.16; 24.2).[43] Both prophets act throughout this narrative 'by the word of Yahweh' (בדבר יהוה, 1 Kgs 13.1, 2, 5, 9, 17, 18, 32), and this word is seen to be inviolable once given, even when the reader wishes it to be otherwise. By the end of 1 Kings 13, the certainty of prophetic fulfilment in Kings is well established: 'The message he proclaimed by the word of Yahweh will certainly happen' (כי היה יהיה הדבר אשר קרא בדבר יהוה, 1 Kgs 13.32).

Von Rad's assessment of this motif was theological. He claimed it was because Dtr wished to present Yahweh's word as 'invariably [achieving] its purpose in history by virtue of its own inherent power'.[44] However, it also functions on a literary level, because once a prophecy is given, the pattern of fulfilment shapes the reader's expectation of how the rest of the narrative will unfold.[45] The various literary mechanisms we examined above can be used to link the individual narratives to these wider arcs, as we saw above with 2 Kings 3. So narrative tension escalates as some as-yet unfulfilled predictions are complicated by the intervening material and look increasingly less likely to come about. Closure is eventually reached when each prophecy is fulfilled. Thus, each prophetic fulfilment resolves a narrative arc that was established when the prophecy was given. There are over 30 such arcs within the book of Kings, and several additional fulfilments of predictions made in other parts of the Primary History. As Bezalel Porten notes, 'the narrative framework for most of the biblical stories is furnished by prophecy–fulfilment'.[46]

2.3.2. *Kings as Narrative Intercalation*

An analysis of the expectations generated by these prophecies will yield something concerning the plot and purpose of Kings, to which we shall return. Before we come to that, we must first notice that the placement of prophecies and fulfilments within Kings is not haphazard. Not only do the prophecy–fulfilment arcs form a pattern, but it is a pattern that correlates with the placement of the regnal formulae as well.

---

43. See also Josh. 8.8, 27. The phrase is used in 1 Kgs 12.24 but there indicates obedience rather than fulfilment.

44. See von Rad, 'The Deuteronomic Theology of History in 1 and 2 Kings', 156.

45. Cohn, 'The Literary Structure of Kings', 114–16. See also Keith Bodner, *1 Samuel: A Narrative Commentary*, HBM 19 (Sheffield: Sheffield Phoenix, 2009), 126.

46. Porten, 'The Structure and Theme of the Solomon Narrative (I Kings 3–11)', 95–9.

As we shall see, the book contains a narrative intercalation.[47] This literary pattern is a type of juxtaposition, occurring when one narrative, coherent on its own, is split apart and made to enclose a second one.[48] I call the two narratives Outer Kings and Inner Kings. These two units do not correspond with the two kingdoms: both Outer Kings and Inner Kings feature both Israel and Judah in different ways. I return to the precise delineation below, but in summary:

Outer Kings A:	1 Kgs 1.1–16.28
Inner Kings:	1 Kgs 16.29–2 Kgs 15.38
Outer Kings B:	2 Kgs 16.1–25.30

Not only is there significant textual and corroborating evidence for this proposal, but as we shall see below, such a structure suggests a way of relating the different parts of the book to one another. The case for this is cumulative, and will occupy the rest of this chapter.

i. *Narrative Arcs and Regnal Formulae*

The main evidence for this structure is the convergence of two structural patterns. First, the narrative arcs that are created by the various prophetic predictions and their fulfilments are not randomly arranged. In Figure 2.1, each curve represents a narrative arc, a prediction linked to its fulfilment across the book of Kings. The chapters of 1 and 2 Kings are indicated along the horizontal axis. For clarity, only arcs that do not begin and end in the same chapter are shown. Arcs that have their origin outside of Kings are noted below the horizontal axis.

---

47. This literary term is more familiar in New Testament studies, where it is also known as a 'sandwich'. E.g. Tom Shepherd, 'The Narrative Function of Markan Intercalation', *NTS* 41 (1995), 522; and F. G. Downing, 'Markan Intercalation in Cultural Context', in *Narrativity in Biblical and Related Texts: La narrativité dans la bible et les textes apparentés*, ed. G. J. Brooke and J. D. Kaestli (Belgium: Leuven University, 2000), 105–8.

48. It is related to *mise-en-abyme*, though often functions through mutual interpretation rather than analogy (see Gilmour, *Juxtaposition and the Elisha Cycle*, 42–5). Downing ('Markan Intercalation in Cultural Context', 106) lists several other possible intercalations in the Old Testament, including Nathan's dialogue with David in 2 Sam. 11.1–12.25, where the inner narratives 'intentionally comment' on the outer, flanking, narratives.

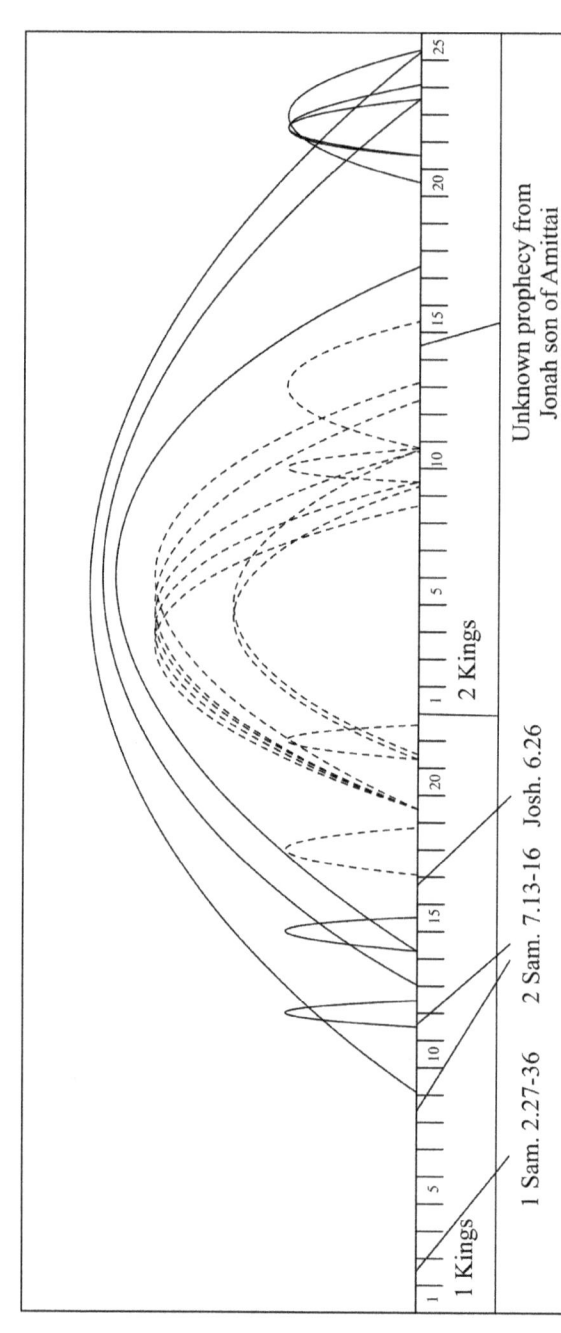

Figure 2.1. *The Narrative Arcs in Kings*

The arcs are generated by the prophecy and fulfilment in Kings are not randomly arranged. There are a series of narratives in the middle section of the book (dashed) that do not intersect with those in the outer sections of the book (solid).

An interesting pattern emerges. A series of narrative arcs develop across the middle section of the book (dashed arcs). These narratives do not intersect with those that develop across the outside sections of the book (solid arcs). There are no predictions made in the outer sections that are fulfilled in the inner section, and similarly *vice versa*. There are, however, several prophetic predictions that are made in the first part of the book that are left in suspense during the middle section, and which find closure in the last part. Because these predictions drive the contract and the plot of the book, this divides the book into two distinct narratives, one embedded within the other. This is a literary intercalation.

A second structural pattern directly supports this observation, which is noticed in the placement of the regnal formulae. Even though the structural significance of the formulae is well noted, the significance of their placement within the narrative has not yet been observed.

Here we are concerned with paired regnal formulae, where the opening and closing formula for a king occurs in the same chapter. The reason for this can be explained in terms of the reader's experience of narrative time.[49] Since regnal formulae mark time within the narrative by recording how many years have passed since the previous formula, a quick succession, as is found in a paired formula, means that many years pass within the narrative in a small number of words for the reader. If multiple paired formulae happen in a chapter, then the increased narrative pace makes the reader aware they have encountered a section of the book where history is summarised. Through this they gain the impression of lack of narratorial interest in the sections, and their attention is focused on the story in the surrounding material.

Figure 2.2 shows how many paired opening and closing regnal formulae occur within each chapter of Kings. The same tripartite structure that we observed in the pattern of narrative arcs can be seen here also. Clumps of paired regnal formulae (1 Kgs 14–16 and 2 Kgs 13–15) are placed in the sections that separate the inner arcs from the outer arcs. We will add precision to these section breaks below, but the general result can be seen already. The summarised material in these sections marks them as transitional, and the book is delineated by these transitions into the same three longer units that we discovered through an analysis of the prophecy–fulfilment pattern, which I have called Outer Kings A, Inner Kings, and Outer Kings B.

---

49. On narratives and time see Amit, *Reading Biblical Narratives*, 105–9; and Bar-Efrat, *Narrative Art in the Bible*, 141.

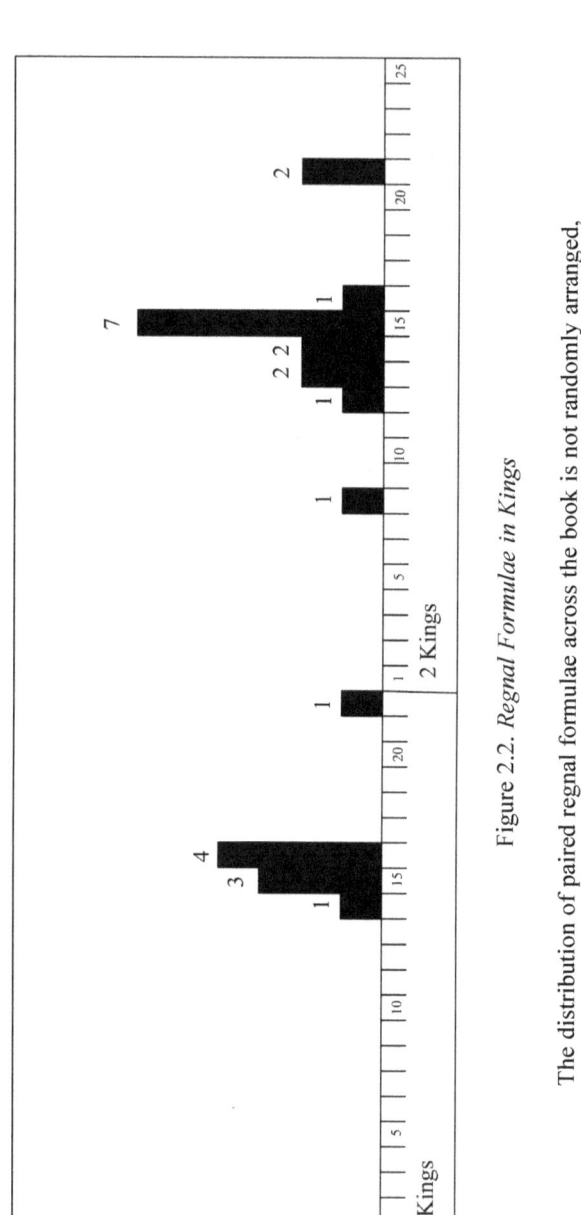

Figure 2.2. *Regnal Formulae in Kings*

The distribution of paired regnal formulae across the book is not randomly arranged, but clumped in two main sections, which provide transitions between the outer and middle sections of Kings.

ii. *Transition Sections*

Is it possible to delineate these transition sections more precisely? We will need to use data from both prophecy-fulfilment and regnal formulae patterns to do so.

The first transition is straightforward. The first paired formula is 1 Kgs 14.21-31, which narrates the reign of Rehoboam with just eleven verses between formulae. This pace of narrated time is matched through chs. 15–16. Thus the transition begins at 1 Kgs 14.21. The endpoint of the transition section is apparent when Ahab's opening regnal formula (1 Kgs 16.29) is not immediately matched by a closing formula. Instead follows a long series of narratives concerning Elijah and Ahab. Thus at 1 Kgs 16.29 we have begun a new narrative section.

The second transition is more difficult and Figure 2.2 masks some of the necessary detail of the text. The first paired formula in the clump is Je(ho)ash of Judah, but his narrative occupies all 21 verses of 2 Kings 12, and follows directly from an episode that also concerned him in 2 Kings 11. There is too much narrative detail here to be summary material.

Many commentators see a new section beginning at 2 Kings 12 or 13, based on the assumption that this part of Kings is telling a story focused on the Northern Kingdom.[50] However, I argue below that the plot of Inner Kings does not revolve around the north particularly, but around the danger brought to the south by intermarriage with the house of Ahab. Furthermore, the note concerning Hazael (2 Kgs 12.17-18 [12.18-19, Heb.]) develops the narrative arc that began in 1 Kgs 19.15.[51] Jehoahaz's and Je(ho)ash's short accounts (2 Kgs 13.1-9; 13.10-13) seem to be summary material, but a long section follows with considerable detail concerning a prediction of deliverance from Syria (2 Kgs 13.14-19), the deaths of Elisha (2 Kgs 13.20-21) and Hazael (2 Kgs 13.22-24), and the predicted restoration of Israel (2 Kgs 13.25).[52] All of these episodes close narrative arcs that began in 1 Kgs 19.15-18 as we shall see when we examine the plot below. Therefore, 2 Kings 13 is also integral to the plot of Inner Kings, not transitional.

The two paired formulae in 2 Kings 14 are once again summary material, followed by seven paired formulae in 2 Kings 15. This is clearly a transitional section. The one paired formula in 2 Kings 16 is for Ahaz, who occupies all 20 verses and once again introduces significant narrative detail. Therefore, the second transition begins in 2 Kgs 14.1 and ends at 2 Kgs 15.38.

---

50. E.g. Walsh, *1 Kings*, 373; Savran, '1 & 2 Kings', 148; and Cohn, 'The Literary Structure of Kings', 110–11.
51. See below on the plot of Inner Kings.
52. On the logic of 2 Kgs 13 see Olley, '2 Kings 13', 199–218.

iii. *The Literary Structure of Kings*

In summary, then, the literary structure of Kings is:

Outer Kings A:	1 Kgs 1.1–16.28
	(including a transition section 14.21–16.28)
Inner Kings:	1 Kgs 16.29–2 Kgs 15.38
	(including a transition section 2 Kgs 14.1–15.38)
Outer Kings B:	2 Kgs 16.1–25.30

This structure can be seen in Figures 2.3 and 2.4 which overlay my labels onto Figures 2.2 and 2.1 respectively.

The narrative pace of each section can also now be tabulated. Outer Kings and Inner Kings each cover approximately five years per chapter, though this is not evenly paced. The transition sections average closer to 30 years per chapter:

Table 2.1. *The Narrative Pace of Kings*

(The narrative pace averages approximately five years per chapter in Inner and Outer Kings, and 30 years per chapter in the transition sections.)

	Section	Kings	Narrative Time (Approx.)	Narrative Pace (Yrs/Ch)
Outer Kings A	I.1.1–14.20[53]	Solomon to Jeroboam	50 years	4
Outer Kings A (transition)	I.14.21–16.28	Rehoboam to Omri	50 years	25
Inner Kings	I.16.29–II.13.25	Ahab to Jehoahaz	75 years	4
Inner Kings (transition)	II.14.1–15.38	Amaziah to Jotham	65 years	32
Outer Kings B	II.16.1–25.30	Ahaz to Josiah (II.23.30)[54]	65 years	6

---

53. Throughout this study I use abbreviated notation in tables. I.1.1 = 1 Kgs 1.1; II.13.25 = 2 Kgs 13.25, etc.

54. The system of regnal formula breaks down in 2 Kgs 23.31–25.30. This has been explained both as a product of a post-Josianic redaction (e.g., Provan, *Hezekiah and the Books of Kings*, 114–31, 134–41), as well as an intentional strategy to highlight the crisis of exile (e.g., Meir Sternberg, 'Time and Space in Biblical [Hi]story Telling: The Grand Chronology', in *The Book and the Text: The Bible and Literary Theory*, ed. Regina M. Schwartz [Oxford: Blackwell, 1990], 111–12).

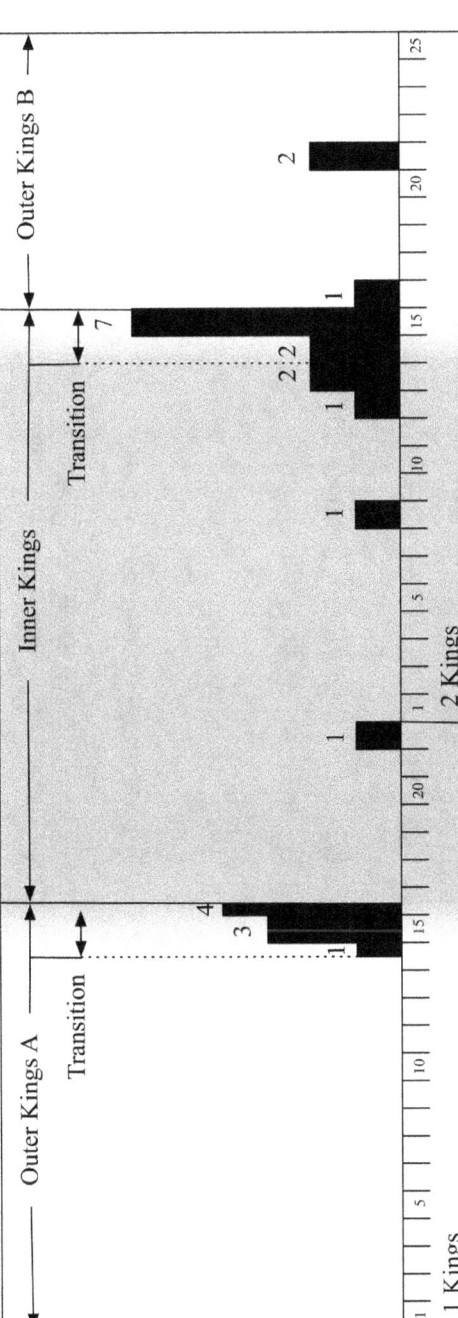

Figure 2.3. *Regnal Formulae, Inner and Outer Kings*

When combined with observations concerning the prophecy-fulfilment arcs, the clumps of paired formulae designate transitional sections between Inner and Outer Kings.

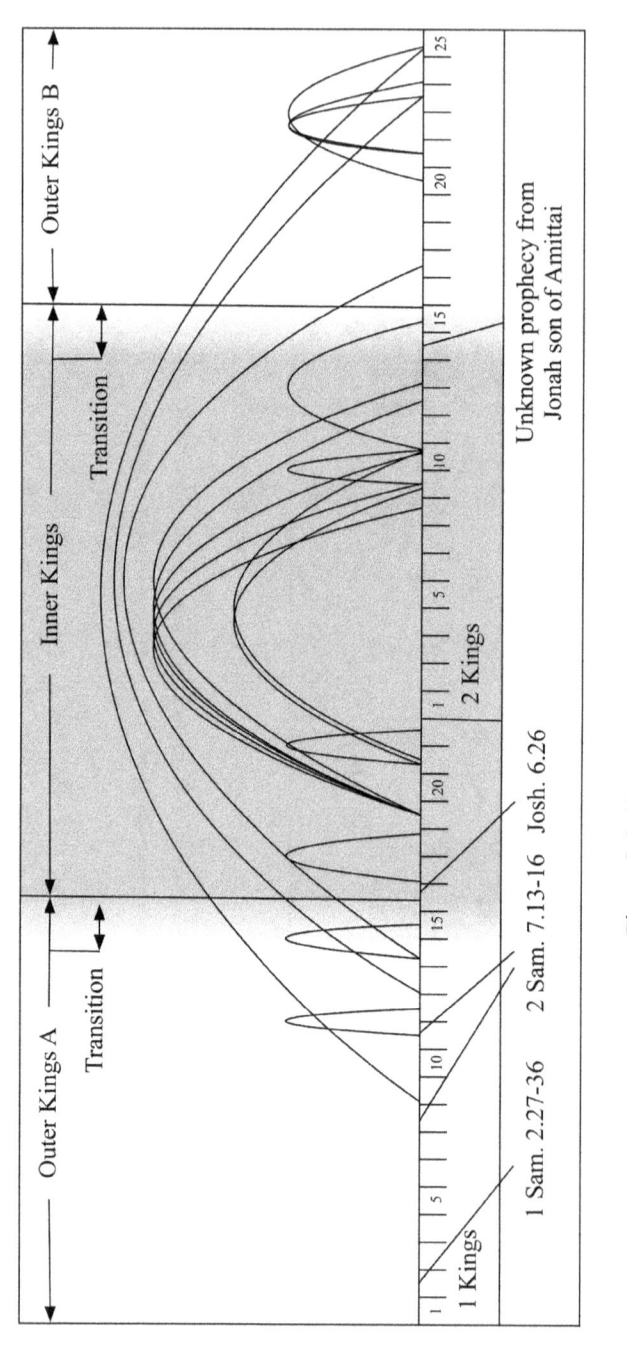

Figure 2.4. *Narrative Arcs, Inner and Outer Kings*

Once the transition sections are identified and Inner and Outer Kings are delineated, narrative arcs in Inner Kings and Outer Kings do not overlap or intersect.

2.3.3. *The Plot: Inner and Outer Kings*

There is further textual evidence to support these structural observations, but it will be useful first to develop an understanding of what these narratives are about. It will be necessary to summarise in the following section, but my purpose here is not to engage in a close reading of the narrative. Rather, I shall cover the key prophecies which create reader expectation and drive the plots of Inner and Outer Kings, leaving the following chapters of this study to demonstrate that other texts also fit this framework, and to defend some of my readings where necessary.

i. *The Plot of Outer Kings*

The plot of Outer Kings is driven primarily by a tension between two different words spoken by Yahweh, each of which have already been established in the Primary History, and are assumed by the book of Kings. On the one hand, Yahweh promises to bless Israel only in the case that Israel obey the covenant (e.g., Deut. 28.1-14). On the other, Yahweh promises David an eternal throne regardless of obedience (2 Sam. 7.13-15).

There are several ways that the book draws the reader's attention to the importance of these promises for the narrative. First, Kings is consistent in its use of covenantal and promissory language.[55] On 22 occasions the book uses 'covenant' (ברית),[56] and with only one exception has the Mosaic covenant from the deuteronomic tradition in mind.[57] In every case it reserves that word to highlight Israel's failure to do what Yahweh commanded. Importantly, Kings never uses ברית to refer to the promise made to David in 2 Samuel 7.[58] Rather, when referring to the Davidic promise, Kings speaks of the word (דבר) that Yahweh spoke to David: fulfilling (מלא, e.g. 1 Kgs 8.15, 24), establishing (קום, e.g. 1 Kgs 8.20), keeping (שמר, e.g. 1 Kgs 8.25), and confirming (אמן, e.g. 1 Kgs 8.26) it. In Kings the word of God is used to explain the progression of history, which occurs 'according to the word of Yahweh'. The covenant is used to explain the failure of Israel to obtain Yahweh's blessings.

---

55. As I explored previously in Lovell, 'The Shape of Hope', 6–8.

56. There are several instances of human covenants that are not relevant for this discussion, e.g. 1 Kgs 5.12 (5.26, Heb.).

57. 2 Kgs 13.23 is the only occurrence of the Abrahamic covenant in Kings, the significance of which I explore below. See also Olley, '2 Kings 13', 208–10.

58. Note that other parts of the history do use ברית for the Davidic covenant, e.g. 2 Sam. 23.5. The word can also be used to speak of Yahweh's promises (e.g., Josh. 2.1). The use I describe here is particular to the book of Kings.

Second, the two motifs are reinforced early in the narrative. Solomon claims that his succession to the throne and completion of the temple is evidence that Yahweh's promise to his father has been fulfilled (1 Kgs 8.20). However, as well as reinforcing this promise,[59] the next chapter makes Solomon's continued success dependent on his fidelity to the covenant (1 Kgs 9.4-5). More ominous is the note, addressed now to a wider audience than Solomon alone,[60] concerning the exile and the destruction of the temple[61] if either Solomon or one of his descendants should ever disobey (1 Kgs 9.6-9). The language of this note is reminiscent of Deuteronomy (e.g., Deut. 29.24-28), which recasts a warning that was originally given to Israel as a whole as one now directed to Israel's line of kings. This is characteristic of the book of Kings, which understands national sin as primarily the result of bad leadership.[62] It also generates a reader expectation concerning the future of Solomon's temple and kingdom. If Solomon or his successors should prove to be unfaithful to Yahweh's covenant then the temple will be torn down, and Israel will be exiled from their land (1 Kgs 9.6-8). As the narrative proceeds Solomon does become unfaithful (1 Kgs 11.6), and so the reader must wrestle with the two contradictory expectations – whether Yahweh will honour the promise to Moses or to David: will he bring national destruction for disobedience or continue to uphold David's kingdom? In this way the basic narrative tension of Outer Kings has been established.

The third way the book draws the reader's attention to the interplay between promise and covenant is by flagging that the Davidic covenant, although 'eternal' (עד־עולם, 2 Sam. 7.13), might be contingent. The first prophetic fulfilment in Kings explores this possibility (1 Kgs 2.27). When Solomon expels Abiathar, the priest who supported his rival Adonijah, the narrator comments that this act fulfilled the prophecy made to Eli in 1 Sam. 2.27-36. That text explicitly revoked a covenant to Eli that

---

59. There are also textual links here to the dream at Gibeon, reinforcing Yahweh's selection of Solomon. See Sweeney, *I & II Kings*, 138.

60. The addressees of vv. 6-9 are plural, which many take to be indicative of a secondary insertion. See Simon J. De Vries, *1 Kings*, WBC 12 (Waco, TX: Word, 2003), 127.

61. Note: that MT has 'this temple will become exalted' (עליון, 1 Kgs 9.8). The suggestion of the editors of *BHS* to emend עליון to 'to rubble' (לעיין, with 𝔈𝔖𝔗) is followed by most translations and is probably correct. The destruction of the temple is implied by its rejection in v. 7 in any case. See Sweeney, *I & II Kings*, 139.

62. We will return to this in Chapters 4 and 6, but see my earlier discussion in Nathan H. Lovell, 'A Text-Linguistics Approach to the Literary Structure and Coherence of 2 Kings 17:7-23', *VT* 68 (2018): 229.

was framed in similar terms to the one made with David: for an 'eternal house' (עַד־עוֹלָם...תיב, 1 Sam. 2.30).[63] This act, one of Solomon's first as king, draws the reader's attention to the ironic possibility that the promise to David for an 'eternal house' (עַד־עוֹלָם...תיב, 2 Sam. 7.16) might be similarly revoked.

However, the narrative does not simply accept this conclusion. Continual reminders are presented throughout the rest of the book of the way Yahweh acts to preserve Jerusalem for the sake of David (e.g., 1 Kgs 11.36; 15.4; 2 Kgs 8.19; 19.34).[64] And so, after 1 Kings 11, the reader has seen Solomon fail and expects both the covenant curse, as promised in 1 Kgs 9.6-8, and also Yahweh's ongoing fidelity (somehow) to the Davidic promise.

The division of the kingdom complicates the plot concerning the fate of David's house. The prophet Ahijah promises Jeroboam a kingdom: a 'sure house' (בית־נאמן) like David's (כאשר בניתי לדוד, 1 Kgs 11.38). The major difference between this and Nathan's earlier promise to David in 2 Samuel 7 is that 1 Kgs 11.31-39 has no clause guaranteeing the future of the kingdom in the case of disobedience. There are, however, several surprising reminders in Adonijah's speech of Yahweh's intention to remain faithful to David in spite of Solomon's sin: Yahweh will ensure David always has a 'lamp' (ניר) before him in Jerusalem (1 Kgs 11.36) and will not humble David 'forever' (אך לא כל־הימים, v. 39). All of this complicates the plot. The reader is left guessing how this will all play out. A series of contradictory expectations has been created that makes the fulfilment of all of these various promises seem unlikely.

Meanwhile, Jeroboam builds the golden calves and receives a series of prophecies that launch several new narrative arcs. Some are concerned with the fate of the Northern Kingdom. The incident of Jeroboam's sick child (1 Kgs 14.1-18) creates an expectation for threefold judgment: personal calamity (vv. 12-13), the demise of his dynasty (v. 14), and the scattering of Israel (vv. 15-16). Others are concerned with the altar at Bethel itself (1 Kgs 13.2-3): that it should be split apart (v. 3) and that a Davidic scion named Josiah should desecrate it (v. 2).

Closure is reached quickly for the prophecies concerning the split altar (1 Kgs 13.5; which must have been repaired, 2 Kgs 10.29), Jeroboam's son (1 Kgs 14.17), and his dynasty (1 Kgs 15.27-28). However, because his golden calves survive his family's demise, the reader wonders about

---

63. On the many similarities between Eli in 1 Sam. 2 and David in 2 Sam. 7 see A. Graeme Auld, *I & II Samuel: A Commentary*, OTL (Louisville, KY: Westminster John Knox, 2011), 51–2.

64. See also Lovell, 'The Shape of Hope', 8–9.

the relationship between Josiah and the end of the Northern Kingdom. These expectations are left unresolved at the end of Outer Kings A.

Inner Kings further complicates these plots, as I explore below, but the expectations are finally resolved in Outer Kings B. The Northern Kingdom is exiled (2 Kgs 17), bringing closure to the Jeroboam arc involving the scattering of Israel, but now complicating the Josianic expectation. The predicted end of Jeroboam's kingdom has not resulted in the demise of his religion (e.g., 2 Kgs 17.28). This final prediction concerning Josiah is fulfilled when he destroys the altar at Bethel (2 Kgs 23.15-20).

Finally, the Southern Kingdom is itself destroyed in 2 Kings 25, along with the temple, closing the arc that began in 1 Kgs 9.6-8.[65] What has become of Yahweh's intention to act for the sake of David?

Throughout this study we will examine several indications that the narrative generates hope for its exilic audience for the future fulfilment of this promise. In Chapter 4 we will see that the exiles are a remnant. In Chapter 5 we shall see that their relationship to Yahweh has not been severed. And in Chapter 6 we will examine the extent to which the release of Jehoiachin from Babylonian prison engenders hope for a future Davidic king (2 Kgs 25.27-30). However, even in the narrative pattern of the book there is already reason to hope. If Josiah could still fulfil the word of God concerning Jeroboam long after the demise of Jeroboam's kingdom, then perhaps there is yet room for a son of David from the context of exile also.

ii. *The Plot of Inner Kings*

Although the stories are interrelated, Inner Kings has its own narrative integrity that operates independently of Outer Kings. The plot focuses particularly on the Northern Kingdom, and the contract is created as a product of Elijah's ultimately unsuccessful attempt to call them to repentance in 1 Kings 18. When he flees to Horeb (1 Kgs 19.1) he is instructed to anoint Jehu, Hazael, and Elisha (1 Kgs 19.16-18), a commissioning that includes two promissory aspects.[66] First, Hazael, Jehu, and Elisha would bring a complete end to Ahab's dynasty: '[It will be]... Jehu will kill and... Elisha will kill...' (והיה...ימית יהוא ו...ימית אלישע...,

---

65. The connection between 2 Kgs 25 and the prophecy in 1 Kgs 9 is not explicit, but commentators have noted the intertextuality between 2 Kgs 25 and 1 Kgs 6–8; e.g. Savran, '1 & 2 Kings', 148. Solomon is mentioned by name and the reader is reminded of the details of his temple in the same order in which they were manufactured (2 Kgs 25.13-17).

66. See also Paynter, *Reduced Laughter*, 149–57. We will revisit the textual details of this section in Chapter 4.

v. 17). Second, that Yahweh would preserve a remnant ('cause to remain in Israel', והשארתי בישראל, v. 18) who would be faithful to him.

These expectations are complicated in several ways as the plot develops. First, Ahab's repentance brings a deferral of judgment from Yahweh (1 Kgs 21.27-29), meaning that his dynasty has time to expand before it is destroyed. As a result, what might have been fulfilled through a simple coup like Zimri's (1 Kgs 16.11-13) becomes a massacre at the hands of Jehu (2 Kgs 9–10, esp. 2 Kgs 9.31). The reader does not encounter Hazael until 2 Kings 8 when he usurps the Syrian throne (2 Kgs 8.7-15), and Jehu comes to power in 2 Kgs 9.1-13.

A second major complication is the increased involvement of Judah in Israel's political sphere. Every appearance of Judah in Inner Kings brings them politically closer to Israel. We saw part of the way this plot develops above when we examined 2 Kings 3. Although they are always at war in Outer Kings, their alliance in Inner Kings is first expressed between Jehoshaphat and Ahab (1 Kgs 22.4), and repeated with Je(ho)ram of Israel (2 Kgs 3.7). Apparently they were close enough that Jehoshaphat named his own son after Je(ho)ram of Israel (2 Kgs 1.17; 8.16). This alliance eventually culminates in intermarriage as Je(ho)ram of Judah marries Athaliah, who is Ahab and Jezebel's daughter (2 Kgs 8.18). Je(ho)ram of Judah also named his son after another of Ahab's children (by then deceased), Ahaziah (2 Kgs 8.24). In this way the Davidic and Omridic lines become mixed, and so the expected destruction of Ahab's dynasty must now involve two kingdoms instead of one.

This development poses a complication not only for the plot of Inner Kings, but for the plot of Outer Kings as well. If David's line is now Omridic, and Ahab's house is destined to be destroyed, will that also bring an end to David? The only reminder in Inner Kings of the Davidic promise is given at a crucial narrative junction, just before Jehu kills the Davidic king and leaves the Omridic queen Athaliah to usurp the throne in Jerusalem (2 Kgs 8.19).

Closure occurs through a series of events. Jehu's revolution systematically destroys Ahab's dynasty (2 Kgs 9–10), including anyone related from Judah found within his reach (2 Kgs 9.27-29; 10.12-14). This fulfils the first promise made to Elijah. However, with Hazael still threatening the Northern Kingdom, the potential remains that the entire Northern Kingdom will be destroyed (2 Kgs 10.32). This leaves open the fulfilment of the promised remnant, but that expectation is deferred while the narrative arc concerning Judah is resolved.

Athaliah, now widowed in the south, and without possibility to return to the north, attempts to usurp the southern throne by killing her own (half-Davidic) children (2 Kgs 11.1-3). Since Athaliah is not part-Davidic her success would result in the end of David's line. However, her coup is thwarted (7 years later!) by a single Davidic heir who was hidden in the temple (2 Kgs 11.4-20). With a Davidic king back on the Judean throne, and the temple repaired, a measure of equilibrium is reached with respect to the Southern Kingdom, and finalised by the removal of Hazael as a threat to the south (2 Kgs 12.17-18 [12.18-19, Heb.]).

Finally, then, the remaining arc concerning the Northern Kingdom is closed also. Elisha's last act is to prophesy alleviation from the threat still posed by Hazael to the Northern Kingdom (2 Kgs 13.14-19), and this is fulfilled after the death of Hazael (2 Kgs 13.22-25). The final unresolved prophecy given in Inner Kings, to Jehu for a dynasty of four generations (2 Kgs 10.30), is fulfilled as the narrative transitions back to Outer Kings (2 Kgs 15.12).

2.3.4. *Supporting Evidence*

Having reached a preliminary understanding of the structure of the book of Kings, we are ready now to look at some corroborating evidence for this structure.

At one level the result is intuitive. Many readers feel that they have encountered a different type of material beginning when Elijah enters the narrative, which is why scholarship has often treated the central section as self-contained,[67] and sometimes excluded it from the wider book.[68] It is also why the central section is widely discussed in redaction-critical scholarship,[69] and why narrative-critical scholarship has so often utilised concentric structures in the book to explain it.[70]

---

67. E.g. Thomas L. Brodie, *The Crucial Bridge: The Elijah–Elisha Narrative as an Interpretive Synthesis of Genesis–Kings and a Literary Model for the Gospels* (Collegeville, MA: Liturgical, 2000), 4–5; Bodner, *Elisha's Profile in the Book of Kings*, 1, 5–11; Brueggemann, *1 & 2 Kings*, 4; Paynter, *Reduced Laughter*, 17–28; Hens-Piazza, *1–2 Kings*, 5; Talshir, 'Towards the Structure of the Book of Kings'; and Volkmar Fritz, *1 & 2 Kings*, trans. Anselm C. Hagedorn, ICC (Minneapolis, MN: Fortress, 2003), 1.

68. McKenzie (*The Trouble with Kings*, 81–100, esp. 99) finds a coherent narrative in Kings if this central section is removed. Sweeney (*King Josiah of Judah*, 77–92) and Knoppers (*Two Nations Under God 1*, 1–12) both pay little attention to the section.

69. Many believe that this material does not suit the interests of the Dtr(s). See Otto, 'The Composition of the Elijah–Elisha Stories', 487–90; Römer, *The So-Called Deuteronomistic History*, 153; and McKenzie, 'The Books of Kings in the Deuteronomistic History', 295.

70. See above on Cohn, 'The Literary Structure of Kings', 110–11; Walsh, *1 Kings*, 373–4; and Savran, '1 & 2 Kings', 148.

For this reason, some textual data I accumulate here has been employed by other methodologies but this is not mutually exclusive with my synchronic use of the data. Even if the literary development of Kings could be convincingly demonstrated, the literary impact of its composition remains. The structure of the final text is the result of a careful and intentional use of source material.

Apart from the main line of evidence concerning the placement of narrative arcs and regnal formulae, I have divided my textual data into two groups: the different narrative focus, that is, how the narrative divides its time between northern and southern kingdoms, and the different narrative styles.

i. *The Narrative Focus of Inner and Outer Kings*

One frequent observation is the emphasis that Inner Kings gives to the Northern Kingdom. This is accomplished primarily through the way the regnal formulae have been employed.

Throughout Kings, the formulae follow a pattern that 'alternates' between northern and southern kingdoms.[71] With some notable exceptions which I discuss below, everything narrated by the book occurs as part of the story of a particular king. That is, every story is told between someone's opening and closing regnal formulae. When one king dies the narrator continues either with Israel's or Judah's next king. In the usual pattern, the narrative alternates to the opposite kingdom if a new king has arisen there within the reign of the king who just died. If not, the narrator continues with the same kingdom.[72]

In general, any material that falls between the opening and closing formulae of a king will be related to the kingdom of that king. Thus, for example, the material between the opening and closing formulae of Ahaz (2 Kgs 16.1-20) relays the events of the Syro-Ephraimite crisis from the perspective of the Southern Kingdom because Ahaz is a southern king. The material between the opening and closing formulae of Ahab (1 Kgs 16.29–22.40) relays events from the perspective of the Northern Kingdom, even when the events do not include Ahab directly (e.g., 1 Kgs 19).

Outer Kings (including the transition sections) provides a roughly even pattern of alternation between kingdoms as long as the two kingdoms coexist (1 Kgs 12.1–16.27; 2 Kgs 14.1–17.40), as can be seen in Table 2.2. The number of verses spent before alternating is shown in the right column.

---

71. On this pattern see Cohn, 'The Literary Structure of Kings', 110–17.
72. I discuss the single exception to this below.

Table 2.2. *The Pattern of Alternation in Outer Kings*

The alternation between northern and southern kingdoms is consistent in Outer Kings (1 Kgs 1.1–16.28; 2 Kgs 14.1–25.30), including in the transition sections that are marked by frequent regnal formulae (RF). Neither kingdom is more prominent.

King	Kingdom	Opening RF	Closing RF	Vv. before Alternating
Outer Kings A				
Jeroboam	North	[I.12.20][73]	I.14.19-20	68
Rehoboam	South	I.14.21-24	I.14.29-31	36
Abijam		I.15.1-5	I.15.7-8	
Asa		I.15.9-14	I.15.23-24	
Nadab	North	I.15.25-26	I.15.31-32	36
Baasha		I.15.33-34	I.16.5-7	
Elah		I.16.8	I.16.14	
Zimri		I.16.15	I.16.20	
Tibni		I.16.21-22	I.16.21-22	
Omri		I.16.23-26	I.16.27-28	
Outer Kings B				
Amaziah	South	II.14.1-4	II.14.18-22	23
Jeroboam (II)	North	II.14.23-24	II.14.28-29	7
Azariah	South	II.15.1-4	II.15.6-7	8
Zechariah	North	II.15.8-9	II.15.10-12	24
Shallum		II.15.13	II.15.14-15	
Menahem		II.15.16-18	II.15.21-22	
Pekahiah		II.15.23-24	II.15.25-26	
Pekah		II.15.27-28	II.15.30-31	
Jotham (Uzziah)	South	II.15.32-35	II.15.36-38	28
Ahaz		II.16.1-4	II.16.19-20	
Hoshea	North	II.17.1-2	[II.17.5][74]	5

From this table we can see that Outer Kings spends approximately 140 verses in southern narration, and 95 in northern, never tarrying too long in either. By contrast, Inner Kings goes to some lengths to position the

---

73. Jeroboam has no opening formula, but since this story is told from his perspective, it should be regarded as northern narrated time.

74. Hoshea has no closing formula, but his story ends here. I argue for my reading of vv. 6-23 in Chapter 4.

formula so that nearly all narrated time is northern narrated time. Strictly, the pattern of alternation does not change, but stories concerning southern kings tend to be narrated from a northern perspective.

Jehoshaphat is a good example.[75] He receives almost no narrated time, but has an opening and closing formula in immediate succession without any events recalled from his perspective (1 Kgs 22.41-50 [22.41-51, Heb.]).[76] He is, however, a relatively well developed character who features in two lengthy narratives. Both of his narratives are told from the perspective of northern kings: the story of Ahab's death (1 Kgs 22.1-40), and the story of the war with Moab (2 Kgs 3). When contrasted with the narrative space devoted to Jehoshaphat in 2 Chronicles 17–20, it is clear that the author has gone to some lengths to focus Inner Kings on northern narrated time by avoiding any extensive account of Jehoshaphat.

The narrative strategy is similar with other southern kings in Inner Kings as well. For example, J(eh)oram of Judah is unknown to Inner Kings outside his regnal formulae (2 Kgs 8.16-24). Ahaziah (of Judah) is perhaps the most interesting case, because of the way his story intersects with the northern queen Athaliah (2 Kgs 8.26). Ahaziah's account opens with a normal regnal formula, but J(eh)oram of Israel's account has not yet closed. For the first time in Kings the reader awaits the closing formula of both kingdoms together. Neither occurs. Instead, Jehu, who receives no opening formula, kills both of them and usurps the northern throne, while the northern queen Athaliah takes the southern throne. All of this story is told from the perspective of the north. The narrative effect of this is to demonstrate the way that the two kingdoms have become reunited through marriage into the Omride dynasty, and so too their fates.

In contrast to Table 2.2, we can see from Table 2.3 that Inner Kings narrates approximately 568 verses from a northern perspective, and only 41 using a southern perspective:

---

75. The many historical readings that claim Jehoshaphat is underrepresented in Kings (e.g., Kyle Greenwood, 'Late Tenth and Ninth-Century Issues: Ahab Underplayed? Jehoshaphat Over-played?', in Arnold and Hess, eds., *Ancient Israel's History*, 286–318) can be accounted for by the narrative strategy I describe here.

76. This is not true in LXX where 1 Kgs 22.41-51 (22.41-52, Heb.) is duplicated after 1 Kgs 16.28, giving a significant section of southern narrated time.

Table 2.3. *The Pattern of Alternation in Inner Kings*

While continuing the pattern of alternation, Inner Kings devotes much more narrative to the Northern Kingdom than the south. This table excludes the transition sections.

King	Kingdom	Opening RF	Closing RF	Vss before Alternating
Ahab	North	I.16.29-33	I.22.39-40	209
Jehoshaphat	South	I.22.41-43	I.22.45-50	10
Ahaziah		I.22.51-53	II.1.17-18	
n/a II.2.1-25	North	n/a		225
J(eh)oram		II.3.1-3	[II.9.24][77]	
J(eh)oram	South	II.8.16-18	II.8.23-24	9
Ahaziah	North + South[78]	II.8.25-27	[II.9.27-29]	
Jehu	North	[II.9.1, 30-31][79]	II.9.34-36	119
Athaliah	North + South[80]	[II.11.1]	[II.11.20]	
J(eh)oash	South	II.11.21–12.3	II.12.19-21	22
Jehoahaz	North	II.13.1-3	II.13.8-9	
Jehoash	North	II.13.10-11	II.13.12-13[81]	15
n/a II.13.14-24		n/a		

One other peculiarity of the narrative focus of Inner Kings is worth mentioning. In addition to the persistent northern focus, the position of the regnal formulae in Inner Kings also creates two events that do not occur within regnal time. Elijah's ascension (2 Kgs 2) and the death of Elisha (2 Kgs 13.14-24) are both related after a regnal closing formula, and before the opening of another. Both narratives involve extraordinary events: a rapture and a resurrection. And both events involve the departure of one of the major prophets who dominate the narrative of Inner Kings. All of this suggests structural intentionality on the part of the compiler of this material.[82]

---

77. J(eh)oram of the south has no closing formula, but his story ends here, as discussed above.

78. Ahaziah is a southern king, told from northern perspective (see above). Strangely, Ahaziah's introductory formula is given again in 2 Kgs 9.29.

79. Jehu receives no opening formula. The story is told from his perspective from 9.1 onwards.

80. Athaliah, as an illegitimate queen in the narrator's eyes, warrants neither opening nor closing formula. As a northern queen, the story is told from northern perspective, but set in Jerusalem.

81. This closing formula is given again in 2 Kgs 14.15-16.

82. Cohn (*2 Kings*, 10, 80) argues that Elijah's ascension is a carefully planned literary strategy, but curiously misses the same observation for Elisha's death.

ii. *The Narrative Style of Inner and Outer Kings*
In his 1903 work, Burney commented that the middle section of Kings had several features that distinguish it from the outer material.[83] He attributed these to the provenance of the source material of that section, which he understood to be the pre-exilic Northern Kingdom. These distinguishing features are linguistic: the Hebrew of the section has several peculiarities; editorial: the narrator explains details of southern geography (e.g., that Beth-Shemesh and Beersheba are 'in Judah', ליהודה; 1 Kgs 19.3; 2 Kgs 14.11); theological: Jeroboam's calves are not blamed for the apostasy of the north, nor even mentioned; and stylistic: these 'North Palestinian Narratives [are]…narratives dealing with the affairs of the kingdom of Israel…[with] stories in most cases of some length…high descriptive power and sympathetic feeling'.[84]

Gary Rendsburg's study has largely confirmed the linguistic results, in which he proposed the peculiarities are best explained as a pre-exilic northern dialect.[85] Even if this explanation is questioned,[86] the data retain a literary role in the book. Burney's theological and editorial observations have also been repeated in redaction-critical studies which note that Dtr language is rare in this part of the book.[87] We can also observe the

---

83. Burney, *Notes*, 207–15.
84. Burney, *Notes*, 207–9.
85. The list of distinctives is too extensive to note here, but include subtleties of phonology, morphology, and syntax. Rendsburg's appendix (*Israelian Hebrew*, 151–4) lists these in concise format. See also 'Morphological Evidence for Regional Dialects in Ancient Hebrew', in *Linguistics and Biblical Hebrew*, ed. Walter Ray Bodine (Winona Lake, IN: Eisenbrauns, 1992), 71–86.
86. Ian Young ('The "Northernisms" of the Israelite Narratives in Kings', *ZAH* 8 [1995]: 63–70) attributes the 'northernisms' in Kings to an intentional literary device. By noticing that they occur primarily in speech, he suggests they may be part of the characterisation of northerners which would suggest southern provenance. On Young's concerns with Rendsburg's method and the (im)possibility of isolating a northern dialect of Hebrew see Ian Young, 'Evidence of Diversity in Pre-Exilic Judahite Hebrew', *HS* 38 (1997): 7–20; and Ian Young, Robert Rezetko, and Martin Ehrensvärd, *Linguistic Dating of Biblical Texts: An Introduction to Approaches and Problems* (London: Equinox, 2008), 173–200. See also William M. Schniedewind and D. Sivan, 'The Elijah–Elisha Narratives: A Test-Case for the Northern Dialect of Hebrew', *JQR* 87 (1997): 303–37; David Talshir, 'The Habitat and History of Hebrew During the Second Temple Period', in *Biblical Hebrew: Studies in Chronology and Typology*, ed. Ian Young (London: T&T Clark, 2003), 251–75; and Naama Pat-El, 'Israelian Hebrew: A Re-Evaluation', *VT* 67 (2017): 227–63.
87. See my discussion in Chapter 1. Briefly, on the incorporation of pre-Dtr 'prophetic' narratives into Dtr see Joseph, *Portrait of the Kings*, 42–5. Critiquing this idea see McKenzie, *The Trouble with Kings*, 10–14.

same trend in language involving David. References to 'David', 'Zion', Yahweh's chosen ruler or place, the temple, and allusions to 2 Samuel 7, are all rare in Inner Kings, which is partly because the narrative is primarily set in the north.

Burney's observation concerning the portrayal of apostasy can be developed. In Outer Kings apostasy is abstract. The kings build monuments to various gods, and the narrator tells us this is sinful. However, as we will discuss further in Chapter 3, apostasy in Inner Kings is explored through Baalism specifically. Baal appears for the first time in the book as Inner Kings opens, giving the reader the impression that he is a Syro-Phoenician import that has appeared alongside Ahab's marriage to Jezebel (1 Kgs 16.31-32).[88] The plot of Inner Kings then explores Baal's defeat and removal from Israel, climaxing in the slaughter of 2 Kgs 10.18-28: 'So Jehu destroyed Baal worship in Israel'. Baal then largely disappears from the narrative after Inner Kings. Like the other idols, he takes his place among the monuments erected by the kings (2 Kgs 17.16; 21.3; 23.4-5).

There are other stylistic differences worth noting as well. There are, for example, differences in the geo-political focus of the stories. There is never a time in Outer Kings when Judah and Israel are not at war, and there is never a time in Inner Kings when they are not allied. Outer Kings explores high-level political interactions with Egypt, Tyre, Assyria, and Babylon, but does so from a narrative setting within Israelite territory. The reader has no insight into the inner workings of these other nations, and the narrative mentions them only when they encroach on Israelite territory. By contrast, Inner Kings regularly detours outside Israel's borders and the reader meets non-Israelite characters who are well-developed in the narrative, gaining insight into these other places and even the inner workings of the Syrian king and his kingdom.

Major characters[89] in Outer Kings tend to be kings or their representatives. Prophets are generally not well-developed characters, and we meet almost no commoners. In Inner Kings, prophets, queens, assistants (Gehazi), widows, lepers, bands of raiders, and foreign generals all play roles alongside the kings, who may or may not be Israelite. There are many narratives where kings do not appear at all.

---

88. The last appearance of Baal in the Primary History was Judg. 6.31-32, a story similar to 1 Kgs 18.

89. Robert Cohn ('Characterisation in Kings', in Halpern and Lemaire, eds., *The Books of Kings*, 91–2) identifies five types of characters by level of narrative development, by increasing order: *minor*, *cameo*, *supporting*, *major*, and *main*.

Finally, and probably due to the prominence of the prophets, much of the miraculous activity in the book is confined to Inner Kings. There are a significant number of miracles, and they tend to gravitate towards several themes: fire from heaven (or flaming angels, flaming chariots, fiery armies, etc.); blindness and sight; and the provision of what is needed for life (food, water, oil, healing, resurrection, etc.). There are miracles in Outer Kings, but far fewer and they concentrate on healing.[90]

These observations are cumulative, contributing in different ways to the very common reader experience we began by noting, that the middle section of the book somehow feels different. Our observations have not been exhaustive. They have rather been an attempt to give substance to this feeling.

2.4. Conclusions: The Narrative Strategy of Kings

It is now possible to draw some conclusions concerning the narrative strategy of the book. Kings is structured through the juxtaposition of smaller narratives and other material, and these are held together primarily by two techniques. The first is the structural frame which is created by the regnal formulae. These indicate progression of narrative time; they mark the transition of scenes and alternate settings from south to north; and they introduce and evaluate many of the characters. The second is the narrative arcs which tie together the pericopes more tightly than juxtaposition alone by drawing them into a wider plot. These arcs are created by the prophecy-fulfilment pattern. The reader is encouraged to expect prophetic fulfilment, and so the details of each pericope can be used to develop, thwart, complicate, or resolve earlier predictions. In this way the book of Kings gains a coherent plot, and each pericope contributes to it.

The placement of the structural devices, the formulae and the prophetic arcs, divides the book into two major narratives: Inner Kings and Outer Kings, separated by their own prophecy-fulfilment arcs. The transitions between them are marked by a concentration of paired formulae, creating sections that summarise many years of history and do not greatly advance the wider plots.

---

90. Unless one counts the unusual behaviour of the lion (1 Kgs 13.24, 28), the only miracles outside of Inner Kings are the salvation of Jerusalem (2 Kgs 19.35), healing Jeroboam's hand (1 Kgs 13.4, 6), and healing Hezekiah's sickness (2 Kgs 20.1-11).

Although the two sections have separate plots, they deal with the same themes from different perspectives. Where Outer Kings tells a story about the fate of the Davidic monarchy, Inner Kings details the story that leads to its greatest moment of threat. In Outer Kings, Israel and Judah are at war, but northern hostility never threatens the Davidic throne. However, as Judah are slowly and peacefully drawn into the circle of the Omrides they are also drawn into their fate. Except for the Babylonian exile itself, Jehu's rebellion and Athaliah's coup are the greatest threat posed by Kings to the promise to David.

The two plots, when read together, complement one another. For example, the short Outer Kings narrative of Zimri's rebellion (1 Kgs 16.9-20) can be juxtaposed with the longer Inner Kings account of Jehu's rebellion (2 Kgs 9–10). There are numerous elements of repetition and parallelism to encourage the reader to form a narrative analogy:[91] Baasha's dynasty falls under the same prophetic condemnation as Ahab's (1 Kgs 16.4; 21.24); Baasha's entire family is struck down by a usurper in fulfilment of prophecy, as is Ahab's (1 Kgs 16.11-13; 2 Kgs 10.17); the usurper Jehu is explicitly compared to Zimri (2 Kgs 9.31); and the prophet who announces Baasha's demise is coincidentally named Jehu (1 Kgs 16.1). Even though we do not know the details of Zimri's rebellion, we can infer the kinds of things that must have happened by analogy with the fuller Inner Kings account.

The purpose of this structure goes beyond narrative art. It also served the interests of the exilic community who first read it. In Chapter 1, I argued that this narrative is a political historiography, a statement of identity for the exilic community. In part, the book demonstrates continuity with their monarchic past. It also gives an explanation for their present situation and it entails hope for the future. As we shall see in Chapter 3, it can do all of this through the promise–covenant dialectic that drives the narrative of Outer Kings.

In Chapters 4–6 we will observe the way that Inner Kings nuances the strong Davidic themes that emerge in Outer Kings. Set in the north, Inner Kings demonstrates the possibility of a faithful form of Yahwism with neither David nor temple. It narrates the formation of a faithful community centred on the prophetic ministries of Elijah and Elisha, and in doing so allows the book to explore the contradiction of Israel's exilic existence. As we noticed, the narrative in Inner Kings takes frequent detours outside of Samaria, into the regions of Sidon and Syria, into the minds and lives of foreigners. It is the narrative of Israel amongst the nations.

---

91. Drawing once again on Gilmour's categories of juxtapositional logic (*Juxtaposition and the Elisha Cycle*, 33–45).

Inner Kings also focuses on the domain of life away from the halls of power, recounting instead the day-to-day lives of ordinary people who suffer because of its misuse. The widow ready to die from the drought proclaimed against Ahab, the woman who fled a famine and had to plead for justice to regain her land, and the lepers who starve outside the city gate in a siege are all nearer parallels to the readers of the book than the great kings Solomon, Hezekiah, and Josiah.

Inner Kings is a story about those who suffer because of a political world they do not control. The characters seem to be separate from Yahweh's promises and plan for Israel, but nevertheless find, serve, and worship him. It is a story about the prophets who straddle the two worlds: royal and ordinary, confronting the former with the God who will act with miraculous power for the benefit of the latter. It is a story of Israel in exile, who gather around the prophets, expecting and hoping that God will act once again.

3

Covenant: What Is Israel?

3.1. *The Mosaic Covenant in Kings*

In Chapter 2 we investigated the role that the Mosaic covenant plays within the literary architecture of Kings.[1] In this chapter we turn to its significance for the national ideology of the book, which operates at two levels.

First, the covenant creates an ideal definition of what it means to be Israel,[2] a concept I shall term *Covenant-Israel* to avoid confusion with other uses of the word 'Israel' in Kings. Although the history in the book recounts Israel's inability to implement this ideal, I shall argue in this chapter that the logic of covenant and promise in Kings creates an expectation for a renewed community that will embody it. This political expectation is known as a destiny: an imagined, hoped-for future shared by the members of the community.[3]

---

1. We are using the book of King's own definition of ברית as we explored in Chapter 2. Kings does not use this word to refer to the Davidic promise, only to the Mosaic covenant. For the most part, though not exclusively, Kings draws on the deuteronomic traditions, as we noted in Chapter 1. I mean by that word, those traditions that came to be recorded in the book of Deuteronomy. This chapter draws on scholarship on Deuteronomy, but does not assume that the author of Kings necessarily knew it in its current form. I do assume the traditions surrounding the Mosaic covenant, and especially its deuteronomic expression, were available to the author. And I argue that the Mosaic covenant was selected intentionally as the primary identifier of national Israel.

2. This is true of the role of divine covenants in political-theological analysis more generally. See e.g. Smith, *Chosen Peoples*, 50–1.

3. See Smith, *Chosen Peoples*, 216–17; and Coakley, 'Mobilizing the Past', 550–2.

Second, the covenant also informs the way the book understands history to work, as von Rad observes:

> It is interesting to note how the [deuteronomist] proceeds from the basic assumption that the history of the two kingdoms is nothing more or less than the historical expression of the will and word of Yahweh.[4]

I shall argue that, by presenting Israel's history as the outworking of the covenant, the book does more than explain the fact of the exile. It also demonstrates through a carefully crafted presentation of history that Israel's adherence to the covenant has been determinative for their future in every historical situation. We shall see that the book creates an argument that the covenant must be kept whether Israel is in a golden era or at the point of annihilation, and that in either case Israel is equally susceptible to failure. In Kings, it is Israel's fidelity to the covenant rather than the ebb and flow of natural history that determines Israel's political success.

3.2. *The Covenant as Destiny: A Framework for Political Identity*

3.2.1. *Deuteronomy and Political Identity*

There is a long heritage of thought that regards Deuteronomy as a political manifesto, or constitution for Israel.[5] This trend has only grown in contemporary scholarship.[6] For example, Sean McBride calls Deuteronomy a

---

4. Von Rad, 'The Deuteronomic Theology of History in I and II Kings', 160.

5. This dates at least to Josephus, who chose the Greek word πολιτεία to speak of what he found in Deuteronomy, rather than νόμος, which he used to refer to the Torah more generally. See McBride, 'Polity of the Covenant People', 229–30, who also notes (p. 230 n. 4) that Baruch Spinoza discussed the constitutional significance of Deuteronomy in the eighteenth century.

6. See, e.g., McBride, 'Polity of the Covenant People', 229–44; Hastings, *The Construction of Nationhood*, 18; Moshe Greenberg, 'Biblical Attitudes Toward Power: Ideal and Reality in Law and Prophets', in *Religion and Law: Biblical-Judaic and Islamic Perspectives*, ed. Edwin B. Firmage, Bernard G. Weiss, and John W. Welch (Winona Lake, IN: Eisenbrauns, 1990), 101–12; Lothar Perlitt, 'Der Staatsgedanke im Deuteronomium', in *Language, Theology and the Bible: Essays in Honour of James Barr*, ed. S. E. Balentine and J. Barton (Oxford: Clarendon, 1994), 182–98; Elazar, *Covenant and Polity in Biblical Israel*; McConville, 'Law and Monarchy', 69–88; Bernard M. Levinson, 'The First Constitution: Rethinking the Origins of Rule of Law and Separation of Powers in Light of Deuteronomy', *Cardozo Law Review* 27 (2006): 1853–88; McConville, *God and Earthly Power*, 74–98, and 'King and Messiah', in *King and Messiah in Israel and the Ancient Near*

'comprehensive social charter', and 'the product of mature reflection on [Israel's] identity'.[7] This makes sense, even if it appears anachronistic at first.[8] At an abstract level, Deuteronomy encodes more than a collection of laws. It also includes traditions and customs (חוקים ומשפטים)[9] that ensure continuity of the community throughout both their territory (e.g., Deut. 16.1-16) and their generations (e.g., Deut. 6.20-25).[10]

As we saw in Chapter 1, national identity is a matter of sharing common 'myths and memories, a public culture, and common laws and customs for all members'.[11] So, as Benedict Anderson phrases it, national identities are 'imagined'.[12] They are an appeal to a group to understand themselves as having these things in common, to ignite a sense of community that 'inspires the collective will and mass emotion'.[13]

When the author of Kings selects the deuteronomic traditions of covenant, he finds such a 'social charter'[14] ready to hand. These traditions embody what Smith calls the 'myth of ethnic election'[15] that sets the Israelite people apart from the other peoples around them (e.g., Deut. 7.1-8). Within it, Israel are imagined as a 'sacred communion of the

---

East: Proceedings of the Oxford Old Testament Seminar, ed. John Day (London: T&T Clark, 2013), 276–81; Berman, *Created Equal*, 51–80; Daniel I. Block, '"You Shall not Covet Your Neighbour's Wife": A Study in Deuteronomic Domestic Ideology', *JETS* 53 (2010): 449–74, and 'The Burden of Leadership: The Mosaic Paradigm of Kingship (Deut 17:14-20)', *BSac* 162 (2005): 259–78, and 'The Joy of Worship: The Mosaic Invitation to the Presence of God (Deut 12:1-14)', *BSac* 162 (2005): 131–49; George E. Mendenhall, 'Covenant Forms in Israelite Tradition', *BA* 17 (1954): 50–76, and 'Ancient Oriental and Biblical Law', *BA* 172 (1954): 26–46. This trend owes much to the recognition that there is a relationship between the literary forms of Deuteronomy and ANE covenant treaty documents.

7. McBride, 'Polity of the Covenant People', 236–7.

8. See Elazar (*Covenant and Polity in Biblical Israel*, 35–8) on the development of ancient covenant-based communities.

9. McBride ('Polity of the Covenant People', 233–4) reads this as a hendiadys meaning 'constitutional matters'.

10. See Norbert Lohfink, 'Distributions of the Functions of Power: The Laws Concerning Public Offices in Deuteronomy 16:18–18:22', in *A Song of Power and the Power of Song*, ed. Duane L. Christensen (Winona Lake, IN: Eisenbrauns, 1993), 336–52; and U. Rutersworden, *Von der politischen Gemeinschaft zur Gemeinde: Studien zu Dt 16,18–18,22*, BBB (Frankfurt: Athenaum, 1987).

11. Smith, *Chosen Peoples*, 24.

12. Anderson, *Imagined Communities*, 145. See also Smith, *Chosen Peoples*, 20–4.

13. Smith, *Chosen Peoples*, 22.

14. McBride, 'Polity of the Covenant People', 238.

15. Smith, *Chosen Peoples*, 48–9.

people'[16] – the great 'assembly' (קהל) who stood at Mount Horeb on the day the covenant was instituted (e.g., Deut. 4.10; 5.22; 9.10; 10.4). There is a strong appeal to Israel as a people united across families and generations (e.g., Deut. 5.3).[17] There is an already established 'distinctive history and culture' with 'a specific ancestral territory', 'a separate public cult that unites its adherents into a single moral community of the faithful', and 'a union of equals who compose a moral community whose members are possessed, at least theoretically, of common rights and duties'.[18] Everything needed to construct an idealised political vision for national Israel is already found within the Mosaic covenant.

In an exilic context, however, the selection of the deuteronomic covenant traditions as the foundation of the book was not inevitable. For that community, much of the political vision idealised in Deuteronomy had been lost, and an alternative ideological framework might have been chosen that addressed more immediate needs.[19] For example, if the author had thought it most urgent to advocate the preservation of cultural distinctiveness against the Babylonian hegemony, then we might have expected the festivals, circumcision, and the Sabbath to have played a greater role in the history of the book. As it stands, these are nearly absent. Or, if the need was the preservation of ethnicity, then a more prominent place might have been allocated to the patriarchal and other familial traditions such as the Abrahamic covenant which is mentioned only once (2 Kgs 13.23). The traditions of tribal heritage, particularly the priestly role of the Levites, barely enter the story of Kings at all,[20] but these traditions were available to Ezekiel (e.g., Ezek. 47.13–48.29).

So it is our task to explore what is gained from the context of exile by imagining Israel as *Covenant-Israel*, as a nation still idealised by the traditions of the covenant.[21] The key will be its relationship to the Davidic promise, and I shall argue here that it is the dialectic between the covenant and that promise which gives it an ongoing validity by re-imagining the covenant as a destiny.

---

16. Smith, *Chosen Peoples*, 32–3.
17. McConville, *God and Earthly Power*, 85–7; Elazar, *Covenant and Polity in Biblical Israel*, 193–224.
18. Smith, *Chosen Peoples*, 32–3.
19. E.g. Habel (*The Land Is Mine*, 36–53) lists six political ideologies of land that are present within Old Testament literature, each with distinctive concerns and characteristics. We shall return to these in Chapter 5.
20. See, e.g., Habel, *The Land Is Mine*, 68.
21. See Chapter 3.

3.2.2. *David within the Covenant*

As we saw in Chapter 2, the logic of promise and fulfilment in Kings drives the narrative of the book because the reader is drawn to expect every promise to be fulfilled.[22] This includes the promise to David in 2 Sam. 7.8-16, which was not conditional on covenant obedience:

> I will be to him a father, and he shall be to me a son. When he commits iniquity, I will discipline him with the rod of men, with the stripes of the sons of men, but my steadfast love will not depart from him… Your house and your kingdom will endure forever before me; your throne will be established forever. (2 Sam. 7.14-16, ESV)

Given this, it is surprising that the book of Kings never states the promise in its unconditional form. Although it reminds the reader of the unconditional nature of the promise through other means,[23] the Davidic promise is always stated conditionally in Kings (e.g., 1 Kgs 2.4; 8.25; 9.4-5). What is the logic of this strange mix of conditionality and unconditionality?

This question rose to prominence in scholarship of the 1970s and 80s, and several proposals have been popular. The diachronic solution understands the conditional elements as a later (exilic) corrective to an earlier (pre-exilic) unconditional promise,[24] but this has not met with general acceptance.[25] One significant objection has been that the ending of the book (2 Kgs 24–25), which can definitely be attributed to the exilic editor, does not link the demise of Judah to a conditional form of the promise.[26] In fact, the Davidic promise is not mentioned in either conditional or unconditional form after Hezekiah.[27] Thus we require a synchronic

---

22. See also von Rad, 'The Deuteronomic Theology of History in 1 and 2 Kings', 156.

23. Particularly the 'burning lamp' *Leitmotif* (e.g., 1 Kgs 11.36; 15.4; 2 Kgs 8.19). See Lovell, 'The Shape of Hope', 8–9.

24. See, e.g., Cross, *Canaanite Myth and Hebrew Epic*, 274–89; Provan, *Hezekiah and the Books of Kings*, 100–131; and Jon D. Levenson, 'The Last Four Verses in Kings', *JBL* 103 (1984): 354–6.

25. Halpern ('Why Manasseh Is Blamed for the Babylonian Exile: The Evolution of Biblical Tradition', *VT* 48 [1998]: 488) accuses the position of invoking a diachronic explanation when a synchronic one is simpler. See also Antti Laato, *A Star is Rising: The Historical Development of the Old Testament Royal Ideology and the Rise of the Jewish Messianic Expectations* (Atlanta, GA: Scholars Press, 1997), 37; and Linville, *Israel in the Book of Kings*, 51–2.

26. Knoppers, *Two Nations Under God 1*, 94–112.

27. For this reason Iain Provan (*Hezekiah and the Books of Kings*, 131–2) attributes both forms of the Davidic promise to the pre-exilic redaction of the book.

solution that explains how the conditional and unconditional elements function in the exilic text.

One such synchronic solution is to understand the unconditional promise as pertaining only to the rule of Judah, while the kingship over greater Israel was always conditional on covenant obedience. Richard Friedman noted that in Kings all the conditional promises refer to the 'throne of Israel' (כסא ישראל, 1 Kgs 2.4; 8.25; 9.4-5) where none of the unconditional ones do, and so he proposed that this phrase refers particularly to the Northern Kingdom.[28] This has found widespread support,[29] but there are good reasons to question whether Kings, or any other Old Testament literature, understands the Davidic promise as operating differently with respect to the northern and southern parts of the kingdom.[30] This would not easily fit the context of 2 Samuel 7, where David already rules a united kingdom when the promise is given. Neither does it fit the context of 1 Kings 8, where the label 'Israel' applies the Davidic promise to both northern and southern tribes (e.g., 1 Kgs 8.16, see below). And, as Linville argues, why does the prophetic announcement of Jeroboam's kingdom (1 Kgs 11.29-39) not offer him the 'throne of Israel' if that term was coined precisely to refer to that political domain?[31]

A second alternative is to understand the Davidic promise as encompassing all of Israel in both its conditional and unconditional forms.[32] Here, the conditionality of the covenant does not call into question Yahweh's ability to fulfil the promise. Rather, it outlines the conditions under which

---

28. Richard E. Friedman, *The Exile and Biblical Narrative: The Formation of the Deuteronomistic and Priestly Works* (Chico, CA: Scholars Press, 1981), 12–13.

29. E.g. Nelson, *The Double Redaction of the Deuteronomistic History*, 100–104; Sweeney, *King Josiah of Judah*, 33–4; Baruch Halpern, *The Constitution of the Monarchy in Israel*, HSM (Chico, CA: Scholars Press, 1981), 99–105; Halpern, *The First Historians*, 155–67; and Halpern and Vanderhooft, 'The Editions of Kings', 242–3.

30. Bruce K. Waltke, 'The Phenomenon of Conditionality within Unconditional Covenants', in *Israel's Apostasy and Restoration: Essays in Honor of Roland K. Harrison*, ed. Avraham Gileadi (Grand Rapids, MI: Baker, 1988), 135–6.

31. Linville, *Israel in the Book of Kings*, 152–3. See also Avraham Gileadi, 'The Davidic Covenant: A Theological Basis for Corporate Protection', in Gileadi, ed., *Israel's Apostasy and Restoration*, 157–63.

32. I have argued for this previously: Lovell, 'The Shape of Hope', 10. See also Lissa M. Wray Beal, *1&2 Kings*, ApOTC (Grand Rapids, MI: IVP, 2014), 75; Waltke, 'The Phenomenon of Conditionality', 135; Gileadi, 'The Davidic Covenant', 157–63; McConville, '1 Kings VIII 46–53', 77–9, and 'Narrative and Meaning', 37–8; and David N. Freedman, 'Divine Commitment and Human Obligation: The Covenant Theme', *Int* 18 (1964): 420–6.

fulfilment might occur. Bruce Waltke, for example, comments on the parallel problem of conditionality and unconditionality in the case of Abraham and Moses:[33]

> The unilateral covenant eternally committing YHWH to Abraham and his descendants, and the bilateral covenant imposing obligations on Israel are, in fact, inseparable. On the one hand, YHWH's faithful discharge of his promise...provides the spiritual basis for Israel to accept and keep the covenant with commandments. On the other hand, the commandments set forth the conditions that qualify one to become a beneficiary of YHWH's grant... In this way YHWH irrevocably commits himself to fulfilling his promises, but not apart from ethical behaviour on Israel's part. This connection between the two covenants explains how the two apparently incompatible kinds of covenants – oath and obligation – could be made with the same people. Under the terms of the oath, YHWH committed himself forever to Israel as a whole; under the terms of *obligation*, he could discipline them individually, even to the point of putting them under curses.[34]

In this understanding, the Davidic promise would not imply that every Davidic son will be automatically blessed (see 2 Sam. 12.11); it would only necessitate that, eventually, one of them is.[35]

i. *Conditionality and Fulfilment: Solomon's Dedication*

This second alternative makes sense of the promise–fulfilment language that permeates Solomon's dedication of the temple (1 Kgs 8). This chapter is the key text in Kings dealing with this relationship between the covenant and the Davidic promise.[36] As Knoppers notes, the construction of the temple is portrayed as beginning a new epoch in the history of

---

33. The logic of this position is well developed in scholarship on the parallel tension in Deuteronomy between the conditional covenantal blessings and the unconditional promise to Abraham. See, e.g., J. Gordon McConville, *Grace in the End: A Study in Deuteronomic Theology* (Grand Rapids, MI: Zondervan, 1993), 134–9; William J. Dumbrell, 'The Prospect of Unconditionality in the Siniatic Covenant', in Gileadi, ed., *Israel's Apostasy and Restoration*, 152–4.

34. Waltke, 'The Phenomenon of Conditionality', 135.

35. E.g. Halpern and Vanderhooft, 'The Editions of Kings', 243–4.

36. See Troy D. Cudworth, 'Yahweh's Promise to David in the Books of Kings', *VT* 66 (2016): 215–16; Gary N. Knoppers, 'David's Relation to Moses: The Contexts, Content and Conditions of the Davidic Promises', in Day, ed., *King and Messiah in Israel and the Ancient Near East*, 91–118; and Christopher J. H. Wright, *God's People in God's Land: Family, Land, and Property in the Old Testament* (Carlisle: Paternoster, 1997), 6–7, 24–43.

Israel (see, e.g., 1 Kgs 6.1),[37] the change of an era from Sinai to Zion.[38] However, Solomon's rhetoric in 1 Kings 8 is not one of abrogation. The covenant finds a place in Solomon's new order (v. 21).[39] The account opens with Solomon's appeal to continuity with Israel's covenantal past (1 Kgs 8.1-9).[40] He honours the bearers of the old order, the priests and Levites (never mentioned again in Kings), by having them bring the old symbols to the temple: the ark of the covenant and its paraphernalia. The text portrays this as Israel's new moment of gathering (קהל, vv. 14, 22, 55, 65; see e.g. Deut. 4.10; 5.22). This time, instead of the gathering at Moses's mountain, they gather at David's city (v. 1), around David's offspring (v. 5).

The rhetoric of Solomon's first speech (vv. 15-21) follows the same strategy of continuity.[41] Solomon uses standard promise–fulfilment language, which we examined in Chapter 2, to relate the way Yahweh has accomplished (מלא, קום, vv. 15, 20) what he promised (דבר) to David. Everything has happened 'just as Yahweh said' (כאשר דבר יהוה, v. 20). That is, according to Solomon, the dawn of this new era is something that was promised by Yahweh long ago.

Solomon's theology of fulfilment represents the book more broadly.[42] The narrator (e.g., 1 Kgs 2.12) and several other characters are positive towards Solomon's claim to embody the fulfilment of the divine promises to David (e.g., David, 1 Kgs 2.4; and Hiram of Tyre, 1 Kgs 5.7 [5.21, Heb.]). The narrator also believes Solomon has established a kingdom that embodies both patriarchal and deuteronomic hopes (1 Kgs 4.20-25 [4.20–5.5, Heb.]; see Gen. 15.5; 22.17; Deut. 8.8) and marks the beginning of a new era in Israel's history (1 Kgs 6.1). The book of Kings further endorses Solomon's agenda in 1 Kings 8 by recalling that

---

37. Knoppers, 'Prayer and Propaganda', 242–4.
38. Knoppers, 'There Was None Like Him', 112–17.
39. Knoppers, 'Prayer and Propaganda', 249–50.
40. I examine the unity of 1 Kgs 8 in some detail in Chapter 5. For now, note that this theme of continuity with Israel's traditions provides a high degree of structural and thematic coherence to the chapter. See Knoppers, 'Prayer and Propaganda', 233–9; and Walsh, *1 Kings*, 112 n. 9.
41. On the structure of 1 Kgs 8 delineated by Solomon's speeches, see Sweeney, *I & II Kings*, 129; or Walsh, *1 Kings*, 108–9.
42. On the possibility that Solomon is an unreliable character, see Jung Ju Kang, *The Persuasive Portrayal of Solomon in 1 Kings 1–11* (New York: Peter Lang, 2003), 240–55; and Walter A. Brueggemann, *Solomon: Israel's Ironic Icon of Human Achievement* (Columbia, MO: University of South Carolina, 2005), 95–6.

the cloud from the tent of meeting re-appeared at Solomon's dedication (1 Kgs 8.10-13; Deut. 1.33; 4.11; 5.22; 31.15).

As Solomon's second speech begins, this language of fulfilment is set alongside a continuing assertion that the covenant must be kept (1 Kgs 8.23-26).[43] The prayer is structured into several parts, beginning with a doxology (vv. 23-24), followed by a general petition (... ועתה יהוה, vv. 25-26), and then a long sequence of petitions relating to possible contingencies (vv. 27-53). The covenant–promise dialectic emerges early in this second speech. Even though Solomon believes Yahweh has fulfilled the promise to David (v. 24), he can still petition Yahweh to fulfil it (vv. 25-26). The key to this logic is in the opening doxology. I will offer a translation below, after resolving some of the difficulties:

23a	יהוה אלהי ישראל
b	אין כמוך
c	↑אלהים[44] בשמים ממעל ועל הארץ מתחת
d	↑שמר הברית והחסד לעבדיך ההלכים לפניך בכל לבם:
24a	↑אשר[45] שמרת לעבדך דוד אבי את אשר דברת לו
b	ותדבר בפיך
c	ובידך מלאת כיום הזה:

Yahweh is incomparable (v. 23b) in three ways (vv. 23c-24a),[46] and the second of these (v. 23d) requires unpacking. It characterises Yahweh as the God who is faithful (a keeper [שמר] of *something*) only to those who 'walk before you with all their hearts', as David did (v. 24a, see 1 Kgs 3.6, 14).[47] What is this *something* to which God is faithful? The phrase is הברית והחסד.[48] Many English translations see this as a hendiadys (e.g.,

---

43. Sweeney, *I & II Kings*, 133–4.

44. The placement of this word in v. 23c requires a verbal ellipsis: '[who is] God in the heavens...' See Neil B. MacDonald, '1 Kings 8:23 – A Case of Repunctuation?' *VT* 53 (2003): 115–17.

45. I take the antecedent of אשר to be אלהים (v. 23a), even though it is distant (so RSV). It cannot be הברית (v. 23d) because the object לו את אשר דברת would not relate to the clause. The only other possibility is to read v. 24a as independent, in spite of the relative pronoun (so NIV, ESV).

46. In my reading, v. 24a explains Yahweh's incomparability: '...there is none like you..., who has kept with your servant...' This exegesis does not affect my argument.

47. So Wray Beal, *1&2 Kings*, 137.

48. Apart from its occurrence in Deut. 7 (see below), this phrase has also been found on the Ketef Hinnom Amulet 1, dating from the seventh century, which may

'keeping your covenant of love', NIV; 'keeping your gracious covenant', NJPS; 'keeping your covenant of kindness', NAB;[49] 'keeping with loyalty...'[50]). In this case the phrase must refer to the Davidic covenant, and would be the only occurrence in the text of Kings where 'covenant' (ברית) is used for that purpose.[51] However, there is little warrant for a hendiadys here.[52]

It is better, with the RSV and ESV, to understand הברית והחסד as two separate ideas: 'keeping the covenant and [showing] covenantal love'.[53] In this case the phrase refers to Yahweh's fidelity to the blessings of the Mosaic covenant if Israel are obedient. Deuteronomy 7.9-12 provides a close comparison to support this reading.[54] The precise phrase (שמר הברית והחסד) occurs in Deut. 7.9, and this verse also shares with 1 Kgs 8.23 notions of the incomparability and faithfulness of Yahweh. In both texts Yahweh keeps הברית והחסד only to those who 'love him and keep his commandments' (Deut. 7.9) or who 'walk before him with all their heart' (1 Kgs 8.23). In Deuteronomy this is further qualified by v. 12 where the two terms are separated. There Yahweh keeps 'the covenant and [also] the covenantal love which he swore to your fathers' (את הברית ואת החסד אשר נשבע לאבתיך, Deut. 7.12). In Deut. 7.9 also, then, the covenant (הברית) is something distinguishable from the covenantal love (החסד).[55]

1 Kings 8.23 can therefore be unpacked. For those who 'walk before you with all their hearts' Yahweh's act of keeping the covenant (ברית) results in the bestowal of his covenantal love (חסד). With David's

---

imply it has become a stock phrase by the time of Kings. See Shmuel Ahituv, *Echoes from the Past: Hebrew and Cognate Inscriptions from the Biblical Period* (Jerusalem: Carta, 2008), 49–50.

49. So also Roger L. Omanson and John E. Ellington, *A Handbook on 1&2 Kings*, UBS Handbook Series (Münster: UBS, 2008), on 1 Kgs 8.23.

50. Cogan, *1 Kings*, 283.

51. See Chapter 2.

52. The support cited for this reading is a small number of poetic texts where the two terms occur in parallel. E.g. Pss. 89.29; 106.45. See Cogan, *1 Kings*, 283.

53. The meaning of חסד is difficult to translate into English, embodying obligation, fidelity and loyalty, as well as affection. It fits the covenantal context well. For discussion see *NIDOTTE*, s.v. 'חָסַד, ḥāsad, II)'.

54. MacDonald ('1 Kings 8:23', 116) notes a number of parallels between this verse and Deuteronomy. Other uses of this phrase in the Old Testament are dependent on this one (2 Chron. 6.14; Neh. 1.5; 9.32; Dan. 9.4).

55. So Adele Berlin, Marc Zvi Brettler, and Michael A. Fishbane, eds. *The Jewish Study Bible* (Oxford: Oxford University Press, 2004), s.v. Deut. 7.12.

offspring, this bestowal of חסד will result in the fulfilment of the Davidic promise (see 1 Kgs 3.6). I suggest the following translation for 1 Kgs 8.23-24:[56]

> [23a]Yahweh God of Israel, [b]there is none like you: [c]God in the heavens above and on the earth below; [d]keeping the covenant and showing covenantal love to those who walk before you with all their heart; [24a]who has kept what you swore to your servant David. [b]What your lips have promised, [c]your hand has fulfilled, as it is this day.

Thus Solomon can petition that Yahweh would 'keep' and 'establish' (imperative of שמר and jussive of אמן, vv. 25-26) what he believes has already been kept (v. 24): the promise made to David. Even though Yahweh's blessing results from an unconditional promise to David, at any point in history he will show covenantal love only to those who remain faithful to the covenant. The certainty of eventual fulfilment is not in question, but there is scope for Yahweh to fulfil the curses promised in the covenant while he awaits a king who will 'walk before him with all his heart'.

By the same logic, Israel also must eventually become Covenant-Israel. The Davidic promise includes an 'established' (כון) and 'enduring' (נאמן ... עד־עלם) kingdom (ממלכו, 2 Sam. 7.12, 16). It encompasses the blessings of the Mosaic covenant by including a promise that Israel will be established in the land as 'my people Israel' (עמי ישראל, 2 Sam. 7.10; e.g. Deut. 4.20; 7.6) where Yahweh will provide 'rest' (נוח, 2 Sam. 7.11; e.g. Deut. 12.10).

Solomon's closing benediction (1 Kgs 8.56-61) draws on the same promise–fulfilment logic we have seen above, but now applies it to the people generally. Like David in vv. 23-24, the people 'at this time' (כיום הזה, 1 Kgs 8.61) are portrayed as faithful with 'hearts committed to Yahweh to walk in his statutes and to keep his commandments' (v. 61). Just as Yahweh keeps covenantal love with David as a result (v. 24), now Yahweh has given 'rest' (נוח) to 'his people Israel' (עמו ישראל) in fulfilment of what was promised (דבר) to Moses (1 Kgs 8.56). And just as Solomon could ask with respect to the Davidic promise that Yahweh still fulfil in the future what he has already fulfilled this day (vv. 25-26), so also he can pray that Yahweh might yet 'incline the hearts [of the people] to him' (להטות לבבנו אליו, 1 Kgs 8.58), so that they might 'walk in obedience to him and keep the commands, decrees and laws he gave our ancestors'.

---

56. Refer to the syntax diagram above.

The certainty of the Davidic promise therefore entails the blessings of the Mosaic covenant for all of Israel also. For the exilic readers it clearly does not imply that every generation of Israel will be blessed in this way. However, the dialectic between covenant and promise does create hope: an expectation that Covenant-Israel will emerge even from the exile, but how?

3.2.3. *The Covenant and Repentance: Josiah's Reforms*

One conclusion that might be drawn from these data is that the message of the book to those in exile is one of repentance: that penitence would precipitate the blessings of the covenant and the Davidic promise, and with these blessings would come the full restoration of Israel. This idea has been proposed,[57] first by Hans Walter Wolff in his thoughts on the message of DtrH:[58]

> However, amid this hour of deepest catastrophe, there is not much brief for teaching hope…but still, if Judges 2 and 1 Samuel 12 are to be believed, there is yet room for hope: the cry to Yahweh, with a confession of guilt, a prayer for deliverance, and a willingness to give renewed obedience, may be efficacious again.[59]

Initially this seems to make good sense. If the malady is covenant disobedience, then the remedy must surely be repentance. Amongst other data, Wolff notices the frequency of the word שוב at key points in the narrative of Kings (e.g., 1 Kgs 8.22-53, 6 times) and reads these in the context of Deut. 30.1-10, where repentance is a prerequisite of Israel's return to the land.[60]

---

57. This idea grew naturally out of Noth's (*The Deuteronomistic History*, 97–9) negativity towards Israel's future. Von Rad (*Old Testament Theology* [Peabody, MA: Prince Press, 2005], 1:341–3) countered that Jehoiachin's release provides hope. There have been a range of mediating positions since. See, e.g., Wolff, 'Kerygma', 91–9; Janzen, 'The Sins of Josiah and Hezekiah', 370, and 'An Ambiguous Ending', 57; Ackroyd, *Exile and Restoration*, 79–81; Murray, 'Of All the Years the Hopes – or Fears?', 263–5; Leslie J. Hoppe, 'The Death of Josiah and the Meaning of Deuteronomy', *LASBF* 48 (1998): 47; Nelson, *The Double Redaction of the Deuteronomistic History*, 123. See also my previous discussion in Lovell, 'The Shape of Hope', 3–5.

58. Wolff, 'Kerygma', 91–3.

59. Wolff, 'Kerygma', 92.

60. Wolff, 'Kerygma', 91–2, 96–8.

Wolff's observations concerning the value of repentance are accurate, but his conclusion that repentance will precipitate blessing is too hasty. The narrative of Kings does not support this belief. For example, Solomon's prayer, dealing with the case of exile, encourages repentance with no explicit hope for restoration (1 Kgs 8.46-49).[61] Solomon prays for forgiveness, and that their 'captives would show them mercy' (v. 50).

More than this, every case of repentance in the narrative of Kings fails in the longer term. The repentance precipitated by Elijah (1 Kgs 18.39) is followed by further Baalism (1 Kgs 19.1). Jehoiada's faithfulness (2 Kgs 12.2 [12.3, Heb.]) and covenant renewal (2 Kgs 11.4) saves the kingdom from Athaliah, but they continue in sin (2 Kgs 12.3 [12.4, Heb.]). Kings from the north who repent have their dynasty extended by several generations (e.g., 1 Kgs 21.25-29; 2 Kgs 22.19), but judgment still comes.[62] Hezekiah's reforms (2 Kgs 18.3-6) are undone by Manasseh (2 Kgs 21.3) and, according to Isaiah, would not have ultimately saved Jerusalem (2 Kgs 20.16-18).

The most compelling evidence is the case of Josiah, who is a test of the value of repentance in the current form of the narrative.[63] By every deuteronomic measure, Josiah's reform is blameless. He is the only king in the book who 'listens' (שמע) to the law of Moses (2 Kgs 22.11, 18-19), who 'reads' (קרא) it (2 Kgs 22.10, 16; 23.2; see also Deut. 17.19), and who 'keeps' (שמר) and 'does' (עשה) it (2 Kgs 22.2, 13; 23.3, 21; see also Deut. 17.19).[64] He is the only person in the Old Testament who is recorded to have repented (שוב) to Yahweh with his 'heart, soul and might' (2 Kgs 23.25; Deut. 6.4).

Even though Josiah's repentance is presented as the right thing to have done (2 Kgs 22.19), there is no hint his reforms will precipitate blessing. Not only does his untimely death subvert that message, but everyone in the narrative knows Josiah's reform will not save Judah. This includes Josiah himself (2 Kgs 22.13), and the prophetess Huldah (2 Kgs 22.16-20). Josiah may have repented (שוב), but Yahweh has not turned (שוב) from his anger (2 Kgs 23.25-26). McConville comments:

---

61. As Wolff ('Kerygma', 99) also recognises.
62. Hoppe, 'The Death of Josiah', 31–47; and Lovell, 'The Shape of Hope', 14.
63. On Josiah's role in the exilic edition of Kings, see Peter J. Leithart, *1&2 Kings*, BTCB (Grand Rapids, MI: Brazos, 2006), 266–71; Linville, *Israel in the Book of Kings*, 229–35.
64. Lovell, 'The Shape of Hope', 13–14.

From the fact that reforms in 1,2 Kings typically fail to secure the covenantal blessings for Judah it follows, not that a better reform might have done the trick (which patently it did not), but that none ever could. The brilliant portrayal of Josiah's efforts makes this point with irony and force.[65]

The reason given is that Josiah's reforms have not undone Manasseh's sin (2 Kgs 23.26-27),[66] as David Janzen observes:

> ...exilic readers can learn from this final form of the last chapters of Kings that, when a monarch causes the people to sin and become even worse than the Canaanites, as Manasseh did, not even a perfect act of repentance will save the nation from destruction.[67]

Although the book of Kings believes repentance and covenant renewal must precede blessing (1 Kgs 8.46-49), it does not imagine that they will precipitate it.[68]

3.2.4. *Covenant, Grace, and Destiny*

If repentance will not precipitate blessing, what message does the dialectic between covenant and promise deliver to those in exile? Or, to return to our original question, to what end is the ideal of Covenant-Israel used in this book?

The only certainty in Kings, as we have seen already, is that the word of Yahweh 'invariably achieves its purpose in history by virtue of its own inherent power'.[69] It is this inevitability – that Yahweh will be faithful to his word even when confronted with Israel's faithlessness – which guarantees the Davidic promise.

However, as we have also seen, Yahweh will not bless apostasy with covenant love. The covenant is therefore employed within Kings not only to explain Israel's exilic situation as the result of the curse, but also to

---

65. McConville, *Grace in the End*, 89. See also McConville, 'Narrative and Meaning', 42–4.
66. See Lovell, 'The Shape of Hope', 15; Hoppe, 'The Death of Josiah', 31–47; Pietsch, 'Prophetess of Doom', 71–80; Nadav Na'aman, 'The "Discovered Book" and the Legitimation of Josiah's Reform', *JBL* 130 (2011): 47–62; Janzen, 'The Sins of Josiah and Hezekiah', 361.
67. Janzen, 'The Sins of Josiah and Hezekiah', 369.
68. The solution to this dilemma can be found in the broader exilic literature: a covenant where sins could simply be forgiven (e.g., Jer. 31.31-34).
69. Von Rad, 'The Deuteronomic Theology of History in 1 and 2 Kings', 156.

show under what conditions the promise to David and the blessings of the Mosaic covenant will certainly be realised. Part of the resolution is that, eventually, there must arise a king in Israel who keeps the covenant.[70] However, Josiah, who is this kind of king, shows that this is not enough. Israel, too, must become obedient to the covenant.

Obedience therefore, rather than repentance, precipitates blessing. This is a subtle but important distinction, because obedience also has a precondition according to Solomon's prayer of dedication. Israel have not been able to accomplish obedience by repenting, but Solomon prays that Yahweh might be with them (1 Kgs 8.57) 'so that' Israel's hearts might be inclined to obey (להטות לבבנו אליו ללכת בכל דרכיו ולשמר מצותיו וחקיו ומשפטיו, v. 58).[71] An act of Yahweh is required.[72]

Covenant-Israel is an ideal that in one sense was lost through exile. However, by the same logic of inevitable blessing, it is also guaranteed by the power of Yahweh's word. By using the deuteronomic covenant as a basic framework of national identity, and by entwining those traditions with the promise to David, the author of Kings provides an anticipated future for its exilic readers, a destiny.[73] The book of Kings encourages its readers to believe that one day Israel will live up to the ideal, and this eventuality relies on Yahweh's grace.

3.3. *The Covenant within the Historiography of Kings: Political Redefinition*

We have been exploring the reason the author of Kings may have used the covenant as the basis of Israel's political definition, even from the context of exile when so much had been lost. One answer was that the relationship between the covenant and the promise in Kings produces hope. Eventually, a covenant-shaped Israel will be realised.

A second reason is that the covenant is used to explain the progress of Israel's history as outcome of Yahweh's fidelity to his word (1 Kgs 9.6-9). At one level this has been frequently observed.[74] The book of Kings

---

70. We explore this idea further in Chapter 6.

71. Note the preposition ל with the infinitive of נטה expressing purpose or result: Paul Joüon and T. Muraoka, *A Grammar of Biblical Hebrew*, SubBi (Rome: Pontificio Istituto Biblico, 2006), 405. Note also that Solomon's apostasy is framed as an inclination (נטה) of the heart (1 Kgs 11.2-4, 9).

72. This logic is paralleled in Deut. 30.1-10 (note v. 6). See McConville, *Grace in the End*, 134–9.

73. Smith, *Chosen Peoples*, 216–17; Coakley, 'Mobilizing the Past', 550–2.

74. Since Noth, *The Deuteronomistic History*, 97–9.

does not view history as a modern historiographer might, purely as the outworking of historical and physical causes and events. Assyrian power is not accounted for by the tides of historical fortune, for example, but because they have been appointed by Yahweh as punishment for apostasy (2 Kgs 17.20; 24.2-4). However, often in Kings, divine will is not accomplished by direct divine intervention. The book does not deny that normal historical cause and effect exists; it simply demonstrates Yahweh's ability to direct even the mundane details of life. A prophecy is given and then, through a series of events that might otherwise have been thought coincidental, somehow, Yahweh's word is fulfilled.

In this way, the covenant in Kings is active behind the scenes of history, so to speak, always directing Israel's historical progress. As Israel disobey the covenant they begin a process of historical transformation, which is summarised by 2 Kgs 17.15:

> They despised his statutes and his covenant that he made with their fathers and the warnings that he gave them. They went after false idols and became false, and they followed the nations that were around them, concerning whom the Lord had commanded them that they should not do like them.

As we shall see, this précis is expanded and repeated throughout the book. It begins with covenant apostasy. As Israel go after 'the false [gods]' (ההבל) they themselves become false (ויהבלו).[75] Then the narrative begins to show how they gradually and increasingly resemble the surrounding peoples rather than the ideal of Covenant-Israel. This is not portrayed as something done to them from an external influence, nor an intentional decision on their part. Political transformation is part of the way Yahweh's word is fulfilled through mundane history. The decision to worship gods other than Yahweh inexorably leads, one way or another, to the semblance of Egypt, Canaan, or Assyria. Mostly, we shall see that this process is conveyed through the careful composition and artistry of the book rather than through the narrator's explicit comment.

Kings, like many works of national historiography, incorporates stories from many stages of the nation's history:[76] its origins, development, golden eras, times of struggle, and national crises. Peter Kaufman explores the religious and ideological language used by nations at various historical moments,[77] categorising them as periods of *conquest* (i.e. national ascendency), *conflict*, and *crisis*.[78]

75. See also Jer. 2.5.
76. Coakley, 'Mobilizing the Past', 542–3; Smith, *Chosen Peoples*, 171–9.
77. Kaufman, *Redeeming Politics*, 3–13, 78.
78. See also O'Donovan, *The Desire of the Nations*, 72–3.

Rhetorically, conquest narratives are often marked by stories of legitimation in which the national deity authorises, endorses, and explains the ascendant political order.[79] Conflict is marked by rival claims when competing factions within the nation can appeal to familiar religious traditions for their own legitimation. And crisis literature recounts times of national undoing, by warfare, disaster, or rebellion, wrestling with the meaning of such events when the nation has, in better times, conflated their own interests with their god's.[80]

Such stories were often composed independently and told for their own purposes. When, later, these narratives become integrated into the historiography of the nation, as has happened with the book of Kings, the rhetoric serves a different end. John Coakley calls these re-contextualised narratives *golden ages*, *ages of struggle*, and *dark ages*.[81]

Coakley observed that golden ages are often recalled in moments of crisis to provide hope:

> First, [golden ages] provide a people that may be suffering from socio-economic and cultural deprivation with a self-validating image of former greatness, one that allows members of the nation to hold their heads high in a context where other nations enjoy much greater power and prestige in the present. Second, it implies a political project for the future that is entirely compatible with the nationalist agenda: the re-establishment of national freedom and unity are seen as prerequisites to the re-establishment of the golden age.[82]

Ages of struggle and dark ages, on the other hand, are often used to appeal to a sense of national unity by vilifying oppressors and recounting the epics of heroes and the battles they fought:[83]

> Nationalist historiography served the useful function of identifying and, where appropriate, demonising the external enemy, in some cases generating a catalogue of brutality and treachery on the part of this group and its agents… [Such] myths of national oppression tend to be closely related

---

79. Kaufman, *Redeeming Politics*, 13.
80. Kaufman, *Redeeming Politics*, 78.
81. Coakley, 'Mobilizing the Past', 546–50. See also Smith, *Chosen Peoples*, 190.
82. Coakley, 'Mobilizing the Past', 546.
83. As Carl Evans ('Naram–Sin and Jeroboam: The Archetypal *Unheilsherrscher* in Mesopotamia and Biblical Historiography', in *Scripture in Context II: More Essays on the Comparative Method*, ed. William W. Hallo, James C. Moyer, and Leo G. Perdue [Winona Lake, IN: Eisenbrauns, 1983], 114) proposes for the source of the Jeroboam 'hero' narratives.

to myths of struggle. If the ills of the nation were attributable to external oppression, then the struggle for freedom became an important theme. If the problem lay in disunity, then the solution was to be found in a rather different direction – in a struggle for unity... In the case of movements for unity, the national struggle is between the nation-building elite and retrogressive, parochial forces that stand as obstacles to unity.[84]

The book of Kings also looks back upon golden ages, like Solomon, periods of struggle, like Elijah, and dark ages like the Assyrian crisis, but the remarkable thing about the historiography of Kings is that it bucks Coakley's trends. The book resists the wistful glorification of Israel's golden eras. Its moments of crisis do not bring reunification and its epic heroes all fail. Neither does Kings demonise Israel's foreign oppressors.

Rather, Kings uses all of its source material – narratives of conquest, conflict, and crisis – to tell the same political story: that of despising the covenant, going after false idols and becoming false like the nations around them (2 Kgs 17.15). The point seems to be that, in every case, no matter what historical contingencies have emerged, Israel's political fortunes have depended on their fidelity to the covenant. No amount of wealth or power secured Israel's future, and no foreign threat jeopardised it. Whether in a golden age or a moment of crisis, the chief threat to the ideal of Covenant-Israel is not the day-to-day affairs of state. Rather the threat is Israel themselves, who through the act of apostasy become just like other nations.

3.3.1. *Conquest: Solomon's Golden Age*

There is little doubt that much of the material from which the Solomon narratives are drawn was literature of legitimation, or in Kaufman's terms, conquest literature.[85] Both the succession narrative (1 Kgs 1–2)[86] and the narratives concerning his kingdom (1 Kgs 3–10) are full of material that

---

84. Coakley, 'Mobilizing the Past', 548–50.
85. Cf. Eric A. Seibert, *Subversive Scribes and the Solomonic Narrative: A Rereading of 1 Kings 1–11* (New York: T&T Clark, 2006), 111–80.
86. The succession narrative is thought to be an earlier source incorporated into both 2 Samuel (11–20) and 1 Kings (1–2). See Roger N. Whybray, *The Succession Narrative: A Study of II Samuel 9–20; I Kings 1 and 2* (London: SCM, 1968). The very name 'succession narrative' implies literature of legitimation, composed as an *apologia* for Solomon's rule; see, e.g., J. Blenkinsopp, 'Another Contribution to the Succession Narrative Debate (2 Samuel 11–20; 1 Kings 1–2)', *JSOT* 38 (2013): 35–58.

aggrandises Solomon and legitimates his rule.[87] We have already examined Solomon's dedication in 1 Kings 8. Outside of this text, Solomon's kingdom is understood to be the fulfilment of the divine promise to the patriarchs and David (e.g., 1 Kgs 4.20-21 [4.20–5.1, Heb.]; 8.24), and the fulfilment of the blessings of the Mosaic covenant (1 Kgs 8.56). Solomon is also personally visited by Yahweh and blessed with wisdom, riches, and honour to rule (1 Kgs 3.10-13). His magnificence not only draws comment from the narrator (e.g., 1 Kgs 4.29-34 [5.9-14, Heb.]), but also from those characters who come into contact with him (e.g., 1 Kgs 3.28; 5.7 [21, Heb.]; 10.3-10). Solomon's marriage to an Egyptian princess (1 Kgs 3.1; 7.8; 9.16, 24; 11.1-2) was an unprecedented diplomatic victory when read in light of Egyptian literature.[88] And his accumulation of gold (e.g., 1 Kgs 10.21) and military hardware (e.g., 1 Kgs 4.26 [5.6, Heb.]) is unparalleled.

There is little doubt that Solomon's era is portrayed as a golden age. But is it recalled in Kings, as Coakley argues of such prosperous times, to provide a national model to which the exiles might aspire?[89] Mullen argues that the Davidic-Solomonic monarchy was the historical ideal by which the exilic community could define itself.[90] In his reading, the pre-monarchic era exposed the inadequacy of prophetic and priestly

---

87. These were possibly sourced from the 'Book of the Acts of Solomon' (1 Kgs 11.41). See Nadav Na'aman, 'Sources and Composition in the History of Solomon', in *The Age of Solomon: Scholarship at the Turn of the Millennium*, ed. Lowell K. Handy, SHANE (Leiden: Brill, 1997), 76–80; Eric W. Heaton, *Solomon's New Men: The Emergence of Ancient Israel as a Nation State* (London: Thames & Hudson, 1974), 15–30; K. Lawson Younger Jr., 'The Figurative Aspect and the Contextual Method in the Evaluation of the Solomonic Empire (1 Kgs 1–11)', in *The Bible in Three Dimensions: Essays in Celebration of Forty Years of Biblical Studies in the University of Sheffield*, ed. David J. A. Clines, Stanley E. Porter, and Stephen E. Fowl (Sheffield: JSOT, 1990), 157–75; McKenzie, *The Trouble with Kings*, 147–52.

88. In the fourteenth century, Pharaoh Amenophis III denied a marriage alliance with a Babylonian king: 'from old, the daughter of an Egyptian king has not been given in marriage to anyone'. Even if this does not reflect actual Egyptian policy, the marriage alliance is mentioned six times in the Old Testament (see also 2 Chron. 8.11), and is clearly intended to display Solomon's diplomatic prowess. See John D. Currid, *Ancient Egypt and the Old Testament* (Grand Rapids, MI: Baker Academic, 1997), 162–5; and Heaton, *Solomon's New Men*, 178.

89. Coakley, 'Mobilizing the Past', 546.

90. Mullen, *Narrative History and Ethnic Boundaries*, 14–15, 38–43, 163–5, 265, 281. In his analysis, Samuel is examined under the heading 'The Golden Age Created: The Ideal Realised', and Kings under 'The Golden Age Lost: The Paradox Recreated'. See also Mullen, *Narrative History and Ethnic Boundaries*, 209, 249.

leadership,[91] and the post-Solomonic kingdoms functioned as a warning not to repeat the mistakes of the past,[92] but, 'With Solomon, Israel reached the pinnacle of statehood; the "golden age" initiated by David found its fulfilment with Solomon'.[93]

However, this positive reading of Solomon's kingdom does not seem likely when the narratives are set within the wider book of Kings. The recontextualised account seems full of contradictions, both in the evaluation of Solomon himself, and his kingdom,[94] and these have invited scholarly scrutiny.[95] To begin with, the conclusion of Solomon's account is a narrative of failure (1 Kgs 11). The new ending not only records Solomon's apostasy, but invites a re-reading of the entire account.[96] The reader finds out (after the fact) that the kingdom had been besieged with adversaries all along (1 Kgs 11.14, 23, 25).[97] We recall that there were a series of four divine encounters, and that each was more negative in tone than the last: 1 Kgs 3.3-15 promised blessing for obedience; 1 Kgs 6.11-13 was similarly positive, but with a warning; 1 Kgs 9.1-9 contained an extended threat for disobedience; and 1 Kgs 11.11-13 announced a curse. When read in an intertextual relationship with Deuteronomy, the report of Solomon's crowning diplomatic achievement, his marriage to

---

91. Mullen, *Narrative History and Ethnic Boundaries*, 163–5.

92. Mullen, *Narrative History and Ethnic Boundaries*, 265, 281.

93. Mullen, *Narrative History and Ethnic Boundaries*, 252.

94. I return to an examination of Solomon's character in Chapter 6. I will focus here on the portrayal of the kingdom itself. On the contextualisation of 1 Kgs 3–10 within DtrH, see Brueggemann, *Solomon*, 24–45.

95. See Yairah Amit, *Hidden Polemics in Biblical Narrative*, Biblical Interpretation Series (Leiden: Brill, 2000), 56–8, on implicit polemics within Hebrew narrative. On Solomon, see J. Daniel Hays, 'Has the Narrator Come to Praise Solomon or to Bury Him? Narrative Subtlety in 1 Kings 1–11', *JSOT* 28 (2003): 155; John A. Davies, '"Discerning Between Good and Evil": Solomon as a New Adam in 1 Kings', *WTJ* 73 (2011): 53–5; Hugh S. Pyper, 'Judging the Wisdom of Solomon: The Two-Way Effect of Intertextuality', *JSOT* 59 (1993): 35; Kim I. Parker, 'Solomon as Philosopher King: The Nexus of Law and Wisdom in 1 Kings 1–11', *JSOT* 53 (1992): 76; Leithart, *1&2 Kings*, 75–82; Steven Weitzman, *Solomon: The Lure of Wisdom* (New Haven, CT: Yale University Press, 2011); Robert D. Miller, 'Solomon the Trickster', *BibInt* 19 (2011): 496–504; Jerome T. Walsh, 'Symmetry and the Sin of Solomon', *Shofar* 12 (1993): 11–27; Kang, *The Persuasive Portrayal of Solomon*, 223–64; and Brettler, 'The Structure of 1 Kings 1–11'; and Keith Bodner, *The Theology of the Book of Kings* (Cambridge: Cambridge University Press, 2019), 52–79.

96. See Yong Ho Jeon, *Impeccable Solomon? A Study of Solomon's Faults in Chronicles* (Eugene, OR: Wipf & Stock, 2013), 68–70.

97. Leithart, *1&2 Kings*, 86.

the Egyptian princess (1 Kgs 3.1), becomes the mechanism that leads to his downfall (1 Kgs 11.1-8, see Deut. 7.3-4; 17.17). And the military and economic prowess of Solomon's kingdom come under similar critique – horses and gold from Egypt (1 Kgs 10.26-29; Deut. 17.16-17).

Despite this, some continue to view Solomon's kingdom positively but need to rethink the relationship between Kings and Deuteronomy to do so.[98] For example, Knoppers proposes that 1 Kings 3–10 and not Deuteronomy 17 is typical of the Dtr's attitude to leadership.[99] In his view, Solomon's is a golden age, the united monarchy is an ideal, and Deuteronomy 17 is out of place. Carol Meyers and Norman Habel argue something similar,[100] but this is a difficult reading in my view. Even without the law of the king, the book of Kings would still understand Solomon as a cautionary tale, simply because of the way his story concludes (1 Kgs 11.1-6), as well as the way the entire book concludes with the deportation of Solomon's kingdom,[101] for which some of the responsibly is placed on Solomon himself (1 Kgs 9.6-9).

The majority view has followed Noth, who believed the book was negative towards Solomon, but incorporated the positive material out of fidelity to his sources.[102] This is also unlikely in my opinion. There is too much positive material to believe that the author of Kings was forced to include so much that did not suit his purpose.

---

98. It is common to date the law of the king (Deut. 17.14-20) to the later monarchy (e.g., Richard D. Nelson, *Deuteronomy: A Commentary*, OTL [Louisville, KY: Westminster John Knox, 2002], 222–5; or Gerhard von Rad, *Deuteronomy*, OTL [London: SCM, 1966], 118–20), so the author of Kings probably knew Deut. 17. It would only strengthen my point if the reverse were true because then the author of Deut. 17 was already reading Solomon's account as a cautionary tale.

99. Gary N. Knoppers has written about this in a number of places. See: 'The Deuteronomist and the Deuteronomic Law of the King: A Re-examination of a Relationship', *ZAW* 108 (1996): 337–46; *Two Nations Under God 1*, 77–134; *Two Nations Under God 2*, 232; 'There Was None Like Him', 122, 134.

100. Meyers argues that Dtr has recast earlier positive material unfairly. Habel argues that the pro-Solomonic ideology existed alongside the Dtr ideology and operated independently from it. Carol Meyers, 'The Israelite Empire: In Defense of King Solomon', *Michigan Quarterly* 22 (1983): 412–28; Habel, *The Land Is Mine*, 17–32.

101. Everything Solomon had made ends the story in Babylon. See Chapter 4.

102. For discussion see McConville, 'King and Messiah', 287 n. 73. See also Hays, 'Has the Narrator Come to Praise Solomon or to Bury Him?'; Leithart, *1&2 Kings*, 82; and Davies, 'Discerning Between Good and Evil', 56–7.

Rather, the key is to see how well the re-contextualisation of the positive material works, assuming it is intentional. When read in its broader context in Kings, Solomon's failure is deeply interwoven into the logic of political conquest and the nature of the covenant.[103] At first, Solomon 'walked in the statutes of David his father' (1 Kgs 3.3). The simple act of taking an Egyptian bride (1 Kgs 3.1) was the means of growing his kingdom (e.g., 1 Kgs 9.16),[104] but also an act of covenantal disobedience (1 Kgs 11.2; quoting Deut. 7.3-4). Similarly, what nation could survive long without a military, and where else but Egypt could horses be obtained?[105] Accumulation of wealth always accompanies political ascendency, but labour gangs are needed to dig the gold out of the ground (1 Kgs 5.13-18 [5.27-32, Heb.]; 9.15-28).[106] The same wisdom that brings justice (1 Kgs 3.28) also resulted in the sale of military hardware to the enemies of the kingdom and Solomon's assassination of political enemies (e.g., 1 Kgs 2.8-9). And so the narrative returns to where it began. Solomon has built a kingdom remembered as a golden age, but in doing so has become 'no longer wholly true to Yahweh his God' because his 'wives turned away his heart' (1 Kgs 11.4).

The strategy of compilation has been to set the narratives of conquest within the wider context of covenant failure. The purpose of this is to discourage an exilic yearning for a return to political ascendancy, replacing it with covenant obedience as a more worthy aspiration. 1 Kings 8 demonstrates that a Solomon-style kingdom is compatible with the realisation of God's promises to David. The memory of Israel gathered around Yahweh in his temple as a worshipping community is treated positively by the historian. However the parallel warning is that even, and perhaps especially, in such times the covenant cannot be forgotten (Deut. 8.10-14). 'Gold, guns and girls', as Peter Leithart quipped,[107] might appear desirable when accompanied by a period of peace and fulfilment. However, these do not in themselves characterise Covenant-Israel. Obedience is more important than prosperity.

---

103. See especially Leithart, *1&2 Kings*, 83–9; and Brueggemann, *Solomon*, 153–6.

104. This was true of all Solomon's 300 brides and 700 concubines. Cogan, *1 Kings*, 329.

105. Gary N. Knoppers, 'Rethinking the Relationship Between Deuteronomy and the Deuteronomistic History: The Case of Kings', *CBQ* 63 (2001): 401–2.

106. Brueggemann, *Solomon*, 154.

107. Leithart, *1&2 Kings*, 82.

i. *Solomon's Egypt*

The consequence of Solomon's gradual slide into apostasy is that the golden age of his kingdom comes to resemble the successes of other ancient kingdoms, in this case Egypt. This is portrayed in the narrative through a series of favourable comparisons. The parallels between Solomon's kingdom and Egypt are extensive and have been noted by a variety of scholars.[108] Leithart, for example, observes:

> Solomon begins acting like a Pharaoh, not only in the obvious sense that he builds stables for his horses and chariots (1 Kgs 9:19; cf. Deut 17:16), but also in that he builds 'cities of storage' (כל־ערי המסכנות) (1 Kgs 9:19), a phrase used elsewhere only in Exod 1:11... Solomon returns Israel to an Egyptian-like state.[109]

There are many parallels between the literary portrayal of Solomon's kingdom and Egypt.[110] We have already observed the frequent mention of Solomon's marriage to an Egyptian princess (1 Kgs 3.1; 7.8; 9.16, 24; 11.1-2). Even though ancient Egypt was renowned for its voluminous wisdom literature, the book of Kings has Solomon out-produce them (1 Kgs 4.31-34 [5.11-14, Heb.]).[111] Solomon's administrative (1 Kgs 4.1-19) and taxation structures (1 Kgs 4.22-24, 27-28 [5.2-4, 7-8, Heb.]) mirror similar systems used in Egypt at his time,[112] but are presented as Solomon's brainchild (1 Kgs 4.29-30 [5.9-10, Heb.]), and are met with

---

108. Baruch Halpern and André Lemaire, 'The Composition of Kings', in Halpern and Lemaire, eds., *The Books of Kings*, 152; Halpern and Vanderhooft, 'The Editions of Kings', 135–7; André Lemaire, 'Toward a Redactional History of the Book of Kings', in Knoppers and McConville, eds., *Reconsidering Israel and Judah*, 446–61; Steven M. Oritz, 'The United Monarchy: Archeology and Literary Sources', in Arnold and Hess, eds., *Ancient Israel's History*, 261; Dever, 'Archeology and the Question of Sources in Kings', 518–19, 537–8. Some see a critique of Babylon, e.g. Hermann Niemann, 'The Socio-Political Shadow Cast by the Biblical Solomon', in Handy, ed., *The Age of Solomon*, 252–99; Knoppers, *Two Nations Under God 1*, 132–3.

109. Leithart, *1&2 Kings*, 76.

110. Many of the comparisons below are developed in Heaton, *Solomon's New Men*.

111. See John D. Ray, 'Egyptian Wisdom Literature', in *Wisdom in Ancient Israel*, ed. John Day, Robert P. Gordon, and H. G. M. Williamson (Cambridge: Cambridge University Press, 1995), 17–29.

112. Donald B. Redford, 'Studies in the Relations Between Palestine and Egypt During the First Millennium B.C.: 1. The Taxation System of Solomon', in *Studies on the Ancient Palestinian World: Presented to Professor F. V. Winnett on the Occasion*

unparalleled success (1 Kgs 10.21). Other proposed comparisons with Egypt[113] include parallels between Solomon's and the Egyptian throne (1 Kgs 10.18-20),[114] shipping enterprises (1 Kgs 10.22),[115] and monumental architecture (1 Kgs 6–7).[116] In every case, Solomon's grandeur is highlighted. The portrayal of his military power is instructive. Solomon buys Egyptian war horses, but he is never said to use them (1 Kgs 4.24-25 [5.4-5, Heb.]). Instead, the narrative has Pharaoh conquering Solomon's political enemies and gifting the plunder to Solomon (1 Kgs 9.16).[117] As Eric Heaton commented, from the point of view of the narrative, 'Egypt had now met its match, and the only recognition it could look for from Solomon's emergent nation was the flattery of wholesale imitation'.[118]

Solomon's kingdom is portrayed as out-Egypting Egypt.[119] By 1 Kings 12 the irony of this has become clear.[120] It may have been a golden age, but the cost was high. Solomon's kingdom of glory (כבד, 1 Kgs 3.13) had become a 'heavy yoke' (עול כבד) that his people could not bear (1 Kgs 12.4). And the labour that Solomon organised to build the temple (1 Kgs 5.13-18 [5.27-32, Heb.]; 9.15, 22-23) had his people complaining of a 'hard service' (העבדה חקשה) that they had not encountered since they were slaves to Pharaoh (1 Kgs 12.4; Exod. 1.14).[121] Through his gradual departure from covenant faithfulness, Solomon had constructed a form of Israel that is not Yahweh's promised kingdom, but just another

---

of his Retirement 1 July 1971, ed. John W. Wevers and Donald B. Redford (Toronto: University of Toronto, 1972), 144; Alberto R. Green, 'Israelite Influence at Shishak's Court', *BASOR* 233 (1979): 59–62.

113. See Currid, *Ancient Egypt and the Old Testament*, 159–71.

114. F. Canciani and G. Pettinato, 'Salomos Thron: Philologische und archäologische Erwägungen', *ZDPV* 81 (1965): 88–108; H. Brunner, 'Gerechtigkeit als Fundament des Thrones', *VT* 8 (1958): 426–8.

115. Alan R. Millard, 'King Solomon in his Ancient Context', in Handy, ed., *The Age of Solomon*, 30–53.

116. The extent of Egyptian influence on Solomon's temple and palaces is debated. See Y. Yadin, 'Solomon's City Wall and Gate at Gezer', *IEJ* 8 (1958): 80–6; and R. B. Y. Scott, 'Weights and Measures of the Bible', *BA* 22 (1959): 26. For the counter-argument, see Redford, 'The Taxation System of Solomon', 144.

117. Leithart, *1&2 Kings*, 75.

118. Heaton, *Solomon's New Men*, 178.

119. Jeon, *Impeccable Solomon?*, 71–5.

120. Many others have arrived at the same conclusion. See, e.g., Leithart, *1&2 Kings*, 91; Heaton, *Solomon's New Men*, 14; Provan, *1 & 2 Kings*, 104; McConville, *God and Earthly Power*, 151–5; and Wray Beal, *1&2 Kings*, 180–2.

121. Lovell, 'The Shape of Hope', 12.

manifestation of Egypt.[122] And Israel in ascendency had become like other ascendant nations. The readers of this account in Babylon perhaps felt this comparison even more poignantly, for by then Egypt's glory days, like their own, had long since passed.

3.3.2. Conflict: Elijah's Struggle for the Soul of Israel[123]

The book of Kings incorporates several conflict narratives. The story of the division of the kingdom (1 Kgs 12) is a prominent example, where Rehoboam and Jeroboam each try to implement a different political version of Israel.[124] Here we shall focus on the contest between Elijah and Ahab, who also have opposing ideals for Israel. Elijah is portrayed as the political and religious conservative, contending for a version of the Northern Kingdom based in the covenant (1 Kgs 18.18; 19.10, 14). Ahab is portrayed as a reformer who, as we saw in Chapter 2, introduced Baal worship through the influence of his foreign wife. Their conflict involves different political visions for the nation, which becomes apparent when each accuses the other of being the 'troubler of Israel' (1 Kgs 18.17-18).

Several parallels exist between Solomon, who was also a religious reformer, and Ahab. Both Solomon and Ahab's father founded their dynasties and built the capital city of their respective kingdoms (1 Kgs 16.24).[125] Like Solomon, Ahab (and not his father) furnished the kingdom with a temple (1 Kgs 16.32). Ahab is also the first king portrayed since Solomon to have exposed his nation to the influence of a foreign god through marriage (1 Kgs 11.5, 7; 16.31). However, as the narrative unfolds, it becomes clear that Ahab is not a king of the calibre of Solomon.[126] Neither is he the chief antagonist of the story. Although he describes Elijah as his 'enemy' (1 Kgs 21.20), Elijah does not fear Ahab (1 Kgs 18.7-16). Rather, Ahab is compliant, obeying every command Elijah gives him on Carmel without comment or question (e.g., 1 Kgs

---

122. I return to this theme specifically with Solomon's wisdom on view in Chapter 6.

123. I owe this title to Patricia J. Berlyn, 'Elijah's Battle for the Soul of Israel', *JBQ* 40 (2012): 52–62.

124. I return to examine this narrative in detail Chapter 4.

125. Omri's historical accomplishments were more significant than 1 Kings records. See Cogan, *1 Kings*, 418–19; and Greenwood, 'Late Tenth and Ninth-Century Issues'.

126. See Cohn, 'Characterisation in Kings', 101–2; and Hayyim Angel, 'Hopping Between Two Opinions: Understanding the Biblical Portrait of Ahab', *JBQ* 35 (2007): 3–10, for an analysis of Ahab's portrayal.

18.17-20, 41-46).[127] During the conflict he remains silent[128] and does not challenge Elijah even when his prophets are arrested and killed (1 Kgs 18.40).

With whom, if not Ahab, does Elijah struggle? He accuses Israel of 'limping on two crutches', that is, of being between two opinions (פסחים על שתי הסעפים, 1 Kgs 18.21), and demands they choose either Yahweh or Baal to follow. However, Baal is not the antagonist of this story either. During the challenge at Carmel, Baal is characterised not as impotent, but as absent (ואין קול ואין ענה/קשב, 1 Kgs 18.26-29).[129] He does nothing when his own prophets mutilate themselves (1 Kgs 18.27), and nothing when they are later slaughtered (1 Kgs 18.40, see 2 Kgs 10.19).

Even before Carmel, Baal is shown to be impotent by a series of miracles that Elijah performs within Baal's normal domain of authority.[130] According to Canaanite religion, Baal was the storm god responsible for bringing rains, fertility, and life.[131] However, in Kings it is Elijah who does these things (1 Kgs 17.2-7, 8-16, 17-24), and he does them in Baal's normal territory of Sidon (1 Kgs 17.9). Alan Hauser comments:

> Baal is shown to have no power at all in the realm that is supposed to be his, the sending of annual rains. He is, in fact, quite dead… If, according to Canaanite mythology, Baal has to struggle periodically with death and lose, in 1 Kings 17–19 Yahweh confronts death, and wins. Yahweh is thus portrayed as the God of life who has ultimate control over death.[132]

The threat to Elijah's vision of Covenant-Israel is neither Ahab nor Baal. It is Jezebel (e.g., 1 Kgs 18.4, 13, 19; 21.25). The prophets of Baal are those who 'eat at Jezebel's table' (1 Kgs 18.19), and Jezebel is the only

---

127. A broader study of Ahab's character agrees with this analysis of royal timidity (in both the MT and differently ordered LXX accounts). See Angel, 'Hopping Between Two Opinions', 7–10.

128. Angel, 'Hopping Between Two Opinions', 6; Walsh, *1 Kings*, 249.

129. Leithart, *1&2 Kings*, 135–6; and Wray Beal, *1&2 Kings*, 246–8.

130. Gunkel (*Elijah, Yahweh, and Baal*, trans. K. C. Hanson [Eugene, OR: Cascade, 2014], 11) believed the account of Elijah's miracles to be haphazard. However, Ugaritic texts show the polemic nature of the textual arrangement. See Leah Bronner, *The Stories of Elijah and Elisha as Polemics against Baal Worship*, Pretoria Oriental (Leiden: Brill, 1968); Alan J. Hauser and Russell Gregory, *From Carmel to Horeb: Elijah in Crisis* (Sheffield: Sheffield Academic, 1990), 9–90; Moshe Garsiel, *From Earth to Heaven: A Literary Study of Elijah Stories in the Book of Kings* (Bethesda, MD: CDL, 2014); and Cogan, *1 Kings*, 430–2.

131. On the Ugaritic texts, see Gunnar Östborn, *Yahweh and Baal* (Lund: Gleerup, 1956).

132. Hauser and Gregory, *From Carmel to Horeb*, 11.

character in the story whom Elijah fears (1 Kgs 19.3). Thus the first step in Ahab's undoing is marrying her (1 Kgs 16.31; 21.25).[133]

By the end of the story of Naboth's vineyard (1 Kgs 21),[134] Jezebel has subverted the covenant's vision for all of Israel's political institutions: the law, the kingship, and the land.[135] She is clearly operating with a different model of kingship and law than the covenantal model:[136] she usurps power to issue orders (v. 8) that result in the perversion of justice (v. 10), the death of one of Ahab's subjects (v. 13), and the illegal acquisition of his property (v. 15). At the start of the narrative she found Ahab sullen and questioned him: 'Do you not rule the kingdom of Israel?' (1 Kgs 21.7). By the end the irony is exposed, that she and not he is in charge.

Jezebel's subversion of the land is linked to the covenant by Naboth's refusal to sell. He will not relinquish the vineyard because he understands that it would be a 'profanity' (חלילה לי מיהוה, v. 3) to give away the 'inheritance of my fathers' (נחלת אבתי). As we shall see in Chapter 5, deuteronomic theology understands the land to belong to Yahweh, and to be given as a perpetual inheritance to Israel divided by her tribes (1 Kgs 8.36, see, e.g., Deut. 4.21, 38; 12.9; 15.4). Jezebel, however, understands it as hers to give to whom she wills (… אני אתן לך, 1 Kgs 21.5).

Because of this theme of covenantal subversion, a story that is about social justice becomes one concerned with covenantal fidelity. In deuteronomic logic, social justice proceeds from the covenant, and so also stems from worship. It is Jezebel's idolatry that leads to injustice in Israel, as Lissa Wray Beal also comments:

> The king is judged for his abuse of social power (vv. 17-19), but this judgment is immediately couched in the underlying issue of covenant sin regarding the worship of YHWH (vv. 20-26)… In this chapter social injustice goes hand in hand with wrong worship, demonstrating the implicit link between belief and practice. As the king worships, so he acts.[137]

The story of Ahab shows that this is true for Israel more generally. This is 2 Kgs 17.15 again: 'They went after false idols and became false'.

---

133. So Angel, 'Hopping Between Two Opinions', 5.

134. Walsh (*1 Kings*, 316–28) has a detailed analysis of this narrative. See also Amit, *Reading Biblical Narratives*, 54–8; Angel, 'Hopping Between Two Opinions', 7–8; Dutcher-Walls, *Jezebel*, 42–54.

135. On the way this narrative draws on the covenantal traditions, see Wray Beal, *1&2 Kings*, 277–8.

136. See Chapter 6 on this model.

137. Wray Beal, *1&2 Kings*, 277.

Conflict narratives, according to Coakley, are often retold to show or create national unity, and this rings true of the Ahab narratives.[138] In this case the polemic against Baal in Inner Kings works just as well as an implicit critique of the Babylonian gods of the exile. The hero's rally cry (1 Kgs 18.21) that unites Israel in the narrative (1 Kgs 18.39) would also carry the same impact in exile. However, this story contends for a view of Israel that is grounded in the covenant specifically, and not just Yahweh worship generally (1 Kgs 18.18; 19.10, 14), so there are other implications besides national unity and monotheism.

Ahab is not portrayed as intentionally abandoning the covenant. In the narrative, it is his weakness of character and his selection of a wife that introduce a non-covenantal vision for Israel (1 Kgs 16.31; 21.25; Deut. 7.3). However, in the logic of history viewed through the lens of the covenant, small acts of disobedience have great consequences, as we saw also with Solomon (1 Kgs 11.1-3). Jezebel introduces the foreign worship of an impotent deity, and in doing so also introduces foreign concepts of land, kingship, law, and (in)justice. Israel is becoming like Canaan.

i. *Ahab's Canaan*
Inner Kings has a similar motif of political transformation to the one we have already observed in the Solomon narratives, except that it invites a comparison with the Canaanite nations rather than Egypt. Leithart calls this a 'reverse-conquest' motif that portrays Jezebel's influence as a process of re-Canaanisation.[139] Sometimes this is done through explicit narrated comment. For example, Ahab is condemned for acting like one of the Amorites 'whom Yahweh drove out from before the people of Israel' (1 Kgs 21.26). More often the motif is subtle, but various elements of it are now well noticed by commentators.[140] There is, for example, a series of allusions to Joshua and Judges running throughout Inner Kings which encourage the reader to relate the story to the theme of conquest.[141] Inner Kings opens with a note that the Canaanite city

---

138. Habel, *The Land Is Mine*, 36–53, but against Cogan (*1 Kings*, 478), who understands the verse to reflect the priestly ideology which sees the land as Yahweh's to be relinquished in the Jubilee.

139. Leithart, *1&2 Kings*, 186 n. 2, also 120, 127, 172–3, 157 n. 5, 232–3, 269.

140. E.g. Leithart, *1&2 Kings*; Bodner, *Elisha's Profile in the Book of Kings*, 39–60; Wray Beal, *1&2 Kings*, 306–8; Mordechai Cogan and Hayim Tadmor, *2 Kings: A New Translation with Introduction and Commentary*, AB 11 (New Haven, CT: Yale University Press, 2008), 143; Provan, *1 & 2 Kings*, 131.

141. Contrast von Rad (*Old Testament Theology*, 1:346–7), who believed that Kings contains no allusions to the Judges cycle.

Jericho has been re-founded, and the five-century-old prophetic curse of Joshua is enacted (1 Kgs 16.34, see Josh. 6.26). Iain Provan comments that this 'reminds us, finally, of the difference between Israel's past under Joshua, and its present under the apostate monarchy. Israel no longer conquers the Canaanites, but instead embraces their religion and courts their fate'.[142]

Then, as Ahab becomes the first (and only subsequent) 'troubler' (עכר) of Israel since Achan (1 Kgs 18.17-18; Josh. 2.25), Elijah becomes the first (and only subsequent) man whose voice Yahweh heeds (וישמע/ לשמע יהוה בקול) since Joshua (1 Kgs 17.22; Josh. 10.14).[143] There are many parallels between Elijah's journey out of the land in 2 Kings 2, and Joshua's conquest, in which Elijah's itinerary mirrors Joshua's, in reverse order, culminating in a dramatic parting of the waters of the Jordan.[144] Finally, at the place where Israel once ate the first fruit of the land (Josh. 5.10-11), they now find a 'pot of death' (2 Kgs 4.40, see also 2 Kgs 2.19).[145]

The narrative effect of these persistent allusions is cumulative, as Bodner notes:

> From the perspective of Elisha's characterization, the sum total of these allusions to Joshua's succession indicate that his agenda will include a conquest of the land... Just as Joshua led the struggle against Canaanite ideology and influence, so we infer that Elisha will be a catalyst for releasing the nation from the grip of the Omrides.[146]

This reversed conquest motif reaches closure only in 2 Kings 13–14, where there is a series of allusions to the book of Judges. After Israel has been reconquered, and freed from the Canaanite religion of Jezebel by Jehu, they find themselves oppressed by a foreign power (2 Kgs 13.3, 7, 22; 14.26), and cry out to Yahweh for salvation (2 Kgs 13.4). Yahweh then raises a saviour to free them (2 Kgs 13.5; Judg. 2.18; 3.9, 15; 2 Kgs 14.27; Judg. 6.36, 37).[147] By the end of Inner Kings, Israel has repeated the pattern known to the reader from the book of Judges, of apostasy → oppression → salvation → restoration.[148]

---

142. Provan, *1 & 2 Kings*, 131; see also Leithart, *1&2 Kings*, 120.
143. Walsh, *1 Kings*, 234; Leithart, *1&2 Kings*, 131–3.
144. Leithart, *1&2 Kings*, 178.
145. There are other less convincing allusions between the battles of Inner Kings and Joshua: Walsh, *1 Kings*, 305–6; Leithart, *1&2 Kings*, 154, 178.
146. Bodner, *Elisha's Profile in the Book of Kings*, 50.
147. Cogan and Tadmor, *2 Kings*, 143; Wray Beal, *1&2 Kings*, 408–9.
148. We shall examine this pattern in detail in Chapter 4.

3.3.3. *Crisis: The Assyrian Dark Ages*

The bulk of the crisis narratives incorporated into Kings do not involve the final exile of the Southern Kingdom (2 Kgs 24–25), but the earlier series of crises involving the Syro-Ephraimite crisis, the Assyrian conquest of the north, and Sennacherib's aborted siege of Jerusalem (2 Kgs 15–19).

It is well recognised that the portrayal of Assyria in the book of Kings is selective.[149] It is clear from extra-biblical sources, for example, that Ahab fought against Assyrian aggression over a century before Assyria first appears in the narrative of Kings (2 Kgs 15.19).[150] Assyria also remained well after the time of Hezekiah, which is their final reported interaction with Judah (2 Kgs 20.6). Historically, it is clear that Manasseh was subject to Assyrian rule (see 2 Chron. 33.11), even though this is not reported in the book of Kings. Kings portrays the Assyrians in relation to just five kings of Israel and Judah: Menahem (2 Kgs 15.16-22), Pekah (2 Kgs 15.27-31), Ahaz (2 Kgs 16.1-20), Hoshea (2 Kgs 17.1-6, 24-28), and Hezekiah (2 Kgs 18–20).[151]

---

149. For a review, see Peter Dubovský, 'Assyrian Downfall Through Isaiah's Eyes (2 Kings 15–23): The Historiography of Representation', *Bib* 89 (2008): 1–5. This selectivity has made the history of the period difficult to reconstruct. See Sandra Richter, 'Eighth-Century Issues: The World of Jeroboam II, the Fall of Samaria, and the Reign of Hezekiah', in Arnold and Hess, eds., *Ancient Israel's History*, 337–49; Richard S. Hess, 'Hezekiah and Sennacherib in 2 Kings 18–20', in *Zion, City of our God*, ed. Richard S. Hess and Gordon J. Wenham (Grand Rapids, MI: Eerdmans, 1999), 23–41; Peter Dubovský, 'Tiglath-Pileser III's Campaigns in 734–732 BC: Historical Background of Isa 7; 2 Kgs 15–16 and 2 Chr 27–28', *Bib* 87 (2006): 153–70; August H. Konkel, 'The Sources of the Story of Hezekiah in the Book of Isaiah', *VT* 43 (1993): 462–82; Antti Laato, 'Assyrian Propaganda and the Falsification of History in the Royal Inscriptions of Sennacherib', *VT* 45 (1995): 198–226.

150. Ahab had helped to lead a coalition of eleven Syrian and Palestinian states against Shalmaneser III in 853 BCE, and Hazael of Damascus had survived an Assyrian assault two decades later. A. F. Rainey and R. S. Notley eds., *The Sacred Bridge: Carta's Atlas of the Biblical World* (Jerusalem: Carta, 2006), 199, 208. Menahem reigns in the Northern Kingdom approximately a century after these events.

151. Assyria only appears in a passing mention in relation to Egyptian troop movements under Josiah (2 Kgs 23.29), which is related to their defeat at the battle of Carchemish in 605 BCE, some 80 years after the conclusion of Hezekiah's reign. See Rainey and Notley, *Sacred Bridge*, 46–50, 59.

What is the reason for this portrayal of Assyria?[152] Peter Dubovský, in an approach that closely harmonises with the narrative structure I proposed in Chapter 2, has argued that all the references to Assyria are part of a single narrative from 2 Kings 15–19.[153] He argues that this narrative has been intentionally constructed to offer an 'interpretation of the collapse of the Assyrian empire'[154] which climaxes with Isaiah's theological explanation (2 Kgs 19.21-28).

However, we shall see it does more than this. It also explores a willingness by the Northern Kingdom to be subject to Assyrian authority. The crisis that the book of Kings explores as it tells this history is not simply the military crisis of an overbearing foreign power. As we have seen with conquest and conflict, crisis is also portrayed in relation to the covenant: it is the religious crisis of voluntary submission when it might have been otherwise.

The Northern Kingdom only progressively become victims of Assyria. For most of the narrative they voluntarily look to this foreign power to establish Israelite political security. However, Assyria is no saviour. Faced with an even more urgent choice, we shall see that Hezekiah chooses a covenant identity for the Southern Kingdom, and is spared the fate of the north. The contrasted outcomes of the two parallel stories provide the exilic community with a case study in foreign relations. Babylon cannot be trusted to secure a political identity; however, even when all seems lost, Yahweh can.

---

152. In this section I draw on Dubovský, 'Assyrian Downfall Through Isaiah's Eyes', 1–16; Phil J. Botha, '"No King Like Him…": Royal Etiquette According to the Deuteronomistic Historian', in *Past, Present, Future: The Deuteronomistic History and the Prophets*, ed. Harry F. van Rooy (Leiden: Brill, 2000), 36–49; Evans, 'The Hezekiah–Sennacherib Narrative as Polyphonic Text'; Ronald T. Hyman, 'The Rabshakeh's Speech (II Kg. 18–25): A Study of Rhetorical Intimidation', *JBQ* 23 (1995): 213–20; Janzen, 'The Sins of Josiah and Hezekiah'; Knoppers, 'There Was None Like Him'; John W. Olley, '"Trust in the Lord": Hezekiah, Kings and Isaiah', *TynB* 50 (1999): 59–77; Dominic Rudman, 'Is the Rabshakeh also Among the Prophets? A Rhetorical Study of 2 Kings XVIII 17-35', *VT* 50 (2000): 100–110; Jerome T. Walsh, 'The Rab Šāqēh Between Rhetoric and Redaction', *JBL* 130 (2011): 263–79; and Hayim Tadmor and Mordechai Cogan, 'Ahaz and Tiglath-Pileser in the Book of Kings: Historiographic Considerations', *Bib* 60 (1979): 498–9.

153. Dubovský, 'Assyrian Downfall Through Isaiah's Eyes', 12–13. We noted in Chapter 2 that the narrative of Outer Kings transitions with the Syro-Ephraimite crisis in 2 Kgs 15, and in Chapter 4 we will examine the relationship between 2 Kgs 17 and 18–19.

154. Dubovský, 'Assyrian Downfall Through Isaiah's Eyes', 1.

i. *Menahem and Pekah*

The first mention of Assyria in Kings occurs within Menahem's reign (2 Kgs 15.19-21), where their brief portrayal is nuanced and they do not come across as aggressively as we know them to be from history.[155] The reader barely learns anything of the Assyrian King Pul.[156] He simply comes upon the land (בא ... על־הארץ, 2 Kgs 15.19). As Dubovský notes, this is a phrase which normally describes aggressive action (e.g., Gen. 6.17; Jer. 25.9), but need not (e.g., Jer. 3.18).[157] Without further context, the NIV's choice to render the phrase as 'invaded' implies destruction where the Hebrew implies perhaps only menace. Rather than military action, the narrative focuses our attention on Menahem's response to the Assyrian presence (2 Kgs 15.19):

19*a*	בא פול מלך אשור על הארץ
b	ויתן מנחם לפול אלף ככר כסף
c	להיות ידיו אתו
d	להחזיק הממלכה בידו

[19a]Pul, king of Assyria, came upon the land. [b]Menahem gave to Pul a thousand talents of silver [c]to gain his favour [d]and to secure his grasp over the kingdom. (2 Kgs 15.19, my translation)

Note that Menahem 'gives to Pul' a thousand talents of silver (ויתן מנחם לפול, Clause *b*). Although it is intended to be understood as a bribe, the narrative does not use the term 'bribe' (שחד) here, reserving it for an escalation in 2 Kgs 16.8 (see below). Neither is it explicitly coerced. Pul does not 'take' (again, see below), Menahem 'gives'.

This gift accomplishes two things (Clauses *c* and *d* above): it establishes a friendship between Menahem and Pul, and it strengthens Menahem's own grip on the kingdom. The gift is excessive and gained from public taxation rather than personal or state resources (v. 20).[158] And so Menahem is portrayed as using Pul's 'visit' to strengthen his own interests at the

---

155. It is known from Assyrian sources that there was military action in Israel at that time of Menahem. See Cogan, *1 Kings*, 172.
156. Also known as Tiglath-Pileser III. See Cogan, *1 Kings*, 171–2.
157. Peter Dubovský, 'Why did the Northern Kingdom Fall According to 2 Kings 15?', *Bib* 95 (2014): 333–4.
158. Dubovský ('Why did the Northern Kingdom Fall?', 338–40) calculates, based on inner-biblical economics, that 1000 talents of silver was enough to purchase most of the Northern Kingdom.

expense of his people.[159] Given the negative portrayal of Menahem to this point (v. 16), we are perhaps not surprised.[160]

This is the first time that the book has explored that the Israelite throne might be secured by a foreign nation rather than by dedication to Yahweh. So far in Kings, it is only Yahweh who has established kingdoms, and who has torn them away (e.g., 1 Kgs 9.5; 11.11). Will Assyria now do what Yahweh has done?

The next mention of Assyria is in relation to the Syro-Ephraimite crisis (2 Kgs 15.29) but the reader is not told the entire story until 2 Kings 16, when it will be recounted from Ahaz's perspective. The 2 Kings 15 account is a summary presented in Pekah's reign. It syntactically mirrors the report we examined in 2 Kgs 15.19.[161] Both summaries are asyndetically juxtaposed with the king's respective judgment formula, and both contain similar language:

ויתן... על־הארץ	בא פול מלך־אשור		2 Kgs 15.19
ויקח...	בא תגלת פלאסר מלך אשור	בימי...	2 Kgs 15.29

This differences between them are suggestive: Where Menahem 'gave' (נתן) to Pul, Tiglath-Pileser 'took' (לקח) from Pekah. Tension has escalated, and it no longer looks like Assyria has an interest in 'strengthening the hand' of the Israelite king (2 Kgs 15.19).

ii. *Ahaz*

A fuller story of the Syro-Ephraimite crisis is now told from the point of view of the southern king, Ahaz (2 Kgs 16.1-20). It details how Pekah had allied with the Syrian king Rezin against Ahaz, who then turned to Assyria to help defend Judah. Once again the account is selective, with details present in the parallel account in Isaiah 7 omitted here. For example, Isa. 7.6 recalls that the motivation for the northern alliance was the removal of Ahaz from power. However, Kings omits this detail. This is because, as it did with Menahem, the account in Kings minimises the compulsion in its portrayal of the relationship between Ahaz and Assyria. This nuance is most clearly seen in contrast with the parallel account in Isa. 7.1:[162]

---

159. So Nadav Na'aman, 'The Deuteronomist and Voluntary Servitude to Foreign Powers', *JSOT* 65 (1995): 39–40.

160. The syntax of v. 16 is unusual, and draws the reader's attention to the horror of the act, on which see Mordechai Cogan, '"Ripping Open Pregnant Women" in Light of an Assyrian Analogue', *JAOS* 103 (1983): 755–7.

161. Dubovský, 'Why did the Northern Kingdom Fall?', 333.

162. I am assuming that neither the Kings nor the Isaiah account is a corruption of the other, but I am not assuming a direction of dependence. My approach is to

	Isa. 7.1	2 Kgs 16.5
a	עלה ... ירושלם	אז יעלה ... ירושלם
b	↑למלחמה עליה	↑למלחמה
c		ויצרו על־אחז
d	ולא יכל להלחם עליה	ולא יכלו להלחם
a	[Rezin and Pekah] came up to Jerusalem	As you know,[163] [Rezin and Pekah] came up to Jerusalem to wage war.
b	to wage war against it,	
c		They besieged Ahaz
d	and he [Ahaz] was not able to fight for it.	but they were not able to fight.

The threat to Jerusalem is more immediate in the Isaiah account than it is portrayed in Kings.[164] In Isaiah, Rezin and Pekah wage war 'against it' (i.e. Jerusalem, Isa. 7.1*b*) and it is Ahaz who cannot defend it (note the singular verb יכל in v. 1*d*). This coincides with the wider portrayal of Ahaz in Isaiah, who is scared in the face of insurmountable military odds (e.g., Isa. 7.2).[165] In Kings, Rezin and Pekah approach Jerusalem, but 'besiege' Ahaz (2 Kgs 16.5*c*),[166] and it is they who cannot fight (note the plural verb יכלו in v. 5*d*). The threat in the Kings account is downplayed, and Ahaz comes across as acting out of self-interest. As with Menahem, Ahaz's submission to Assyrian rule is a voluntary action, precipitated by crisis perhaps, but not a last resort. Ironically, Ahaz calls on Assyria to save him

---

understand the nuance of the Kings account by contrast with the way Isaiah tells the same story. For the source-critical discussion see Sweeney, *I & II Kings*, 383.

163. For various explanations of אז with a *yiqtol* verb, see Jan Dus, 'Gibbon – eine Kultstätte des SMS und die Stadt des benjaminitischen Schicksals', *VT* 10 (1960): 358; John C. L. Gibson, *Davidson's Introductory Hebrew Grammar: Syntax* (Edinburgh: T&T Clark, 1994), 72; and Bruce K. Waltke and Michael P. O'Connor, *An Introduction to Biblical Hebrew Syntax* (Winona Lake, IN: Eisenbrauns, 1990), 498–9. Cogan ('For We, Like You, Worship your God: Three Biblical Portrayals of Samaritan Origins', *VT* 38 [1988]: 186) is probably correct when he takes it to be evidential: 'As you know, …'

164. The purpose of this presentation in Isaiah is to draw a parallel between Ahaz's test of faith and Hezekiah's similar situation (e.g., compare Isa. 7.3 with 36.2). Where Ahaz fails, Hezekiah succeeds. See, e.g., John N. Oswalt, *The Book of Isaiah, Chapters 1–39*, NICOT (Grand Rapids, IN: Eerdmans, 1986), 54–60.

165. Note also the alternate version of the story in 2 Chron. 28.5-21, in which the invasion is severe. See Sweeney, *I & II Kings*, 383.

166. There is no reason to follow *BHS* editors and assume that 'he besieged Ahaz' (ויצרו על־אחז) is an error. צור is well attested with a personal object (e.g., 1 Sam. 23.8; 2 Sam. 20.15). See Na'aman, 'The Deuteronomist and Voluntary Servitude to Foreign Powers', 42–3.

from a people that were 'not able to fight' (ולא יכלו להלחם) and he delivers a bribe (שחד, 2 Kgs 16.8) to secure his throne (v. 7).[167]

There is also a parallel drawn between Menahem and Ahaz. The introduction of the Syro-Ephraimite invasion mirrors the unusual syntax that introduced Menahem's military exploits in the previous chapter (asyndetic אז + *yiqtol*, 2 Kgs 15.16; 16.5). Both kings, through their voluntary submission to Assyria, thrust the Assyrians into a position that has so far been occupied in the narrative only by Yahweh. Menahem asks the Assyrians to 'strengthen his hand'. However, until Ahaz makes a similar request, only Yahweh had acted as a 'saviour' (עלה והושעני, 2 Kgs 16.7, see e.g. 1 Kgs 1.29; 2 Kgs 5.1, 6-7; 6.26-27; 14.27; 19.35). Ahaz, by his own admission, is a 'son and servant' of Assyria (עבדך ובנך אני, v. 7), rather than of Yahweh.[168]

iii. *Ahaz's Damascus*

Like Solomon with Egypt, and Ahab with Canaan, Ahaz's Judah comes to resemble the surrounding nations as he 'walks in the way of the kings of Israel', and follows the 'despicable practices of the nations around him' (2 Kgs 16.3). In this case, it is the conquered Damascus that Judah mimics.

In 2 Kings 16 this process is portrayed through the replica (את־דמות המזבח ואת־תבניתו, v. 10) of the Damascene temple that Ahaz constructs in Jerusalem. The incident has confused scholars.[169] Why would Ahaz replicate in Jerusalem an altar he found in a conquered city (v. 9)?

One proposed solution is that Assyria forced upon both Damascus and Jerusalem their own cultic practices,[170] but this seems unlikely for several reasons. First, the tradition followed by Chronicles (2 Chron. 28.23) and

---

167. See Tadmor and Cogan, 'Ahaz and Tiglath-Pileser in the Book of Kings', 504–5; and Na'aman, 'The Deuteronomist and Voluntary Servitude to Foreign Powers', 45–6.

168. It is common for kings to express submission to Assyria using 'servant' language, but the inclusion of sonship here has created discussion. It is unclear whether a rejection of Israelite royal ideology is intended (e.g., Ps. 2.7). See Na'aman, 'The Deuteronomist and Voluntary Servitude to Foreign Powers', 43; Tadmor and Cogan, 'Ahaz and Tiglath-Pileser in the Book of Kings', 504–5; Cogan and Tadmor, *2 Kings*, 187; and Stuart A. Irvine, *Isaiah, Ahaz, and the Syro-Ephraimitic Crisis*, SBLDS (Atlanta, GA: Scholars Press, 1990), 87–8.

169. For a history of the discussion, see John W. McKay, *Religion in Judah Under the Assyrians, 732–609 BC*, SBT (Naperville, IL: A. R. Allenson, 1973), 6.

170. This was common in earlier scholarship. See, e.g., A. T. Olmstead, *History of Assyria* (Chicago, IL: University of Chicago Press, 1968), 452.

the archaeological data both conclude that Ahaz copied a Phoenician design, rather than an Assyrian one.[171] Second, there is no evidence that Assyria imposed cultic practices on their vassals.[172] And third, even if, historically speaking, the action was imposed upon him, the text does not portray compulsion at any stage of the incident. The verbs on the narrative mainline tell a different story: Ahaz 'goes' (וילך), 'sees' (וירא), and 'sends' (וישלח) the plan for the altar (v. 10). As with everything about Ahaz's portrayal, this is a voluntary action and so compulsion to worship Assyria cannot be the point of the narrative.

Ahaz is not portrayed as abandoning Yahwism anyway.[173] His sacrifices continue to follow Yahwistic (and not Assyrian) practices (2 Kgs 16.12-15; see Lev. 6–7; Num. 15). It is probable that by recounting Ahaz's renovations, the narrative is portraying the way Judah expressed her new relationship with Assyria. Sweeney comments, 'With Assyria as Judah's overlord, symbols of royal privilege and YHWH's protection would now be removed to recognize Assyria's new role as Judah's protector'.[174]

This is something which must have just happened in Damascus also (2 Kgs 16.9), and so it is this architectural expression of subservience, and not the worship of a foreign god, that Ahaz learns there. Wray Beal concludes:

> '[Ahaz's] fault is…that the altar stands as a symbol of Judean subservience to Assyria. Assyria had conquered Damascus and thus placed its god in subservient relationship to the gods of Assyria. By copying the Damascene altar, that same subservience is implied of YHWH to Assyria and its god, Asshur… Thus while Ahaz continues Yahwistic worship at the temple, such worship is conducted in subservience to a foreign king and god. This is the evil of Ahaz' altar.[175]

Having met the conqueror of Damascus, Tiglath-Pileser, and called him 'saviour', Ahaz's Jerusalem begins to look like conquered Damascus. Such is the nature of Assyrian salvation.

---

171. Cogan, *1 Kings*, 193; Klaas A. D. Smelik, 'The New Altar of King Ahaz (2 Kings 16): Deuteronomistic Re-Interpretation of a Cult Reform', in Vervenne and Lust, eds., *Deuteronomy and Deuteronomic Literature*, 274–5.

172. McKay, *Religion in Judah Under the Assyrians*, 5–12; Morton (Mordechai) Cogan, *Imperialism and Religion: Assyria, Judah, and Israel in the Eighth and Seventh Centuries B.C.*, SBL Monographs (Missoula, MT: Scholars Press, 1974), 74–7.

173. Wray Beal, *1&2 Kings*, 441–3.
174. Sweeney, *I & II Kings*, 384–5.
175. Wray Beal, *1&2 Kings*, 443.

iv. *Sennacherib's Invasion*

As Dubovský notes, the account of Sennacherib's invasion of Judah in 2 Kings 18–19 is the climax of the narrative arc involving Assyria in Kings.[176] Unlike Menahem's and Ahaz's capitulation, this invasion is portrayed as a moment of genuine conflict. As with Baal in Inner Kings, it is not the Assyrian gods pitted against Yahweh; it is rather the Assyrian kings who have overcome the gods of the nations (2 Kgs 19.11-12). The Assyrian gods are not even mentioned.

In the various speeches of his envoy, Sennacherib comes offering a rival covenant (2 Kgs 18.19-25, 28-35; 19.10-13).[177] In language familiar from Israel's various rebellions against Yahweh, Hezekiah has rebelled against Sennacherib (כי מרדת בי, 2 Kgs 18.7, 20, e.g. Num. 14.9; Josh. 22.16-19; Ezek. 2.3) by relying on Egypt (vv. 21, 24), and by worshipping another god (in this case Yahweh, v. 22). So Sennacherib's terms of surrender are covenant-like, mirroring the phraseology of Deuteronomy: a life 'eating from your own vine and fig tree, drinking from your own cistern', a 'land of grain and wine, bread and vineyards, olive trees and honey', that 'you may live and not die' (2 Kgs 18.31-32; see e.g. Deut. 8.7-10; 1 Kgs 4.25 [5.5, Heb.]). His rhetoric, 'which of the gods of the nations has delivered his people...?' (vv. 33-35) mirrors the argument of Deut. 4.32-35. Dominic Rudman concludes: 'What is promised to Jerusalem's inhabitants is nothing less than a new Exodus with the Assyrian king usurping the place of Yahweh as the warrior god at their head who will lead them to their new land "like their own"'.[178]

For Menahem, the Assyrian king was a rival king-maker; for Ahaz, he was a rival saviour. Here the portrayal of the Assyrians has reached its zenith: the king is a rival god, and 2 Kings 18 presents a test of the viability of Covenant-Israel in a moment of crisis.[179]

The language of trust (נצל, בטח) is central to 2 Kings 18–19 and, as we shall see when we return to this theme in Chapter 4, it is also particular to it.[180] Hezekiah's choice at that moment is one of whom to

---

176. Dubovský, 'Why did the Northern Kingdom Fall?', 8–12.

177. The Rab-Shakeh's rhetoric is well studied. I present a summary of the results here. See Walsh, 'The Rab Šāqēh Between Rhetoric and Redaction', 263–79; Rudman, 'Is the Rabshakeh also Among the Prophets?'; Olley, 'Trust in the Lord'; Hyman, 'The Rabshakeh's Speech'; Hess, 'Hezekiah and Sennacherib'; Cohn, *2 Kings*, 128–39; and Evans, 'The Hezekiah–Sennacherib Narrative as Polyphonic Text'.

178. Rudman, 'Is the Rabshakeh also Among the Prophets?', 106–7.

179. Cohn, *2 Kings*, 132–3.

180. Eighteen of the 19 uses of נצל and בטח in the book occur in 2 Kgs 18–19. See also David Bostock, *A Portrayal of Trust: The Theme of Faith in the Hezekiah Narratives*, Biblical Monographs (Colorado Springs, CO: Paternoster, 2006), 167–204.

trust (מה הבטחון הזה אשר בטחת, 2 Kgs 18.19, also 2 Kgs 18.20, 21, 22, 24, 30; 19.10). Since Sennacherib's offer comes in the form of a rival covenant, Hezekiah's response must comprise covenantal allegiance. And so his faith in Yahweh is a choice for Yahweh's vision of Israel rather than Sennacherib's. The sudden and climactic rescue of Israel (2 Kgs 19.35-36), and the humbling of Sennacherib and his god, who is mentioned for the first time (v. 37), shows with no doubt Yahweh's superiority over Assyria, vindicating both Hezekiah's faith and the covenant vision for Israel.[181]

Those living in exile lived under a Babylonian vision for Israelite identity. However, in such moments of crisis, there is no hope in the nations. Assyria, or Babylon, may offer salvation and peace; but the narrative arc concerning Assyria in Kings shows that voluntary servitude is still slavery, and apostasy as well. It also demonstrates that even in such moments of crisis Yahweh can be trusted to do what he promised. Because of this, the vision of Covenant-Israel, though threatened by exile, need not be abandoned.

3.3.4. *Why the Exile? Manasseh as Culmination*

In the historiography of the book, the exile is inevitable after 1 Kings 11 because it is demanded by Yahweh's fidelity to his promises. Even without considering the various curses of Deuteronomy 28–29, Yahweh's warning of calamity to Solomon (1 Kgs 9.6-9) is enough to explain Nebuchadnezzar's invasion, because of the same promise–fulfilment theology that saved Jerusalem from Sennacherib.

The author of Kings had several other explanations for the exile on which to draw, had he wished. For example, the exile might have been explained as the result of the cumulative sin of the Judean kings. Halpern remarks that this was the strategy of the Chronicler, and would have seemed to fit the agenda of the Dtr as well.[182] And, in fact, the book comes close to offering this explanation when it implies that Judah had become entangled in the sin (and fate) of Israel (2 Kgs 17.19-20).[183] Or, the book might have portrayed Zedekiah's sin as the straw which broke the camel's back, as it nearly does in 2 Kgs 24.18-20.

However, the book stops short of explicitly blaming the exile on Solomon, the Judean kings, or Zedekiah. Instead of these, the explicit blame

---

181. See also Leithart, *1&2 Kings*, 256–9; Olley, 'Trust in the Lord', 66; and Janzen, 'The Sins of Josiah and Hezekiah', 355–9.

182. Halpern, 'Why Manasseh Is Blamed for the Babylonian Exile', 474–85.

183. The exegesis of these verses requires discussion, which I undertake in Chapter 4.

is placed on Manasseh (2 Kgs 21.10-15; 23.26-27; 24.3).[184] Manasseh's evil is unmatched in the book of Kings with a long litany of offences (2 Kgs 21.2-9, 16). He is portrayed flatly,[185] avoiding more positive traditions (e.g., 2 Chron. 33.10-13), as a 'characterless, cardboard villain'.[186] And even though, historically, Manasseh was an Assyrian vassal,[187] within the narrative world of Kings, Assyria has already been removed as a threat (2 Kgs 19.35-37).[188] So Manasseh's sin is portrayed as un-coerced.

This partisan portrayal has confused scholars. The normal solution has been diachronic:[189] that the pre-exilic Dtr knew nothing of Josiah's death and presented him as the hero of DtrH. Then, because of this, the exilic Dtr needed a way of explaining Josiah's failure without denigrating the hero of the narrative. He turned to Manasseh as a scapegoat.[190]

Putting the issue of textual history to one side, the claim that Manasseh is a scapegoat for Josiah in the exilic narrative is overstated. It is true that he is portrayed with no morally redeeming qualities. However, his portrayal is also a rich tapestry designed to recall the major motifs of the book. Manasseh's idolatry provides an occasion to remind the readers of the Davidic promise (2 Kgs 21.7), its fulfilment in the construction of the temple (v. 4), the Mosaic covenant (vv. 8, 15), and the remnant motif that has been developed throughout the book (v. 14).[191] His various sins are in every case an explicit violation of the covenant[192] and are recounted

184. So Cogan, *1 Kings*, 270–3.
185. Cohn, 'Characterisation in Kings', 93; Israel Gutman, 'Manesseh – Was he Judah's Worst King?', in *Homage to Shmuel: Studies in the World of the Bible*, ed. Zipora Talshir, Shamir Yona, and Daniel Sivan (Jerusalem: Ben-Gurion University Press, 2001), 49–66; and Michael Avioz, 'The Book of Kings in Recent Research (Part 2)', *CBR* 5 (2006): 22–3.
186. Nelson, *The Double Redaction of the Deuteronomistic History*, 126. See also Stuart Lasine, 'Manasseh as Villain and Scapegoat', in *The New Literary Criticism and the Hebrew Bible*, ed. J. Cheryl Exum and David J. A. Clines, JSOTSup 143 (Sheffield: JSOT, 1993), 163–7.
187. Lasine, 'Manasseh as Villain and Scapegoat', 165.
188. So Dubovský, 'Assyrian Downfall Through Isaiah's Eyes', 1–5.
189. The literature is voluminous. See, e.g., Sweeney, *King Josiah of Judah*, 52–63; Michael Avioz, 'Josiah's Death in the Book of Kings: A New Solution to an Old Theological Conundrum', *ETL* 83 (2007): 359–66.
190. So Halpern, 'Why Manasseh Is Blamed for the Babylonian Exile', 513. Alternatively, Manasseh may be a scapegoat for the woes of the exilic audience, e.g., Lasine, 'Manasseh as Villain and Scapegoat', 182–3; and Konrad Schmid, 'Manasse und der Untergang Judas: "Golaorientierte" Theologie in den Königsbüchern?', *Bib* 78 (1997): 87–99.
191. I explore this motif in Chapter 4.
192. See Würthwein, *Die Bücher der Könige*, 441.

in such a way as to remind the readers of all the acts of apostasy of his predecessors.[193] Not only is he compared to Ahab (vv. 3, 13) but there is a long string of allusions to various other acts of apostasy that have occurred in the book,[194] and to the general condemnation of 2 Kgs 17.6-20:

Table 3.1. *The Intertextuality between Manasseh's Sin and the Sins Ascribed to Various Other Kings of Judah and Israel, as well as the Narrative Précis of 2 Kgs 17.6-20*

	Mann.	Sol./ Reh.	Jerob.	Ahab	Ahaz	II.17, vv.
Comparison with the nations who were driven out before Israel	II.21.2, 9	I.11.5, 14.24			II.16.3	8, 15
Note on rebuilding the high places	II.21.3	I.3.3	I.12.31		II.16.4	9, 11
Built an altar for Baal	II.21.3			I.16.32		
Made an Asherah	II.21.3, 7	I.11.5		I.16.33		9, 16
Worshipped all the host of heaven and served them	II.21.3			I.22.19		16
'Built altars in the house of the Lord'	II.21.4, 5, 7	I.11.7, 8.29				
Human sacrifice	II.21.6					17
Used divination	II.21.6					17
Provoked (כעס) Yahweh to anger	II.21.6		I.14.9	I.16.33		11, 17
Followed Amorite gods	II.21.11			I.21.26		
'Caused' Israel/Judah to sin (החטיא)	II.21.11, 16		I.14.6, etc.			
Destruction like the house of Ahab	II.21.12					
Shed innocent blood, filling Jerusalem	II.21.16					

---

193. Cohn, *2 Kings*, 147.

194. For allusions between Manasseh and Ahab see William M. Schniedewind, 'History and Interpretation: The Religion of Ahab and Manasseh in the Book of Kings', *CBQ* 55 (1993): 649–61; between Manasseh and Jeroboam see Lasine, 'Manasseh as Villain and Scapegoat', 167–73. See also Percy S. F. Van Keulen, *Manasseh Through the Eyes of the Deuteronomists: The Manasseh Account (2 Kings 21:1-18) and the Final Chapters of the Deuteronomistic History* (Leiden: Brill, 1996), 146–9.

A caricature this may be, but it is hardly one-dimensional. Rather, Manasseh is presented as the culmination and summation of everything that has gone before.[195] In the pattern of redefinition we have observed, Manasseh's Judah has become indistinguishable from the nations who occupied the land before them (2 Kgs 21.2), and done even more evil (vv. 9, 11). If those nations were 'destroyed' (שמד, v. 9), then what should become of Israel? Because of this (... יען אשר, v. 11) Yahweh gives Judah over to their enemies (v. 14). The role Manasseh plays in the exilic narrative, then, is not as a scapegoat for Josiah's death. The exile is blamed on Manasseh because this king encapsulates and concludes a process that began 'the day their ancestors came out of Egypt' (v. 15, see also 2 Kgs 17.7).

3.4. Conclusions

The book of Kings advocates the Mosaic covenant as a framework for the creation of political identity in the exilic community. The author found within those traditions several foundational elements of communal identity: a national election, a sacred gathering, elements of shared history, traditions, legal frameworks, and cultic and religious beliefs. His agenda was to create in the exilic imagination, through the retelling of Israel's history, a notion of 'Israel' that would withstand the challenges of exile. This imagined ideal is an appeal to a shared vision, and we have termed this Covenant-Israel.

The challenge facing the author of Kings is that elements of the covenant are unavailable from the context of exile, several of which are essential to political identity like the land, the cult, and the monarchy. 'Israel scattered' cannot be 'Israel gathered' at the same time.

His strategy, in response, is to create a dialectic between the Mosaic covenant and the Davidic promise. On the one hand, he will not allow the promise to override the covenant as the primary anchor of social identity. However, on the other, because of the promise, neither will he allow a vision of Covenant-Israel that does not include a Davidic monarchy. Therefore, the promise, which is guaranteed by the logic of Yahweh's word in the book, guarantees the covenant also. Covenant-Israel is not simply an ideal, it becomes a destiny. Equally, the covenant gives content to the promise. Not any Davidic offspring will rule, but only one who can remain faithful to Yahweh's covenant.

---

195. See Wray Beal, *1&2 Kings*, 486–95.

The historiography of Kings explores this ideal of Covenant-Israel with respect to various historical contingencies. In doing so it shows that Israel's faithfulness to the covenant, and not those circumstances of history, will give political definition to the nation.

Several motifs recur throughout Kings, which combine to warn of the dangers of covenant apostasy and reinforce this covenant identity. The danger of apostasy is the same as that of integration: Israel cannot simultaneously 'follow after the nations that are around them' (2 Kgs 17.15) while being 'separated out from all the peoples of the earth' (1 Kgs 8.53). Therefore, at no point in Kings is the threat to the covenant phrased only in terms of religious worship. The great danger to the covenant lies in political compromise.

Royal intermarriage with foreign powers is one danger to be avoided, having led to both Solomon's and Ahab's downfall. The admonition of Deut. 7.3-4 lies close in the background of both stories (e.g., 1 Kgs 11.2), warning of the cultural compromise induced by marriages that cement political treaties with foreign powers. However, as we have seen with Menahem and Ahaz, any kind of voluntary political submission will also bring Israel undone, because it exposes their trust in a power other than Yahweh.

Such alliances begin a process by which Israel is reshaped politically. They come to resemble the surrounding nations and finally join them in their fate. In times of conquest, prosperity is no guarantee of faithfulness because other empires were also prosperous. As Solomon's Israel comes to resemble Egypt, we are shown that obedience is preferable to kingdom-building wisdom. In moments of conflict, the choice between Baal and Yahweh is also a choice between a covenantal and a Canaanite version of Israel. And in times of crisis, to serve other nations is to abandon Yahweh. Israel will be like Damascus if they trust Assyria, but Yahweh can be trusted to deliver them from foreign powers so that Covenant-Israel can be realised.

Since the covenant is Israel's constitutional document, Israel is only Israel to the extent that they keep it. From the context of exile, how might Israel become Israel once again? The answer lies in both religious and political restoration of the covenant ideals. For the author, this is something Yahweh will do, but only through the process of covenantal repentance and renewal.

4

NATIONHOOD: WHO IS ISRAEL?

4.1. *Nationhood: The Name 'Israel'*

The most basic element in the construction of political identity is a name, by which members of the group are identified to each other and to those outside. As Smith argued, nations are firstly 'named human populations'.[1] In the book of Kings, who is Israel? Already we have the intuition that Israel are those who inherit the obligations of the Mosaic covenant and the destiny of what we have labelled Covenant-Israel. However, due to the history of division and exile recorded by the book, it is not apparent in Kings who this is. Neither is the relationship between any of the old monarchic kingdoms and the exilic community straightforward. In what sense do exiled Israel continue to be 'Israel'? With whom do they claim continuity such that they inherit the covenant and promise? It is because the book of Kings addresses these questions that McConville called it 'the most significant Old Testament treatise on the nature of Israel after Deuteronomy'.[2]

Our task in this chapter is therefore to examine the way the book of Kings presents the concept of Israel. The first complication is the plot. The division of the kingdom into northern and southern tribes is portrayed as exploiting a pre-existing tribal fault line.[3] The words of northern rebellion had been heard before on the lips of Sheba, who rebelled against David's initial attempt to unify the tribes (1 Kgs 12.16; 2 Sam. 20.1).[4] However,

---

1. Smith, *Chosen Peoples*, 24.
2. McConville, *God and Earthly Power*, 157.
3. Linville, *Israel in the Book of Kings*, 114–22.
4. Even the earlier revolt was the result of an existing fault-line (2 Sam. 2.10; see also Gen. 37.7-11; 49.8-12, 22-36), and was not repaired by the opening of Kings (e.g., 1 Kgs 1.35; 2.32; 4.20, 25 [5.5, Heb.]).

even if Solomon managed to maintain the deuteronomic ideal of unity,[5] the situation deteriorated as a result of his policies (1 Kgs 12.4),[6] and Rehoboam's failure to correct this error resulted in the division of the kingdom into two (1 Kgs 12.14-16). The rest of the book wrestles with the paradox of two divided kingdoms set against a covenant-based identity that presumes unity.

This problem is compounded by a second, which is that Kings does not use its labels consistently. Most of the time, the label 'Israel' refers to the Northern Kingdom. However, within Kings there is a series of titles and references to various parts of Israel, which are not used the same way in different parts of the narrative:

Table 4.1. *The Title 'Israel' in Kings*

'Israel' as a title is not used consistently in Kings; meaning must be sought from context.

Label for 'Israel'	Referent
ישראל/יהודה	Can refer to the northern/southern kingdoms, the people in those regions, or the ideal of Covenant-Israel in phrases like עמי/עמך (again, never עמי־יהודה) and אלהי־ישראל (never אלהי־יהודה).
בני־ישראל	Can refer to the peoples that inhabit either kingdom: the inhabitants of Judah are still בני־ישראל, never בני־יהודה (e.g., I.12.17). It normally has the nuance of populace rather than a political entity (e.g., I.8.63; 9.22). It is the preferred term for pre-monarchical Israel (e.g., I.6.1; 8.9).
כל־ישראל	Can refer to all the tribes together, all the peoples that inhabit both kingdoms, or the Northern Kingdom.
כל־זרע־ישראל	Used only in II.17.21, with debated meaning. Either referring to the Northern Kingdom or to the people of both kingdoms.
בית־ישראל/יהודה	Refers specifically to the northern and southern kingdoms as political entities, never the people.
כסא־ישראל	Also debated, see Chapter 3 where I argued it referred to the authority to govern all Israel.

This variety can cause confusion. Since the referent of each must be decided by context, it is possible to read the same texts but understand them to be referring to different things. We shall not be able to decide the question of Israel by observing how Kings uses the name.

---

5. See Chapter 3, and John D. W. Watts, 'Deuteronomic Theology', *Review & Expositor* 74 (1977): 325–30.

6. On Solomon's domestic policy specifically (1 Kgs 4.7-19), see Walsh, *1 Kings*, 85–6; and Sweeney, *King Josiah of Judah*, 100–101.

Instead we must interrogate how the narratives portray Israel and Judah. Some positions are easy to rule out. Despite their use of the name 'Israel', the continued emphasis on the Davidic promise is enough to prevent the reader from forming the idea that the Northern Kingdom alone becomes the focus of covenantal hope. And, given the deuteronomic focus on unity, neither is it tenable to posit that both kingdoms separately realise the covenantal ideal of 'Israel', as if there are two Israels. Three basic possibilities remain: (1) that Covenant-Israel was only realised in the united monarchy and lost after that; (2) that the kingdom of Judah alone retains the possibility of realising Covenant-Israel after the separation of the kingdoms; and (3) that none of the kingdoms in the book can implement Covenant-Israel, but they are all related to it. I will argue for this third possibility. We can supplement this definition by noticing that the nations can also be obedient to the stipulations of the covenant, without themselves becoming members of the covenant community.

After settling this question, my thesis in this chapter is that the book of Kings utilises the concept of 'remnant' both to solve the problem of demonstrating political continuity between the exilic community and their monarchic forebears, and to show what kind of hope exists for the future. Israel in exile are those who remain of monarchic Israel after the covenant curses have fallen and, having survived judgment, they are the seed from which Covenant-Israel can be grown.

4.1.1. The United Monarchy

A first approach is to understand the united monarchy under David and Solomon as the only true expression of Covenant-Israel in the book, which is then lost when the kingdoms divide. This was the position of much early exegesis. For example, Carl Keil and Franz Delitzsch draw attention to the 'wrong which the seceding ten tribes had done in claiming the name of Israel for themselves, whereas it really belonged to the whole nation'.[7]

This position has much to commend it from a canonical point of view. It makes good sense of a network of salvation-historical motifs that run throughout the Old Testament, reaching a climax at Solomon's dedication of the temple, and declining after that point.[8] It also creates a point of

---

7. Carl Friedrich Keil and Franz Delitzsch, *Commentary on the Old Testament*, trans. James Martin (Grand Rapids, MI: Eerdmans, 1988), 3:248.

8. E.g. Graeme Goldsworthy, *According to Plan: The Unfolding Revelation of God in the Bible* (Grand Rapids, MI: IVP, 2002), 168–71; James M. Hamilton Jr., *God's Glory in Salvation Through Judgment: A Biblical Theology* (Wheaton, IL: Crossway, 2010), 178–80; Andreas J. Köstenberger and Peter Thomas O'Brien, *Salvation to the Ends of the Earth* (Grand Rapids, MI: IVP, 2001), 40–2.

continuity with the book of Chronicles, which remembers David and Solomon's kingdom as the golden age of Israel's history.[9] And it is easy for Christian readers accustomed to connecting the Davidic covenant with Jesus (e.g., Mt. 1.1; 12.23) to understand the early monarchy as the climax of Yahweh's purposes for Israel in the Old Testament.[10] Also, we have already seen in Chapter 3 that some regard Solomon's kingdom as a golden age, to be regained once the exilic community learn the lessons of the past.[11]

However, this position is difficult to maintain as the message of Kings. In Chapter 3 we examined several reasons to reject that the book of Kings opines for a return to Solomon's golden age. Because it does not advance Solomon's kingdom as a model of aspiration for the exiles, neither can the ideology of the book be one which understands the Israelite ideal to have been embodied by that kingdom. In summary, even at its greatest, Solomon's kingdom does not portray the same political ideal for Israel as is presented in the covenant traditions,[12] and so it cannot function as the defining paradigm for Covenant-Israel.

4.1.2. *Judah*

A second approach is that, after the division of the kingdom, the hope of Covenant-Israel lies exclusively with the Southern Kingdom. This proposal is appealing given the way the Davidic promise functions in the logic of the covenant. It is also appealing for those, like Sweeney, who understand the initial compilation of Kings to function as an *apologia* for Josiah's reform of centralisation and reunification (2 Kgs 23.15-20):[13]

---

9. Williamson, *Israel in the Book of Chronicles*, 87–96; Mark A. Throntveit, 'The Relationship of Hezekiah to David and Solomon in the Books of Chronicles', in *The Chronicler as Theologian: Essays in Honour of Ralph W. Klein*, ed. M. Patrick Graham, Steven L. McKenzie, and Gary N. Knoppers, JSOTSup 371 (London: T&T Clark, 2003), 118–21; John Goldingay, *Israel's Gospel* (Downers Grove, IL: IVP, 2003), 614–16.

10. E.g. Iain W. Provan, 'Solomon', *NDBT*, 788–9; Provan, 'The Messiah in the Book of Kings', 76–81.

11. In particular we examined Mullen (*Narrative History and Ethnic Boundaries*, 14–15, 38–43, 209, 249), and saw that Knoppers ('The Deuteronomist and the Deuteronomic Law of the King', 337–44; *Two Nations Under God 1*, 77–134) understands Solomon's era as a golden age, but has to propose that Deut. 17 is not typical of the Dtr ideology to do it.

12. See McConville, 'King and Messiah'; Knoppers, 'The Deuteronomist and the Deuteronomic Law of the King'.

13. Sweeney, *King Josiah of Judah*, 175–7.

> Essentially, the Josianic DtrH presents Josiah as the monarch who not only rules on the basis of the promise...but as the monarch who rectifies the problems of the past created by both David and Solomon. Overall, it is designed to demonstrate that the northern tribes are not capable of ruling themselves...but that Davidic rule under Josiah represents their only chance to achieve the promises of the Deuteronomic covenant of a secure people, centred on the worship of YHWH at the central shrine (Jerusalem).[14]

Sweeney's argument rests on two pillars: first, that the Northern Kingdom is presented as illegitimate from the beginning, and second, that Kings has an interest in the restoration of the northern tribes to Davidic rule.

In Sweeney's understanding, this thesis accounts for the book's extended sections that narrate the history of the north, showing the failure of their self-rule. He can also find textual support for reunification. For example, he argues that many passages in DtrH which seem to presuppose the exile, such as Deut. 30.1-10,[15] and (importantly for our purposes) 1 Kgs 8.46-51,[16] are Josianic in origin, functioning as an *apologia* for the then exiled northern tribes to return to the south. Thus, even though the Northern Kingdom may have inherited the name, they are only being Covenant-Israel when they are ruled by a Davidic heir and worship at the temple in Jerusalem.

Sweeney's is not a final-form reading of the text and owes much to the reconstruction of a Josianic edition of Kings.[17] However, even if we grant the plausibility of the reconstruction, we would have reason to question whether the exilic version of the book continued to encourage this belief for its readers. Sweeney's reading of 1 Kgs 8.46-51, for example, relies on the Josianic edition of the book, where Solomon's call to pray towards the temple from exile is directed to the wayward northern tribes of Josiah's day.[18] It is unlikely that the exilic author intended his readers to understand it this way. If he did, why is the theology not mirrored by other Dtr texts, such as 2 Kgs 17.34-40?[19]

Reading the exilic text, it is difficult to find textual support for either of the two pillars of Sweeney's thesis. First, Jeroboam's crime does not

---

14. Sweeney, *King Josiah of Judah*, 176.
15. Sweeney, *King Josiah of Judah*, 177.
16. Sweeney, *King Josiah of Judah*, 102 n. 12. Cf. Cross (*Canaanite Myth and Hebrew Epic*, 287), who believed they were targeted towards the exilic Judahites.
17. Sweeney, *King Josiah of Judah*, 170.
18. Sweeney, *King Josiah of Judah*, 102.
19. Sweeney does not deal with this text in his treatment (*King Josiah of Judah*, 81–8) of 2 Kgs 17. I return to it later in this chapter.

seem to be separation from the Davidic kingdom.[20] It is true that his motivation is portrayed as political: Jeroboam feared that the pull of the Davidic-Solomonic political synthesis together with the temple in Jerusalem would eventually turn the loyalty of the people back to the south (1 Kgs 12.26-28).[21] However, if the exilic author intended to make the case that the Northern Kingdom was illegitimate, then he has done a poor job. The inception of Jeroboam's kingdom is portrayed as Yahweh's initiative.[22] The language of Ahijah's prophecy is similar to the Davidic promise (1 Kgs 11.29-40; 2 Sam. 7.8-16), granting Jeroboam a divine mandate over the northern tribes.[23] The only difference between the two is

20. See, e.g., Knoppers, *Two Nations Under God 2*, 35; and Juha Pakkala, 'Jeroboam Without Bulls', *ZAW* 120 (2008): 501–25. Beginning with Wellhausen (*Prolegomena to the History of Israel* [Eugene, OR: Wipf & Stock, 2003], 283), many have argued that the Josianic Dtr required a villain to explain the anomaly of the Northern Kingdom in Israel's history, so that Josiah could be portrayed as the hero who reunited the kingdoms. See also, e.g., Cross, *Canaanite Myth and Hebrew Epic*, 73–4; William F. Albright, *Yahweh and the Gods of Canaan* (Bristol: Athlone, 1968), 43, 197–8; John Gray, *I and II Kings*, OTL (Philadelphia, PA: Westminster John Knox, 1970), 290–3; Bill T. Arnold, 'The Weidner Chronicle and the Idea of History in Israel and Mesopotamia', in *Faith, Tradition, and History: Old Testament Historiography in its Near Eastern Context*, ed. Alan R. Millard, James K. Hoffmeier, and David W. Baker (Winona Lake, IN: Eisenbrauns, 1994), 138–40; Marsha White, 'The Elohistic Depiction of Aaron: A Study in the Levite–Zadokite Controversy', in *Studies in the Pentateuch*, ed. John A. Emerton, VTSup 41 (Leiden: Brill, 1990), 149.

21. The administration of a kingdom without the cult would have seemed like an almost impossible task in ANE context; see, e.g., Knoppers, *Two Nations Under God 2*, 35–6; drawing on Henri Frankfort, *Kingship and the Gods: A Study of Ancient Near Eastern Kingship as the Integration of Society and Nature* (Chicago, IL: University of Chicago Press, 1948), 267–74; Würthwein, *Die Bücher der Könige*, 163–5; Richard J. Clifford, 'The Temple in the Ugaritic Myth of Baal', in *Symposia Celebrating the Seventy-Fifth Anniversary of the Founding of the American Schools of Oriental Research (1900–1975)*, ed. Frank M. Cross, Zion Research Foundation Occasional Publications (Cambridge: American Schools of Oriental Research, 1979), 137–45; John Gray, *Near Eastern Mythology*, rev. ed. (New York: Peter Bedrick, 1985), 53–62, 92–102; and Victor A. Hurowitz, *I Have Built You an Exalted House: Temple Building in the Bible in Light of Mesopotamian and Northwest Semitic Writings*, JSOTSup 115 (Sheffield: Sheffield Academic, 1992), 32–128.

22. Sweeney (*King Josiah of Judah*, 33–4) recognises this, introducing an unresolved tension into his reading.

23. Critical scholarship has wrestled with this Jeroboam-positive material. If we owe the negative portrayal (1 Kgs 12–14) to the Josianic Dtr, then who is responsible for the positive (1 Kgs 11) material? It sits poorly within a southern context, and so a

that the Davidic promise is unconditional, and Jeroabom's is conditional on covenant obedience. Anyway, Rehoboam is prevented by a prophetic oracle from reuniting the kingdoms because 'this thing is from [Yahweh]' (1 Kgs 12.24). Likewise, Jeroboam's sin is always explained in relation to covenant disobedience, and never separation from David.[24] Comparison with David is only made to reinforce that David, and not Jeroboam, had kept the covenant (e.g., 1 Kgs 14.8-9).

It seems likely that the reader is to understand Jeroboam's motivation as political, but the actual sin as religious pragmatism: inventing a false cult to serve political ends. The text goes to some lengths to explore Jeroboam's cult as something he 'made' (עשה), using that word nine times in those five verses (1 Kgs 12.28-33). As Deuteronomy recollects, to make a cult for oneself (עשו להם) is to turn aside from the covenant (Deut. 9.12).[25] This leads to a remarkable conclusion that separates the ideal of worship in Jerusalem from political support for a Davidic king, as Linville comments:[26]

> Jeroboam, therefore, was supposed to remain faithful to the proper religion of the Jerusalem temple. [This implication...] puts an odd condition on his rule and on the interdependence of his kingdom. The central shrine for his people is to be found outside of the kingdom... One could only wonder whether the producers of Kings were implying that, had Jeroboam remained faithful to Jerusalem's temple, there would have been two 'houses' worthy of their fond memory, that of David and, perhaps, even more so, that of Jeroboam.[27]

northern origin story is proposed from which the Josianic author drew. See, e.g., Evans, 'Naram–Sin and Jeroboam', 114. However, why did the southern redactors include it if their intention was to portray Jeroboam as the archetypal sinner? On this problem see Joseph, *Portrait of the Kings*, 110–16; Knoppers, *Two Nations Under God 2*, 30–3; and Gary N. Knoppers, 'Aaron's Calf and Jeroboam's Calves', in *Fortunate the Eyes that See: Essays in Honour of David Noel Freedman in Celebration of his Seventieth Birthday*, ed. A. B. Beck et al. (Grand Rapids, MI: Eerdmans, 1995), 92–104.

24. I demonstrate later in this chapter that neither does 2 Kgs 17.21 support a separatist explanation of Jeroboam's sin, cf. Marc Z. Brettler, 'Ideology, History and Theology in 2 Kings XVII 7-23', *VT* 39 (1989): 268–82.

25. See Leithart, *1&2 Kings*, 97; Provan, *1 & 2 Kings*, 109–10.

26. See also Bodner, *Jeroboam's Royal Drama*, 79–96; Linville, *Israel in the Book of Kings*, 163–75; Knoppers, *Two Nations Under God 2*, 35–44; and Stuart Lasine, 'Reading Jeroboam's Intentions: Intertextuality, Rhetoric and History in 1 Kings 12', in *Reading Between Texts: Intertextuality and the Hebrew Bible*, ed. Danna N. Fewell (Louisville, KY: Westminster John Knox, 1992), 133–52.

27. See Knoppers, *Two Nations Under God 2*, 37. I return to the issue of centralisation in Chapter 5.

The second of Sweeney's contentions is that Kings has an interest in the restoration of the northern tribes to Davidic rule. The evidence for this is also slender. Although the prophecy of the unnamed man of God against Jeroboam implies the return of a Davidic king to Bethel (1 Kgs 13.2), this is fulfilled in the narrative without reunification (2 Kgs 23.15). Aside from this text, there is little else.

Contrast this with the book of Chronicles, which certainly contains an *apologia* for northern Davidic rule.[28] In that version of the history, Hezekiah writes letters to the northern tribes, urging them to return to Jerusalem (2 Chron. 30.1-12), and many do (v. 11). Everyone who had 'set their hearts to seek Yahweh, God of Israel' returns to Jerusalem after Jeroboam's secession (2 Chron. 11.13-17), leaving (it would seem) the Northern Kingdom devoid of faithful Yahwists (see also 2 Chron. 15.9-10). And, on three occasions in Chronicles, the Southern Kingdom is prophetically condemned for drawing too close to their northern counterparts (2 Chron. 19.2-3; 21.12-15; 25.7-11). The point here is not that these traditions have been omitted from Kings where they might have been included, but that Chronicles demonstrates that it is possible to tell the story differently, and in a way that would have accorded with the Josianic historian's interests.

Not only is there no implicit call for reunification in Kings, but the opposite is true. The prophetic activity of Elijah and Elisha is portrayed as one of covenant faithfulness, without ever advocating a return to Jerusalem (1 Kgs 18.31, 36-37; 19.10, 14). Elijah's cry to the northerners, 'If Yahweh is God, follow him!' (1 Kgs 18.21), presupposes the possibility. Elijah's altar on Mount Carmel is built not only in the name of Yahweh (1 Kgs 18.32), but also with reference to the twelve tribes who descended from the patriarch Jacob (בני יעקב, 1 Kgs 18.31). And the community (בני־הנביאים) that Elijah and Elisha gather (e.g., 1 Kgs 20.35; 2 Kgs 2.3-15; 4.1, 38; 5.22; 6.1; 9.1) are represented as faithful Israelites with no connection to the Southern Kingdom. This activity is too extensive to act as a foil to expose the ineptitude of the northern kings. That Yahweh acts to deliver the Northern Kingdom for 'the sake of the promise made to Abraham' implies that they have a continuing place in Yahweh's purposes (2 Kgs 13.23).

---

28. Williamson, *Israel in the Book of Chronicles*, 87–118; Japhet, *The Ideology of the Book of Chronicles*, 267–9, 308–24; Ehud Ben Zvi, 'The Secession of the Northern Kingdom in Chronicles: Accepted "Facts" and new Meanings', in Graham, McKenzie, and Knoppers, eds., *The Chronicler as Theologian*, 61–88.

The Judah–exclusivist position, therefore, is not supported by the text. Sweeney may still be correct: that this was the position of the Josianic redactor. However, if this is true, it is no longer the ideology of the book in the exilic version.

4.1.3. *Both Peoples, but Neither Kingdom*

The final possibility is that the kingdom of Israel has been politically divided, but that this does not thereby imply that two unrelated kingdoms have been created. In this view, Kings understands a certain continuity between the covenant ideal and its expression in the divided kingdoms, and yet neither kingdom fully embodies that ideal without the other. Linville, for example, explores this thesis:[29]

> The interwoven history in Kings which follows the schism implies that neither Israel nor Judah can really exist without the other and maintain a sensible hold on to the past that made them the people of Yahweh. The perversity of the situation is intimated in the twisted recollections of that common history which are contained in the story of the division. While this ensures that greater Israel is reaffirmed in the midst of its political dissolution, it becomes a parody of itself...these new 'Israels' are at once mutually referential and exclusive. They preserve the 'ideal' only by the fascinating and engaging way that it taxes that ideal's integrity... The myth of the schism is strangely perverse; it produces two liminal 'Israels', neither one complete, and neither one expendable, and yet it fulfils the divine will expressed in the prophecies of [1 Kgs 11].[30]

Linville has an understanding of 'Israel' (for which he uses quotation marks) within Kings that supports this claim. This 'Israel' is not quite the same thing as what I have termed Covenant-Israel, because Linville does not view it as an ideal or destiny. For him it is a theological construct: the authority to carry the name of the covenantal community.

Linville's reading of Kings has three major exegetical foundations. First, he contends that the metaphor of tearing a garment is used within Kings to show that the division has not created two independent kingdoms. For example, note the language of 1 Kgs 11.11-13, 'I will surely tear the kingdom from you and give it to your servant' (קרע אקרא את־הממלכה מעליך ונתתיה לעבדך, 1 Kgs 11.11-13, see also vv. 30-31; 12.21, 26; 14.8; 2 Kgs 17.21). A garment remains a single garment once torn. So also,

---

29. Linville's treatment of this theme is Part 2 of his *Israel in the Book of Kings* (114–225).

30. Linville, *Israel in the Book of Kings*, 171, 75.

Linville reasons, Israel remains a single kingdom in two pieces after the division.[31] The 'kingdom' (הממלכה) known as 'Israel' has been torn from Solomon, and 'one tribe' given to him in its place (1 Kgs 11.13). Judah is never called a 'kingdom' (ממלכה/מלכות) in the book,[32] which Linville takes as further evidence that it is still part of Israel. Throughout Kings, Judah is the part of the kingdom (ממלכה) that was not given to Jeroboam. Israel is the part of the kingdom (ממלכה) in 'rebellion against the house of David' (1 Kgs 12.16-19). And Yahweh remains the God of 'Israel', never the God of 'Judah'.

Second, and building from this, Linville maintains that the proper use of 'Israel' is lost to the south when they are torn away. It is inherited by the north, which is why they keep the name Israel. He claims this is not only implied by a close reading of the same tearing metaphor in Ahijah's prophecy,[33] but also by the use of the term '*prince*' (נגיד) in the book.[34] Linville understands the term to represent a special kind of king: the 'divinely appointed answer to threats to the theocracy, or moments of transition in its history'.[35] He claims Solomon loses this title during the separation (compare 1 Kgs 1.35 to 1 Kgs 11.34), and this office is transferred to the northern monarchs: first Jeroboam (1 Kgs 14.7), and then Baasha (1 Kgs 16.2), and only back to the south under Hezekiah (2 Kgs 20.5). The implication is that it is the northern monarchy that represents the locus of kingship over Israel, and Solomon had lost the kingdom.

Third, for Linville, this loss is not permanent, nor does it separate Judah from Israel permanently. Even though Solomon has lost the kingdom, 'Jeroboam is given no leverage to claim that Judah is not part of greater Israel, or that the city [of Jerusalem] does not have a role to play for the whole Israelite people'.[36] His reading of the 'burning lamp' (ניר) *Leitmotif* (1 Kgs 11.36; 15.4; 2 Kgs 8.19) ensures this. Against traditional readings, which understand these promises to protect Judah against foreign annihilation because of covenant infidelity,[37] Linville believes they protect Judah

---

31. Linville, *Israel in the Book of Kings*, 165, 75.
32. However, note that in 2 Kgs 11.1 the Judean kings are the 'royal' (ממלכה) family.
33. Linville, *Israel in the Book of Kings*, 159–63.
34. Linville, *Israel in the Book of Kings*, 139–49.
35. I discuss this in more detail in Chapter 6.
36. Linville, *Israel in the Book of Kings*, 161.
37. For a discussion of the interpretive options, see Ehud Ben Zvi, 'Once the Lamp Has Been Kindled: A Reconsideration of the Meaning of the MT nîr in 1 Kgs 11:36; 15:4; 2 Kgs 8:19 and 2 Chr 21:7', *ABR* 39 (1991): 19–30; and Nadav Na'aman,

against premature re-assimilation into the wider kingdom of Israel. Only the restoration of the peoples of both kingdoms, and their subsequent unification under one Davidic monarch, can result in the realisation of 'Israel'. However, this does not occur in the book:[38]

> The division of the kingdom is not intended to portray the birth of two fundamentally opposed peoples, but to show how a single people were sadly divided against themselves [where the] unity of the claimed normative religion, and singularity of ethnicity are implied.[39]

Linville's solution is better supported by the text than either of those that see the United Monarchy or Judah as the sole heirs of the covenant. There are still shortcomings: the standard readings of both the ניר and נגיד motifs are probably correct,[40] and Linville's idiosyncratic reading of both of these have led to his understanding the name 'Israel' to be something that can be passed around like a baton. The book does not suggest a transfer of 'Israel-ness' (or even that such a thing exists) between the kingdoms, which Linville seems to imply: 'Judah had lost and then regained the symbolic leadership of Yahweh's people'.[41] However, his primary conclusion, that what it means to be 'Israel' need not be attached to the boundaries between administrations of northern and southern monarchies, is warranted.

This is already implied by the narrative of separation. Even though the events of 1 Kings 12 see a new political administration formed, there are strong indicators that their political identity remains undivided. The people remain 'brothers' (1 Kgs 12.24), and both are still people of Israel (בני-ישראל, 1 Kgs 12.17, 24). Also, the Northern Kingdom is thought of as remaining 'in rebellion against the house of David' (1 Kgs 12.19), which implies a continued ideal of unity. Perhaps the strongest indication that they remain one people is the continued assessment of both kingdoms through the lens of the Mosaic covenant which grounds the political identity of north and south alike as equal heirs of the 'good word' spoken to Moses (1 Kgs 8.54-61).

'A ניר for David in Jerusalem', *JNSL* 39 (2013): 29–38. For the standard interpretation see Knoppers, *Two Nations Under God 1*, 191–7; Provan, *Hezekiah and the Books of Kings*, 94–8.

38. Linville, *Israel in the Book of Kings*, 163.
39. Linville, *Israel in the Book of Kings*, 165.
40. See, e.g., Cogan, *1 Kings*, 339–44.
41. Linville, *Israel in the Book of Kings*, 146.

We shall add further exegetical support to this observation later in this chapter when we examine 2 Kings 17. However, already we can see that Judah and Israel can be portrayed as separate kingdoms, without also implying a division in political identity. Even though modern Western minds often equate political identity with political administration, anyone familiar with the relationship between tribal and national identity in much of the Developing World knows these two things are not always the same.[42] So too the book of Kings, which encourages the exiles to imagine themselves as part of a community both grounded in and destined to embrace both north and south.

All of this implies that the particular form of political administration is tangential to Yahweh's ability to fulfil his purposes for his people.[43] Whether ruled by one king or two, Israel is united by other factors:

> ...the patriarchal covenant, and other statements of Yahweh's abiding concern, suggest that the 'davidic model' is but one of several institutionalised alternatives for imagining Israel, [...and that] different models of the core of Israel's 'proper' religion persist: that of patriarchal covenants, Mosaic law, Davidic theology, temple worship, or leadership based on revelation through those accorded the status of 'prophet'.[44]

Such 'myths and memories, public culture, and common customs for all members'[45] can be shared by a people straddling two political administrations. They can also ground the identity of a people without a political administration at all. It is not the monarchy that defines who Israel is, it is their connection to the covenant. And for the exilic readers, who have no monarch, this is a key point in the historiography of the book.

---

42. The anthropological literature often uses the term *ethnie* to denote cultural identity, and *nation* to denote political identity. See, e.g., Thomas Hylland Eriksen, 'The Problem of African Nationhood', *Nations and Nationalism* 22 (2016): 222–31. The literature on the relationship is vast. Some representative examples will suffice: Haala Hweio, 'Tribes in Libya: From Social Organization to Political Power', *African Conflict and Peacebuilding Review* 2 (2012): 111–21; Charles F. Swagman, 'Tribe and Politics: An Example from Highland Yemen', *Journal of Anthropological Research* 44 (1988): 251–61; and M. Tamarkin, 'Tribal Associations, Tribal Solidarity, and Tribal Chauvinism in a Kenya Town', *The Journal of African History* 14 (1973): 257–74.
43. So also McConville, *God and Earthly Power*, 156–65.
44. Linville, *Israel in the Book of Kings*, 178–9.
45. Smith, *Chosen Peoples*, 24.

4.2. *Israelite Boundary Markers and the Nations: The Resettlement of 2 Kings 17*

The name 'Israel' is a core component of national identity, and thus those who use it are a key concern of the narrative of Kings. A second way to examine the boundaries of national identity is to ask what customs and practices separate those in the community from those outside, but the book of Kings does not deal with cultural boundary markers at any length: circumcision, the Sabbath and other festivals, customs and the like. However, we can phrase this question in deuteronomic categories of thought as well: what separates an Israelite who keeps the covenant from a non-Israelite who does the same?

The book envisages that some kind of belief in Yahweh is possible for non-Israelites. There are many texts which illustrate this:[46] the widow of Zarephath and her son, whose god is not Yahweh at first (1 Kgs 17.12) but who come to recognise Yahweh's word as truth (1 Kgs 17.24); the Syrian general who learns that 'there is no God in all the world but Israel' (2 Kgs 5.15); and the Queen of Sheba and the Tyrian king who blesses Yahweh (1 Kgs 10.9; 5.7 [5.21, Heb.]). All of these accord well with Solomon's prayer that 'everybody' (כל בני־אדם, 1 Kgs 8.39) and 'all the peoples of the earth' (כל־עמי הארץ, 1 Kgs 8.43) might come to fear Yahweh, and Hezekiah's prayer that 'all the kingdoms of the earth' might know Yahweh (כל־ממלכות הארץ, 2 Kgs 19.19).

Does the book propose that a non-Israelite could become one of, and be identified with, the people of the covenant? The only text in which the nations come into direct contact with the covenant is 2 Kgs 17.25-41. This narrative records the fate of the territories that used to be controlled by the Northern Kingdom as they are repopulated by the nations.[47] There are two textual sub-units[48] which bring the nations into proximity with the covenant: Unit 1 is concerned with the new inhabitants, who are

---

46. Linville, *Israel in the Book of Kings*, 215–16. There is the tantalising possibility that Elijah the 'Tishbite' (מתשבי) may have been an immigrant. See *HALOT*, s.v. 'תּוֹשָׁב'; and Walsh, *1 Kings*, 226. Given the uncertainty (see Cogan, *1 Kings*, 425) it seems best not to place too much exegetical weight on it. Keith Bodner (*Elisha's Profile in the Book of Kings*, 24) notes that in either case his origin on the east of the Jordan places him outside the normal territory associated with Israel.

47. For an overview of the exegetical issues see Magnar Kartveit, 'The Date of II Reg 17,24-41', *ZAW* 126 (2014): 31–2.

48. Following Wellhausen: Kartveit, 'The Date of II Reg 17,24-41', 32. See, e.g., Cogan, *1 Kings*, 213–14; or Sweeney, *I & II Kings*, 392. Earlier commentators further sub-divided Unit 1 into the report of the lion plague (vv. 24-28 with v. 41) and the report of syncretism (vv. 29-34*a*); see, e.g., James A. Montgomery, *A Critical and*

non-Israelite (2 Kgs 17.24), and Unit 2 incorporates covenantal material that is explicitly deuteronomic.

Unit 1	vv. 25-33	A narrative ('When they first inhabited...') concerning the new inhabitants of the land, and how it is they came to fear Yahweh.
Unit 2	vv. 34-40	A discussion of the current practice ('until this day') of idolatry in light of the covenant, and a re-presentation of the covenant itself, summarised as a matter of fearing Yahweh.
Unit 1'	v. 41	A resumption by *inclusio* of vv. 33-34, summarising the former narrative 'until this day', and so bringing the two parts together.

The question is the relationship between the two units.[49] Are those who are critiqued by the stipulations of the covenant (Unit 2) the same as those who have been brought by Assyria to repopulate the land (Unit 1)? Does the writer go so far as to speak of the foreigners as 'sons of Jacob whom Yahweh called Israel' and bind them to the covenant (vv. 34, 35, and 37)?

Although a first reading may indicate that they are, scholarship has thought otherwise. The tensions between the two units – do they fear Yahweh (v. 33) or not (v. 34)? – have produced a consensus that the two units describe different groups (because they originate from different periods).[50] Unit 1 is often thought to be speaking about the new inhabitants of the land, while Unit 2 is thought to be either a later addition relating to the post-exilic Samaritan cult who self-identify as Yahweh's covenant people (e.g., Ezra 4.2),[51] or a misplaced critique that was directed towards

---

Exegetical Commentary on the Books of Kings, ICC (Edinburgh: T&T Clark, 1951), 471; Gray, *I and II Kings*, 640; Weippert, 'Die "deuteronomistischen" Beurteilungen'. This tri-partite division remains popular amongst those who see two pre-exilic redactional layers in Kings; see, e.g., Lemaire, 'Redactional History of the Book of Kings', 446–61.

49. Frankel, *The Land of Canaan and the Destiny of Israel*, 200–217.

50. The possibility of dating the two units by the presence of unusual linguistic elements has recently been explored by Kartveit ('The Date of II Reg 17,24-41', 34–7). For an overview of scholarship on the text-history, see Frankel, *The Land of Canaan and the Destiny of Israel*, 200–204; or Gary N. Knoppers, 'Cutheans or Children of Jacob? The Issue of Samaritan Origins in 2 Kings 17', in *Reflection and Refraction: Studies in Biblical Historiography in Honour of A. Graeme Auld*, ed. Robert Rezetko, Timothy H. Lim, and W. Brian Aucker, VTSup 113 (Leiden: Brill, 2007), 223–32.

51. E.g. Montgomery, *A Critical and Exegetical Commentary on the Books of Kings*, 471, who follows most German redaction-criticism. See also Kartveit, 'The Date of II Reg 17,24-41', 32; and the comment in Cogan and Tadmor, *2 Kings*, 214.

either the Northern Kingdom[52] or the Israelites who remained in the land after Assyrian deportation.[53] In these cases, Unit 2 is misplaced and does not relate to the nations with which Unit 1 is concerned.

For some, only the diachronic explanation is possible. Mordechai Cogan, for example, finds it 'highly unlikely that any post-exilic writer would speak of the foreigners as "sons of Jacob", bound by the covenant obligations of the Torah (vv. 34, 35, 37)'.[54] If it is the case that no synchronic reading is coherent, then it is unlikely that the ancient author intended to bring the nations into the textual proximity of covenant relationship with Israel's God, and the incoherence would have been noted by his audience. David Frankel opts for this explanation, for example, by arguing that vv. 34-40 were inserted specifically to avoid the implication (of the earlier text) that the 'Lord had made a covenant with the newly arrived colonists'.[55]

We should not too hastily reach this conclusion. The question of the relationship between the covenant material in vv. 34-40 and the narrative of the nations that surrounds it hinges on v. 34:

↓עד היום הזה		34a
הם עשים כמשפטם הראשנים		b
אינם יראים את־יהוה		c
ואינם עשים כחקתם וכמשפטם וכתורה וכמצוה		d
↑אשר צוה יהוה את־בני יעקב		e
↑אשר־שם שמו ישראל		f
ויכרת יהוה אתם ברית ...		35a

> [34a]Until this day [b]they [the nations] continue doing as they did at first: [c]they neither fear Yahweh, [d]nor practise their statutes and customs – the teaching and commandments [e]that Yahweh commanded the sons of Jacob, [f]whose name he called Israel. Yahweh made a covenant with [Israel]...' (2 Kgs 17.34-35a, my translation).

The antecedent of the 3mpl pronouns and suffixes (v. 34b and c) is the nations who have repopulated the former northern territories: '[The nations] continue doing as they did at first...' Specifically they are not doing what 'their statutes and customs – the teaching and commandments...' required (v. 34d). These nations seem to have made their own at least some of the

---

52. E.g. Sweeney, *I & II Kings*, 392.
53. So Cogan and Tadmor (*2 Kings*, 213), who see the phrase 'to this day' in v. 34 as resumptive repetition (*Wiederaufnahmne*) of v. 23.
54. Cogan and Tadmor, *2 Kings*, 213–14.
55. Frankel, *The Land of Canaan and the Destiny of Israel*, 204.

requirements of the covenant, as the 3mpl suffixes indicate: 'their statutes and customs' (כחקתם וכמשפטם, v. 34*d*, agreeing with vv. 28, 32-33). These are grouped with, and qualified further by 'the teaching, and commandments that Yahweh commanded…' (וכתורה וכמצוה אשר צוה יהוה…, v. 34*d*, without suffixes). This then implies that the nations have adopted some of the requirements of the covenant, even if the thrust of the verse is that they did not keep them or misunderstood them.

This conclusion stops short of identifying the nations as a new covenant community. Note that the clause in v. 34*e* identifies the covenant, not the nations. Against Cogan's reading, it is not naming the nations as 'sons of Jacob'. Rather, it is answering the question: 'Which statutes, customs, teaching, and commands had the nations adopted and were now expected to follow?'[56] The answer is, 'the ones Yahweh gave to the Sons of Jacob who were called Israel'. The antecedent of the 3mp suffix ('He made with *them* a covenant…', v. 35*a*) is the sons of Jacob (בני יעקב), and not the nations, as v. 36 also implies. Nowhere are the nations addressed as if they were 'Israel', and neither does the text assert that Yahweh has made a covenant with them. However, this text does expect the nations to adhere to the norms that the covenant once required of Israel, and it accepts that the nations had adopted those norms as if the covenant were their own.

The following material in Unit 2 (vv. 35-39) then summarises these 'statutes, customs, teaching, and commandments' through the concept of fearing (ירא) Yahweh, which is mentioned in every verse, five times in all. This is important for two reasons. First, outside 2 Kings 17, the phrase occurs only five times in Kings, and is used particularly in situations where nations are in view. We saw above that Solomon's dedication of the temple included two petitions that included the phrase (1 Kgs 8.37-40, 41-43) and expressed hope that 'everybody' (כל בני־אדם, v. 39) and 'all the peoples of the earth' (כל־עמי הארץ, v. 43) might come to 'fear Yahweh'. In Inner Kings the same phrase is used to imply true covenant faithfulness in contrast to Ahab's kingdom who was unfaithful (e.g., 1 Kgs 18.3, 12; 2 Kgs 4.1). In both cases the phrase is used to show that peoples who are outsiders to the community named 'Israel', might come to be obedient to the covenant.

The second reason it is important is because fearing Yahweh has been the subject of Unit 1 of 2 Kgs 17.25-41, and the source of contention concerning the structure of the passage. As the resettlement narrative begins, the imported nations did not fear Yahweh (לא יראו את־יהוה, v. 25). Because of this, Yahweh sent lions, so the Assyrian king allowed a priest to return to 'show them how they might fear Yahweh' (מורה אתם איך יראו

---

56. Linville, *Israel in the Book of Kings*, 214–15.

את־יהוה, v. 28). It was not to be. In the narrative of Kings, these nations do what they did in their former territories (כמשפט הגוים אשר הגלו אתם משם ..., v. 33).

The obvious tension between 'it was Yahweh they were fearing' (את יהוה היו יראים, v. 33) and 'there were no fearers of Yahweh among them' (אינם יראים את יהוה, v. 34) is difficult, and it is compounded by unusual syntax.[57] It is also resolvable:

את יהוה היו יראים	33*a*
ואת אלהיהם היו עבדים	*b*
↑כמשפט הגוים אשר הגלו אתם משם	*c*
↓עד היום הזה	34*a*
הם עשים כמשפטם הראשנים	*b*
אינם יראים את יהוה	*c*
ואינם עשים כחקתם וכמשפטים וכתורה וכמצוה	*d*
↑ אשר צוה יהוה	*e*

> [33a][At that time...] they feared Yahweh [b]but served their gods [c]according to the customs of the nations that were driven from there. [34a]Until this day [b]they continue doing as they did at first: [c]they neither fear Yahweh, [d]nor practise their statutes and customs – the teaching, and commandments [e]that Yahweh commanded...' (2 Kgs 17.33-34, my translation)

Clauses 33*a* and 34*c* both have a syntactic parallel which qualify them. Clause 33*a* is qualified by 33*b*: '...they feared Yahweh but served their gods'. This 'fearing' in v. 33*a* therefore cannot imply full covenant fidelity. Just the opposite, they are practicing the 'customs of the nations' (כמשפט הגוים, v. 33*c*), and 'their former practices' (כמשפטם הראשנים, v. 34*b*). Specifically, they are not practising the stipulations of the covenant (כמשפטים ... אשר צוה יהוה, v. 34*d*). The contradiction of v. 34*c* is semantic only, because in both verses they do not 'practise the statutes, customs, teaching and commandments which Yahweh commanded'. There was a sense in which they worshipped Yahweh (v. 33), but this did not extend to keeping the covenant that was made with the former inhabitants.

The irony of the situation is that by the time Sennacherib had invaded the north, he had mistakenly identified the gods of Samaria to have been the same gods that ended up being worshipped there anyway (2 Kgs

---

57. The repeated presence of the ויהי + ptcpl construction implies something other than the preterite translation which is commonly used. See Gibson, *Introductory Hebrew Grammar*, 138; Waltke and O'Connor, *An Introduction to Biblical Hebrew Syntax*, 628–30. There are several other unusual verbal constructions, such as אין + ptcpl and prn + ptcpl. The issue is not the meaning of these forms in themselves, but what semantic distinction is implied by contrasting these verbal forms with each other.

17.24, 30-31; see 2 Kgs 18.34). The Northern Kingdom was so much like the nations that their worship was indistinguishable from the nations who replaced them.[58]

What would have happened had these nations obeyed the covenant? Sadly, we can only guess. On the one hand, Covenant-Israel maintains a historical (העלה אתכם מארץ מצרים, v. 36) and genetic (בני יעקב, v. 34) element to its construction of identity. The phrase 'sons of Jacob' alludes in both 2 Kgs 17.34 and 1 Kgs 18.31 to the tradition of the patriarch wrestling with Yahweh and receiving the name 'Israel' (Gen. 32.28).[59] In both instances the purpose of the allusion seems to do with Israelite identity. In 2 Kings 17, as we have seen, it identifies the covenant as the one Yahweh made in history with Jacob. In 1 Kings 18, as we also noted above, it reinforces the genuinely Israelite nature of Elijah and his sacrifice in spite of their location in the Northern Kingdom.

Israel, then, cannot be replaced by the nations who do not share these historical connections. However, that those who do not share this heritage can still be critiqued by the covenant and expected to obey it implies a possibility. It can still be 'their' covenant, even though it was not made with them. Various foreigners in the narrative have come to fear Yahweh: Naaman, the widow of Zarephath, and others. And so 2 Kings 17 likewise implies that through proximity to Israel the nations might come to worship Israel's God and keep Israel's covenant, joining Israel as members of the covenant community.[60]

This would assure the exilic readers of Kings of their ongoing importance within the purposes of Yahweh. It would also challenge them to be open to the continued possibility of welcoming foreigners. As they live their lives amongst the nations, perhaps some of these might also come to fear Yahweh through their new proximity with Israel. Might Babylon, or at least some Babylonians, also join the covenant community?

4.3. *Israel-Incipient: The Preservation of a Remnant*

As we have seen, the narrative of Kings asserts that, together, the pre-exilic kingdoms embody the concept of Covenant-Israel, but neither fully nor independently from the other. This is because, even though Kings asserts the continued role of the Davidic promise, it advocates a national identity that is grounded in the deuteronomic traditions, rather than one that is

---

58. So, e.g., Wray Beal, *1&2 Kings*, 452.

59. These are the only two occurrences of the phrase in the entire Primary History outside of Genesis. (The other four occurrences are: Mal. 3.6; Pss 77.16; 105.6; and 1 Chron. 16.13.)

60. See also Knoppers, 'Prayer and Propaganda', 251.

based in the political administration of the monarchic period. How does the exilic audience relate to this definition? By what rights do they, living in the post-monarchic era, inherit a pre-monarchic statement of identity? Here we explore how Kings builds a connection between its exilic audience and the deuteronomic traditions, through identification with the concept of a remnant.

The remnant motif in Kings has often been overlooked in recent scholarship.[61] It was explored in the German tradition-critical scholarship of last century,[62] which was concerned to find the origin and development of the idea within Israel's religious history. The Elijah–Elisha narratives were understood to be an important datum, reflecting an early stage in Israel's religious development.[63] Gerhard Hasel labelled the Elijah narrative in 1 Kings 18–19:

> ...the *locus classicus* of the promised remnant in the sense that we meet in this passage for the first time in the history of Israel the promise of a future remnant that constitutes the kernel of a new Israel.[64]

However, these tradition-critical studies differ from our focus, which is the role that the concept plays in the narrative theology of the book.[65] We

---

61. For example, the concept of 'remnant' does not even have an entry in B. T. Arnold and H. G. M. Williamson, eds., *Dictionary of the Old Testament: Historical Books* (Downers Grove, IL: IVP, 2005).

62. E.g. W. E. L. Müller's 1939 thesis, republished and expanded by H. D. Preuss, *Die Vorstellung vom Rest im Alten Testament*, 2nd ed. (Neukirchen-Vluyn: Neukirchener Verlag, 1973); see also von Rad, *Old Testament Theology*. Other studies include H. Gressmann, *Der Ursprung der israelitisch-jüdischen Eschatologie* (Göttingen: Vandenhoeck & Ruprecht, 1905); Herbert Dittmann, 'Der heilige Rest im Alten Testament', *TSK* 87 (1914): 603–18; and O. Schilling, '"Rest" in der Prophetie des Alten Testaments' (Ph.D. diss., Universität Münster, 1942).

63. Müller (*Die Vorstellung vom Rest*, 46) developed his idea from 1 Kgs 18–19 and 2 Kgs 9–10. This line of inquiry seems to have concluded with Gerhard Hasel's seminal work *The Remnant: The History and Theology of the Remnant Idea from Genesis to Isaiah* (Berrien Springs, MI: Andrews University, 1972), 172–3.

64. Hasel, *The Remnant*, 172–3.

65. This different focus has necessitated a different treatment of the remnant passages in the book. For example, the prominent Isaianic remnant passages (such as 2 Kgs 19.4, 29-31 = Isa. 37.4, 30-32) are thought to represent a separate stage in Israel's religious development than 1 Kgs 18–19, and so are often treated in isolation. Hasel (*The Remnant*, 331–9) judged these narratives to be traditions dating from Isaiah of Jerusalem's late ministry, whereas I read them alongside the Elijah–Elisha narratives as part of a single exilic theology of remnant represented by the completed work.

shall need to pave our own way because this theme has not yet received close attention in the literature.

The concept of the remnant in the Old Testament is often associated with a restricted lexical range of words, primarily שאר, יתר, and פלט.⁶⁶ These words can take a range of meanings depending on the context, and so scholarship has used three primary analytical categories to specify what is meant in each instance:⁶⁷

1. *Tone*: is the remnant spoken of positively (a remnant will survive!) or negatively (only a remnant will survive)?⁶⁸
2. *Temporal Location*: is the remnant a surviving group from some past catastrophe, a promised group that will survive a coming disaster, or an eschatological hope?⁶⁹
3. *Composition*: is the remnant composed of survivors of some catastrophe, or are they more narrowly described as a faithful community who has been purified through judgment?⁷⁰

What kind of remnant does the narrative of Kings portray? The lexica give us a place to start and help to identify key texts within Kings where the concept appears. However, we must move beyond isolated texts because, although the use of these words provides substantial corroborative evidence, at times, Kings portrays the preservation of a remnant without using them. As we shall see below, there are a number of editorial comments that allude to the theme without using the words explicitly (e.g., 2 Kgs 14.27). We must therefore investigate the way the idea of remnant has shaped the narrative of Kings.

---

66. See *NIDOTTE*, s.v. 'שָׁאַר'; and also Hasel's discussion in 'Semantic Values of Derivatives of the Hebrew Root šā'ar', *AUSS* 11 (1973): 152–69.

67. These categories are my attempt to distil the main lines of thought into useful distinctions. Others treat the remnant theme differently. For example, Hasel denotes a temporally future remnant that is positive in tone as the 'eschatological' remnant.

68. E.g. Eric W. Heaton, 'The Root שאר and the Doctrine of the Remnant', *JTS* 3 (1952): 28; Lester V. Meyer, 'Remnant', *AYBD*, 670–1; von Rad, *Old Testament Theology*, 2:165–6.

69. E.g. Hasel, *The Remnant*, 169–70.

70. E.g. Gerhard F. Hasel, 'Review of *Die Vorstellung vom Rest im Alten Testament*. By Werner E. Muller. Edited by Horst Dietrich Preuss', *AUSS* 13 (1975): 90; and von Rad, *Old Testament Theology*, 2:187; cf. Müller and Preuss, *Die Vorstellung vom Rest*, 1–40. We will see the motif of purification in all of the remnant cycles. Kings, however, does not develop the thought of Deut. 30.6 that this kind of purification requires Yahweh to 'circumcise your heart'. This is an eschatological thought that suits the prophets better. E.g. Jer. 9.26; 24.7; 31.33; 32.39-41; Ezek. 3.7; 11.19; 36.26.

When we do this we find that there are three narratives within the book concerned to develop this theme, each of which follows the same general pattern:

1. *Sin and Prophecy*: Israel sin by worshipping some false god, and Yahweh pronounces judgment on them which is executed through a foreign power.
2. *Judgment*: The judgment comes, and purifies Israel of their idolatry, but even after their idolatry is removed, the judgment remains so severe that it looks like it may not leave a remnant.
3. *Deliverer*: Yahweh acts graciously and sends a saviour for the sake of his commitment to David or Abraham, and Israel is restored through the remnant that survived.

The three narratives are nested within one another as follows:

Table 4.2. *The Three Judgment Cycles in Kings, Leading to the Remnant Theology of the Book*

	Sin and Prophecy	**Judgment**	**Deliverer**
Ahab Cycle	Sin of Ahab→ Elijah at Horeb	Jehu and Hazael	J(eh)oash (delivers Judah) Jehoahaz, J(eh)oash, Jeroboam II (delivers Israel)
Jeroboam Cycle	Sin of Jeroboam I→ Ahijah's Prophecy	Assyria	The Angel of Yahweh
Solomon Cycle	Sin of Solomon→ Yahweh's Speech	Babylon	?

Solomon Cycle – Sin	1 Kgs 9.6-9
Jeroboam Cycle – Sin	1 Kgs 14.7-16
Ahab Cycle – Sin	1 Kgs 16.31-33
Ahab Cycle – Judgment	2 Kgs 8–11
Ahab Cycle – Deliverer	2 Kgs 12.17-18; 13.5
Jeroboam Cycle – Sin (Reprise)	2 Kgs 17.7-20
Jeroboam Cycle – Judgment	2 Kgs 17–19
Jeroboam Cycle – Deliverer	2 Kgs 19.35
Solomon Cycle – Judgment	2 Kings 24–25
Solomon Cycle – Deliverer	?

The innermost, which follows the plot-line of Inner Kings, deals with the apostasy of Ahab. The next, an Outer Kings narrative, begins with the sin of Jeroboam and concludes with the exile of the Northern Kingdom and the salvation of Jerusalem from Sennacherib. And the outermost follows the same pattern but remains incomplete at the end of the book. Judgment has come for Solomon's sin in the form of exile, but a deliverer has not been found.

This pattern, of sin followed by judgment and then salvation, is familiar from the Judges cycle. This intertextuality is probably intentional; for example, other than 2 Kgs 17.20, Judges has the only other instance of Israel being given 'into the hand of the plunderers' (ביד שסים, Judg. 2.14; compare also 2 Kgs 17.10-12 with Judg. 2.11-13, or 2 Kgs 13.5 with Judg. 2.16).[71] However, there are several key differences between the cycles in these two books.[72] In Judges, the judgment and salvation follow immediately from the acts of sin and repentance.[73] In Kings, salvation can come without repentance, as with Jehoahaz (2 Kgs 13.1-6), and the removal of apostasy does not result in immediate salvation, as when Baal worship is destroyed but Israel continue to be oppressed (2 Kgs 10.28, 32-33). The cycle of judgment and salvation can also be interrupted and delayed in Kings, as with Ahab whose repentance delays the expected appearance of Jehu and Hazael by eight chapters (1 Kgs 21.27-29; 2 Kgs 8–9; see 1 Kgs 19.15-18).

The protraction of the pattern is important in Kings, because it allows prolonged periods between sin and judgment and between judgment and restoration. It is this period between judgment and restoration that creates the narrative space for the concept of a remnant to emerge: a group who survive through the judgment in order for Israel to be restored on the other side. It is also this prolonged period which allows the exilic readers of Kings to see themselves as part of the story: they are those who have survived the judgment of Yahweh, who await a deliverer on the other side, and from whom Covenant-Israel might re-emerge.

4.3.1. *The Ahab Cycle: From Baal to Jeroboam's Yahwism*

The remnant motif in the book first emerges when it becomes the subject of an extended treatment by Inner Kings, where the complete sin → judgment → deliverer pattern is established. The narrative can be diagrammed as follows:

---

71. Barry G. Webb, *The Book of Judges* (Grand Rapids, MI: Eerdmans, 2012), 140–8; Cogan, *1 Kings*, 143; Sweeney, *I & II Kings*, 355.

72. So von Rad, *Old Testament Theology*, 1:342–44. See also Timo Veijola, 'Martin Noth's *Überlieferungsgeschichtliche Studien* and Old Testament Theology', in McKenzie and Graham, eds., *The History of Israel's Traditions*, 113 n. 6.

73. Webb, *The Book of Judges*, 147–8.

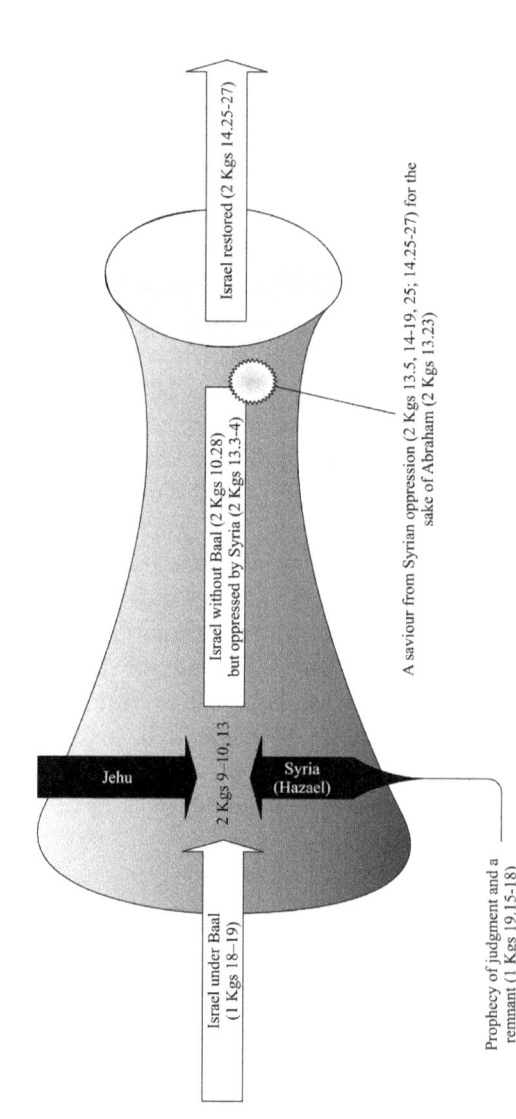

Figure 4.1. *The Ahab Remnant Cycle*

In the Ahab remnant cycle Israel worships Baal, a prophetic announcement of judgment is given. Judgment follows, removing Baal, but is severe and looks like it will not leave a remnant at all. Eventually Yahweh raises a saviour for the sake of his promises to Abraham and Israel is restored.

i. *Sin and Prophecy: Elijah on Carmel*

The story begins with Ahab and Jezebel's imposition of the Tyrian Baal cult upon Israel.[74] So determined is Jezebel that she slaughters Yahweh's prophets (1 Kgs 18.22, see 18.4, 13) until Elijah complains that he alone remains (יתר) of them. After the showdown at Carmel, Elijah believes he has become the only remnant (יתר) of faithful Israel (1 Kgs 19.10, 14). Yahweh's response is given in 1 Kgs 19.15-18, outlining a mandate for Elijah (vv. 15-16), a promise of judgment (v. 17), and a promised remnant (v. 18).

Yahweh intends to deal with Ahab's apostasy through Elisha, Jehu, and the Syrian king Hazael. The use of משׁח three times in vv. 15-16 is striking and includes the anointing of a prophet and a foreigner. The term does not have messianic overtones here (cf. 1 Sam. 2.10), simply meaning to 'install into office'.[75] However, the parallelism groups the three commissionings together, as the three appointed agents by whom Yahweh intends to bring judgment on Ahab.[76]

Verse 18 details Yahweh's purpose to preserve a remnant through this judgment. This verse is sometimes misunderstood. Taken as a contradiction of Elijah's complaint that only he is left amongst Israel (1 Kgs 19.10, 14), v. 18 would imply that he is not alone because there are yet 7000[77] who have not bowed the knee to Baal. This is a common misunderstanding,[78] but this interpretation is not supported by the syntax:[79]

---

74. This portion of Kings has been well studied with respect to its remnant theology. Below I draw from the findings of Hasel, *The Remnant*, 159–73; Müller and Preuss, *Die Vorstellung vom Rest*; and particularly von Rad, *Old Testament Theology*, 2:18–23.

75. Walsh, *1 Kings*, 278.

76. De Vries, *1 Kings*, 236.

77. An 'adequate or ample quantity'. See Walsh, *1 Kings*, 298; and Cogan, *1 Kings*, 457.

78. E.g. KJV: 'Yet I have left *me* seven thousand...'; NET: 'I still have left in Israel seven thousand...'; CEV: 'Yet seven thousand Israelites have refused to worship Baal...'; ELBER05: 'Aber ich habe siebentausend...'; Bodner, *Elisha's Profile in the Book of Kings*, 29–30: 'I have kept...' Even so, Elijah's complaint (vv. 10, 14) is probably sincere, even if hyperbolic (he just met Obadiah). See Hauser and Gregory, *From Carmel to Horeb*, 130–1, 152, and Cogan, *1 Kings*, 456–7.

79. So von Rad, *Old Testament Theology*, 2:21. Note the LXX has *2nd* person future (καταλείψεις): 'Yet you will leave...'

	ויאמר יהוה אליו	wy	15a
	לך │	impv	b
	שוב לדרכך מדברה דמשק │	impv	c
	ובאת │	wq	d
	ומשחת את חזאל למלך על ארם: │	wq	e
	ואת יהוא בן נמשי תמשח למלך על ישראל │	wx-y	16a
	ואת אלישע בן שפט מאבל מחולה תמשח לנביא תחתיך: │	wx-y	b
	והיה הנמלט מחרב חזאל ימית יהוא │	MSM[80]+y	17a
	והנמלט מחרב יהוא ימית אלישע: │	wx-y	b
	והשארתי בישראל שבעת אלפים │	wq	18a...
	כל הברכים │		...a
↑אשר לא כרעו לבעל		x-q	b
	וכל הפה │		...a
↑אשר לא נשק לו:		x-q	c

¹⁵ᵃYahweh said to him, ᵇ'Go, ᶜtake the road to the wilderness of Damascus and ᵈenter there. ᵉAnoint Hazael to be king over Syria, ¹⁶ᵃbut Jehu son of Nimshi you shall anoint to be king over Israel, ᵇand Elisha son of Shaphat from Abel-Meholah you shall anoint to be prophet in your place. ¹⁷ᵃThe one who escapes the sword of Hazael Jehu will put to death, ᵇand the one who escapes the sword of Jehu Elisha will put to death, ¹⁸but I will preserve seven thousand in Israel, ᵃevery knee ᵇthat has not bowed to Baal, ᵃand every lip ᶜthat has not kissed him. (1 Kgs 19.15-18, my translation)

The pertinent word is והשארתי (v. 18*a*), which is a *hifil weqatal*. The *hifil* adds a causative nuance to שאר: 'I will cause to remain' → 'I will preserve'. The *weqatal* is a sequential verb form,[81] which in this context continues the future sequence that began with Verse 17*a*: 'Jehu will kill (MSM + *yiqtol*)…Elisha will kill (ו+*x-yiqtol*)…but I will preserve (*weqatal*)'. Thus 1 Kings 19.17-18 constitutes a promise of judgment (Hazael and Jehu), that looks like it will leave no remnant (… הנמלט ימית, v. 17). However, it is also a promise of Yahweh's preservation (v. 18).

This reading is confirmed by the various prophetic interactions between Elijah and Ahab. Elijah draws on a motif of complete destruction to predict the total end of Ahab's dynasty (1 Kgs 21.21-24). This motif, involving birds, dogs, and male offspring (משתין בקיר), is used in Kings

---

80. 'MSM' denotes macro-syntactic marker. See Gibson, *Introductory Hebrew Grammar*, 89–90, 97–100.

81. Waltke and O'Connor, *An Introduction to Biblical Hebrew Syntax*, 523.

when no remnant of a dynasty remains after judgment (Jeroboam in 1 Kgs 14.10-11; 15.29; Baasha in 1 Kgs 16.4, 11; see also 1 Sam. 25.22, 34).[82]

ii. *Judgment: Jehu's Revolt, and Hazael*

Once Hazael becomes king of Syria (2 Kgs 8.7-15) and Jehu is anointed king of Israel (2 Kgs 9.1-13), the promised judgment follows. By that time, Judah also has fallen under judgment as they have intermarried and followed the sin of the Omride dynasty (2 Kgs 8.16-19, 26-29). At first the narrative focuses on Jehu's role. 2 Kings 9–10 relate a series of five massacres: against the southern king J(eh)oram and the northern king Ahaziah (9.14-28); against Jezebel (9.30-37); against Ahab's children (10.1-11); against Ahab's relatives (10.12-17); and finally against the prophets of Baal (10.18-27). The narrator comments five times in these episodes that Jehu, as predicted, left no remnant (שאר, פלט, 2 Kgs 9.15; 10.11, 14, 17, 21). Hazael plays a supporting role in Jehu's coup (2 Kgs 9.14-15), but he continues to be problematic afterwards (2 Kgs 10.32-33).

Following Jehu's coup, the specific threat brought by Ahab, which is Baalism, has been removed from Israel (2 Kgs 10.28), and this fulfils the commissioning of 1 Kgs 19.17-18 and 2 Kgs 9.7-10.[83] The immediate juxtaposition of Hazael (2 Kgs 10.32-33) encourages the reader to link 1 Kings 19 with 2 Kings 10, and to notice that this moment is a prophetic fulfilment.[84]

This connection between the Jehu narrative and the commissioning of 1 Kgs 19.15-18 resolves some dilemmas that arise when one reads the Jehu stories in isolation.[85] David Lamb, for example, wonders what to make of Dtr's strategy in the Jehu narratives. He examines 2 Kings 8–10 and concludes that Dtr has endorsed Jehu (2 Kgs 10.28, 30), but critiqued his successors.[86] From this he draws a lesson regarding the concept of

---

82. On the ANE background and other elements to this formula, see Cogan, *1 Kings*, 379–80; and Gray, *I and II Kings*, 337–8.

83. So Sweeney, *I & II Kings*, 223–4. Cf. Campbell, *Of Prophets and Kings*.

84. This placement is strategic, not 'tacked on'; cf. Fretheim, *First and Second Kings*, 172.

85. So Wray Beal, *The Deuteronomist's Prophet*, 155–6.

86. David T. Lamb, *Righteous Jehu and his Evil Heirs: The Deuteronomist's Negative Perspective on Dynastic Succession*, Oxford Theology and Religion Monographs (Oxford: Oxford University Press, 2008), 22–7, 256–62.

dynastic succession,[87] but he must set aside the negative evaluation of Jehu to do it: 'To mention Jehu in connection with the sins of Jeroboam need not be a sign of Dtr disfavour'.[88]

This is unnecessary when the story is set in its wider prophecy-fulfilment framework. We can conclude that Jehu has done right, insofar as he has done what Yahweh 'had in mind to do' (v. 30), which the reader already knows to be the destruction of Ahab's family (2 Kgs 10.17). Because of that act he is rewarded for obedience to the prophets, even though neither he nor his successors return Israel to covenantal fidelity (2 Kgs 10.29, 31; 13.2, 11; 14.24).[89]

As we have seen, the narrative pattern of sin, judgment, and deliverance in Kings allows for a protracted time between phases, which is true here. Israel find themselves free of Baal, but not free from trouble. Syrian oppression remains severe throughout Hazael's time and into the reign of his son Ben-Hadad (2 Kgs 13.3), who oppressed Jehoahaz (2 Kgs 13.22) and left no remnant (שאר) of his army (2 Kgs 13.7). By the time of Jeroboam II, the judgment has been 'very severe', even bringing Israel's future into doubt (2 Kgs 14.26).

What sort of remnant has been left? Since Baal's followers have all been killed in the temple massacre, those who remain are those who, by definition, have 'not bowed the knee to Baal' (1 Kgs 19.18). Bodner notes:

> Two binary categories are formed: those who are killed versus those who are not killed, and from this we can extrapolate that those who bow before Baal are differentiated from those who do not. The latter category is numbered at 7,000, and also is variously interpreted, but the figure is best understood as metaphorically referring to those citizens who have withstood the pressures to follow the ideological and political path blazed by Ahab and Jezebel.[90]

This is accurate, but given the note about continued apostasy in 2 Kgs 10.29, the reader senses that this is, perhaps, not good enough. Elijah's original complaint was about fidelity to the covenant in general, not Baalism in particular (1 Kgs 18.22; 19.10, 14).

87. Lamb, *Righteous Jehu and his Evil Heirs*, 256–62.
88. Lamb, *Righteous Jehu and his Evil Heirs*, 25.
89. This resolves several readings that understand the narrator to be ambivalent (e.g., Cohn, *2 Kings*, 75) or that rely on diachronic solutions (e.g., Campbell, *Of Prophets and Kings*).
90. Bodner, *Elisha's Profile in the Book of Kings*, 32.

During the protracted time of judgment, it is tempting to connect the enigmatic 'sons of the prophets' (בני־הנביאים) with the remnant of 2 Kgs 19.18 (see, e.g., 1 Kgs 20.35; 2 Kgs 2; 4.1, 38; 5.22; 6.1; 9.1).[91] We do see embodied within this group a faithful Israel, so this identification would bring the idea of the remnant in Inner Kings into closer alignment with the prophetic concept of a remnant as a faithful Israel within Israel.[92] However, the narrative does not encourage this identification. The text lacks any connection between them and the promise of 1 Kgs 19.18, and neither does it connect them to the judgment of Hazael and Jehu.

I take it, then, that the composition of the remnant is neither those who simply happen to survive, nor specifically those who are faithful to Yahweh's covenant. It comprises those who did not follow Ahab and Jezebel's Baalism.

iii. *Deliverer: Jehoahaz, Jehoash, and Jeroboam II*

Into the seemingly hopeless context of 2 Kings 13, Yahweh promises a saviour (מושיע, 2 Kgs 13.5).[93] This salvation works out through 2 Kings 13 and 14,[94] bringing closure to the arcs of Inner Kings, and eventually restoring Israel's borders to their former extent (2 Kgs 14.25; see 2 Sam. 8; 1 Kgs 8.65).

There is debate concerning the exact identity of this saviour figure.[95] The most likely candidates are Jehoahaz, since this announcement is a response to his prayer for salvation (2 Kgs 13.3-4), his son J(eh)oash, and his grandson Jeroboam II. If the announcement of a saviour (v. 5) is proleptic, then its fulfilment can be linked to all the events of 2 Kings 13–14 as follows:[96] the final sign-act of Elisha's ministry (2 Kgs 13.14-19) announces an 'arrow of salvation' (תשועה) from

---

91. As I also have done in the past. See Lovell, 'The Shape of Hope', 17–18.

92. See Hasel, 'Semantic Values of Derivatives of the Hebrew Root šā'ar', 169–70.

93. Note that Judah's salvation from the same Syrian oppression has already been provided by J(eh)oash (2 Kgs 12.17-18 [12.18-19, Heb.]).

94. Olley, '2 Kings 13'.

95. E.g. Hobbs (*2 Kings*, 167–8) reads it as Elisha. For further discussion see Cogan and Tadmor, *2 Kings*, 143.

96. See, e.g., Olley, '2 Kings 13', 199–218; Fretheim, *First and Second Kings*, 182–6; Cohn, *2 Kings*, 87–90; Wray Beal, *1&2 Kings*, 420–1; and Sweeney, *I & II Kings*, 355.

Syria (2 Kgs 13.17), which predicts a partial alleviation that J(eh)oash accomplishes (2 Kgs 13.24-25). Jeroboam II finally completes it (ויושיעם, 2 Kgs 14.27), restoring Israel's borders, and so Israel can 'dwell in their homes as before' (2 Kgs 13.5).

What has motivated this salvation? It is not the obedience to the covenant by those who survived Jehu and Hazael. Note that the provision of a saviour (2 Kgs 13.4) is phrased to avoid the conclusion that it is a response to Jehoahaz's piety, and no penitence is implied on his part:

4a	ויחל יהואחז את פני יהוה
b	וישמע אליו יהוה
c	↑כי ראה את לחץ ישראל
d	↑כי לחץ אתם מלך ארם

⁴ᵃJehoahaz desperately sought the face of Yahweh, ᵇand Yahweh listened to him ᶜbecause he saw the oppression of Israel, ᵉthat the King of Syria oppressed them. (2 Kgs 13.4, my translation)

Sweeney reads repentance into the verb ויחל, expecting to find the cycle familiar from the book of Judges.⁹⁷ However, the root חלה (v. 4a) is not used elsewhere for repentance.⁹⁸ It implies sickness or weakness, and can be used as an entreaty on occasions of desperation (e.g., Exod. 32.11; 1 Kgs 13.6),⁹⁹ which fits this context (v. 7). Yahweh hears Jehoahaz's entreaty but is not motivated by his penitence as he was with Ahab (1 Kgs 21.29). Rather, on this occasion, Yahweh is motivated by Israel's oppression (לחץ, v. 4c-d). This makes sense of the way that Yahweh's promise of salvation (2 Kgs 13.4-5) is bracketed by Jehoahaz's negative evaluation (vv. 2-3, 6). This is not a contradiction because the reason given for salvation is one of grace, not repentance: 'he turned towards them because of his covenant with Abraham, Isaac, and Jacob, and would not destroy them...' (2 Kgs 13.23).¹⁰⁰ 2 Kings 13 records a remarkable deliverance by Yahweh, but not a return to covenant fidelity by Israel.

---

97. Sweeney, *I & II Kings*, 360.
98. *HALOT*, s.v. 'I חלה'.
99. Hobbs, *2 Kings*, 166.
100. This is the only reference to the Abrahamic promise in Kings, and occurs here because of the northern setting of the narrative. Elsewhere Kings prefers to use the similar promise to David as a basis for Yahweh's faithfulness.

Von Rad detected this same note of grace much earlier in Ahab Cycle, commenting on 1 Kings 19:

> [...Israel] will only consist of a remnant. But it is to be noted that this is spoken of as if it already existed: there is no antecedent condition (a remnant will remain if some are found who have not bowed the knee to Baal). God appoints the remnant...[that] doubtless consists of those who had remained faithful: but their preservation had been decided even before the start of the coming troubles.[101]

However, von Rad did not continue his analysis into the fulfilment of this prediction in 2 Kings 13–14, so it is possible to give a more specific reason. The remnant exists not because 'Yahweh had not finished with Israel',[102] but because while ever some small part of Israel remains, so too does the potential that Yahweh's promises might be kept. Yahweh 'had not said he would blot out the name of Israel from under heaven' (2 Kgs 14.27).

So, as Hasel observed,[103] the remnant preserves the core of Israel through Yahweh's judgement, so that Israel might once again be reconstituted on the other side. But as we have seen, the book uses the concept of the remnant for a broader purpose than this. It not only ensures the continued existence of Israel, but also functions in relation to the promises of Yahweh. The remnant is, in fact, a correlate of Yahweh's fidelity to his word. If he does not act in judgment, then he will undo the Mosaic covenant, but if he does not act in mercy, then he will break the promise once made to Abraham (2 Kgs 13.23). It is this divine dilemma that drives the logic of remnant in Kings, presenting the concept as the solution to one of the main theological difficulties of the book: that Yahweh has promised both destruction and blessing.

4.3.2. *The Jeroboam Cycle: From Israel to Judah*[104]

Outer Kings has two remnant narratives, but only one is complete. This one deals with the sin of Jeroboam, and can be summarised:

---

101. Von Rad, *Old Testament Theology*, 2:21.
102. Von Rad, *Old Testament Theology*, 2:21.
103. Hasel, *The Remnant*, 387–8.
104. This section draws on my previous work: 'A Text-Linguistics Approach to the Literary Structure and Coherence of 2 Kings 17:7-23', 220–31.

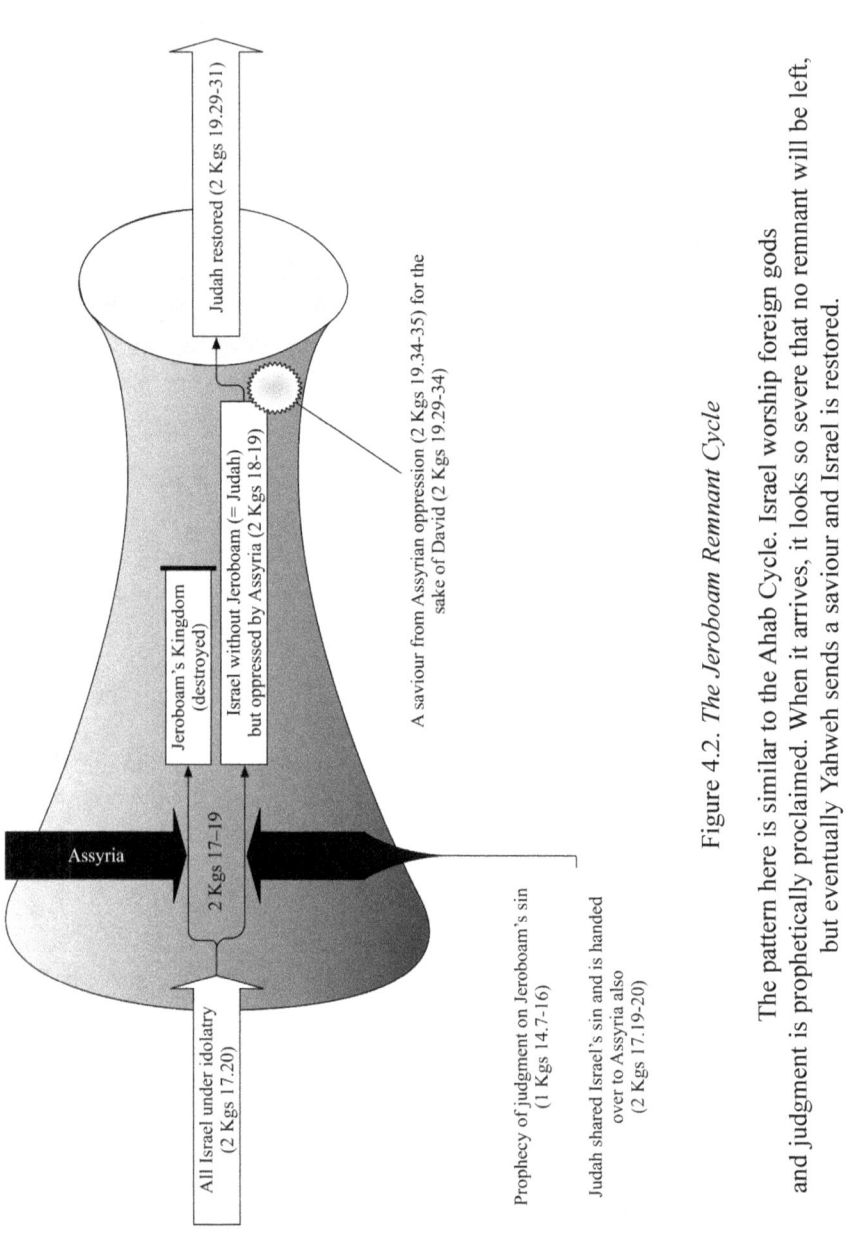

Figure 4.2. *The Jeroboam Remnant Cycle*

The pattern here is similar to the Ahab Cycle. Israel worship foreign gods and judgment is prophetically proclaimed. When it arrives, it looks so severe that no remnant will be left, but eventually Yahweh sends a saviour and Israel is restored.

i. *Sin and Prophecy: The Narrative Précis of 2 Kings 17*

The destruction of the Northern Kingdom was announced as a response to the sin of Jeroboam (1 Kgs 14.7-16), which we examined earlier in this chapter, but there is a long re-telling of the history leading to its demise in 2 Kings 17 which we will focus on here. Analysis of this chapter has proven to be problematic. The reason for this is that it has been considered to be Dtr's climactic speech, a homily concerning the fall of the Northern Kingdom. Since Noth proposed this, nearly every reconstruction of DtrH has found this chapter to be one of the keys that unlocks the entire history.[105] However, I treat this text as a narrative précis that summarises the rest of the book and supplies a perspective that includes Judah.

The present form of 2 Kings 17 is structured into five sections by clauses that provide a temporal frame of reference for what follows. Although this structure is not standard,[106] I have defended it elsewhere.[107]

A	2 Kgs 17.1-5	Hoshea's regnal summary	בשנת שנים עשרה לאחז ...
B	2 Kgs 17.6	Report of captivity	בשנת התשיעית ...
C	2 Kgs 17.7-20	Israel's history recounted as a narrative of apostasy	ויהי כי־חטאו בני־ישראל ...
D	2 Kgs 17.21-24	History of the Northern Kingdom	כי־קרע ישראל ...
E	2 Kgs 17.25-41	Subsequent history of the former Northern Kingdom	ויהי בתחלת שבתם שם ...

105. See my literature review in 'A Text-Linguistics Approach to the Literary Structure and Coherence of 2 Kings 17:7-23', 220–2. For a recent overview of some of the literature, see Kartveit, 'The Date of II Reg 17,24-41', 31–3; or McKenzie, *The Trouble with Kings*, 140–2. On the Dtr flavour of the text, see Weinfeld, *Deuteronomy and the Deuteronomic School*, 320–65; and Noth, *The Deuteronomistic History*, 6, 73.

106. The majority of proposals understand 2 Kgs 17 as a complex literary creation emerging in a series of redactions, but with little scholarly agreement on the details. See Noth, *The Deuteronomistic History*, 6, 73; Sweeney, *King Josiah of Judah*, 81–4; Mordechai Cogan, 'Israel in Exile: The View of a Josianic Historian', *JBL* 97 (1978): 207; Ronnie Goldstein, 'A Suggestion Regarding the Meaning of 2 Kings 17:9 and the Composition of 2 Kings 17:7-23', *VT* 63 (2013): 393–407; Cohn, *2 Kings*, 118–19; Cross, *Canaanite Myth and Hebrew Epic*, 281, 88; Gray, *I and II Kings*, 645–50; Long, *2 Kings*, 180–90; John MacDonald, 'The Structure of II Kings XVII', *Glasgow University Oriental Society* 23 (1970): 29–41; Brettler, 'Ideology, History and Theology', 268–82; Nelson, *The Double Redaction of the Deuteronomistic History*, 55–63; Provan, *Hezekiah and the Books of Kings*, 71; Hartmut N. Rösel, 'Why 2 Kings 17 Does Not Constitute a Chapter of Reflection in the "Deuteronomistic History"', *JBL* 128 (2009): 85–90; and Dietrich, *Prophetie und Geschichte*, 41–6.

107. Lovell, 'A Text-Linguistics Approach to the Literary Structure and Coherence of 2 Kings 17:7-23', 223–7. For a comparable literary analysis see Pauline A. Viviano, '2 Kings 17: A Rhetorical and Form-Critical Analysis', *CBQ* 49 (1987): 548–59.

Of relevance here are sections C and D. These two sections recount and summarise the story of Kings from different perspectives. Section C is a narrative précis that retells the history of Israel and Judah from the point of view of covenant apostasy, and Section D summarises the story of Jeroboam.[108] Section C has traditionally been understood to be Dtr's homily on the events described in v. 6,[109] as in the major English and German versions,[110] such as NRSV:

> In the ninth year of Hoshea the king of Assyria captured Samaria… This occurred because the people of Israel had sinned against the Lord their God… (2 Kgs 17.6-7)

This translation is not suggested by the syntax of the Hebrew: ויהי כי־חטאו בני־ישראל (v. 7).[111] If this reading were correct, the subject of ויהי would need to be implied by v. 6 ('This [i.e. v. 6] occurred…'), which then would connect causally with v. 7 ('…because…', כי).[112] However, as I have demonstrated elsewhere, this would be the only occasion in the Hebrew Bible where the construction ויהי כי + *qatal* + *wayyiqtol* operates this way.[113] Instead, v. 7 should be understood to begin a temporal reference point for a narrative that follows, and might be translated:

> When the children of Israel sinned against Yahweh their God who had brought them up out of the land of Egypt, from under the hand of Pharaoh, king of Egypt, they feared other gods… (2 Kgs 17.7, my translation)

---

108. Cf. Brettler ('Ideology, History and Theology', 281–2) who thinks this continues Section C and provides a second explanation of the exile that assigns blame to Jeroboam for breaking from David. This is syntactically unlikely and creates a contradiction with 1 Kgs 12. See Lovell, 'A Text-Linguistics Approach to the Literary Structure and Coherence of 2 Kings 17:7-23', 227.

109. This view has been ubiquitous since Noth (*The Deuteronomistic History*, 73).

110. So NRSV, RSV, KJV, NKJV, NIV, ASV, SCH1951/2000. Luther (1545) has (v. 7): 'Denn da die Kinder Israel wider den Herrn, ihren Gott, sündigten …'

111. Neither is it suggested by the LXX: καὶ ἐγένετο ὅτι ἥμαρτον οἱ υἱοὶ Ισραηλ …Note 𝔊^Luc has an explicit subject (καὶ ἐγένετο ὀργὴ κυρίου ἐπὶ τὸν Ισραηλ ὅτι ἥμαρτον …) which commentators often take as superior but not original, e.g. Burney, *Notes*, 331; and Montgomery, *A Critical and Exegetical Commentary on the Books of Kings*, 478.

112. So Omanson and Ellington, *A Handbook on 1&2 Kings*.

113. Lovell, 'A Text-Linguistics Approach to the Literary Structure and Coherence of 2 Kings 17:7-23', 224–5. Hobbs (*2 Kings*, 231) calls it 'extremely rare' but then parses it the usual way.

The subsequent narrative (vv. 7-20) recounts a story that begins in the pre-monarchic era and then, working through the monarchic era,[114] contrasts the fates of Israel and Judah within the context of the Assyrian crisis.[115] Through this contrast, it explores the way Judah becomes the remnant of wider Israel. The labels applied to the kingdoms in this narrative are noted in the table below, and follow the same chronological sequence, supported by inter-textual allusion to different periods in the narrative of Kings:[116]

Table 4.3. *Allusions to Israel's Various Historical Eras in the Narrative Précis of 2 Kgs 17.7-20*

11.17	Era	Referent	Intertextual Allusions
7-8	Pre-Monarchy	בני־ישראל[117]	Fearing other gods, walking according to the ways of the nations
9-12	Early Monarchy	בני־ישראל	High places, pillars, Asherim, high hills and green trees, like the nations before them
13-16	Middle Monarchy	ישראל ויהודה	Golden calves, Asherah, Baal
17	Assyrian Context		Child sacrifice, divination, omens
18		ישראל	
18-19		יהודה	
20		כל־זרע ישראל	Summary

The focus of the narrative initially is the בני־ישראל. Who is this group? It is a common phrase in Kings, occurring 32 times, but never refers to the Northern Kingdom. It can draw a distinction between the nation and its inhabitants (e.g., v. 22; 1 Kgs 12.17; 20.15); it can imply a distinction between ethnic Israelites and those who inhabit Israelite territory (e.g.,

---

114. This is often understood as a product of the redaction that sought to apply the lessons of the northern exile to a later time. See, e.g., Sweeney, *I & II Kings*, 391; Cogan and Tadmor, *2 Kings*, 207; Brettler, 'Ideology, History and Theology', 281–2.

115. The alternating focus on Israel and Judah is sometimes understood as a product of the redaction that sought to apply the lessons of the northern exile to a later time. See, e.g., Sweeney, *I & II Kings*, 391; Cogan and Tadmor, *2 Kings*, 207; Brettler, 'Ideology, History and Theology', 281–2.

116. See Lovell, 'A Text-Linguistics Approach to the Literary Structure and Coherence of 2 Kings 17:7-23', 228–31.

117. The nominal ומלכי ישראל in v. 8 is awkward but is probably glossed from 2 Kgs 16.3. See Burney, *Notes*, 332; Cogan and Tadmor, *2 Kings*, 204. Its retention would not impact my argument.

1 Kgs 9.20-22); or it can refer to the pre-monarchical people of Israel (e.g., 1 Kgs 8.9). In v. 7, the term 'children of Israel' (בני־ישראל) fits this pre-monarchical context well.[118] The language of idolatry used in vv. 7-8 seems to be drawn from Israel's wilderness and conquest traditions, and is infrequent in Kings. For example, Kings nearly always understands idolatry to be the result of the king's actions, who 'cause [the people] to sin' (*hifil* of חטא, e.g. 1 Kgs 14.16; 2 Kgs 21.16). However, this narrative ascribes sin to the people (בני־ישראל) which is common in pre-monarchic history (e.g., Lev. 4.2; 24.15; Num. 18.22; Judg. 10.10, 15; 1 Sam. 7.6).[119] Similarly, Kings has not used phrases such as 'fearing other gods' (v. 7), or 'walking according to the ways (חקים) of the nations' (v. 8). These seem to be drawn from Israel's wilderness traditions (Deut. 5.7; 6.13, 24; 10.12; 26.17; Lev. 18.3, 30; 20.23; see also 2 Kgs 17.37-38). As the narrative progresses, the descriptions of idolatry use phrases that we associate with elsewhere in Kings. The sins of vv. 9-12[120] are familiar from the early monarchic period, Rehoboam in particular, which is the only other place in Kings that ascribes idolatry to the people rather than the king (1 Kgs 14.22-24).[121]

In vv. 13-17 Israel and Judah together become the focus of this narrative. When used together in Kings, these labels always refer to the Northern and Southern Kingdoms.[122] The language of idolatry in these verses similarly shifts to what we have seen in the middle (vv. 13-16) and latter (v. 17) parts of Kings. Prophetic warnings (v. 13) against idolatry began with Jeroboam (v. 16), and are common in the Elijah–Elisha narratives. The gods Asherah and Baal (v. 16) enter the narrative of Kings with Asa and Ahab respectively (1 Kgs 15.13; 16.32). The sins of v. 17 are associated with Assyria (2 Kgs 16.3; 21.6).[123]

---

118. The title is used 506 times in the pre-monarchical traditions (Genesis–Judges) and only 134 times in the entire rest of the Old Testament.

119. So Rösel, 'Why 2 Kings 17 Does Not Constitute a Chapter of Reflection in the "Deuteronomistic History"', 87–8. Notably, Rehoboam's story is also the only place in Kings other than the present text which ascribes idolatry to the people rather than the king.

120. The verb of clause *e*, חפא, is a *hapax* with uncertain meaning. See Goldstein, 'A Suggestion', 393–407.

121. So Brettler ('Ideology, History and Theology', 272–3) who suggests this is a misplaced justification for the Babylonian exile.

122. It is often claimed that וביהודה in v. 13 is a later gloss, but there is no evidence on which to base this, and no need to maintain this in my reading of the text. See Lovell, 'A Text-Linguistics Approach to the Literary Structure and Coherence of 2 Kings 17:7-23', 230 n. 40.

123. See Cogan and Tadmor, *2 Kings*, 205–6; and Brettler, 'Ideology, History and Theology', 275–6.

Verses 18-19 then isolate Israel (v. 18) and Judah (v. 19), and then summarise the fate of 'every Israelite' (כל־זרע ישראל, v. 20). I have argued elsewhere that the term כל־זרע ישראל is best understood to refer to the people of Israel and Judah together.[124] This conclusion, then, draws a contrast between the two kingdoms who have both been rejected (מאס) and handed over to the plunderers (שסים) – Assyria (note also 2 Kgs 21.14). They began their journey into idolatry together as the children of Israel, but by the end Israel is removed and Judah is spared (שאר, v. 18).[125] Judah will be the remnant of Israel that survives the Assyrian crisis.

ii. *Judgment: The Assyrian Invasion*

Assyria comes upon both Israel and Judah in Kings because of their shared history of apostasy (2 Kgs 17.20).[126] As we saw with Jehu's rebellion, this judgment removes the idolatry that occasioned it without bringing closure to the wider issues of the narrative. The Northern Kingdom is destroyed in 2 Kings 17 (also 2 Kgs 18.9-12), but Judah has also been placed 'in the hand of the plunderers' (2 Kgs 17.20) and the story of the Assyrian invasion continues in 2 Kings 18–19. Assyria capture 'all the fortified cities of Judah' (2 Kgs 18.13) until eventually only a remnant of Judah remains (שאר, 2 Kgs 19.4). Isaiah responds in 2 Kgs 19.31 with the promise of a 'remnant' (שארית), and a 'band of survivors' (פליטה).

iii. *Deliverer: The Angel of Yahweh*

Yahweh responds with a saviour (וגנותי ... להושיעה, 2 Kgs 19.34), who delivers Jerusalem from the Assyrian threat, and Judah continues as the remnant of Israel (2 Kgs 21.14). What has motivated salvation on this occasion?

However tempting it may be to link Hezekiah's unusual faithfulness (2 Kgs 18.5)[127] to the salvation of Jerusalem,[128] this is not a connection

---

124. Lovell, 'A Text-Linguistics Approach to the Literary Structure and Coherence of 2 Kings 17:7-23', 230. On the difficulties of this phrase, see Nelson, *The Double Redaction of the Deuteronomistic History*, 56; and Provan, *Hezekiah and the Books of Kings*, 70. It occurs nowhere else in Kings, and only four times in the Old Testament (2 Kgs 17.20; Isa. 45.25; Jer. 31.37; Ps. 22.23) which cannot be determinative for its meaning here.

125. This anticipates 2 Kgs 18–19. See Sweeney (*King Josiah of Judah*, 82–4) who explores this connection.

126. See Chapter 3 on the presentation of Assyria in Kings.

127. See Chapter 6.

128. E.g. Bostock, *A Portrayal of Trust*, 159–65; Cohn, *2 Kings*, 138. Most interpretations of the salvation of Jerusalem are diachronic, placed within the pro-Zion Josianic layer; see, e.g., Nelson, 'The Anatomy of the Book of Kings', 41; Cogan

that the Hezekiah narrative draws. Language that relates deliverance (נצל) to faith (בטח) is prominent in 2 Kings 18–20 and is clustered in these chapters,[129] but Hezekiah's faith is not directly linked to the salvation of Jerusalem. The theme of trust neither accounts for the inclusion of these narratives in the history, nor the salvation of Jerusalem in the logic of the history.

David Bostock argues that the key is to note how this theme of trust in Yahweh is developed and contrasted with other potential saviours.[130] We have already seen in Chapter 3 that Assyria is presented as a rival saviour to Yahweh, with a rival covenant offer. In this way of reading, the issue of the narrative is not whether Hezekiah's faith can save, it is whether salvation comes from Yahweh or some other place. For example, Sennacherib's envoy, the Rab-Shakeh, makes several speeches to the inhabitants of Jerusalem and Hezekiah's representatives to persuade them to surrender (2 Kgs 18.19-25, 28-35; 19.10-13). During these speeches he continually asserts that Yahweh will neither be able to defend Jerusalem (e.g., 2 Kgs 18.33-35), nor be willing, even if he could (e.g., 2 Kgs 18.22, 25).[131] Bostock comments:

> The way in which בטח is used indicates that trust in YHWH is contrasted with other sources of supposed strength such as horses and other nations... [The] theme of a contest between YHWH and other gods [means that] the book might be understood as a polemic against the worship of gods other than YHWH... It is in connection with this theme that the Hezekiah narratives, especially as they give expression to the notion of trust, may be seen to fit into the book of Kings.[132]

---

and Tadmor, *2 Kings*, 239, 243; Hobbs, *2 Kings*, 283–4; Long, *2 Kings*, 202–3; and Sweeney, *I & II Kings*, 419.

129. Of the 19 instances of נצל and בטח within Kings, 18 occur in these chapters which are largely common to Kings and Isaiah (36–39). This suggests an Isaianic origin might be necessary to explain the language that is not typical of the Primary History; see, e.g., Olley, 'Trust in the Lord', 62–6; Nelson, 'The Anatomy of the Book of Kings', 47. Studies on Isaiah's use of Assyrian imperial rhetoric have suggested the same thing: see Aster, *Reflections of Empire in Isaiah 1–39*, 248. Robb Andrew Young (*Hezekiah in History and Tradition*, VTSup 155 [Leiden: Brill, 2017], 150) understands some but not all of the text as native to Isaiah. Bostock (*A Portrayal of Trust*, 1–11, 30–2, 149, 167–204) examines trust as a *Leitmotif* within the Hezekiah narrative of both books.

130. Bostock, *A Portrayal of Trust*, 167–204.

131. See Rudman, 'Is the Rabshakeh also Among the Prophets?'; Walsh, 'The Rab Šāqēh Between Rhetoric and Redaction'; Hyman, 'The Rabshakeh's Speech'.

132. Bostock, *A Portrayal of Trust*, 162.

Bostock's point is that the theme of trust in the Hezekiah narrative is developed not in connection with the Davidic *Leitmotif* and Zion,[133] but in connection with potential rival deities, alternative sources of security, and ways of life.[134] John Olley has argued something similar:

> There is nothing in the contexts of בטח that links it with either the Davidic covenant or a 'protection of Zion' theology. Overwhelmingly it is associated with...the worship of one God alone, who is incomparable and who is to be recognised as God by all nations... A link with the temple, Zion and the Davidic covenant is secondary. It is YHWH who is 'King'.[135]

This reading is correct. Even Hezekiah's introduction as a king unparalleled in faith is phrased (through fronting a prepositional phrase) so as to emphasise not the faith itself, but the object of that faith: 'It was in Yahweh the God of Israel that Hezekiah trusted...' (... ביהוה אלהי ישראל בטח, 2 Kgs 18.5). The salvation of Jerusalem is only ever explained by Yahweh's fidelity to David (2 Kgs 19.34; 20.6).[136]

Therefore, though Hezekiah proves faithful to Yahweh in the face of the Assyrian threat, his faith is vindicated rather than rewarded. As was the case with the Inner Kings narrative, the preservation of the remnant is understood to be a correlation of Yahweh's promises, not Israel's faithfulness. And so on the other side of judgment, Israel can once again be restored, free of the sin of Jeroboam (2 Kgs 19.29-31).[137]

4.3.3. *From Judah to Exile*

The final remnant narrative in Kings follows the same pattern that we have already seen twice, but remains incomplete at the end of the book. This allows the implied exilic reader to identify themselves with the remnant that is created in this narrative:

---

133. So also Nelson, 'The Anatomy of the Book of Kings'.
134. See also Olley, 'Trust in the Lord', 71.
135. Olley, 'Trust in the Lord', 71.
136. So Janzen, 'The Sins of Josiah and Hezekiah', 355-9 and McConville, '1 Kings VIII 46-53'.
137. The continued existence of either kingdom would suffice for the fulfilment some promises, but this is not true for the promise made to David (1 Kgs 8.25-26). Judah is not spared because of their greater fidelity (2 Kgs 17.19), but because of Yahweh's commitment to David (2 Kgs 8.19). This accounts for the asymmetry between Israel and Judah in the Assyrian crisis. See also Janzen, 'An Ambiguous Ending', 49–58.

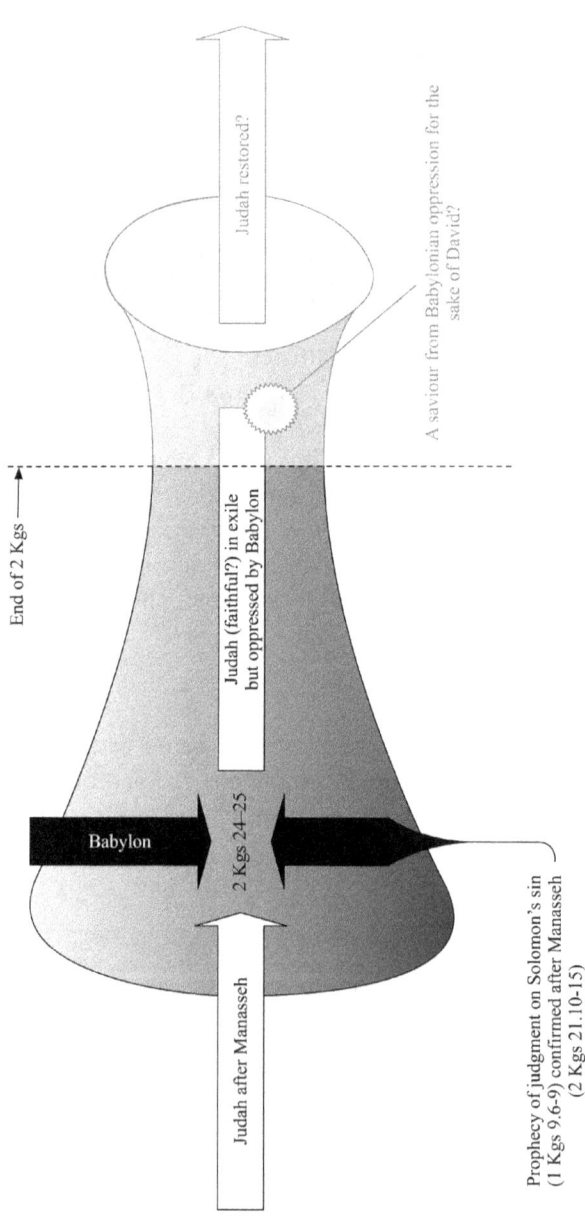

Figure 4.3. *The Judah to Exile Remnant Cycle*

The pattern of judgment and deliverance is now well established from both the Ahab and Jeroboam cycles. Judah in exile has been judged and now awaits a saviour.

i. *Sin and Prophecy: Solomon*
The original announcement of judgment, including destruction of the temple and exile, was conditional on Solomon's disobedience (1 Kgs 9.6-9). These conditions were met in 1 Kgs 11.1-8, which leads the reader to expect ultimate disaster even from this early point. The first unconditional prophecy of the end of Judah was given to Hezekiah, even before they were delivered from Assyria (2 Kgs 20.16-18),[138] confirmed under Manasseh (2 Kgs 21.12-15), and unchanged after Josiah's reforms (2 Kgs 22.16-20).[139]

ii. *Judgment: Babylonian Exile*
The prophecy of destruction is fulfilled in 2 Kings 24–25, and we will return in Chapter 5 to examine how this judgment is narrated. For now we should note that the book stops short of completing the pattern we have seen in the other remnant cycles, ending amid this judgment.[140]

Is there a remnant at the end of Kings or has Israel been destroyed by exile? The final chapters use remnant language for two different groups of people: the 'poorest people of the land', who are left behind by Babylon (שאר, 2 Kgs 24.14; 25.12, 22), as well as those taken to Babylon (שאר, יתר, 2 Kgs 21.14). However, the book only invests hope in the latter group; the narrative gives the impression that those who remained in the land (both 'small and great') eventually find themselves in Egypt (2 Kgs 25.26).[141] Not so, however, with the group taken into exile. In deuteronomic theology, exile does not dissolve all future hope of political identity (e.g., Deut. 4.29-31; 30.1-10), and this is also true within Kings (1 Kgs 8.46-53). Israel can be 'cut off from the land', as promised to Solomon (1 Kgs 9.7), but even when this happens, the book reserves hope for political reformation through those who survive (שאר, יתר, 2 Kgs 25.11).

The concept of a remnant, then, draws a line of continuity between Israel's pre-exilic polity and their hoped-for future. The community in Babylon has everything they need to reform Covenant-Israel when Yahweh sends a deliverer, because it is not only the remnant of the

---

138. 2 Kgs 20 is set chronologically prior to the events of 2 Kgs 18–19 (see 2 Kgs 20.6, 12).

139. We examined in Chapter 3 the reason why Manasseh is blamed for the exile in Kings.

140. On the ending of Kings, see Lovell, 'The Shape of Hope', 3–5; Janzen, 'An Ambiguous Ending', 351–2; Levenson, 'The Last Four Verses in Kings', 354–6; Murray, 'Of All the Years the Hopes – or Fears?' 263–5; Wolff, 'Kerygma', 93–7.

141. Roger S. Nam, '"The Poorest of the Land": Perception and Identity of the Remnant in 2 Kings and Jeremiah', *Journal of Religion and Society* 10 (2014): 61–9.

people who were taken to Babylon in the exile (2 Kgs 25.11). Rather, the narrator provides an extensive list (24.14-16), including the king (2 Kgs 24.12) who gains freedom by the end of the book (2 Kgs 25.27-30). The temple also, albeit in dismantled form, but including everything Solomon had made, ends the story in Babylon (2 Kgs 24.13; 25.13-17;[142] see also 1 Kgs 9.7). By the end of 2 Kings 'all Jerusalem' (כל־ירושלם, 2 Kgs 24.14) resides in Babylon: people, temple and king, which is a microcosm of everything essential to Israelite polity.[143] As with Jerusalem in Hezekiah's time (2 Kgs 19.30-31), the exilic community constitutes a seed which Yahweh might yet deliver and from which a new Israel might grow.

iii. *A Deliverer?*

The narrative pattern we have been examining has been repeated and interrupted by the ending of Kings, presumably because the compiler of the book is working from exilic context and does not know the future. The expectation that the pattern might repeat, however, constitutes a statement of hope. It provides the exilic Israelites with an understanding both of their connection with Israel in the past, and their relation to Covenant-Israel, which is their expected future. If history were to repeat itself, then several things should be expected:

1. Just as the Northern Kingdom was purged of Baal by the destruction of Ahab, and Jeroboam's influence was removed from Israel by the destruction of the Northern Kingdom, now the exile should result in the removal of all idolatry, which was Solomon's original sin. Kings expects repentance to precede restoration (1 Kgs 8.46-53). The remnant passing through exile should be the faithful remnant of the prophets.
2. Even once that occurs, Babylonian oppression would continue until Yahweh raised up a saviour to deliver them. The book of Kings knows nothing of 'Cyrus my [anointed] shepherd' (Isa. 44.28–45.1) who will eventually deliver Israel from Babylon, but the literary pattern we have observed anticipates him.
3. Israel should be restored so they might 'live in their homes as formerly' (2 Kgs 13.5), where the remnant might 'take root' in Jerusalem and Zion and 'bear fruit upward' (2 Kgs 19.30-31).

---

142. This list mirrors the list of (bronze) things that Solomon made for the temple in 1 Kgs 7.

143. So Leithart, *1&2 Kings*, 273–4; and Hobbs, *2 Kings*, 360.

4.4. Conclusions

The author of Kings faces several challenges in his construction of political identity for those in exile. His primary task, as we have seen in the previous chapter, is to imagine a political destiny for the exiles based on the covenantal traditions. This raises an issue of continuity. By what right does the exilic community lay claim to the covenant, when they have clearly broken it?

The book of Kings asserts that Covenant-Israel is a political ideal inherited by all whose ancestors Yahweh had rescued from Egypt, founded on Israel's shared pre-monarchical traditions. This remains true throughout the different periods of Israel's history, even after the dissolution of the Northern Kingdom. The united monarchy inherited the covenant, but failed to be covenantally shaped, showing that Israel can fail its ideals even in a Davidic golden age. After the division, neither the Northern Kingdom nor Judah were the exclusive heirs of the covenant, because the ideal required unity amongst all the sons of Jacob. Israel in exile is thus still Israel. The definition allows a partial inclusion of the other nations. Even though there is no hint that the nations can replace Israel as the covenantal people, they can be held to a covenantal standard and become 'fearers of Yahweh'.

The continuity between those who inherited the covenant, namely monarchic Israel, and those who broke it, namely exilic Israel, is provided through the concept of a remnant. The pattern is established in the Inner Kings narrative, in which Ahab and Jezebel's apostasy is judged so severely through Jehu and Hazael that Israel threatens to dissolve. However, Yahweh preserves a remnant, sends a saviour, and Israel is restored. The same pattern is then used to explain the dissolution of the Northern Kingdom. Assyria is Yahweh's judgment on Israel, where Judah becomes the remnant of Israel preserved in Jerusalem. Through an unfinished third repetition of the pattern, the exiles can then understand their own situation. Even if they are unable from this context to implement the ideal of Covenant-Israel, they are the seed from which it will be grown when Yahweh sends a saviour.[144]

---

144. We have seen the motif of purification in all of the remnant cycles. Kings, however, does not develop the thought of Deut. 30.6 that this kind of purification requires Yahweh to 'circumcise your heart'. This is an eschatological thought that suits the prophets better. E.g. Jer. 9.26; 24.7; 31.33; 32.39-41; Ezek. 3.7; 11.19; 36.26.

In Kings, such salvation is always from Yahweh (e.g., 1 Kgs 1.29), and never available from human kings (2 Kgs 5.6-7; 6.26-27; see also 2 Kgs 5.1). The saviour is sometimes angelic (e.g., 2 Kgs 19.35), and sometimes human, but in both cases an agent of Yahweh: '*Yahweh* saved them by the hand of Jeroboam' (ויושיעם [יהוה] ביד ירבעם, 2 Kgs 14.27). Yahweh's salvation now functions to preserve a seed, a microcosm of Israel, from which a new nation might emerge (2 Kgs 19.29-31). Thus the book is encouraging its readers to understand the exile as purposeful and restorative, and not simply retributive.

5

Land: Where Is Israel?

5.1. *The Political Significance of the Promised Land*

Land is a central concept in the construction and reflection on national identity.[1] As we noted in Chapter 1, land is more than just where people happen to live. Human connection to the land operates on many social levels: from personal rootedness, through community sustenance and legal jurisdiction, to the larger levels of national power and the construction of political identity.[2] Some of the concepts related to these connections are modern inventions – Anderson, for example, argued that the advent of modern cartography was necessary before nations could be imagined as 'sovereignty exercised within a bounded territory'.[3] But, as Smith demonstrates, the relationship between land and political identity has always existed in one form or another.[4] One example is the phenomenon of 'territorialization of memory':

---

1. Smith, *Chosen Peoples*, 131–8, 139–65; Leeman, *Political Church*, 117–18; Coakley, 'Mobilizing the Past', 552–3; Bartholomew, *Where Mortals Dwell*, 167–242.

2. David Storey, 'Land, Territory and Identity', in *Making Sense of Place: Multidisciplinary Perspectives*, ed. Ian Convery, Gerard Corsane, and Peter Davis (Suffolk: Boydell, 2012), 12–14, 14–17. See also John A. Anderson, 'Nationalist Ideology and Territory', in *Nationalism, Self-Determination and Political Geography*, ed. R. J. Johnston, D. Knight, and E. Kofman (London: Croom Helm, 1988), 18–39, and David Delaney, *Territory: A Short Introduction* (London: Blackwell, 2005).

3. Anderson (*Imagined Communities*, 174–81) explores how many pre-modern monarchies operated as polities with fixed centres but fuzzy boundaries. Democracies, he claims, require cartography and the census, because it is necessary to know whose vote counts and where it should be enforced.

4. Smith, *Chosen Peoples*, 131–3.

> This term refers to a process by which particular places evoke a series of memories, handed down through the generations, and it summarizes a tendency to root memories of persons and events in particular places and through them create a field or zone of powerful and peculiar attachments.[5]

Israel's patriarchal and deuteronomic traditions are full of these 'territorialized memories' of places. Israel, that is, the covenant ideal, is also a territorially bounded nation (e.g., Deut. 1.7-8; 11.24), because the promise of Yahweh specified its extent (e.g., Deut. 1.8; 6.10; 34.4). In deuteronomic tradition, Yahweh has apportioned other lands to other nations (e.g., Deut. 2.9; 32.8), and Israel's allotment is realised under Solomon (1 Kgs 4.21 [5.1, Heb.]).

Because of this, it is only within the land that the covenant can be properly enacted. Although Israel were given the commands at Sinai, much of Deuteronomy is focused on the future context of Canaan as the location of obedience (e.g., Deut. 11.31-32; 12.8-11). Frankel calls it the '"playing ground" where "biblical religion" is supposed to occur'.[6] Israel can only be Covenant-Israel from the context of the land.

The deuteronomic traditions also remember that Yahweh promised to select a place within Israel's territory and to set his own name there (Deut. 12.5, 11, 21; 14.23-24; 16.2, 6, 11; 18.22; 26.2). This too is realised under Solomon (1 Kgs 5.5 [5.19, Heb.]; 8.29, 35, 43), which creates a geographical centre to Israel's bounded territory.[7] From that time (e.g., 1 Kgs 3.2) Israel's worship of Yahweh is an issue of location. With worship come implications for political identity:[8] the 'symbols, memories, myths and traditions that form the distinctive heritage of the nation'[9] are all associated with what happens at the geographical centre of the land. Given all of this, it is the loss of land during the exile that most threatens Israel's political identity.

---

5. Smith, *Chosen Peoples*, 134.

6. Frankel, *The Land of Canaan and the Destiny of Israel*, 16.

7. The placement of a temple in ANE context creates a 'divinely ordered centre [in the] mythological universe'. Martti Nissinen, 'Prophets and Prophecy in Joshua–Kings: A Near Eastern Perspective', in Jacobs and Person Jr., eds., *Israelite Prophecy and the Deuteronomistic History*, 122.

8. O'Donovan (*The Desire of the Nations*, 43, 46–9) demonstrates how worshipping communities are political. Worship shapes community identity around a shared tradition and creates a focus of group loyalty.

9. Smith, *Chosen Peoples*, 24–5.

Nevertheless, the author of Kings does have several traditions on which to draw that do not rely on the promise of land. He might have, for example, made greater use of the pre-conquest era: 'A wandering Aramaean was my father...' (Deut. 26.1-11). If Israel began with a promise to a wanderer which became the hope of oppressed sojourners (e.g., Deut. 10.19), then the book of Kings might have been expected to create a new hope that Yahweh might do the same again (e.g., Deut. 4.25-31; 30.1-10).[10] However, the narrative never takes this path.[11]

Our task in this chapter, therefore, is to investigate what path the book does take. To what extent could the remnant in Babylon be Covenant-Israel, even in embryonic form, without the land? And, because there is a relationship between land and worship, is it even possible for the remnant to worship Yahweh from Babylon: 'How can we sing the song of Yahweh in a foreign land?' (Ps. 137.4). In order to do justice to these two questions, we shall need a third: what is the relationship between Yahweh and the land?

Daniel Block's study on ANE national theology provides a useful framework, since it investigates similar questions.[12] Block draws a triangle with the top vertex labelled 'deity' and the two across the bottom labelled 'people' and 'land', and then examines the relationship between these concepts within the context of ANE national ideologies:

> In the picture that emerges [of ANE political thought] it quickly becomes clear that, among other factors, the territorial and theological factors were viewed as critical throughout the region [of the ANE...]. The three-dimensional nature of the northwestern Semitic perspective may be illustrated by a triangle in which each of the members represents an apex: [deity, people, and land.] In this scheme of things each element is vital, not only because it is related to both of the other elements, but also because it has a significant bearing on the bond that unites the opposite members... Consequently, it is impossible to examine the relationship of a god and his/her subjects in isolation from the ties of both deity and population to the land.[13]

---

10. Similar to the 'new-exodus' theme prevalent especially in Isa. 40–55. E.g. H. M. Barstad, *A Way in the Wilderness: The 'Second Exodus' in the Message of Second Isaiah* (Manchester: University of Manchester Press, 1989).

11. As McConville ('1 Kings VIII 46–53', 67–79) notes, the theology of exile in 1 Kgs 8.46-53 seems to be consciously set against Deut. 30.1-10.

12. Block, *The Gods of the Nations*. Block recognises (pp. 19, 73) the anachronism of using the word 'nation'. See my discussion in Chapter 1.

13. Block, *The Gods of the Nations*, 20.

He argues that generally in ANE cultures the priority lies with the deity–land relationship.[14] That is, deities were not associated with specific people groups delineated along ethnographic lines, but were rather identified with particular territories. The only exception he discovers is the Hebrew Bible, which clearly prioritises the deity–people relationship.[15] As we noted, in deuteronomic thought Israel were God's people well before they reached the land: 'Has any God ever attempted to go and take a nation for himself from the midst of another nation…which Yahweh your God did for you in Egypt?' (Deut. 4.34). The answer, apparently, was 'No. Deities do not do that sort of thing.'

This chapter will confirm that Block's finding is also true of the historiography of Kings. The primary focus of political identity for Israel is presented in Kings as their relationship to Yahweh rather than the land. And this is important when the exilic context of the historiography is considered. The exile effectively, even if temporarily, severs the relationship between the people and the land, but it does not sever the relationship between the people and Yahweh. This creates the possibility of a genuine community focused on the worship of Yahweh from the context of exile, gathered around the prophetic ministry instead of the temple. The relationship between Yahweh and the land is nuanced. We shall see that in exile Yahweh's presence can still be found in the land. Since Yahweh does not abandon the land when the exile occurs, in an important sense a return to the land will also be a return to Yahweh's presence. This implies both the necessity of return, and the possibility of renewed covenant blessing.

5.2. *Centralisation of Worship in the Book of Kings*

Before we can begin to examine the general ideology of land in Kings, the first step will be to establish the narrative's position with regards to centralisation of worship. It has long been argued by the Harvard School of composition that this theme is one of the major factors giving rise to the pre-exilic composition of the book, because that version of the text was written to support Josiah's reforms.[16] The moral mandate for centralisation is provided by Deuteronomy 12, which is often thought

---

14. Block, *The Gods of the Nations*, 21–32. See also Cogan, *1 Kings*, 466.
15. Block, *The Gods of the Nations*, 25–32.
16. The literature was reviewed in Chapter 1. For overviews of the theme of centralisation of worship in Kings see particularly McConville, 'Law and Monarchy', 21–30; or Knoppers, *Two Nations Under God 2*, 121–40.

to have been composed at the same time.¹⁷ However, our interest is the exilic text, which is often overlooked in the discussion. To what extent does the exilic narrative continue to endorse centralisation, whether by intention or oversight? If, for example, Jerusalem remains the only valid centre of worship in the final form of the book, then how should the exilic community think about their faith?

Three clusters of material in Kings contribute to the centralisation motif: (1) the nature of Jeroboam's sin; (2) the way Kings interacts with the deuteronomic 'place where Yahweh will set his name'; and (3) the theme of decentralised shrines (במות).¹⁸

We have already done the necessary work for the first of these. In Chapter 4, I argued that in the exilic version of the book Jeroboam's sin consists in apostasy, not in breaking away from Judah and the temple. In other words, his sin is not one of decentralisation. Similarly, I concluded that the problem with his cult was not its location outside of Jerusalem.¹⁹ Rather, the text acknowledges that the separation from David imposes a real political problem on Jeroboam, but holds out the possibility that

---

17. The relationship between Deuteronomy and the 'book of the law' that Josiah finds (2 Kgs 22.8) is thus critical to the analysis of the literary history of the book. For an overview of recent approaches to this question see David Henige, 'Found but Not Lost: A Skeptical Note on the Document Discovered in the Temple under Josiah', *JHebS* 7 (2007): 5–8. A spectrum of positions from conservative to sceptical is represented by Provan, *1 & 2 Kings*, 271; Christof Hardmeier, 'King Josiah in the Climax of the Deuteronomic History (2 Kings 22–23) and the Pre-Deuteronomic Document of a Cult Reform at the Place of Residence (23.4-15): Criticism of Sources, Reconstruction of Literary Pre-Stages and the Theology of History in 2 Kings 22–23', in *Good Kings and Bad Kings*, ed. Lester L. Grabbe, LHBOTS 393 (New York: T&T Clark, 2007), 130, 135–6; Sweeney, *King Josiah of Judah*, 14–20; and Henige, 'Found but Not Lost', 15–16. On the 'pious fraud' theory, see A. J. Droge, 'The Lying Pens of the Scribes: Of Holy Books and Pious Frauds', *MTSR* 15 (2003): 117–47. The Göttingen School often attributes the origin of the centralisation theme, along with the text of Deut. 12, to the time of Josiah also; e.g. Timo Veijola, *Das fünfte Buch Mose: Kapitel 1,1–16,17*, ATD 8/1 (Göttingen: Vandenhoeck & Ruprecht, 2004), 1–3; Römer, *The So-Called Deuteronomistic History*, 3, 10, 49–55; and Thomas C. Römer, 'Transformations in Deuteronomistic and Biblical Historiography: On "Book-Finding" and Other Literary Strategies', *ZAW* 109 (1997): 1–11.

18. 'High place' is an unlikely translation of במה. I have chosen to render it as 'shrine' instead. The lexeme probably refers to sacred spaces in rural settings. Their frequent occurrence on hills lead to the LXX translation ὑψηλά and from that 'high place'. Note Jer. 32.35. See Humphrey H. Hardy II and Benjamin D. Thomas, 'Another Look at Biblical Hebrew bəmā "High Place"', *VT* 62 (2012): 175–88.

19. Cf. Sweeney, *King Josiah of Judah*, 175–7.

Jeroboam could have reigned over a kingdom like David's if he had been obedient to the covenant (1 Kgs 11.38). This implies the possibility of obedience to the covenant after separation from Judah. This is important for two reasons. First, because it shapes the way we understand Josiah, who is still portrayed as the solution to Jeroboam (1 Kgs 13.2), and we shall return to this below. Second, it suggests at an early point in the narrative of Kings that faithful worship of Yahweh can occur without the temple. This is a thought that becomes more explicit as the narrative of Kings progresses.

5.2.1. Name Theology, Sacrifice, and Prayer

The second motif contributing to the theology of centralisation in Kings is the way the book draws on name theology, which has been a standard component of Deuteronomistic thought.[20] Much of the scholarly literature on this motif is concerned with the extent to which Yahweh's actual presence is thought to be in the temple, and how Israel's belief may have changed over time.[21] The question revolves around the relationship between P (כבוד) and Dtr (שם) theologies of presence,[22] but here we shall focus particularly on the implications for centralisation of worship.

There is nothing in 1 Kings 8 that insists worship should be exclusive to the temple, but it is often deduced through the intertextuality with Deuteronomy 12. Solomon's prayer reveals the temple to be a 'place for Yahweh's name' (e.g., v. 29), and Deuteronomy 12 mandates that worship, or more accurately, sacrifice, should only occur in the place Yahweh will eventually choose to 'set his name' (e.g., Deut. 12.5, 11, 21). It follows for many, then, that the author – normally understood to be the

---

20. E.g., Weinfeld, *Deuteronomy and the Deuteronomic School*, 191–209; and Gerhard von Rad, *Studies in Deuteronomy*, trans. David M. G. Stalker, SBT (London: SCM, 1953), 37–44.

21. See J. Gordon McConville, 'God's "Name" and God's "Glory"', *TynB* 30 (1979): 149–63; Sandra L. Richter, *The Deuteronomistic History and the Name Theology: lešakkēn šemôšām in the Bible and the Ancient Near East* (New York: de Gruyter, 2002); and Tryggve N. D. Mettinger, *The Dethronement of Sabaoth: Studies in the Shem and Kabod Theologies*, Coniectanea biblica, Old Testament (Lund: C. W. K. Gleerup, 1982), esp. 38–79.

22. The Dtr 'name' section is vv. 12–53 and the 'glory' section sometimes ascribed to P is vv. 1–11. On the thematic unity of the chapter see Knoppers, 'Prayer and Propaganda', 233–9, and Walsh, *1 Kings*, 112 n. 9. On the question of a P redaction in 1 Kgs 8, see McKenzie, *The Trouble with Kings*, 138–40; Sweeney, *I & II Kings*, 130; Antony F. Campbell and Mark A. O'Brien, *Unfolding the Deuteronomistic History: Origins, Upgrades, Present Text* (Minneapolis, MN: Fortress, 2000), 349–50.

pre-exilic (Josianic) redactor at this point – believed that worship should be centralised at the temple.

We should begin by noticing that the two texts have different emphases.[23] Solomon's prayer, and the book of Kings more broadly, show a persistent emphasis on prayer as the proper use of the temple (פלל, 1 Kgs 8.30, 33, 35, 44, 48; 2 Kgs 19.15).[24] However, Deuteronomy 12 does not mention prayer, focusing instead on the issue of where sacrifice should be performed. This second issue, the location of sacrifice, is not taken up by Kings. Although Solomon does perform sacrifices at the temple (1 Kgs 8.1-5, 62-66; 9.25), Yahweh's name is not mentioned in those sections, and the book does not mention the temple in the context of sacrifice after that. The altar in Solomon's prayer is an ongoing place of justice rather than sacrifice (1 Kgs 8.31, see Exod. 22.11). Furthermore, there are legitimate sacrifices in Kings that are not performed at the temple (e.g., 1 Kgs 18.31-38), to which we return later in this chapter, and there are places where sacrifice might be expected but does not appear in the narrative, such as in relation to Josiah and Hezekiah. If the theology of Deuteronomy 12 stands behind the presentation of these king's reforms, then why does neither king offer sacrifice at the temple?[25]

It is probable that Deuteronomy and Kings are drawing on name theology for different reasons.[26] According to Block, Deuteronomy uses the 'place where Yahweh will choose to set his name' as a focal point of community: the imperatives in Deuteronomy 12 are 'go', 'gather', 'eat', and 'rejoice' (Deut. 12.7, 18).[27] With what is Yahweh's name associated in Kings?

---

23. Richter (*The Deuteronomistic History and the Name Theology*, 69–90) makes a similar observation to mine, that the two passages are textually not as close as many have supposed.

24. The MT locates Hezekiah's prayer in העיר התיכנה ('the middle city') but this is a textual corruption of חצר התיכנה ('middle court'), one of the courts of the temple structure. See Cogan and Tadmor, *2 Kings*, 254.

25. So Knoppers, 'Prayer and Propaganda', 231.

26. A common explanation has been to propose that Deut. 12 draws on early sacrificial traditions and 1 Kgs 8 'demythologises' or 'spiritualises' Israel's temple by focusing on prayer. Weinfeld, *Deuteronomy and the Deuteronomic School*, 191–243; Moshe Weinfeld, 'Deuteronomy's Theological Revolution', *BR* 12 (1996): 38–41, 44. See, e.g., Y. Kaufmann, *The Religion of Israel from Its Beginnings to the Babylonian Exile* (Chicago, IL: University of Chicago Press, 1960), 269; Noth, *The Deuteronomistic History*, 93–5; Martin Noth, *Könige*, BKAT (Neukirchen-Vluyn: Neukirchener Verlag des Erziehungsvereins, 1968), 168–93.

27. Block, 'The Joy of Worship', 143–9.

In the speeches of Solomon (1 Kgs 8.12-53),[28] name theology is linked to prayer (e.g., v. 29) and revelation of Yahweh amongst the nations (v. 43). It is also linked to the fulfilment of the Davidic promise. Solomon's second speech (vv. 15-21), which we already examined in Chapter 3,[29] repeats the idea of building (בנה) a house (בית) for God's name six times (vv. 16, 17, 18, 19 [×2], 20). This language is familiar only from 2 Sam. 7.13: 'He shall build a house for my name (ובנה־בית לשמי), and I will establish the throne of his kingdom forever'. In both 2 Samuel 7 and 1 Kings 8 the temple is built to house the ark (2 Sam. 7.2; 1 Kgs 8.1-9), which is called by the name 'Yahweh' in both books (see esp. 2 Sam. 6.2) but never in Deuteronomy where it is only ever the Ark of the Covenant (Deut. 10.8; 31.9, 25-26). It is 2 Samuel 7, more than Deuteronomy 12, that lies in the background of most of the name theology in the book of Kings (e.g., 1 Kgs 5.3-5 [5.17-19, Heb.]). Sandra Richter calls the Davidic promise the 'catalyst for name theology in Kings', commenting:

> [Solomon's] dedicatory prayer makes it clear that the [temple] is the ultimate symbol of Yhwh's past and present relationship with his people – a symbol which serves to memorialise and perpetuate Yhwh's acts of redemption in the midst of Israel *and* the nations. The reputation (*šēm*) of Yhwh, about which David was so concerned in 2 Samuel 7, has found its memorial in the temple.[30]

That is not to deny a place to Deuteronomy in the rest of Kings. Deuteronomy uses a different cluster of terms than 2 Samuel 7, speaking of a place (מקום) Yahweh chooses (בחר) to set (שים) his name. This language arises in Kings on four occasions (1 Kgs 11.36; 14.21; 2 Kgs 21.4-7; 23.27), each time referring to Jerusalem rather than the temple. Manasseh's account shows this is not coincidental. The text accuses him of building altars to foreign gods in the temple, but still uses name theology with reference to Jerusalem: 'And he built altars in the house of the Lord, of which the Lord had said, "In Jerusalem will I put my name"' (2 Kgs 21.4).

There is only one text in Kings that associates the temple with Deuteronomy 12-style name theology that would imply centralisation (1 Kgs 3.2), and we shall examine this in the section below. There is one other that associates Yahweh's name with sacrifice (1 Kgs 18.24), but this does not occur at the temple and we shall return to this below as well. These two texts aside, there is very little evidence for centralisation so far. Kings affirms that the temple is suitable for these activities because it was

---

28. On the syntactic structure of 1 Kgs 8 delineated by Solomon's speeches, see Sweeney, *I & II Kings*, 129.

29. See also Knoppers, 'Prayer and Propaganda', 233–9.

30. Richter, *The Deuteronomistic History and the Name Theology*, 90.

built for Yahweh's name. For the same reason the temple is the fulfilment of what was promised to David. Kings also affirms that Jerusalem was chosen by Yahweh as a place for his name. However, all of this stops short of affirming the exclusivity of worship to those places.

5.2.2. *The Shrine (במות) Theme: Yahweh or Apostasy*

The third motif contributing to the theology of centralisation in Kings is the shrine (במות) theme. This theme, too, has played an integral part in the reconstruction of the literary history of the book and a Josianic edition carrying the theme of centralised worship.[31] The argument runs thus: before Josiah, worship at the shrines was the norm practised in Israel (e.g., 1 Sam. 9.12-13). However, Josiah's agenda of centralisation required an *apologia* for temple-exclusive worship, and so the theme has been retrospectively incorporated into Israel's history by Dtr. After the temple is constructed (1 Kgs 3.2), the narrator rebukes otherwise good kings who do not remove these alternate places of worship (Asa, 1 Kgs 15.14; Jehoshaphat, 1 Kgs 22.43 [22.44, Heb.]; J(eh)oash, 2 Kgs 12.3; Amaziah, 2 Kgs 14.4; Azariah, 2 Kgs 15.4; Jotham, 2 Kgs 15.35). The motif disappears from the narrative after Josiah removes the shrines (2 Kgs 23.19-20), and so Josiah is presented as the solution to Solomon's and Jeroboam's sin of constructing them (1 Kgs 11.7; 12.31).[32]

Our question is not the accuracy of this historical reconstruction, but how the narrative of Kings makes sense of the shrine theme. When the otherwise good kings are being rebuked for their failure to remove the shrines, does the narrative encourage its readers to understand this as neglect of the law of centralisation, or as permitting the worship of foreign gods? How would the exilic audience have understood the text?

As with other traditions from Samuel, Kings presupposes that its readers are familiar with stories that associate shrines with Samuel (e.g., 1 Sam. 9.11-26), Saul (e.g., 1 Sam. 10.5-13), and David (e.g., 2 Sam. 1.25; 22.34). The author of Kings provides a rationale that excuses them from obedience to the altar law, on the basis that the temple has not yet been built.[33]

---

31. See, e.g., Provan, *Hezekiah and the Books of Kings*, 55–90; Wissmann, 'He Did What Was Right', 247.

32. Norbert Lohfink, 'The Cult Reform of Josiah of Judah: 2 Kings 22–23 as a Source for the History of Israelite Religion', in *Ancient Israelite Religion: Essays in Honor of Frank Moore Cross*, ed. J. M. Miller, P. D. Hanson, and S. D. McBride (Philadelphia, PA: Fortress, 1987), 459–75.

33. Cogan, *1 Kings*, 184. Note that even though the author of Kings thought such a note necessary, the author of Samuel apparently did not. No equivalent note in that book exonerates Samuel in the same situation (1 Sam. 9.12-25).

> The people were sacrificing at the shrines, however, because no house had yet been built for the name of the Lord. (1 Kgs 3.2)[34]

This also excuses Solomon who, in context, is on his way to a shrine at Gibeah (1 Kgs 3.4). The reminder, however, performs a second function. There is good reason to suspect that an exilic reader's initial interpretation of the shrines would have been apostasy,[35] rather than decentralisation, and so the author of Kings wanted to remind them that there was a time in Israel's history when shrines were a legitimate place for Yahwistic worship.

The link between shrines and apostasy is strong both in Kings and other exilic literature, and so without 1 Kgs 3.2, an exilic audience may have simply assumed Gibeah was an apostate shrine too. As early as Solomon, they become associated with foreign gods in the south (1 Kgs 11.7; 14.23) and with Jeroboam's cult in the north (1 Kgs 12.31). We found in Chapter 3 that Jeroboam's sin is presented as one of apostasy, rather than decentralisation. The association between shrines and apostasy is strengthened by the note that Ahaz used them for child sacrifice (2 Kgs 16.3-4), by their close proximity to the Asherah, foreign worship, cult prostitution, and idolatry (e.g., 1 Kgs 14.23-24; 2 Kgs 17.10-12), and by the note about the syncretism of the repopulated northern territory (2 Kgs 17.32-33). When Hezekiah tears the shrines down, the text is not making a point about centralisation. By that stage of the narrative they are associated with the Nehushtan and other problematic objects (2 Kgs 18.4). However, even if the association between shrines and apostasy had not come from the narrative of Kings, the exilic readers may have picked it up from their wider cultural milieu (e.g., Deut. 12.1-5; Jer. 7.31; 19.5; 32.35; 48.35; Ezek. 6.3-6; 20.29).[36]

Because of this, the note to the reader in 1 Kgs 3.2 serves a double function to the exilic audience. First, it reminds its readers that the temple was not always available, and so the law of centralisation did not

---

34. The combination of name theology with the mention of the shrines in this verse creates a definite allusion to Deut. 12. See Sweeney, *I & II Kings*, 78–9.

35. On the exilic understanding of the term, see De Vries, *1 Kings*, xxviii; and Cogan, *1 Kings*, 185. Even some modern commentators understand the word to entail syncretism; e.g. Montgomery, *A Critical and Exegetical Commentary on the Books of Kings*, 103, 268, 468; Gray, *I and II Kings*, 120.

36. The translators of the LXX made a distinction. When used for orthodox worship (i.e. in association with Samuel, Saul, David, or Solomon), they transliterate במות as βαμά. In cases where they are used for worship of other gods, a variety of other words are used, often ὑψηλὰ. See J. T. Whitney, "Bamoth' in the Old Testament', *TynB* 30 (1979): 127 n. 11.

always apply.[37] This exonerates Solomon's sacrifice at Gibeah. Second, it reassures its readers that worship at shrines was not automatically a matter of apostasy. It was permissible to worship Yahweh at the shrines when the temple was not available, as had been done prior to this point of Israel's history. This would not violate the law of centralisation if worship was possible at the temple.

There are examples in Kings of worship that occurs outside of Jerusalem, but is nevertheless considered orthodox (i.e. covenantal). The most prominent of these is Elijah's sacrifice at Carmel, which happens at the 'time for sacrifice' (1 Kgs 18.29), at the 'altar of Yahweh', and where Elijah 'calls on the name of Yahweh' (1 Kgs 18.24).[38] Just prior to this sacrifice, Elijah's complaint had been that Israel had forsaken the covenant through the very act of tearing down Yahweh's altars:

> He said, 'I have been very jealous for the Lord, the God of hosts. For the people of Israel have forsaken your covenant, thrown down your altars, and killed your prophets with the sword...' (1 Kgs 19.10, see v. 14)

There is no hint of Jerusalem in any of these texts, and neither is Elijah portrayed as advocating a non-covenantal form of Yahwism. Rather, the exilic author of the book sees no contradiction.[39] The law of centralisation is not intended to be understood in an absolute sense in the final form of Kings. Since it was not feasible for Elijah to drag Ahab and the prophets of Baal to Jerusalem, 1 Kgs 3.2 exonerates Elijah as well.

The shrine theme climaxes in Josiah's reforms. Josiah explicitly destroys the shrines constructed by Solomon (2 Kgs 23.13), Jeroboam (v. 15), and the other northern kings (v. 19). The narrative portrays some of these shrines as orthodox, like Elijah's. The shrines Josiah finds in Jerusalem's vicinity are clearly associated with apostasy (vv. 4-7) and so Josiah kills their priests along with the priests of Jeroboam's shrines (vv. 5, 20). He does not do this with the shrines he finds from Geba

---

37. Early commentators explored situations in which Deut. 12 may have been suspended, or the extent to which it was temporary; see Whitney, '"Bamoth" in the Old Testament', 125–30; and Cogan, *1 Kings*, 442.

38. We will return below to the extensive parallels between Elijah's sacrifice and temple worship, but see Nicholas P. Lunn, 'Prophetic Representations of the Divine Presence: The Theological Interpretation of the Elijah–Elisha Cycles', *JTI* 9 (2015): 50–2.

39. The contradiction that critical scholarship has detected assigns these texts to non-Dtr editors or explains them as Dtr's reluctant fidelity to inconvenient source material. See, e.g., McKenzie, *The Trouble with Kings*, 81–100; Knoppers, *Two Nations Under God 2*, 229–54.

to Beersheba (vv. 8-9).⁴⁰ The priests associated with these shrines are returned to Jerusalem unharmed and permitted to re-join their brothers, suffering only exclusion from temple duties (v. 9). The narrative does not intend its readers to understand worship at every shrine as apostasy, or these priests would have been killed also. The shrines from Geba to Beersheba are Yahwistic. Josiah's reforms therefore deal with both shrine-problems: shrines where other gods are worshipped are destroyed, as are their priests; shrines where Yahweh is worshipped are centralised, as are their priests.⁴¹

Some historical questions remain,⁴² but the narrative portrayal of the shrine theme is consistent. In practice, shrines could be used to worship any god, and worshipping any god but Yahweh was apostasy. Once the temple becomes available, the law of centralisation (Deut. 12) demands that only the temple should be used for sacrifice (1 Kgs 3.2). However, on occasions when the temple is unavailable, orthodox Yahwism can be practised at the shrines without violating the law of centralisation.

2.3. *Centralisation of Worship: Summary*

The theme of centralisation of worship has played a prominent part in the critical discussion of Dtr literature, but it has been our purpose to discover what the exilic narrative of Kings advocates. The temple and Jerusalem are both portrayed as places where Yahweh's name dwells, but the book does not conclude from this that worship should be exclusive to that location. There are no instances of worship in Kings that are portrayed as apostate simply because they were not done in Jerusalem. This includes Jeroboam's, which is condemned only for apostasy, not for decentralisation. Kings does affirm the law of centralisation now found in Deuteronomy 12: once the temple becomes available, it should be used

---

40. On the relationship of these verses and Deut. 12, see Christoph Uehlinger, 'Was there a Cult Reform under King Josiah? The Case for a Well-Grounded Minimum', in Grabbe, ed., *Good Kings and Bad Kings*, 279–316; or Lohfink, 'The Cult Reform of Josiah of Judah', 466. On Deut. 18.6-8, see Ernest W. Nicholson, 'Josiah and the Priests of the High Places (II Reg 23,8a.9)', *ZAW* 119 (2007): 501–3.

41. This is the majority reading. See Cogan and Tadmor, *2 Kings*, 286–7; Hobbs, *2 Kings*, 334. Nicholson's alternative reading of the syntax ('Josiah and the Priests of the High Places', 503–5; 'Once Again Josiah and the Priests of the High Places (II Reg 23,8a.9)', *ZAW* 124 [2012]: 358–63) proposes that the priests do not go to Jerusalem, in which case this text knows nothing of centralisation. He hypothesises an exilic provenance instead.

42. What was the nature of worship at the shrines during Israel's monarchic period? And how extensive were Josiah's reforms? Lohfink, 'The Cult Reform of Josiah of Judah'.

(at least for sacrifice). Accordingly, Josiah's reforms are portrayed as centralising a distributed orthodox worship of Yahweh back to Jerusalem. However, in the case when the temple is unavailable, worship of Yahweh remains possible at other places. This includes calling on Yahweh's name, as Elijah does on Carmel. The message of Kings to the exilic audience who have no temple is clear: covenantal Yahwism is still possible from this context, even though it would be better to have the temple.

5.3. *Israel's Relationship to the Land: The Status of the Land during the Exile*

We return now to Block's geographical–theology triangle, to examine the relationship between Israel and the land in the book of Kings. The original readers of this work understood their own situation to result from the history of land loss that the book narrates. Given that the land is inseparable from the covenant, it would seem to follow that the ideal of Covenant-Israel is entirely lost without it.

However, we have already discovered much in Kings that indicates the opposite. The idea of the remnant in the book encouraged the exiles to understand themselves as Covenant-Israel, in embryonic form, awaiting a restoration. In the centralisation theology of the book we have already discovered a hint of that which we will develop here: that genuine relationship with Yahweh is possible without the land. So we shall see that the land is still required for fulfilment of everything Yahweh has promised, but not required for hope. The book of Kings does portray Israel's relationship to the land as severed by exile, but in doing so it also re-defines the concept of land to help its readers to integrate the possibility of hope and restoration.

5.3.1. *The 'Empty Land' Motif and Land Ideology*

How does the book of Kings understand the status of the land during the exile? In one way this is an unusual question. The issue has normally been addressed by scholarship more broadly than from the point of view of any single book. Scholars have argued that Israel's exilic works – Jeremiah and Ezekiel mainly – regard the land as empty at the end of Judah's occupancy.[43] This 'empty land' motif portrays the Babylonian exile as

---

43. Christoph Levin, *Die Verheißung des neuen Bundes in ihrem theologiegeschichtlichen Zusammenhang ausgelegt*, FRLANT 29 (Göttingen: Vandenhoeck & Ruprecht, 1985), 165–9, 200–209. See also Karl-Friedrich Pohlmann, *Studien zum Jeremiabuch: Ein Beitrag zur Frage nach der Entstehung des Jeremiabuches*, FRLANT 118 (Göttingen: Vandenhoeck & Ruprecht, 1978), 193–1; Pohlmann,

the complete removal of all orthodox Yahwism from Judah, such that the remaining inhabitants are theologically inconsequential.[44] Christoph Levin, for example, claims that these works 'settle the question of who was authorised to represent the Jewish tradition legitimately in the Persian period'.[45] A history that represented the land as vacated by the exile served the interests of the returning Babylonian community.

Levin's recent work integrates the narrative of Kings into this wider argument.[46] Although Kings makes no direct observation regarding the status of the land after the conquest, Levin detects a hint in the literary history behind 2 Kings 24–25 that agrees with the consensus.[47] He claims, for example, that in the records of the first deportation (2 Kgs 24.8-17) the important Judahites are removed to Babylon,[48] but the records of the second deportation (2 Kgs 25.1-21) have been edited to avoid giving the same impression:[49]

> Significantly, for the second deportation no destination is given. The deportees are not thought to have joined the community of the first golah that went to Babylon with Jehoiachin, but to be spread amongst the nations like the inhabitants of Samaria. From now on, the true Judah is to be found exclusively among the exiles of 597... The author declares the Judeans who have remained in Palestine to be simply non-existent.[50]

Ezechielstudien: Zur Redaktiongeschichte des Buches und zur Frage nach den ältesten Texten, BZAW 478 (Berlin: de Gruyter, 1992); and Hermann Joseph Stipp, *Jeremia im Parteienstreit: Studien zur Textentwicklung von Jer 26:36–43 und 45 als Beitrag zur Geschichte Jeremias, seines Buches und judäischer Pareien im 6. Jahrhundert*, BBB 82 (Frankfurt: Anton Hain, 1992), 278–84. For further references see Levin's brief literature review, 'The Empty Land in Kings', 62. Contrast Jakob Wöhrle, 'The Un-Empty Land: The Concept of Exile and Land in P', in Ben Zvi and Levin, eds., *The Concept of Exile in Ancient Israel and its Historical Contexts*, 189–206, for the later view of P.

44. Often, scholars see this as contrary to historical fact in which a significant proportion of Judah is thought to have remained behind. E.g. Robert P. Carroll, 'The Myth of the Empty Land', *Semeia* 59 (1992): 79–93.

45. Levin, 'The Empty Land in Kings', 62.

46. Levin, 'The Empty Land in Kings'.

47. Levin's analysis ('The Empty Land in Kings', 88–9) is diachronic, and he does not ascribe these all to the same revision of the book. In his analysis Kings was originally ambiguous as to the status of the land during the exile and the ideology of land as empty was progressively introduced through a series of exilic redactions.

48. Levin, 'The Empty Land in Kings', 63–70.

49. Note Jer. 52.28-30 does list deportees from this event.

50. Levin, 'The Empty Land in Kings', 81, 84–5.

For Levin, the demise of Zedekiah and the exile of Jehoiachin fits this pattern as well. Judah's king had been relocated to Babylon in the first deportation, and the later editors give the impression that only Jehoiachin remains of the Davidic line. Contrast this with the fate of Zedekiah's sons, whose deaths emptied the land of the Davidic line who remained behind, or Gedaliah's murder, which serves to de-theologise the remaining 'poorest of the land', rendering them unimportant.[51]

Many of Levin's observations are plausible, but his argument is diachronic and relies on incomplete evidence of the book's literary history. His literary reconstruction allows him to find the same 'empty land' theology in Kings that is well recognised in Jeremiah and Ezekiel, but should we necessarily expect this?[52]

Habel's *The Land Is Mine*[53] enumerates six ideologies of land in the Old Testament, each of which summarises a broad conception of the way the people relate to land. He labels these ideological approaches: *royal, theocratic, prophetic, ancestral, agrarian,* and *immigrant*. In general, these can be distinguished easily by their distinctive use of 'inheritance' (נחלה).[54] A brief summary will be useful:

1. The *royal* ideology understands the land as the source of royal wealth and power, an inheritance (נחלה) granted by Yahweh to his chosen king, which expanded over time to embrace the entire Earth (e.g., Ps. 2.8).[55]

---

51. Levin, 'The Empty Land in Kings', 82–5.
52. See also Cogan and Tadmor, *2 Kings*, 327.
53. Habel, *The Land Is Mine*. Other ideological analyses are similar. E.g. Gerhard von Rad, 'The Promised Land and Yahweh's Land in the Hexateuch', in *The Problem of the Hexateuch and Other Essays* (London: SCM, 1984), 79–93. Wright, *God's People in God's Land*, 1–9; and Eryl W. Davies, 'Land: Its Rights and Privileges', in *The World of Ancient Israel: Sociological, Anthropological and Political Perspectives*, ed. R. E. Clements (Cambridge: Cambridge University Press, 1989), 349–69. Various dissertations have explored this idea also, e.g., W. Malcolm Clark, 'The Origin and Development of the Land Promise Theme in the Old Testament' (Ph.D. diss., Yale, 1964); Herbert S. Bess, 'Systems of Land Tenure in Ancient Israel' (Ph.D. diss., University of Michigan, 1963); Arthur Mason Brown, 'The Concept of Inheritance in the Old Testament' (Ph.D. diss., Columbia University, 1965).
54. The word נחלה is not easily translatable, and scholars debate whether it is primarily territorial inheritance (e.g., Wright, *God's People in God's Land*, 19 n. 29; von Rad, 'Promised Land', 19–20; and Brown, *The Concept of Inheritance in the Old Testament*) or feudal entitlement (e.g., Habel, *The Land Is Mine*, 33–5; *NIDOTTE*, s.v. 'נָחַל'). This discussion does not impact my argument.
55. Habel, *The Land Is Mine*, 17–34.

2. The *theocratic* ideology understands the land as Yahweh's undeserved gift to all Israel as an inheritance (נחלה) conditional on covenantal obedience.[56] Obedience guaranteed not only continued habitation but also ongoing blessing within the land (e.g., Deut. 28.4-6). Disobedience resulted in removal from the land as divine punishment.
3. The *prophetic* ideology understands the land as Yahweh's inheritance (נחלה, e.g. Jer. 2.7). It considers the land as virgin territory before the conquest, and Israel's sin as pollution (e.g., Jer. 16.18). The land itself is personified, suffers and is redeemed.[57]
4. The *agrarian* ideology does not use inheritance (נחלה), preferring categories often assigned to Priestly literature like Jubilee (Lev. 25.10-54) and the Sabbath of exile (Lev. 26.34).[58]
5. The *immigrant* ideology is found within the patriarchal traditions, where the land is a host to foreigners. Although it involves the future hope of inheritance (נחלה), it emphasises peaceful relations with the nations in the meantime.[59]
6. The *ancestral* ideology is related to the theocratic ideology but is primarily found in Joshua.[60] Where Deuteronomy, for example, is concerned with Israel as a united people, the ancestral ideology is concerned with the tribal allotments that focus on families and clans in which Joshua becomes the leader of an ideal 'household' (e.g., Josh. 24.15).

Each ideology would answer the question of the status of the land from a different perspective. The agrarian ideology, for example, understands the land to be in Sabbath during exile, recovering from Israel's misuse (Lev. 26.34). In the prophetic schema, Jeremiah's redemption of the field of Anathoth is an explicit indication of hope for future habitation in a way that is continuous with Israel's pre-exilic land rights (Jer. 32.8). And the theocratic ideology envisages not only post-exilic restoration but also that renewed national prosperity would exceed the former times (e.g., Deut. 30.5).

---

56. Habel, *The Land Is Mine*, 36–53. See also von Rad, 'Promised Land', 19–20.
57. Habel, *The Land Is Mine*, 75–96. See also Block (*The Gods of the Nations*, 113–48), who understands the exile through the motif of divine abandonment common in the prophetic literature (e.g., Jer. 14.10).
58. See von Rad, 'Promised Land', 79–93.
59. Habel, *The Land Is Mine*, 115–32.
60. Habel, *The Land Is Mine*, 54–74.

What is the overall position of the book of Kings? The actual term נחלה, as well as words frequently associated with it such as ירשה and הלק, are surprisingly infrequent in Kings, but the overall position of the narrative is easy to identify as theocratic. The ideology of conditional grant and disciplinary retribution is explicit in the major speeches that look forward to the exile (e.g., 1 Kgs 8.46-51; 9.6-9; 2 Kgs 17.7-24), as is the assertion that the Canaanite nations were dispossessed of the land so that Israel might possess (ירש) it (e.g., 1 Kgs 21.19; 2 Kgs 16.3; 17.8; 21.2). The two passages in the book that directly utilise the root נחל are theocratic. In Solomon's prayer (1 Kgs 8) the land properly belongs to Yahweh (ארצך, e.g. v. 36) but is given to Israel as their inheritance (נחלה, v. 36). The language is also present in the story of Naboth when he refused to sell his inheritance (נחלה) to Ahab (1 Kgs 21.3, 4), so Jezebel 'possessed' it (ירש, vv. 15, 16, 18, 19).

Although Habel draws extensively from the Solomon narratives (1 Kgs 3–10) to demonstrate royal ideology,[61] Kings is not explicitly royal. It is true that in 1 Kings 4 the land is the King's source of wealth and power (e.g., 1 Kgs 4.1, 7) that expands over time to embrace the earth (e.g., 1 Kgs 4.24 [5.4, Heb.]). However, Kings never portrays the land as Yahweh's gift to Solomon. It is only ever given to Israel (e.g., 1 Kgs 8.34, 40, 48; 14.15; 2 Kgs 21.8).

Importantly, there is never any sign of prophetic land ideology in Kings, which we would expect if Levin's reconstruction of the prophetic 'empty land' motif in Kings were accurate. Israel, and not the land, is Yahweh's inheritance in Kings (e.g., 1 Kgs 8.51, 53). The land was not *terra nullius* prior to the exile in Kings (contrast, e.g., 1 Kgs 14.24 with Jer. 2.7 or 3.19), and there is no explicit hope of post-exilic territorial continuity.[62] We must take care not to simply assume that Kings will make precisely the same point as the prophets.[63] In fact, a synchronic reading of 2 Kings 24–25 yields a more nuanced view that is also consistent with the wider narrative in Kings.

---

61. Habel, *The Land Is Mine*, 17–34.
62. Bodner (*The Theology of the Book of Kings*, 152) notes that the Shunammite woman has land returned to her after her 'exile' might be suggestive in exilic context (2 Kgs 8.1-6).
63. Neither does Kings make the same point as Deuteronomy, as McConville notes ('1 Kings VIII 46-53', 71, 79).

5.3.2. Land, City, and Temple: 2 Kings 24–25

The narrative of exile in 2 Kings 24–25 has received little scholarly attention in contrast to the Josiah (2 Kgs 22–23) and Jehoiachin (2 Kgs 25.27-30) narratives that enclose it. Given that the regular progression of regnal formulae breaks down in this section,[64] many have assumed it to be an appendix to the history, created by the (often thought careless) exilic Dtr to update what he found in Dtr_1.[65] Terrence Fretheim calls these chapters '[a] relentless litany of one thing after another being destroyed and removed'.[66]

Even though they may be a later addition, these chapters are not as careless or 'relentless' as we might suppose, and their significance for the theology of exile in the book is often overlooked. As Robert Cohn notes, there is a neat two-stage symmetry of exile present in these chapters,[67] which does not correspond to the two historical invasions of Babylon in 597/8 and 586/7.[68]

The two-stage structure of these chapters forms a narrative of progressive loss, highlighting first the role of Egypt, and then the role of Babylon in the loss of the land:

Table 5.1. *The Two-Stage Exile of 2 Kings 24–25*

The structure of the final chapters of Kings reveals a parallel between Egyptian and Babylonian invasions. Where Egypt takes the 'land', Babylon takes 'Jerusalem'.

2 Kgs 23.31–24.7 – Egyptian Exile	2 Kgs 24.8–25.7 – Babylonian Exile
Jehoahaz reigns for 3 months	Jehoiachin reigns for 3 months
Jehoahaz imprisoned by Pharaoh	Jehoiachin imprisoned by Nebuchadnezzar
Pharaoh installs Eliakim on the throne and names him Jehoiakim	Nebuchadnezzar installs Mattaniah on the throne and names him Zedekiah
Pharaoh takes Jehoahaz to Egypt	Nebuchadnezzar takes Jehoiachin to Babylon
Jehoiakim reigns 11 years	Zedekiah reigns 11 years
Jehoiakim rebels against Nebuchadnezzar	Zedekiah rebels against Nebuchadnezzar
God sends attackers	God sends attackers

---

64. See Chapter 2 and also Cohn, 'The Literary Structure of Kings', 108–9; Halpern and Lemaire, 'The Composition of Kings', 131–2; and Provan, *Hezekiah and the Books of Kings*, 33–56.

65. Cross, *Canaanite Myth and Hebrew Epic*, 285–9; McKenzie, *The Trouble with Kings*, 135–46.

66. Fretheim, *First and Second Kings*, 223.

67. Cohn, *2 Kings*, 163–4; see also Leithart, *1&2 Kings*, 273–4.

68. Both of these invasions are reported in the second stage of the narrative.

The first stage narrates the loss of 'land' (ארץ) to Egypt. Even though Israel remain in the land after their submission to Egypt, executive control of the land is lost, as Pharaoh Neco is able to 'tax the land' (ויתן־ענש על־הארץ, 2 Kgs 23.33) and to 'exact silver and gold from the people of the land' through his proxy king, Jehoiakim (2 Kgs 23.35). By the close of the Egyptian cycle, Egypt had acquired (כל אשר היתה למלך מצרים) everything from 'the river of Egypt to the river Euphrates' which is the precise territory once governed by Solomon (2 Kgs 24.7, see 1 Kgs 4.21 [5.1, Heb.]). The land once ruled by Solomon is lost, and Judah has been 'turned away from [Yahweh's] presence' (להסיר מעל־פניו, 2 Kgs 24.3).

The second stage no longer speaks of the loss of 'land', but rather focuses on the capture of 'Jerusalem' by Babylon. Nebuchadnezzar comes against Jerusalem, not Judah or 'the land' (2 Kgs 24.10-17; 25.1-7; contrast e.g. 2 Kgs 15.19, 37; 17.5-6). As we saw in Chapter 4, the subsequent events of 2 Kings 25 relay how the contents of Jerusalem are taken into exile. This final summary is introduced by its own date formula, and through a chiastic structure focuses on the temple as a microcosm of Jerusalem (2 Kgs 25.8):[69]

2 Kgs 25.8	Summary introduction that Babylon has come to Jerusalem
2 Kgs 25.9-12	Jerusalem destroyed, beginning with the temple
2 Kgs 25.11-12	Jerusalemites taken to Babylon
2 Kgs 25.13-17	Temple contents taken to Babylon
2 Kgs 25.18-20	Leaders killed, beginning with the temple officials
2 Kgs 25.21	Summary statement that Babylon completed the exile[70]

The sequence that is discernible in these chs. 24–25, then, is one where the land is reduced by Egypt to Jerusalem, which is in turn conquered by Babylon, climaxing with the temple. Thus the 'land' can be thought of as a layered concept, which can be slowly stripped away by successive invasions. All of these layers are associated with Yahweh's name and presence in Kings:

> The central sanctuary, the city of Jerusalem, [and] the promised land…are all identified as that place where Yhwh has [chosen to set his name]… The relationship between these various locales is not so much an evolutionary development in the mind of the biblical authors, as it is the result of the microcosmic nature of sacred space in ANE thought… Yhwh 'plants' Israel

---

69. See also Hobbs, *2 Kings*.
70. Paired with 2 Kgs 17.23. See Cogan and Tadmor, *2 Kings*, 327; Wray Beal, *1&2 Kings*, 528.

in the 'place of his enthronement' and the resulting human kingdom is spoken of as Yhwh's 'sanctuary.[71]

This same sequence of layers, land → city → temple, recurs at various points throughout the narrative of Kings. It was found in Hulda's prophecy to Josiah, which appears to set the agenda for these closing chapters:

> And Yahweh said, 'I will also turn Judah away from my presence (אסיר מעל פני, see 24.3), just as I have turned Israel away, and I will reject this city that I have chosen, Jerusalem, and this house of which I have said, 'my name will be there'. (2 Kgs 23.27)

It can also be found in Solomon's prayer for the people in exile where Israel should:

> ...repent with all their heart and their soul...and pray to you towards their land which you gave to their fathers, the city that you have chosen, and the house that I have built for your name... (1 Kgs 8.48).

It also appears in full or in part throughout other parts of the narrative (e.g., 1 Kgs 8.16, 44; 9.7-8; 2 Kgs 11.3, 20). In the book of Kings, the land is a house for Yahweh's name, in a city Yahweh chooses to place his name, within territory Yahweh grants to Israel:

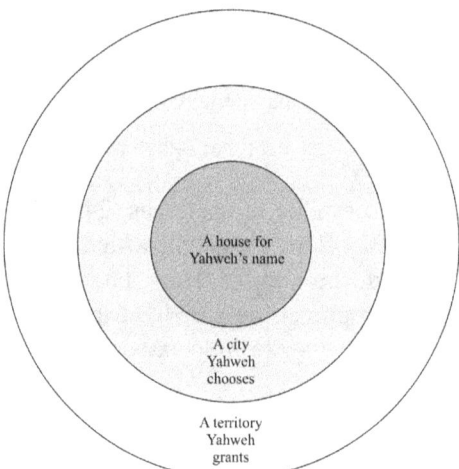

Figure 5.1. *Land in Kings*

The book of Kings has a consistent way of talking about land and territory, revealing a concentric definition: a house for Yahweh's name, in a city Yahweh chooses, in a territory Yahweh grants.

71. Richter, *The Deuteronomistic History and the Name Theology*, 95–6.

Throughout the narrative, this definition is used to sometimes extend and sometimes decrease the land known as 'Israel'. The exile is akin to stripping away the layers, until there is no 'land' left, while restoration movements, such as Josiah's, progressively reincorporate the lost layers. The reforms begin at the temple and radiate outwards to Jerusalem then Judah, culminating with the former northern territory (2 Kgs 23.4-20):[72]

    2 Kgs 23.4-7   Temple
    2 Kgs 23.8-12   Jerusalem
    2 Kgs 23.13-20   Judah → Bethel → Samaria

Thus, when Israel prosper, it begins with the temple and radiates outward. When they are exiled, it moves in the opposite direction, peeling the land like an onion, until finally the temple itself is destroyed.[73]

5.3.3. *The Empty Land in Kings*

Is the land at the end of Kings then 'empty' as we have seen Levin argue? In an important sense, yes. However, this is not because the account of Gedaliah's murder (2 Kgs 25.22-26) demonstrates the theological irrelevance of those who remained after the Babylonian invasion.[74] Rather, the Gedaliah narrative implies that even those who 'remained in the land of Judah' (2 Kgs 25.22) end up leaving for Egypt (2 Kgs 25.26): 'all the people, both small and great, and the captains of the forces…' The land is empty because everyone in the narrative has either departed or been taken.

In another sense, however, the land is not 'empty'. In contrast to the prophetic ideology, there are repeated and numerous hints that Yahweh's presence does not depart the land with the exiles, but remains behind. Even though Kings remembers the cloud of glory that filled the temple (1 Kgs 8.10-11), there is no parallel to Ezekiel's account in which it moves east towards Babylon with the exiles (Ezek. 11.23). As we saw in Chapter 4, when the territory of the former Northern Kingdom was repopulated, the people were plagued by lions from Yahweh because they did not know the customs of the 'God of the land' (אלהי הארץ), who was still present in it (2 Kgs 17.26). A priest is sent back to Bethel so that

---

72. Cohn, *2 Kings*, 156–60; Wray Beal, *1&2 Kings*, 506–9.
73. All of this coheres well with the concept of a centred rather than bounded territory. See Anderson, *Imagined Communities*, 174–81; and Nissinen, 'Prophets and Prophecy in Joshua–Kings', 122.
74. Levin, 'The Empty Land in Kings', 82–5. See also Cogan and Tadmor, *2 Kings*, 327.

worship of Yahweh might continue there (2 Kgs 17.28).⁷⁵ Similarly, after the Babylonian invasion, Solomon's petition encourages Israel to pray for mercy from captivity 'in the direction of their land' (והתפללו אליך דרך ארצם, 1 Kgs 8.48).⁷⁶ Although it does not necessarily imply restoration, the exilic readers of the book would have understood Solomon's prayer to mean that even during the exile the land remained that which was 'given to their fathers', and Jerusalem, 'the city you have chosen'.⁷⁷

In the same way, the ruined house remains a place of revelation, though perhaps not for the expected reason. When, in 1 Kgs 9.6-9, Yahweh warns Israel⁷⁸ of the consequences of disobedience, he expects that the nations would interpret the destruction of the temple as a testimony to his faithfulness to carry out the curse of the covenant (1 Kgs 9.9). Thus, even in its rejection and destruction (1 Kgs 9.7) the temple remains a place where Yahweh's covenant fidelity can be discovered.

The people have been removed 'out of [Yahweh's] sight' (2 Kgs 17.23), which is to say, away from where Yahweh's 'eyes' are (1 Kgs 9.3). Yahweh's eyes remain with his presence, which can still be found in the ruins of the house for his name, in a city he chooses, within territory he granted to Israel. In Kings, the land during the exile is 'emptied' only of Israel; Yahweh remains. Why should this be the case?

5.4. *Yahweh's Relationship to the Land*

The second of the sides in Block's geographical–theology triangle is that between Yahweh and the land. We concluded the previous section by noting that, although the exile severs Israel from the land, Yahweh does not abandon the land. What is implied by this? The simplest answer would be henotheism: that Yahweh remains in the land because he is in some way attached to it.⁷⁹ However, this cannot be the case. Within Inner Kings, there are many narratives that demonstrate Yahweh's activity outside of

---

75. We examined this text in Chapter 4.
76. In Sweeney's analysis (*King Josiah of Judah*, 33–4), these verses were originally directed towards the refugees of the exiled Northern Kingdom after 722 but prior to the destruction of the temple in 586. If this is the case, then the exilic redactor still left them untouched.
77. So Frankel, *The Land of Canaan and the Destiny of Israel*, 169.
78. Note that v. 6 switches to plural, indicating that it is no longer only Solomon being addressed. See Hobbs, *2 Kings*, 127, or Cogan, *1 Kings*, 296–7.
79. On this possibility see Block, *The Gods of the Nations*, 21–5.

Israel's boundaries. The reader is often transported into foreign lands, or into the minds of foreign characters. Many of these Inner Kings narratives intentionally use the Jordan as a moment of transition from interior to exterior:[80]

Table 5.2. *Inner Kings' Narrative Settings Outside of Israel*

Inner Kings utilises narrative settings outside of Israel on many occasions. The Jordan is often the place of transition.

	Activity Outside of Israel
I.17	The reader follows Elijah as he crosses the Jordan and goes to Zarephath in Sidon where numerous miracles happen.
I.19	The reader follows Elijah through Judah and the wilderness to Horeb to meet with Yahweh.
I.20	The war with Syria gives the reader insight into the mind of the Syrian king Ben Hadad, and shows Yahweh to be the god of the plains (in Syria) as he is of the hills (in Ephraim).
I.22	The reader follows the kings of Israel and Judah to Ramoth Gilead, contested territory east of the Jordan, for a battle with Syria.
II.2	The reader follows Elijah and Elisha as they cross the Jordan for Elijah's ascent in the desert, then we return with Elisha as he re-crosses the Jordan on his way back into the land.
II.3	The reader follows the kings of Israel and Judah into battle in Moab and observes several miracles.
II.5	The reader follows Naaman from Syria to Israel and back again, and watches his healing via bathing in the Jordan.
II.6.1-7	The reader is with Elisha and the 'sons of the prophets' (בני־הנביאים), as one of them loses an axe head in the Jordan and has it miraculously restored.
II.6.8-23	The reader learns of the Syrian king's concerns with Elisha, and follows the Syrian army into Israel only for them to be led (blind) into Samaria and given a feast.
II.8.7-15	The reader follows Elisha to Damascus where he anoints Hazael.
II.9	The reader follows one of the 'sons of the prophets' to Ramoth Gilead where Jehu is anointed, then rides with Jehu back into Jezreel.

---

80. On the narrative significance of the Jordan crossings, which are used in Inner Kings as moments of character as well as geographical transition, see Jeremy M. Hutton, *The Transjordanian Palimpsest: The Overwritten Texts of Personal Exile and Transformation in the Deuteronomistic History*, BZAW 396 (Berlin: de Gruyter, 2009), 4; Long, *2 Kings*, 26; Bodner, *Elisha's Profile in the Book of Kings*, 50.

As Cogan comments concerning these:

> The [narratives are] an expression of 'ancient Israelite universalism', an idea which surfaces frequently in the Elijah–Elisha cycles of stories. Through His prophets, YHWH works abroad and is recognised as the sole god (e.g., 1 Kgs 17.14; 19.15; 2 Kgs 5.1; 8.13).[81]

However, these Inner Kings narratives still maintain a particular relationship between Yahweh and the land that is not true of Yahweh's relationship to other places. As we examine the deity–land side of Block's triangle, it will be our task to explore this dialectic. What is special about Yahweh's relationship to geographical Israel and to the temple that is not also true of other places?

5.4.1. *Yahweh Uncontainable: God Over Every Land*

i. *Isaiah's Taunt and Hezekiah's Prayer*

In the first place, Yahweh is portrayed as the god over every land. There is a sense in which Yahweh's relationship to Israelite land is different from other territories, but not with respect to his sovereignty. Isaiah's taunt in 2 Kings 19 illustrates this well.[82] Yahweh's relationship with surrounding lands is explored by juxtaposing several perspectives on Sennacherib's campaign,[83] constructed as a dialogue between Yahweh and Assyria, with the overall goal of exposing the incongruity of Assyrian pride. Note that the victims of Assyrian aggression are voiceless in this poem, but Yahweh speaks for them (v. 21). Only Assyria dares speak to Yahweh:[84]

---

81. Cogan and Tadmor, *2 Kings*, 67.

82. We have examined the Hezekiah narratives twice already in this study. In Chapter 3 we surveyed the presentation of Assyria as a rival saviour, covenant maker, and deity to Yahweh. In Chapter 4 we considered Yahweh's victory over Assyria and noted that it was Yahweh's promise that saved Jerusalem. However, where the theme of the Davidic promise gave us the reason why Yahweh saved Zion, the theme of Yahweh's sovereignty we examine here indicates how he is able to do so. Many commentators discern two layers of redaction in this chapter (e.g., Cogan and Tadmor, *2 Kings*, 243) but they are well integrated into the wider narrative: note, e.g., the allusion to 2 Kgs 18.17-35 in 2 Kgs 19.23. See Hobbs, *2 Kings*, 278–9.

83. Dubovský ('Assyrian Downfall Through Isaiah's Eyes') and Evans ('The Hezekiah–Sennacherib Narrative as Polyphonic Text') both explore the way that the different perspectives of the various characters are presented in the Assyrian narratives. As we have already noted, one Assyrian perspective on the invasion is represented in the Rab-Shakeh's words which deify Sennacherib (2 Kgs 18.33).

84. So Dubovský, 'Assyrian Downfall Through Isaiah's Eyes', 8.

2 Kgs 19.21-22	Stanza 1	Yahweh's perspective
2 Kgs 19.23-24	Stanza 2	Assyria's perspective
2 Kgs 19.25-28	Stanza 3	Yahweh's perspective

Stanzas 2 and 3 are of interest. The Assyrian perspective portrays their campaign as a great feat they have accomplished in language that mimics Assyria's own imperial propaganda, blending conquest with exploration as feats equally worthy of praise:[85]

By the hand of your messengers	ביד מלאכיך	23a
you have mocked the Lord.	חרפת אדני	b
You said,	ותאמר	c
'In my many chariots	ברב[86] רכבי	d
I have ascended the heights of the mountains,	אני עליתי מרום הרים	e
the extremes of Lebanon.	ירכתי לבנון	f
I have cut down its highest cedars,	ואכרת קומת ארזיו	g
its finest fir trees.	מבחור ברשיו	h
I have come to its farthest lodging,	ואבואה מלון קצה	i
its most fertile forest.	יער כרמלו:	j
It is I who have dug wells	אני קרתי	24a
and I have drunk foreign waters,	ושתיתי מים זרים	b
I have dried up with the soles of my feet	ואחרב בכף פעמי	c
every stream in Egypt'. (translation mine)	כל יארי מצור:	d

The stanza is constructed to emphasise the Assyrian accomplishment as much as possible. It is introduced as their own perspective (v. 23c). The 1cs pronouns in clauses 23e and 24a are emphatic,[87] as is the fronted prepositional phrase (with a pronominal suffix) in clause 23d (ברב רכבי), which might be (over)translated: 'In *my* many chariots, it is *I* who have gone up...' Each bicolon in the Assyrian stanza begins with a stich containing a 1cs verb that is gapped in the second stich (vv. 23e, g, i; 24c). This gives the stanza a steady rhythm that emphasises the Assyrian perspective of autonomy: 'I did this…and this…I did this…and this…'

Yahweh's counter-perspective is then given in the third stanza:

---

85. Aster, *Reflections of Empire in Isaiah 1–39*, 244–73. Liverani (*Assyria*, 41–54) demonstrates the way that exploration and conquest are related in Assyrian imperial propaganda. This is not only true of Assyria, but of most empires with frontiers.

86. Reading with the Qere. Note that the adjective רב often precedes the noun: Joüon and Muraoka, *A Grammar of Biblical Hebrew*, 488.

87. Waltke and O'Connor, *An Introduction to Biblical Hebrew Syntax*, 293–5.

Have you not heard?	הלא שמעת	25a
From long ago I did it.	למרחוק אתה עשיתי	b
In the ancient days I planned it,	למימי קדם ויצרתיה	c
now I bring it to pass:	עתה הביאתיה	d
that they should become devastations – ruinous heaps,	ותהי להשות גלים נצים	e
the fortified cities,	ערים בצרות:	f
their inhabitants disempowered,	וישביהן קצרי יד	26a
are dismayed and ashamed.	חתו ויבשו	b
They have become like the grass of the field,	היו עשב שדה	c
green shoots,	וירק דשא	d
or grass on the roof,	חציר גגות	e
that is scorched before it has grown.	ושדפה לפני קמה:	f
But your sitting down, and your going out,	ושבתך וצאתך	27a
your coming in – I know them –	ובאך ידעתי	b
and your raging against me.	ואת התרגזך אלי:	c
Because of your raging against me	יען התרגזך אלי	28a
and because your insolence has come up to my ears,	ושאננך עלה באזני	b
I have set my hook in your nose	ושמתי חחי באפך	c
and my bridle in your mouth,	ומתגי בשפתיך	d
and now I return you	והשבתיך	e
on the way from which you came.	בדרך אשר באת בה:	f

(translation mine)

The 1cs verbs throughout v. 25 are placed unusually in the final position of their clause, this time to emphasise Yahweh's activity: 'Haven't you heard? From long ago *I* did it; from ancient days *I* planned it; now *I* bring it to pass' (see also ידעתי in v. 27*b*). In contradiction to Assyria's claim, 'it' (note the 3fs pronoun, v. 25*b, c, d*) is something that Yahweh has done. This refers to the Assyrian campaign in the first half of the poem, but it is never nominalised here. It is only described as destruction (vv. 25*e-f*, 26). In Yahweh's perspective, Assyria's actions are more violent and less intrepid than their own claim made them seem. In spite of this, Yahweh's rhetoric avoids assigning even the grisly glory of battle to Assyria, refusing to allow Assyria to become the subject of any active verbs. Against the major English versions, the bicolon in v. 25*e-f* contains no 2ms pronoun: 'That they should become devastations – ruinous heaps; the fortified cities'. The series of infinitives in vv. 27 and 28 does the same, avoiding acknowledging Assyria as the instigator of their own invasion: '…because of your raging against me…' rather than (e.g., NIV): '…because you rage against me…' (v. 28).

In Yahweh's perspective it is he, and not Assyria, who planned (v. 25c) and brought to pass (v. 25d) this destruction, who intimately knows Assyria's role in it (v. 27), and who can halt Assyrian aggression (v. 28). Significantly, Yahweh began this 'long ago' (v. 25c-d), and his sovereignty incorporates the entire campaign that brought them to this moment: 'coming out and going in' (v. 27) is idiomatic for military movements.[88] And so Assyrian pride is unwarranted, because this campaign has been Yahweh's doing, even when it occurred outside of Israel. Yahweh has been as sovereign in Assyrian territory as he is at Zion, and 'blasphemous Sennacherib does not understand the basis of his own power'.[89]

Hezekiah's prayer (2 Kgs 19.15-19) gives a second, stronger perspective on the relationship between Yahweh and the nations. It extends the assertion of universal sovereignty to a statement of full monotheism. While Hezekiah's prayer concedes the Assyrian point that they have overcome the gods of the nations, he argues that this is because the gods of the nations were not gods (כי לא אלהים המה, 2 Kgs 19.17-18, see 19.9-13). Since the God of Israel is the creator of the heavens and earth (v. 15), and the living God (v. 17), Assyria's experience in Zion will be different:

15a	יהוה אלהי ישראל
b	↑ישב הכרבים
c	אתה הוא האלהים לבדך לכל ממלכות הארץ
d	אתה עשית את השמים ואת הארץ:

[15a]Yahweh God of Israel, [b]who dwells between the cherubim, [c]you are God alone to all the kingdoms of the earth, [d]you have made the heavens and the earth. (2 Kgs 19.15, my translation)

The relationships between Yahweh and Israel on the one hand, and Yahweh and the 'kingdoms of the earth' on the other are asymmetric. The prayer combines an acknowledgement of Yahweh's location in the temple

---

88. E.g. Deut. 28.6, 19; 31.2; Josh. 14.11; 1 Kgs 3.7. Hobbs and Cogan note the comprehensiveness implied by the merism. Hobbs, *2 Kings*, 281; Cogan and Tadmor, *2 Kings*, 237.

89. Sweeney, *I & II Kings*, 418–19. See also Ronald E. Clements, *Isaiah and the Deliverance of Jerusalem: A Study in the Interpretation of Prophecy in the Old Testament* (Sheffield: JSOT, 1984), 72–89; Ben C. Ollenburger, *Zion: The City of the Great King*, JSOTSup 41 (Sheffield: JSOT, 1987), 13–19; and Cogan and Tadmor, *2 Kings*, 238.

in Israel (v. 15*a-b*)⁹⁰ with an assertion that Yahweh is God everywhere else as well (v. 15*c*). However, the syntax of clause *c* is different to that of clause *a*. Yahweh is the God *of* Israel (using the construct form, v. 15*a*), but he is God *to* all the kingdoms of the earth (using a preposition, v. 15*c*).⁹¹ Israel's God exercises sovereignty over the nations as well – God *to* them – but God *of* Israel alone.

ii. *The Temple and the Universal God*

Surprisingly, this theme of Yahweh's sovereignty over all nations is an important part of the broader temple theology of the book.⁹² This can be demonstrated through the intertextuality between the key temple passages: Hezekiah's prayer and Solomon's dedication. At first, the link is drawn by the observation that Hezekiah is the first (and only) person in the narrative after Solomon to use the temple for prayer. However, there is also language shared between these two texts that appears nowhere else in Kings, for example, references to the cherubim (1 Kgs 6.23-35; 7.29-36; 8.6; 2 Kgs 19.15) and the merism 'heavens and earth' (1 Kgs 8.23, 27, 36, 43; 2 Kgs 19.15). The two passages also share several other ideas: that Yahweh is God alone (1 Kgs 8.23, 60; 2 Kgs 19.15, 19), that Yahweh's eyes and ears should be open to see and hear (1 Kgs 8.29, 52; 2 Kgs 19.16), and that all the kingdoms of the earth should know Yahweh (1 Kgs 8.60; 2 Kgs 19.20).

Much of this language belongs to the semantic domains of creation and exclusive monotheism,⁹³ and has been assigned to the exilic Dtr,⁹⁴ along with the similar themes in Moses's address in Deuteronomy 4:⁹⁵

---

90. Note also v. 16 has several allusions to Solomon's dedication. Cogan and Tadmor, *2 Kings*, 236.

91. The syntax is unique in the Old Testament to this verse, apart from the parallel in Isa. 37.16.

92. Frankel, *The Land of Canaan and the Destiny of Israel*, 162–9. Cogan and Tadmor, *2 Kings*, 236.

93. Cogan and Tadmor, *2 Kings*, 236; Weinfeld, *Deuteronomy and the Deuteronomic School*, 39. See, e.g., Josh. 2.11.

94. The themes of creation and monotheism are typically thought to be exilic. Note also the lack of pro-David or pro-Zion language in these portions of the text. See Nelson, *Deuteronomy*, 60–71; Weinfeld, *Deuteronomy and the Deuteronomic School*, 39; Cogan and Tadmor, *2 Kings*, 240–4; Sweeney, *I & II Kings*, 278. See also Brevard S. Childs, *Isaiah and the Assyrian Crisis*, SBT (London: SCM, 1967), 99.

95. This text is also nearly always attributed to the exilic deuteronomist. See J. Gordon McConville, *Deuteronomy* (Leicester: Apollos, 2002), 102.

Table 5.3. *Intertextuality between 2 Kings 19, 1 Kings 8 and Deuteronomy 4*

Intertextuality between Hezekiah's prayer at the temple,
Solomon's dedication of the temple and the conclusion of Moses's first
address at Horeb reveals that universal, monotheistic language
is common in temple contexts.

Hezekiah's Prayer (II.19)	Solomon's Dedication (I.8)	Moses's Address (Deut. 4)
ישב הכרבים (v. 15)	The only other references to כרבים are 1 Kgs 6.23-35; 7.29-36; 8.6.	
הוא/אתה האלהים לבדך (vv. 15, 19)	אלהי ישראל אין כמוך אלהים בשמים ממעל ועל הארץ מתחת (v. 23) הוא האלהים אין עוד (v. 60)	יהוה הוא האלהים אין עוד מלבדו (vv. 35, 39)
אתה עשית את השמים ואת הארץ (v. 15)	The only other references to השמים and הארץ together are vv. 23, 27, 36, 43.	vv. 36, 39
מעשה ידי אדם עץ ואבן (v. 18)		מעשה ידי אדם עץ ואבן (v. 28)
פקח יהוה עיניך וראה ושמע (v. 16)	היות עיניך פתחות ... לשמע (vv. 29, 52)	לא יראון ולא ישמעון (v. 28)
וידעו כל ממלכות הארץ ... (v. 20)	למען דעת כל עמי הארץ ... (v. 60)	אתה הראת לדעת ... (vv. 35, 39)

Why should this universal, monotheistic language be common to the temple sections of the book, when the temple supposedly represents Yahweh's particular relationship to geographical Israel?[96] The question is only more pressing if one attributes these texts to the hand of the exilic author who had no temple.[97] Part of the answer must be that the temple does not constrict Yahweh's presence or action in any way (1 Kgs 8.27). We return to the importance of the temple in Kings below, but its role is not to demarcate Yahweh's territory. The temple theology of the book incorporates the idea that Yahweh acts wherever he pleases.

This explains why the same universal and monotheistic language occurs frequently in Inner Kings, in contexts associated with Yahweh's activity. Other than Hezekiah's and Solomon's prayers (which both contain requests for divine deliverance, note also Deut. 4.34), Solomon's

---

96. See Frankel, *The Land of Canaan and the Destiny of Israel*, 164, 169.
97. Wissmann, 'He Did What Was Right', 254.

phrase 'Yahweh, he is God' (יהוה הוא האלהים) can be found on the lips of the Israelites who witness Elijah's victory on Mt. Carmel (1 Kgs 18.39, see also v. 24).[98] Naaman makes a similar claim, having been healed of leprosy (2 Kgs 5.15). 1 Kings 20 is perhaps the best example. In that episode the Syrians lead a coalition of 32 kings against the Northern Kingdom (1 Kgs 20.1-22). When routed by only 7000 Israelite soldiers, they assumed it was because Israel's gods ruled the hilly, central region of the Northern Kingdom.[99] The Syrian advisors suggested fighting in the north-eastern Transjordan plain, not in order to maximise the benefit of their chariots, but because they assume their gods will be able to bring victory there (vv. 23-25).[100] However, Yahweh proves victorious in Syrian territory as well. The Syrian survivors flee to Aphek, a town in the western regions of Syria,[101] where a wall falls upon the remaining 27,000 soldiers (vv. 29-30) and Yahweh is shown to be God alone in the plains of Syria as well as the hills of Ephraim. This occurs, like the other contexts, so that 'they might know that Yahweh is God' (1 Kgs 20.28).

The language of universalism in Outer Kings is found in the temple prayers of Hezekiah and Solomon. In Inner Kings the same language is found smattered throughout the various times that Yahweh acts in and around the Northern Kingdom. Inner Kings is demonstrating what Outer Kings states: 'Behold, heaven and the highest heaven cannot contain you; how much less this house that I have built!' (1 Kgs 8.27). Whatever other roles the temple may play in the narrative, it does not demarcate a territorial limit to Yahweh's sovereignty, or action. In Kings, Yahweh is uncontainable. This is an important premise for the exilic audience who live their lives in the shadow of gods that are 'the work of human hands' (מעשה ידי אדם, 2 Kgs 19.18).

5.4.2. *Yahweh Locatable: Found in a Place*

i. *Yahweh and the Land: The Case of Naaman*

Our conclusion so far has been that the temple theology of the book of Kings incorporates Yahweh's universal activity. However, we have also discovered that the book upholds centralisation, as per Deuteronomy

---

98. Angel, 'Hopping Between Two Opinions'. See also Chapter 3.

99. On the geography of the region see Carl G. Rasmussen, *Zondervan Atlas of the Bible*, rev. ed. (Grand Rapids, MI: Zondervan, 2009), 23–4.

100. The term מישור (vv. 23, 35) is probably a reference specifically to the transjordan tableland north of the wadi Arnon, not a general word for plain. See Cogan and Tadmor, *2 Kings*, 466; and Deut. 3.10, Josh. 13.16. The generalised term for מישור is עמקים ('valleys'), imagining a wide, flat area between mountain ranges (v. 28).

101. Cogan and Tadmor, *2 Kings*, 466.

12, when the temple is available. Why? What is gained within Israel's geographical bounds that cannot be gained outside of it?

The story of Naaman's conversion addresses this question. The power dynamics of this narrative are often noted,[102] as is the universalism,[103] but the geographical implications are less frequently observed.[104] Naaman's post-conversion confession is universal, sharing the language we have already seen on the lips of Solomon, Hezekiah, and the unnamed prophet of 1 Kings 20: 'There is no other God in all the earth...' (אין אלהים בכל־הארץ..., 2 Kgs 5.15). We might expect, then, the completion of this statement as follows: '...except Yahweh' (כי אם־יהוה...). It is interesting that Naaman's confession is actually geographical: '...except in Israel' (כי אם־בישראל...).

Naaman's cleansing story involves the land at every point. The story opened with an assertion of Yahweh's sovereignty over the nations, that '...by [Naaman] Yahweh had given victory to Aram' (v. 1). The Israelite girl advised him to find the prophet 'who is in Samaria' (v. 6), and Elisha sent for Naaman so that 'he might know that there is a prophet in Israel' (v. 8, see also 2 Kgs 1.3, 6). Naaman's expectation that Elisha would act 'in the name of Yahweh' with some hand-waving was thwarted (v. 7). Instead, his healing involved him forsaking the 'better' waters of Damascus (טוב...מימי ישראל) for the Jordan river instead (vv. 10-12). This is not only a story about a powerful man who learns humility.[105] This is also a story about Naaman's journey to Israel, where he discovers that the god in that land is the only God.

There is no geographic restriction placed on Naaman's worship. His request for 'two mule loads of earth' (v. 17) would have been understood by the readers as enough soil to build an altar[106] which would attest that Naaman's intention is to return to Syria and perform public sacrifice (עלה וזבח, v. 17). We should not interpret this as inward, secret worship. Much of the discussion concerning his request for pardon to 'bow himself in the temple of Rimmon' (v. 18) assumes that Naaman intends to worship Yahweh secretly while outwardly adhering to the

---

102. E.g., Leithart, *1&2 Kings*, 192–7; Long, *2 Kings*, 69–77; and Cohn, *2 Kings*, 35–42.

103. E.g. Provan, *1 & 2 Kings*, 191–4; Cogan and Tadmor, *2 Kings*, 66–8; and Wray Beal, *1&2 Kings*, 336–8.

104. Wray Beal's commentary notes many of the geographical features (*1&2 Kings*, 338).

105. Leithart, *1&2 Kings*, 192–7.

106. Wray Beal, *1&2 Kings*, 335.

official cult.¹⁰⁷ However, we should avoid reading the story of Daniel into the silence of the narrative here.¹⁰⁸ The extent to which Naaman would have been free to sacrifice publicly to Yahweh in Syria at the time is difficult to determine. It is possible that his duty to Rimmon was only a function of his official position as the 'right-hand man' of the king (v. 1), and that he was free to offer sacrifices to whatever god he wished when not acting in that capacity.¹⁰⁹ Neither does it seem likely that Elisha is granting leave to Naaman to begin an 'insider movement'¹¹⁰ of secret Yahweh followers in Syria, nor to carry on a charade that only inwardly, and never publicly acknowledges Yahweh.¹¹¹ All of this argues from silence, and much of it reads modern analogies into the text. The only thing asserted by the narrative is that Naaman will worship Yahweh in Syria (v. 17), and this remains true no matter what one makes of v. 18.

Once Naaman has learned that there is 'no other God in all the earth except in Israel' (v. 15), the narrative indicates that he is free to worship from anywhere. Why, then, does it recount that he took the soil?

---

107. Rimmon is also known as Hadad, head of the Aramaean pantheon. See Cohn, *2 Kings*, 39.

108. This 'bowing down' probably does not entail sacrifice (v. 17): Wray Beal, *1&2 Kings*, 335; Cogan and Tadmor, *2 Kings*, 65.

109. So Cohn, *2 Kings*, 39.

110. The missiological literature on the application of this text is vast. For a contemporary missiological reading of 2 Kgs 5, see John Span, 'God Saves. Go in Peace: Wholeness Affirmed or Promotion Piece (2 Parts)', *Biblical Missiology* (2013); or Allan Effa, 'Prophet, Kings, Servants, and Lepers: A Missiological Reading of an Ancient Drama', *Missiology* 35 (2007): 305–13. One example of its use in missiology is the 'insider movement' which understands a category of Christianity that outwardly adheres to some other religion (usually Islam), while inwardly worshipping Jesus. See Phil Parshall, 'Danger! New Direction in Contextualisation', *Evangelical Missions Quarterly* 34 (1998): 404–10; John J. Travis, 'The C-Spectrum: A Practical Tool for Defining Six Types of "Christ Centred Communities" Found in Muslim Contexts', in *Perspectives on the World Christian Movement: A Reader*, ed. Ralph D. Winter and Steven C. Hawthorne, 4th ed. (Pasadena, CA: William Carey, 2009), 664–7; and in the same volume Rebecca Lewis, 'Insider Movements: Retaining Identity and Preserving Community', 673–6.

111. Elijah says only two words: לך לשלום. The many possible interpretations include Fretheim, *First and Second Kings*, 153; Long, *2 Kings*, 73–4; Cogan and Tadmor, *2 Kings*, 65; Fritz, *1 & 2 Kings*, 260; Lasine, '"Go in peace" or "Go to hell"', 5–6; von Rad, *Old Testament Theology*, 2:30–2; and Alexander Rofé, *The Prophetical Stories: The Narratives about the Prophets in the Hebrew Bible; Their Literary Types and History* (Jerusalem: Magnes, 1988), 111–12.

Does Naaman believe Yahweh is somehow attached to it?[112] Von Rad comments:

> The request [for soil] has more than once led commentators to express a poor opinion of Naaman's faith. But they are wrong... Even an Israelite reading the story must have felt that there was something odd in the request...[but] he would have been touched by the way in which a man who had encountered the God of Israel here expresses his eager desire to be able to continue to worship him on heathen soil. Indeed, since he believed that the land which Jahweh granted was the saving gift par excellence, he would have felt that, in the difficult situation in which Naaman was placed, the latter was perfectly in order in seeking to give his faith what might be called a point of sacramental attachment.[113]

In this reading, Naaman takes the soil not because Yahweh can only be worshipped on Israelite turf, but because he wishes to remember that the god he worships was the one he found by coming to Israel.[114] All the critical moments in Naaman's story of revelation and healing are mediated through the land. It was only the happenstance of the captured Israelite servant girl that led Naaman to seek the prophet 'who is in Samaria' (v. 3). The king in Damascus was right to send him to Israel (v. 5), and the king in Samaria was rebuked for refusing him (vv. 7-8). Naaman was not cured until he washed in the Jordan (vv. 12-14).

This story is typical of the book. In Kings, Yahweh's commitment to Israel means that characters normally do not come to know Yahweh unless from within the territory of Israel, and do not normally receive Yahweh's blessing except through someone or something from Israel. Once they have found the God of Israel in Israel, they can worship him anywhere.

ii. *The Temple as a Guarantee of Blessing*

We saw above that the theology of centralisation found within the narrative of Kings means that the temple should be used for worship if it is available, even though it does not contain or constrain Yahweh in any way. However, it is possible to say more than this because of Yahweh's commitment of attentiveness to the temple. The temple guarantees his action in response to prayer.[115] Solomon's dedication lists seven historical contingencies in which Yahweh's presence ought to be sought:

---

112. Cogan and Tadmor, *2 Kings*, 67; Hobbs, *2 Kings*, 66.
113. Von Rad, *Old Testament Theology*, 2:31.
114. So Wray Beal, *1&2 Kings*, 335; Fretheim, *First and Second Kings*, 153; Leithart, *1&2 Kings*, 192–7.
115. See Knoppers, 'Prayer and Propaganda', 245.

Table 5.4. *The Function of the Temple in Solomon's Prayer*

The function of the temple within the contingencies of Israel's history according to the seven petitions in Solomon's prayer of dedication (1 Kgs 8.31-51).

1.8	#	In the case of:	Prayer at/towards the temple provides:
31-32	1	Sin leading to interpersonal conflict	Judgment, justice
33-34	2	Sin against God leading to military defeat	Forgiveness and restoration
35-36	3	Sin against God leading to drought	Forgiveness, instruction, and rain
37-40	4	General calamity, personal or communal (famine, enemies, sickness, etc.)	Yahweh will act according to their need, fear of God
41-43	5	A foreigner comes to seek Yahweh	Access to Yahweh for the foreigner, international reputation for Yahweh
44-45	6	General warfare	Victory in warfare
46-51	7	Sin against God leading to exile, followed by repentance	Forgiveness and compassion

These petitions are formulaic,[116] but the symbolism of seven petitions, along with the individual variations, lead the reader to understand that prayer at the temple is a solution to 'the total or all-embracing threat which man experiences'.[117] The temple mediates blessings for both individuals (petitions 1, 4–5) and Israel as a whole (petitions 2–4, 6–7). It is for both Israel (petitions 1–4, 6–7) and foreigners (petition 4–5).[118] Some petitions have to do with sin (petitions 1–3, 7), while others deal with other situations (petitions 4–6). In both cases the blessings are contingent on obedience to the covenant (petitions 2, 3, 7),[119] sincerity of heart (petition 4), and, for foreigners, fear of Yahweh (petitions 4–5).[120] The temple is capable of mediating Yahweh's blessing to all people, Israel and the nations, individually or corporately, in every situation of life.

116. Knoppers, 'Prayer and Propaganda', 236.
117. O'Kennedy, 'The Prayer of Solomon', 84.
118. Petition 4 is focused on those in the land, but it does specify that כל־אדם (v. 38) and כל־בני האדם (v. 39) will be heard. The universalism is missing in the LXX.
119. See Terence E. Fretheim, *The Suffering of God: An Old Testament Perspective* (Philadelphia, PA: Fortress, 1984), 35–44; and Samuel E. Balentine, *Prayer in the Hebrew Bible: The Drama of Divine–Human Dialogue* (Minneapolis, MN: Fortress, 1993), 37–8.
120. See my discussion on foreigners fearing Yahweh in Chapter 4.

It is, however, Yahweh's own commitment rather than Solomon's request that makes the temple significant. In response to this prayer, Yahweh guarantees:[121]

> ...I have heard your prayer and your plea, which you have made before me. I have consecrated (הקדשתי) this house that you have built, by putting my name there forever. My eyes and my heart will be there for all time. (1 Kgs 9.3)

As Cogan notes, the idea that Yahweh consecrates (קדש) something for human use is unique in this verse,[122] giving the temple a special significance. It is the location where Yahweh guarantees that prayers will be forever heard and answered. Given the scope of Solomon's request, the temple should mediate Yahweh's blessing to Israel in every contingency of life.[123] This gives the temple an ironic role in the narrative[124] because apart from Hezekiah, it is never used for prayer. The further irony is that every prayer in Kings is, indeed, answered.[125] The historiography of the book suggests that all of Judah's catastrophes might have been avoided, if only they had prayed at the temple.

iii. *The Prophets as the Mediators of Blessing*

Even though the kings of the book rarely pray, the prophets do. And except for Isaiah, the location of prayer is not the temple. Elijah prays several times both inside and outside the land of Israel (e.g., 1 Kgs 17.20; 18.36-37) and, remarkably, 'Yahweh listens to Elijah's voice' (וישמע יהוה בקול אליהו, 1 Kgs 17.22).[126]

Functionally, Elijah and Elisha perform the same role as that which Solomon's prayer envisages for the temple. We noted above that the prayer presents seven historical contingencies and requests a specific response in each case (1 Kgs 8.31-51). In Inner Kings, with only the exception of exile, each contingency occurs and Yahweh responds through the prophetic ministry. There are narratives in which the prophets

---

121. See Hobbs, *2 Kings*, 127. Note that the link between the prayer and Yahweh's response is stronger still in the LXX: πεποίηκά σοι κατὰ πᾶσαν τὴν προσευχήν σου. See Cogan, *1 Kings*, 295.

122. Cogan, *1 Kings*, 295.

123. O'Kennedy, 'The Prayer of Solomon', 84–5.

124. As is flagged even by the verses, 1 Kgs 9.6-9. See Sweeney, *I & II Kings*, 138–9.

125. Leithart, *1&2 Kings*, 129.

126. The authors of the New Testament found this remarkable as well (Jas 5.16-17).

function as judges or ensure justice (1 Kgs 20.38-43; 2 Kgs 8.1-6),[127] mediate restoration after military defeat (2 Kgs 6.24–7.20), bring rain in times of drought (1 Kgs 17.1; 18.41-46; 2 Kgs 3.17), relief in other times of general calamity (1 Kgs 17.8-16, 17-24; 2 Kgs 4.1-7, 18-37, 38-44; 6.1-7), provide access to Yahweh for a foreigner who seeks him (2 Kgs 5.1-14), and provide victory in warfare (1 Kgs 20.26-30).

Thus, in Inner Kings, the prophets do what the temple was supposed to do in Outer Kings.[128] Like the temple, the prophets are associated with Yahweh's name (1 Kgs 18.24; 22.16; 2 Kgs 2.24; 5.11). Like the temple, they are a place of revelation where Yahweh can be found (e.g., 1 Kgs 17.24; 18.36-37; 20.13, 28; 2 Kgs 5.15). Also like the temple, they function as the centre of a worshipping community. Elisha gathers around himself a community of faithful Yahweh worshippers, the 'sons of the prophets' (בני־הנביאים).[129] These people are portrayed as faithful followers of Yahweh, like the priests in Outer Kings, who are invariably faithful (1 Kgs 8.3-11; 2 Kgs 11.9-20; 12.2, 4-16; 19.2-4; 22.8-14; 23.2-4, 24).[130]

The 'sons of the prophets' are first encountered in 1 Kgs 20.35 without introduction and they re-appear throughout the narratives involving Elisha's ministry (2 Kgs 2; 4.1, 38; 5.22; 6.1; 9.1). They lack the temple, but receive instead the blessings of the prophetic ministry:[131]

---

127. In Chapter 6 we will investigate whether the prophets subvert the king's duty in this regard (as in, e.g., Bodner, *Elisha's Profile in the Book of Kings*, 47).

128. On the relationship of prophets and priests in DtrH more broadly, see Mark Leuchter, 'Samuel: A Prophet like Moses or a Priest like Moses?', in Jacobs and Person Jr., eds., *Israelite Prophecy and the Deuteronomistic History*, 147–68. On Elijah and Elisha's priestly ministry, see, in the same volume, Marvin A. Sweeney, 'Prophets and Priests in the Deuteronomistic History: Elijah and Elisha', 48–9. John T. Noble ('Cultic Prophecy and Levitical Inheritance in the Elijah–Elisha Cycle', *JSOT* 41 [2016]: 56–8) argues that Elijah and Elisha are Samuel-like prophet-priests. See also Gilmour, *Juxtaposition and the Elisha Cycle*, 222.

129. The historical identity of the בני־הנביאים, as well as their origin and composition, is probably now irrecoverable with any degree of certainty. See J. R. Porter, 'בני־הנביאים', *JTS* 32 (1981): 423–9; Cogan and Tadmor, *2 Kings*, 31–2; Johannes Lindblom, *Prophecy in Ancient Israel* (Philadelphia, PA: Fortress, 1962), 29–70, 183–4; and J. G. Williams, 'The Prophetic "Father"', *JBL* 85 (1966): 344–8. On their literary function as a community of worshippers, see Bodner, *Elisha's Profile in the Book of Kings*, 47.

130. Uriah is the exception in Outer Kings (2 Kgs 16).

131. If Elijah's ascension is included then these miracles account for all but two of the references to the בני־ישראל in the book (the others are 1 Kgs 20.35 and 2 Kgs 9.1). Sattherthwaite ('The Elisha Narratives', 3–9) explores the idea that this group represents faithful Israel. See also Leithart, *1&2 Kings*, 198–203.

Table 5.5. *The (Non-Military) Miracles Performed by Elisha*

The (non-military) miracles performed by Elisha are usually for the benefit of the 'sons of the prophets'.

	Miracle	For the benefit of:
II.2.19-22	Healing Waters at Jericho	'The men of the city', i.e. the בני־הנביאים at Jericho (v. 15)
II.4.1-7	The Widow's Jar of Oil	The wife of one of the בני־הנביאים
II.4.38-41	Purifying the Stew	The בני־הנביאים
II.4.42-44	Feeding a Hundred Men	Feeding the same men as 4.38-41 above
II.6.1-6	The Floating Axe Head	One of the בני־הנביאים

Nicholas Lunn explored several further parallels between Elijah and Elisha and concepts associated with the temple,[132] concluding that the textual depiction of Elijah and Elisha represents a significant theological development within Israel's thought:

> What we are witnessing [in the Elijah–Elisha narratives...] is a major new juncture in the notion of the indwelling of God's presence among his people, and one that is remarkable in comparison with what has gone before. Here in fact may be traced a theological development that transcends the conventional Hebraic ideology respecting the temple as the dwelling place of Yahweh. For with regard to Elijah and Elisha there is now introduced the idea of human personhood connected with the sanctuary and theophany. A crucial move has occurred from visual and structural representation to human representation... Elijah and Elisha, we submit, testify to a significant new development in the whole theology of God-manifestation.[133]

Lunn marshals the following evidence, from which he intends to build a cumulative case:[134]

1. The Carmel narrative contains many parallels with temple and sacrificial language as we explored already in this chapter.[135]
2. Elijah and Elisha's movements are told using the language of divine theophany.[136] Accounts of theophanies often use the *nifal*

---

132. Lunn, 'Prophetic Representations'.
133. Lunn, 'Prophetic Representations', 61–2.
134. Lunn ('Prophetic Representations', 57–9) lists several additional tentative observations.
135. Lunn, 'Prophetic Representations', 50–2.
136. Lunn, 'Prophetic Representations', 53.

stem of the verb ירא followed by אל ('Yahweh appeared to...', e.g. Gen. 12.7; Num. 20.6) as Kings also does of Elijah (see, e.g. 1 Kgs 18.1, 15). Similarly, people's response to Elijah and Elisha's presence is recounted using language of theophanies (לעמד לפני, 'to stand before...', e.g. Deut. 4.10; 10.8, etc.; see 2 Kgs 4.12; 5.15, etc.)

3. Elijah speaks in first person singular as God (e.g., 1 Kgs 21.20-21).[137]
4. There are numerous linguistic parallels between Elijah calling fire down from heaven (2 Kgs 1.9-15) and the events at Sinai (e.g., 2 Kgs 1.9-10; see Exod. 19.20; 24.17).[138]
5. Elements of theophanic manifestation are commonly associated with Elijah and Elisha: the chariots of fire, fire from heaven, and whirlwind (2 Kgs 2.11; 6.17, see, e.g., Ps. 68.17; Isa. 29.6; 66.15; Hab. 3.8; Ezek. 1.4, 13, 15).[139]
6. The Shunammite woman essentially constructs a temple for Elisha to dwell in.[140] Since Elisha is a 'holy man of God' she makes 'a small chamber on the roof with a bed, a table, a chair, and a lamp' (2 Kgs 4.9-10). The word for 'bed' (מטה) is consonantally the same as the word for Aaron's 'staff' which was placed 'before the Testimony' (Num. 17.8-10). All of the other objects are present in the temple also: the table (Exod. 25.23), the chair (i.e. throne, כסא, see Isa. 6.1; Ps. 93.2), and the lamp (Exod. 25.31). Significantly the 'lamp' she gives is a מנורה which is a word used elsewhere exclusively in cultic context. The more regular word for lamp is ניר. Even the sequence of construction (עשה then שים) resembles the construction of the temple (2 Kgs 4.10; see Exod. 25.1, 4, 7, 17; 40.3, 5, 19, etc.). Elisha's designation as 'holy' is unique to this context, and the only other person called 'holy' in Kings is Yahweh (2 Kgs 19.22).
7. Those that meet Elijah and Elisha pay obeisance to them (e.g., 1 Kgs 18.7; 2 Kgs 1.13; 2.15; 4.37). Both Elijah and Elisha are called 'Lord' (אדני, 1 Kgs 18.7; 2 Kgs 2.19; 4.16, 28; 6.5).[141]

---

137. Lunn, 'Prophetic Representations', 53–4.
138. Lunn, 'Prophetic Representations', 54.
139. On Elijah and Moses/Joshua, see David J. Zucker, 'Elijah and Elisha: Part 1—Moses and Joshua', *JBQ* 40 (2012): 225–9; also Hauser and Gregory, *From Carmel to Horeb*, 30–6, 47–54.
140. Lunn, 'Prophetic Representations', 55–7.
141. Lunn, 'Prophetic Representations', 57.

Lunn summarises that all of this language, used in Kings in connection with Elijah and Elisha, is elsewhere associated with either the sanctuary or theophany,[142] and thus the interpretation of it is 'to be sought in the sphere of divine presence'.[143] Lunn's argument is more persuasive in some parts than others, but the cumulative case that there is an intentional connection between the temple and these prophets is strong.

We can now draw together the two threads we have been investigating: that Yahweh's presence and blessing is guaranteed at the location of the temple, and that Yahweh can act through prophetic mediation in other places when he wants to. First, the significance to the exilic audience is one of encouragement: that they might receive some of the blessings of the temple even in its absence. Exilic Israel's historical situation is a much nearer parallel to the בני־הנביאים under Ahab than to any stage of the Southern Kingdom. They find themselves dislocated from the Davidic promise, without access to the temple, and ruled by a king who neither knows nor fears Yahweh. However, Kings assures its readers that this extraordinary historical situation does not prevent an active relationship with Yahweh. Prayers might yet be heard and blessings for Israel might yet be obtained through the ministries of the prophets. The remnant community that can no longer fully realise Covenant-Israel can nevertheless still embody the hope of its renewal. They are the seed from which Israel might yet be grown, because their relationship to Yahweh is maintained by the prophets.

Second, because Yahweh's presence is not removed from the land, and because he continues to guarantee revelation and blessing only within the land, any hope generated by the prophetic ministry is a restless hope. The community cannot find satisfaction in Babylon, because Yahweh has never been found outside of Israel. As we saw with Namaan, characters in Kings must come to Israel's land to find Israel's God. Similarly, Yahweh guarantees blessing only through the temple, and so the temple cannot be replaced entirely by prophetic ministry. The land remains an important part of the constitution of Covenant-Israel, determinative for their national identity, because it is the only place where they know for certain that the God of all the earth will make himself known and hear their prayers.

---

142. Lunn, 'Prophetic Representations', 59–63.
143. Lunn, 'Prophetic Representations', 59.

5.5. Conclusions

The book of Kings defines the land theologically, as a house for Yahweh's name, in a city Yahweh chooses, within territory Yahweh grants. The narrative is careful to portray to its exilic audience an ongoing significance of each of these levels within Yahweh's purposes for Israel.

At the level of a house for Yahweh's name, we have seen that the book reaffirms centralisation of worship as per Deuteronomy 12 when the temple is available. The theology of the temple in the book also makes that place a unique location where Yahweh commits himself to hear and answer prayer for every historical contingency. It is a place of promise, for care, provision, and action. And we have seen this remains true even once the temple lies in ruins. The exilic audience would understand this to reaffirm a sense of urgency for restoration.

Jerusalem, the city Yahweh chooses, is also a place of promise, but this time connected with Yahweh's promise to David (e.g., 1 Kgs 11.32, 36; 15.4; 19.34). As we have seen in Chapter 3, this promise functions within the historiography of the book to encourage Israel to imagine their destiny as a people of covenant faithfulness. This, along with what we said above concerning the temple, is enough to ensure that the exiles understood Jerusalem also to have an ongoing significance.

At the level of the land of Israel, we have seen that the book reaffirms Yahweh's continued presence there even after the exile. We have also seen that the land is portrayed as the place of Yahweh's revelation. Yahweh may be sovereign and act internationally, but only those who seek the God who is in Israel find the God of the whole earth. This also remains true in the exile.

The significance of the land, then, relates to the concentric definition. Yahweh's commitment to the temple and Jerusalem ensures they are understood as places associated with Yahweh's promises. These circles sit within the land as the only place within Kings where Yahweh can be found. And this circle sits within another, which is the realm of Yahweh's sovereign action, the entire earth. Within the narrative of Kings, Yahweh is portrayed as transcendent over all the earth, and not located specifically anywhere within it. He governs foreign nations and territories, overcomes foreign gods, and determines the fate of kingdoms:

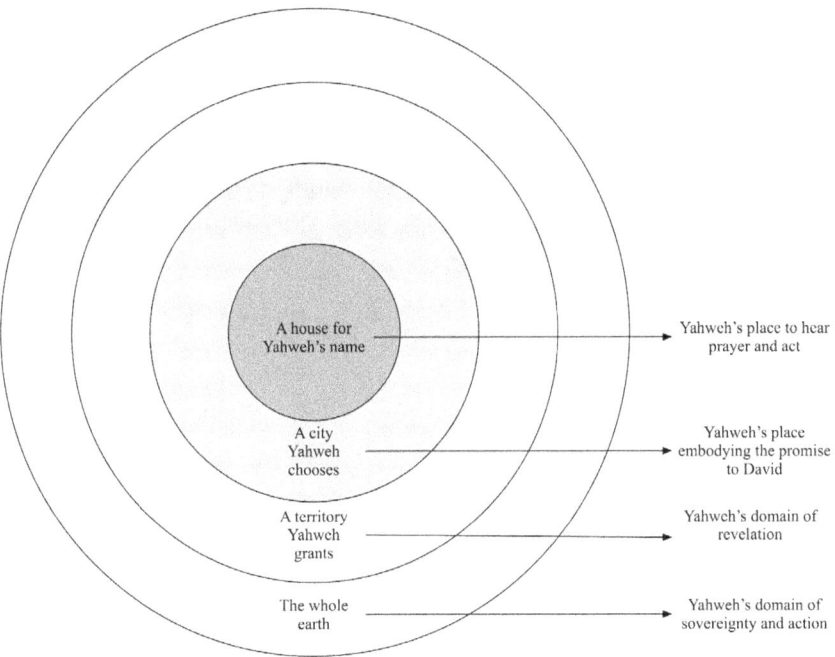

Figure 5.2. *Land and Yahweh's Domain in Kings*

The theological idea of land in the narrative of Kings consists of:
(a) a house for Yahweh's name, where Yahweh guarantees his attention
and the provision of blessing; within (b) a city Yahweh chooses, a place
of promise which Yahweh will preserve for David's sake; within (c) a
territory Yahweh grants; a place of revelation where, through Israel, all
people can come to know that Yahweh is the God of all the earth; within
(d) the entire earth, in which Yahweh sovereignly acts according to his
own purpose.

Recalling Block's theological–geography triangle, all of this means that the deity–land side remains intact during the exile. The people–land side, however, has been severed. To be cast out of Yahweh's presence in Kings (2 Kgs 17.23; 24.20) is to be removed from the place promised to mediate both revelation and blessing. Babylon is not a place for the fulfilment of promises. In order to realise Covenant-Israel, the seed of the remnant will have to be replanted in the territory Yahweh granted; the city Yahweh chose and the house for Yahweh's name must be rebuilt.

In the meantime, the book constructs an alternate community focal point for their exile.[144] In the absence of the temple, and ruled by apostate kings who re-Canaanised the northern territories, a faithful form of Yahwism emerged in the north centred on prophetic ministry. The position of the book is that exilic Israel should likewise construct a social identity around the ministry of the prophets. Although Israel cannot realise the ideal of the covenant from Babylon, their continued relationship with Yahweh encourages hope for restoration.

---

144. Note that Frankel (*The Land of Canaan and the Destiny of Israel*, 136) argued similarly concerning the incorporation of the Sinai traditions into DtrH, to show Israel as 'an extraterritorial religious order'.

6

Rule: The King after Exile

6.1. *Royal Ideology and the Book of Kings*

It is our final task in this study to identify the royal ideology that the narrative of the book endorses. The history of scholarship on Kings warns us that this task may not be easy, and some might say impossible. Two royal ideologies have been perceived in Kings (and DtrH). The perceived tension between these has endured for the last four decades of scholarship as a key sign that the book comprises multiple redactions. And, as we saw in our review in Chapter 1, this is true for both the Göttingen and Harvard Schools of redaction-criticism. The Harvard School has made this tension a central pillar to its thesis. We shall label the two ideologies the Zion and deuteronomic ideals.[1]

In the Harvard model, Zion ideology belongs to the pre-exilic redaction. It supports Judean kingship (Josiah or Hezekiah), Yahweh's selection of David and Jerusalem, and centralisation of worship. In the Göttingen model it is assigned to Dtr_G, who was interested in Israel's history.[2] Many components of Zion ideology are thought to be adopted from Israel's surrounding cultures (see 1 Sam. 8.5, 20).[3] John Day articulates the central

---

1. The Zion ideal is referred to as 'Royal' ideology by some, though I prefer to reserve this term for discussion of ANE kingship more broadly. In my nomenclature, Zion ideology is Israel's particular kingship model.

2. Veijola, *Die ewige Dynastie*, 24–6; Veijola, *Das Königtum in der Beurteilung der deuteronomistischen Historiographie*, 122.

3. See John H. Walton, *Ancient Near Eastern Thought and the Old Testament: Introducing the Conceptual World of the Hebrew Bible*, 2nd ed. (Grand Rapids, MI: Baker Academic, 2018), 256–68; or K. M. Heim, 'Kings and Kingship', *DOTH*, 610–23. For detailed analysis see the essays in Day, ed., *King and Messiah in Israel and the Ancient Near East*: by Wilfred Lambert ('Kingship in Ancient Mesopotamia',

components of Zion ideology, understanding them to have been adapted from the pre-Davidic Jebusite cult:[4]

1. The king was a priest-king, who oversaw the affairs of both state and cult, and who mediated access to the state god.[5]
2. The king was chosen and anointed by god[6] and adopted as 'son of god'.[7] With a few exceptions, only Egypt claimed actual divinity for their kings. Other nations saw their kings as superhuman, but mortal.[8]
3. The state god offered divine protection of the king and inviolability of the central royal–divine sanctuary.[9]

54–71), John Day ('The Canaanite Inheritance of the Israelite Monarchy', 72–90), and John Baines ('Ancient Egyptian Kingship', 16–53). See also Keith W. Whitelam, 'Israelite Kingship: The Royal Ideology and its Opponents', in Clements, ed., *The World of Ancient Israel*, 120–2; Brueggemann and Hankins, 'The Affirmation of Prophetic Power', 58–9; and Gottwald, *The Politics of Ancient Israel*, 146–7. Laato (*A Star Is Rising*, 81–95) explores the uniqueness of the Israelite monarchy. More comprehensive earlier treatments include Ivan Engnell, *Studies in Divine Kingship in the Ancient Near East* (Oxford: Blackwell, 1967); and S. H. Hooke, ed., *Myth, Ritual, and Kingship: Essays on the Theory and Practice of Kingship in the Ancient Near East and in Israel* (London: Clarendon, 1960). I summarise some of this material below. See also Gerald E. Gerbrandt, *Kingship According to the Deuteronomistic History*, SBLDS 87 (Atlanta, GA: Scholars Press, 1986), 192.

4. On the early origins of Zion theology, see J. J. M. Roberts, 'Zion in the Theology of the Davidic-Solomonic Empire', in *Studies in the Period of David and Solomon and Other Essays*, ed. Tomoo Ishida (Winona Lake, IN: Eisenbrauns, 1982), 93–108. See also Day, 'The Canaanite Inheritance of the Israelite Monarchy'. See also Carol Meyers, 'Kinship and Kingship', in *The Oxford History of the Biblical World*, ed. M. D. Coogan (Oxford: Oxford University Press, 1998), 221–71; and Henri Cazelles, 'Sacral Kingship', *AYBD*, 5:863–6.

5. Day ('The Canaanite Inheritance of the Israelite Monarchy', 78–80) develops this view from Ps. 110 and Gen. 14, by claiming that 'Elyon' was the Jebusite god, whom David appropriated and re-identified as Yahweh when he captured Jerusalem.

6. Day, 'The Canaanite Inheritance of the Israelite Monarchy', 80–1.

7. The phrase 'son of god' is well attested throughout the ANE as a royal designation, so we can conclude that divine adoption was a standard component of ANE royal ideology. See Day, 'The Canaanite Inheritance of the Israelite Monarchy', 81–5.

8. E.g. Baines, 'Ancient Egyptian Kingship', 24–41; Lambert, 'Kingship in Ancient Mesopotamia', 55–66; and Walton, *Ancient Near Eastern Thought and the Old Testament*, 260–1.

9. Day, 'The Canaanite Inheritance of the Israelite Monarchy', 79.

4. The king managed the maintenance and well ordering of the nation, including civic and military responsibilities, and was divinely imbued with the supernatural traits (strength, wisdom, etc.) to accomplish this task.[10]

Scholars likewise understand some of Israel's literature as royal *apologia* of the same type found elsewhere in the ANE.[11] Keith Whitelam comments:

> The heavy investment of early state societies in the ideological justification of kingship through written, graphic and ceremonial means indicates the importance of understanding the nature of royal ideology and the way that it functioned or was addressed to different audiences to overcome opposition and thus maintain royal power. The use of force was too costly and on the whole inefficient in means to propagate the royal symbolic universe.[12]

In the Old Testament, the Zion model of kingship is most frequent in the book of Isaiah[13] and the Royal Psalms (e.g., Pss. 2; 18; 72; 89; 110).[14] In the book of Kings it is present in the section common with Isaiah (2 Kgs 18–20), in the Solomon narratives (1 Kgs 3–10, especially

---

10. Day, 'The Canaanite Inheritance of the Israelite Monarchy', 82, 86–7.

11. See Day, 'The Canaanite Inheritance of the Israelite Monarchy', 72–3; J. J. M. Roberts, 'Davidic Origin of the Zion Tradition', *JBL* 92 (1973): 329; Roberts, 'Public Opinion, Royal Apologetics, and Imperial Ideology: A Political Analysis of the Portrait of David, "A Man After God's Own Heart"', *Theology Today* 69 (2012): 116–32; John H. Walton, *Ancient Israelite Literature in its Cultural Context: A Survey of Parallels Between Biblical and Ancient Near Eastern Texts* (Grand Rapids, MI: Zondervan, 1990), 111–19; and Gottwald, *The Politics of Ancient Israel*, 146–9, 156–7. As Knapp observes, *apologetic* is not a genre but rather a literary 'mode' that can be comprised of a variety of genres. The book of Kings is not an *apologetic* but some of its sources may originally have had apologetic intent. Knapp analyses the succession narrative as one example, but it comprises such a small section of Kings (1 Kgs 1–2) that we will not focus on it in this chapter. See Andrew Knapp, *Royal Apologetic in the Ancient Near East*, WAWSup (Atlanta, GA: SBL, 2015), 41–5, 249–76.

12. Whitelam, 'Israelite Kingship', 121; see also Keith W. Whitelam, 'The Symbols of Royal Power: Aspects of Royal Propaganda in the United Monarchy', *BA* 49 (1986): 166–73.

13. J. J. M. Roberts, *First Isaiah*, Hermeneia (Minneapolis, MN: Fortress, 2015), 4–6.

14. Ollenburger, *Zion*, 23–52; H. A. Thomas, 'Zion', *DOTP*, 907–14; Clements, *Isaiah and the Deliverance of Jerusalem*; John H. Hayes, 'Tradition of Zion's Inviolability', *JBL* 82 (1963): 419–26; Thomas, 'Zion', 907–14.

ch. 8),[15] and in the various statements about David and Jerusalem (e.g., 1 Kgs 11.32-36; 14.21; 15.4; 2 Kgs 8.19; 21.4-7).[16] Martti Nissinen and Michael Avioz claim the Davidic promise which lies behind many of these texts (2 Sam. 7) and Solomon's succession (1 Kgs 2) also belong to this category.[17]

The second ideology is referred to as deuteronomism, since it is linked to the wider discussion of the book's composition.[18] This terminology may, however, cause some confusion. Some understand the Zion model to have been the ideology of the pre-exilic Dtr, and thus it too is technically 'deuteronomistic'. However, in this context, deuteronomism specifically refers to the ideology of the exilic editor.

The Harvard School understands deuteronomic ideology to be an exilic reaction in response to the failure of the Zion model. The Göttingen School assigns it to either Dtr_P or Dtr_N, who perceived the limitations of human monarchy and recognised instead Yahweh's direct kingship.[19] In both cases, the redaction superimposes a more reserved, sometimes negative, assessment of the monarchy onto the Zion theology present in, or retained by, an earlier layer (see e.g. Deut. 17.14-20; Judg. 8.22-23; 9.7-20; 1 Sam. 8.1-22).[20] In many redaction-critical models

---

15. Note that Habel's *royal* land ideology (*The Land Is Mine*, 17–32), which we examined in Chapter 5, is an extension of this royal ideological model. See also Keith W. Whitelam, *The Just King: Monarchical Judicial Authority in Ancient Israel* (Sheffield: JSOT, 1979), 119–21.

16. We reviewed this literature in Chapter 1. See Cross, *Canaanite Myth and Hebrew Epic*, 287, 241–3, 246–7, 255; and Nelson, *The Double Redaction of the Deuteronomistic History*, 28; and Sweeney's similar view ('The Critique of Solomon in the Josianic Edition of the Deuteronomistic History', *JBL* 114 [1995]: 622), which we discussed in Chapter 4.

17. Nissinen, 'Prophets and Prophecy in Joshua–Kings', 115; Avioz, *Nathan's Oracle*, 16–24. See also J. J. M. Roberts, 'In Defense of the Monarchy: The Contribution of Israelite Kingship to Biblical Theology', in *Ancient Israelite Religion: Essays in Honor of Frank Moore Cross*, ed. Patrick D. Miller, Paul D. Hanson, and Sean D. McBride, repr. (Minneapolis, MN: Fortress, 2009), 381–2; and John T. Willis, 'David and Zion in the Theology of the Deuteronomistic History: Theological Ideas in 2 Samuel 5–7', in *David and Zion: Biblical Studies in Honor of J. J. M. Roberts*, ed. Bernard F. Batto and Katheryn L. Roberts (Winona Lake, IN: Eisenbrauns, 2004), 125–40.

18. See Chapter 1.

19. Veijola, *Das Königtum in der Beurteilung der deuteronomistischen Historiographie*, 122; see also Gerbrandt, *Kingship*, 33.

20. This idea predates even the DtrH hypothesis, to at the latest Julius Wellhausen (*Prolegomena*, 247–60), who understood the monarchy as the high-point of Israelite

these two ideologies are irreconcilable. One is pro-monarchic, and one anti-monarchic.[21]

This method of literary reconstruction is well recognised in Kings, but the recognition that Kings contains two royal ideologies is not a satisfactory explanation of the theology of the exilic text. Antti Laato comments, for example:

> Scholars have frequently suggested that some of these distinctive theological viewpoints originate from different redactions. However, it is difficult to accept the notion that the intention behind the present form of the Deuteronomistic history was to argue that no particular version of the Israelite royal ideology is correct and that readers have liberty to simply choose between the several alternatives presented in the text. There is reason to suppose that attempts were made to harmonise the various theological outlooks of the traditions so that a single, relatively coherent view was placed in high relief.[22]

This assessment is likely. If the purpose of the final form of the book was to offer Israel a history by which they might understand their political identity, then it makes little sense that the redactor would be careless enough to leave untouched in so many places the same Zionist ideology he intended to critique.[23]

Even early forms of the DtrH hypothesis sometimes attempted to integrate the two views. Noth, for example, accepted the basic proposition of a pro-monarchic and anti-monarchic source,[24] but thought the two

---

development, and the post-monarchic source as a (fictional) retrojection. Neither is it always still associated with the DtrH hypothesis. Hamilton, for example, posits both a pro-monarchic and counter-monarchic (not anti-monarchic) tendency within First Isaiah. See Hamilton, *A Kingdom for a Stage*, 112–13.

21. E.g. Levinson, 'The Reconceptualisation of Kingship'; Christophe Nihan, 'Rewriting Kingship in Samuel: 1 Samuel 8 and 12 and the Law of the King (Deuteronomy 17)', *HBAI* 2 (2013): 338, 343; and Ian D. Wilson, *Kingship and Memory in Ancient Judah* (Oxford: Oxford University Press, 2017), 68–73.

22. Laato, *A Star Is Rising*, 33–4. See also Sang-Won Lee, 'Die Königsbeurteilungen und die Literargeschichte des Deuteronomistischen Geschichtswerks Anmerkungen zu einer kontroversen Diskussion', *VT* 68 (2018): 581–605.

23. Neither is the addition of conditional clauses to the dynastic promise in Kings evidence of such 're-touching' of earlier theology, as I argued in Chapter 3. See also Laato, *A Star Is Rising*, 37; and Sweeney, 'The Critique of Solomon', 622. For a similar treatment of Isaiah's royal theology see Hamilton, *A Kingdom for a Stage*, 107–12. In Hamilton's model, both stages co-exist prior to the exile; see Mark W. Hamilton, 'Isaiah 32 as Literature and Political Meditation', *JBL* 131 (2012): 665–6.

24. Noth, *The Deuteronomistic History*, 63–5.

traditions existed side-by-side within Israel's history.[25] Von Rad agreed.[26] He noted the pro-monarchic elements of the Davidic promise (election, anointing, adoption, and protection) were well integrated into DtrH and argued that it was not possible to excise them.[27] The possibility of parallel literary development has since been bolstered by anthropological[28] and comparative studies.[29]

McConville picks up this line of integration when he proposes that Dtr intends to relativise and demythologise the 'Zion–Davidic Synthesis'.[30] By understanding the positive monarchic elements as an instance of 'divine accommodation',[31] McConville reads DtrH as a critique of a model of kingship that was always intended to be provisional. He argues that the entire matrix of Zion ideology is an ideology borrowed from the ANE, and its demise in exile is to 'undo measures that were originally unwelcome to Yahweh'.[32]

There are other ways to integrate the data. Jon Levenson proposed that the two ideologies were separated by geography: the Zion texts were an *apologia* for the southern monarchy and deuteronomism was a response from the north. In his model the two traditions, 'Sinai and Zion', were forced together when the northern refugees fled to Hezekiah's Jerusalem.[33] Walter Brueggemann gives a theological reading of the history which

25. Agreeing with Halpern, *The Constitution of the Monarchy in Israel*, 227–47. See also McConville, 'King and Messiah', 288–93.

26. Von Rad, *Old Testament Theology*, 1:339–47.

27. See Dennis J. McCarthy, 'II Samuel 7 and the Structure of the Deuteronomic History', *JBL* 84 (1965): 131–8, for the standard defence of this statement following Wellhausen (see n. 20). For discussion, see Laato, *A Star Is Rising*, 33–47; Knoppers, 'David's Relation to Moses', 96–101; and McConville, 'King and Messiah in Deuteronomy', 282–5.

28. E.g. Crüsemann's anthropological study (*Der Widerstand gegen das Königtum: die antiköniglichen Texte des Alten Testamentes und der Kampf um den frühen israelitischen Staat*, WMANT [Neukirchen-Vluyn: Neukirchener Verlag, 1978]) concludes that the anti-establishment texts are the products of a socio-economic group present in the early monarchy, faced with Solomon's oppressive taxation and labour practices.

29. E.g. Mendelsohn's comparative analysis of the treatment of kingship themes in the book of Samuel and Ugaritic literature ('Samuel's Denunciation of Kingship in the Light of Akkadian Documents from Ugarit', *BASOR* 143 [1956]: 22).

30. McConville, 'Law and Monarchy', 74–5; and *God and Earthly Power*, 156.

31. McConville, 'Law and Monarchy', 75.

32. McConville, *God and Earthly Power*, 156.

33. Jon D. Levenson, 'Who Inserted the Book of the Torah?', *HTR* 68 (1975): 227–30; Levenson, *Sinai and Zion: An Entry into the Jewish Bible* (New York: Harper, 1987), 188–206.

moves from anti-monarchic to pro-monarchic and back again.[34] And Knoppers proposes that the tension lies between Deuteronomy (which he believes to be anti-monarchic) and the rest of DtrH (which he reads as pro-monarchic).[35]

Given the wide range of possibilities, it is unlikely that the book of Kings is best understood as a simple *apologia* either for or against the monarchy. Neither is it the careless product of a redactional composite.[36] So far we have been able to find a coherent synthesis of several related issues – centralisation of worship, for example, or covenant and promise – which gives us hope that the same will be true here. We will follow the same strategy. We shall assume that whatever combination of ideologies we find in the narrative were intentionally deployed, and we shall seek a synthesis that explains what the author's agenda might be. Rather than asking whether the book is positive or negative towards kingship, the key will be to ask, as Gerald Gebrandt did, what kind of 'unified concept of kingship'[37] would be suitable for the covenant people of Yahweh?

As we saw above, many treatments of this topic begin with Zion theology and move forward to its deuteronomic critique. There is a logic to this, but one disadvantage is that treatments often portray a negative deuteronomic layer that does little to present a viable alternative to Zion theology. This is not the case. The deuteronomic theology of the book portrays a positive and nuanced ideal. It is with this model of kingship that we shall begin.

6.2. *The Deuteronomic Ideal for Kingship*

6.2.1. *The Exemplary Role of David*

The most obvious locations in Kings to search for the deuteronomic ideal of kingship are the regnal formulae, which assess the kings of

---

34. Walter A. Brueggemann, *The Land: Place as Gift, Promise, and Challenge in Biblical Faith*, OBT (London: SPCK, 1978), 84–5.

35. Knoppers, 'The Deuteronomist and the Deuteronomic Law of the King', 345; 'Rethinking the Relationship', 406. For more on the tension between Deuteronomy and DtrH see Mark W. Hamilton, 'Critiquing the Sovereign: Perspectives from Deuteronomy and Job', *RQ* 47 (2005): 240–5; Tryggve N. D. Mettinger, *King and Messiah: The Civil and Sacral Legitimation of the Israelite Kings*, ConB (London: Coronet, 1976); Levinson, 'The Reconceptualisation of Kingship'; and G. E. Mendenhall, 'The Monarchy', *Int* 29 (1975): 155–70.

36. So Hamilton, *A Kingdom for a Stage*, 51; and Roberts, 'In Defense of the Monarchy', 380–1.

37. Gerbrandt, *Kingship*, 192, see also. pp. 189–90.

Israel and Judah according to the particular standards of the covenant.[38] As we saw in Chapter 2, these formulae belong to the frame structure of the book because they are voiced by the narrator, and therefore speak with an authoritative, evaluative voice. Kings can be good (e.g., Josiah), evil (e.g., Manasseh), or good with the sole exception that they have not removed the shrines (במות, e.g. Asa). This indicates that the book intends its readers to understand that their kings should live up to the standard of the covenant.

The formulae move beyond covenant evaluation by their comparative clauses. When, for example, Amaziah 'does right but not like David' (2 Kgs 14.3), or when Ahab 'walks in the way of Jeroboam son of Nebat', the formulae have in mind examples against which kingship can be measured. These comparisons are also formulaic even though there is some minor variation. In general:

1. Every northern king is compared to Jeroboam son of Nebat;
2. Good kings of Judah are compared either to their father (e.g., Jehoshaphat) or to David (e.g., Hezekiah, Josiah);[39] and
3. Bad kings of Judah are compared either to their father (e.g., Jehoahaz, Jehoiakim), to the nations that were removed from the land (e.g., Rehoboam), or to Israel and/or Ahab (e.g., Jehoram).[40]

David, then, because he is the only positive basis of comparison, functions as the exemplar monarch within the book of Kings. What does a king have to do to be judged 'like David'? Only Asa, Hezekiah, and Josiah are so judged (1 Kgs 15.11; 2 Kgs 18.3; 22.2), which leaves out several good kings like Jehoshaphat (1 Kgs 22.42).

Some have suggested that only explicitly reforming kings earn a comparison to David.[41] However, as Provan notes,[42] this is an unlikely

---

38. We examined the regnal formulae in relation to apostasy in Chapter 3 and in relation to centralisation in Chapter 5. The standard treatment of the contents of regnal formulae, with comparisons to ANE literature, is Long, *1 Kings*, 160–4.

39. Minor variants include Amaziah who does right but 'not like David', only 'like his father' (2 Kgs 14.3), and Je(ho)ash is the only king who 'does right because he was instructed by a priest' (2 Kgs 12.2 [12.3, Heb.]).

40. Minor variants include Abijam and Ahaz who do what is wrong, unlike David (e.g., 1 Kgs 15.3).

41. E.g. E. Cortese, 'Lo schema deuteronomistico per i re di Giuda e d'Israel', *Bib* 56 (1975): 44; Joseph, *Portrait of the Kings*, 90; Greg Goswell, 'King and Cultus: The Image of David in the Book of Kings', *JESOT* 5 (2017): 175–9; Halpern and Vanderhooft, 'The Editions of Kings', 183–90; and Weippert, 'Die "deuteronomistischen" Beurteilungen'.

42. Provan, *Hezekiah and the Books of Kings*, 94.

solution.⁴³ First, what would account for the omission of Jehoshaphat? According to the traditions available to the Chronicler, at least, Jehoshaphat was a reforming king (2 Chron. 17.9).⁴⁴ Second, even if the author of Kings did not have access to that tradition, then the inclusion of Asa is anomalous (1 Kgs 15.12-14).⁴⁵ Asa's reforms do not extend to the removal of the shrines (v. 14), but he still earns a positive comparison to David (v. 11). The hypothesis that reformation of the cult makes a king 'like David' cannot be sustained.

My own proposal is that the book of Kings prefers to compare both good and evil kings of Judah to their fathers if possible. Without exception, if it is possible to compare a good king with a good father, the book does this: Jehoshaphat, Amaziah, Azariah, and Jotham. Following this pattern, only good kings with bad fathers are compared directly to David: Asa, Hezekiah, and Josiah. This pattern also indirectly makes sense of the observation concerning reforms. Only good kings with bad fathers need to implement reforms: good kings with good fathers can maintain the status quo.

This would mean that the Davidic comparison is implicitly applied to every good king. When Jehoshaphat, for example, 'walks in all the ways of Asa his father' (1 Kgs 22.43), how else is the reader to understand this except that he, like Asa, 'did what was right in the eyes of the Lord as David had done' (1 Kgs 15.11)? Even though the Davidic prototype is mentioned explicitly only in three cases, it functions implicitly for every good king who belongs to a line of kings that are all like David.

What, then, if not reforming the cult, makes a king 'like David'?⁴⁶ Joseph enumerates the elements of the Davidic comparisons.⁴⁷ Other than reforming the cult, which Joseph includes, there are two factors that consistently and only arise with kings that are compared positively to David: (1) that the king does 'what is right in the eyes of Yahweh' (הישר בעיני יהוה); and (2) that king has a certain type of heart (לב).

The first of these, doing what is right in Yahweh's eyes, is standard deuteronomic language (e.g., Deut. 12.25, 28; 13.18; 21.9) equivalent to covenant obedience (Deut. 6.18; 1 Kgs 11.33, 38; etc., 29 times in Kings). The narrative of Kings claims that David also 'did what was right in the eyes of Yahweh' (e.g., 1 Kgs 11.38; 14.8; 15.5).⁴⁸ It is also the opposite

43. Note that David, prevented by Nathan, is not a reforming king (2 Sam. 7.4-11).
44. Jehoshaphat is compared to David by the Chronicler (2 Chron. 17.3).
45. As Joseph (*Portrait of the Kings*, 90) also notes.
46. See also Goswell, 'King and Cultus', 174–9.
47. Joseph, *Portrait of the Kings*, 83–93. See also Goswell, 'King and Cultus', 174–9.
48. '…[E]xcept in the matter of Uriah the Hittite' (1 Kgs 15.5).

of the negative deuteronomic phrase, 'doing what is right in [one's] own eyes' (e.g., Deut. 12.8), which was what people did before there was a king in Israel in deuteronomic tradition (e.g., Judg. 17.6; 21.25).

The second is a statement about the heart (לֵב)⁴⁹ of the king.⁵⁰ Such statements about the inclination of the heart are also standard in the language of Deuteronomy (e.g., Deut. 4.9; 6.4, 6; 10.12), and also include the idea of covenant obedience in Kings (e.g., 1 Kgs 2.4; 8.61).⁵¹ In its use of this heart language, however, Kings moves beyond what both the covenant traditions and the traditions of David himself understand as possible.

In Deuteronomy, even though Israel are often enjoined to 'love God with all your heart' (Deut. 6.5), 'worship God with all your heart' (11.13), and 'write the law on your heart' (11.18),⁵² the book envisages failure.⁵³ The people have fearful (1.28; 7.17), 'stiff necked' (10.16; see also 5.29), and disobedient hearts (9.5, see also 8.2). The command that they should 'circumcise their hearts' and 'no longer be stiff necked' (10.16) is met only with promises of Yahweh's grace on the other side of exile (Deut. 4.29; 30.1-2, 10, 14), that Yahweh will 'circumcise their hearts', and then place the law on their hearts (Deut. 30.6, 15). The law of the king also has two warnings about the heart of the king in particular (Deut. 17.17, 20). In Deuteronomy, then, Israel (and their king) are enjoined to have hearts that are predisposed to Yahweh and covenant fidelity, but this is not possible.⁵⁴

---

49. The 'heart' metaphor refers to more than the domain of emotions often associated with the word in Western contexts. It refers to one's inner self, inclinations, dispositions, will, reason, and conscience. See *HALOT,* s.v. 'לֵב'; Daniel I. Block, 'How Many Is God? An Investigation into the Meaning of Deuteronomy 6:4–5', *JETS* 47 (2004): 201–4.

50. Joseph (*Portrait of the Kings*, 82 n. 11) notes that, generally, scholars have not included the לב statements in their analysis of the regnal formulae. Von Rad is an exception (*Old Testament Theology*, 163–4).

51. Wray Beal, *The Deuteronomist's Prophet*, 157.

52. See also Deut. 4.9, 39; 8.5, 14, 17; 9.4; 10.12; 11.16; 15.7, 9, 10; 20.3; 26.16; 29.18; 30.17; 32.46.

53. For explorations of this theme, see Paul A. Barker, *The Triumph of Grace in Deuteronomy: Faithless Israel, Faithful Yahweh in Deuteronomy* (Eugene, OR: Wipf & Stock, 2004). The divergence in theology between Deuteronomy and Kings is part of Knoppers's argument ('The Deuteronomist and the Deuteronomic Law of the King') and noted by McConville (*Deuteronomy*, 283–4).

54. Also in Dtr theology generally. See, e.g., McConville, *Grace in the End*, 134–8; and Daniel I. Block, 'The Grace of Torah: The Mosaic Prescription for Life (Deut 4:1-8; 6:20-25)', *BSac* 162 (2005): 3–22.

In the same way, David, as he is portrayed in Samuel, is never said to have a heart that is committed to Yahweh or his covenant.⁵⁵ David was a man 'after Yahweh's heart' (כלבבו, 1 Sam. 13.4) but in the historiography of Samuel this shows Yahweh's choice, rather than David's disposition.⁵⁶ Far from embodying an attitude of resilient covenantal obedience, the metaphor of David's heart is used in Samuel to show his fear (1 Sam. 21.12; 27.1; 28.5) and tender conscience (1 Sam. 24.5; 2 Sam. 24.10).⁵⁷

However, the book of Kings remembers David differently, and not always consistently.⁵⁸ The narrative of transition (1 Kgs 1–2)⁵⁹ continues the fallible portrayal of David that was found in Samuel into the frailty of old age (see also 1 Kgs 15.5).⁶⁰ In relation to the Davidic promise, as we have seen in Chapter 2, the book remembers and affirms David as the pioneer of the monarchy and of Zion theology.⁶¹ However, neither of these contribute to the deuteronomic ideal of kingship in the book. In relation to that ideal, the book of Kings constructs a covenantally obedient

---

55. Note that the people in Samuel are still commanded to do this (1 Sam. 12.20, 24).

56. George Athas, 'A Man after God's Own Heart: David and the Rhetoric of Election to Kingship', *JESOT* 2 (2012): 196–7; Goldingay, *Israel's Gospel*, 557; Bodner, *1 Samuel*, 123.

57. On the relationship between the mixed portrayal of David in Samuel and the intent of the book to legitimate his kingship, see Knapp, *Royal Apologetic*, 218–42.

58. That the David of Kings is sometimes unlike the David of Samuel has led to significant discussion. E.g., Provan, *Hezekiah and the Books of Kings*, 91–131; Auld, *Kings Without Privilege*, 90–3; von Rad, *Old Testament Theology*, 164; and Goswell, 'King and Cultus', 179–83. On the significance of this for the literary history, see Moshe Garsiel, 'The Book of Samuel: Its Composition, Structure and Significance as a Historiographical Source', *JHebS* 10 (2010): 21, 42; and Wilson, *Kingship and Memory*, 135–47.

59. On the so-called succession narrative source (2 Sam. 11–20; 1 Kgs 1–2) see, classically, Whybray, *The Succession Narrative*; Blenkinsopp, 'Another Contribution to the Succession Narrative Debate'; and Hans Jørgen Lundager Jensen, 'Desire, Rivalry and Collective Violence in the "Succession Narrative"', *JSOT* 55 (1992): 39–59.

60. Fretheim, *First and Second Kings*, 23–9; and Leithart, *1&2 Kings*, 29–35. The reason for this portrayal may be the desire to validate Solomon's ascent to power. See Knapp, *Royal Apologetic*, 218–42; who limits his study of royal apology to 1 Kgs 1–2, after which with respect to Solomon there is 'no apparent apologetic function' (p. 254).

61. E.g. 1 Kgs 2.4, 24; 3.6, 7; 6.12; 8.15-18, 20, 24-26; 9.5; 11.12-13, 32-39; 15.4-5; 2 Kgs 8.9; 19.34; 20.6; 21.7-8. Provan (*Hezekiah and the Books of Kings*, 91–131) also observes that David is portrayed differently for different purposes.

David. Solomon recalls his father as a man who 'walked before [Yahweh] in faithfulness, righteousness, and uprightness of heart' (1 Kgs 3.6), and several chapters later Yahweh affirms this view (1 Kgs 9.4; 11.4).

Through statements like this, the narrative creates in the reader's mind a picture of a 'good' king as one who, like David, can (more or less, 1 Kgs 15.5, 14) whole-heartedly keep the covenant. Nothing we have said so far amounts to the rejection of the Zion model of kingship, but it does relativise the value of the roles associated with the monarch in that model.[62] As we shall see below, David-like kings are not defined by their relation to the cult. Neither are they David-like because of their military or civic accomplishments: about such things the book of Kings seems uninterested (e.g., 1 Kgs 14.19; 15.23; 22.39). Kings are good, like David, only if they are faithful to the covenant (note 1 Kgs 8.58, 61; see also Deut. 17.20).

6.2.2. *The Paradigmatic Virtues of the Incomparable Kings*

The observation that, within the historiography of the book, David-like monarchs are covenant-keeping brings us to Josiah.[63] Even though kings do not have to be perfect to be David-like, Josiah's characterisation is unblemished.[64] As the only king to accomplish Deut. 6.4-5, Josiah is incomparable (2 Kgs 23.25).[65] Even David does not compare.[66]

Alongside Josiah there are two other incomparable kings. Josiah's covenant obedience is matched by Hezekiah's faith (2 Kgs 18.5) and Solomon's wisdom (1 Kgs 3.2). How should these incomparable formulae be understood?

The traditional solution is to assume that each formula means to say the same thing: that this king is the best. Scholars have then assigned these statements to different redactional layers, a Hezekian one and a

---

62. See above, or Day, 'The Canaanite Inheritance of the Israelite Monarchy'.

63. On Josiah and the Davidic prototype, see Joseph, *Portrait of the Kings*, 147–86.

64. We discussed Josiah in Chapter 3 and his reforms in Chapter 5.

65. On the incomparability formulae, see Knoppers, 'There Was None Like Him'. Note that Moses received a similar commendation (Deut. 34.10-12).

66. Sweeney, *King Josiah of Judah*, 173; Joseph, *Portrait of the Kings*, 152–65. This observation has often been used to support the double-redaction theory of the book. Since Josiah is a more perfect David than David, perhaps the ideal was constructed for his benefit? See, e.g. Provan, *Hezekiah and the Books of Kings*, 153–5; Nelson, *The Double Redaction of the Deuteronomistic History*, 84; Cross, *Canaanite Myth and Hebrew Epic*, 274–78. For discussion see Knoppers, 'Theories of the Redaction(s) of Kings', 70–8; Knoppers, and 'There Was None Like Him', 430–1.

Josian one.⁶⁷ However, this is not convincing and assumes at least one careless redactor.⁶⁸ Knoppers's suggestion is better: that since Solomon is incomparable in wisdom, Hezekiah in faith, and Josiah in obedience, the book intends to explore these virtues in relation to the royal ideal.⁶⁹ This suggestion is likely, and can be strengthened by the observation that wisdom, faith, and obedience are all related to the heart (לב) in the book of Kings (1 Kgs 3.9; 2 Kgs 20.3; 23.25). So, as with the Davidic exemplar, these three paradigms of virtue also explore the inward disposition of the king.

i. *The Virtue of Obedience*

Josiah's obedience is paradigmatic within Kings. What is entailed by a king's obedience to the covenant? The pertinent text is the law of the king (Deut. 17.14-20). This law has six components, each of which Josiah seems to follow. The king: (1) must be Israelite, (2) must not acquire a large military, especially from Egypt,⁷⁰ (3) must not acquire a large harem, (4) must not acquire excessive silver and gold, (5) must submit to the law with priestly oversight, and (6) must not exalt himself above other Israelites. Josiah is never shown to contradict any of these stipulations, and so appears to keep the letter of this law. However, when the law of the king is set within its wider context, not everyone agrees that Josiah earns his narratorial commendation.⁷¹ In Deuteronomy, the law of the king is part of a larger program that distributes the powers of the state.⁷² Different institutions had their own responsibilities: local courts (Deut. 16.18; 17.2-7), a central court (Deut. 17.8-13), a levitical priesthood (Deut. 18.1-8), and the prophets (Deut. 18.15-22).⁷³ Because of this,

---

67. Cross, *Canaanite Myth and Hebrew Epic*, 286; Friedman, *The Exile and Biblical Narrative*, 7; and Nelson, *The Double Redaction of the Deuteronomistic History*, 84–5.

68. So Knoppers, 'There Was None Like Him', 430–1.

69. Knoppers, 'There Was None Like Him'; see also Provan, 'The Messiah in the Book of Kings', 76–81.

70. Ironically, Josiah's military was not large enough to defeat Egypt.

71. E.g. McConville, *Deuteronomy*, 283–4; McConville, 'King and Messiah', 292; Joseph, *Portrait of the Kings*, 153. Knoppers ('Rethinking the Relationship', 399–406) understands Josiah's commendation to be genuine, and the book of Kings to critique Deut. 17.

72. See my discussion in Chapter 3, and Knoppers, 'Rethinking the Relationship', 397–8.

73. On the separation of powers in Deuteronomy, see Rutersworden, *Von der politischen Gemeinschaft zur Gemeinde*; McBride, 'Polity of the Covenant People', 229–44; or Lohfink, 'Distributions of the Functions of Power'.

Josiah's reforms, which centralise power in the monarchy at the temple, invite questions. Knoppers comments:

> The whole point of apportioning authority among several authorities is to ensure that no one person aggrandises or monopolises power. In this respect, the Deuteronomic legislation does not seem to permit one authority to usurp the prerogatives of another...[74]

Does Josiah's fervour to centralise the cult cause him to overstep his deuteronomic jurisdiction? Knoppers wonders, for example, why the book fails to condemn Josiah for usurping the power of the priests to lead the people in the Passover.[75] Knoppers understands the ideal deuteronomic king as a 'symbolic head of state' or 'model Israelite' without actual power. He notes that the only positive function indicated by Deuteronomy 17 is to write a copy of the covenant that the priests would authorise. Absent from Deuteronomy, Knoppers notes, are those features of rule associated with ANE royal ideology like the exercise of justice and a role in centralisation of worship.

This argument has been persuasive. McConville used it, for example, to argue that Deuteronomy 17 could not have arisen from the context of Josiah's reforms because no actual king would have tolerated such limitations.[76] This argument is also common amongst those who understand the exilic Dtr to be correcting the excesses of Zion theology.[77]

It is also overstated. Take Knoppers's own example of the Passover. The deuteronomic traditions are silent concerning who should lead the Passover. The law in Deut. 16.1-8 mentions sacrifice,[78] perhaps implying through synecdoche that it was the duty of the priests, but this is not explicit. Deuteronomy makes the people, and not the priesthood, responsible for sacrifice. For example, the imperatives of Deut. 16.1-2 refer to the same antecedent as the pronoun in v. 3: 'Sacrifice (וזבחת) the Passover...because you left (יצאת) Egypt in haste'. (See also Deut. 12.5-14.) The law of priesthood is only concerned that the priests receive their allotted portion to eat from the people's sacrifice (Deut. 18.1-8). Nowhere does the deuteronomic tradition forbid anyone, let alone the king, from

---

74. Knoppers, 'Rethinking the Relationship', 403–4.
75. Knoppers, 'Rethinking the Relationship', 399–405.
76. McConville, *Deuteronomy*, 283–4.
77. See Römer, *The So-Called Deuteronomistic History*, 139–43.
78. Note that the deuteronomic version of this law requires a central sanctuary and thus becomes a pilgrimage festival (cf. Exod. 23.14-17; 34.18, 21-23). See Nelson, *Deuteronomy*, 206–7.

performing sacrifices. Note also that 1 Kgs 8.62-66 does not apportion a role to the priests in Solomon's sacrifice, even though they were present according to vv. 1–11. Josiah is not portrayed as violating the covenant in his administration of the Passover.

Sweeney has argued that this is true of the other functions of royal authority, such as centralisation or the administration of justice:

> The 'Torah of the King' does not restrict royal authority; it merely defines the conditions by which it may be exercised. It does not compromise the judicial role of the king...[79]

Sweeney is correct. There is every sign that the author is providing a deuteronomic assessment of Josiah in good faith.[80]

More than this, the roles that Knoppers thinks are denied to the king, such as the administration of justice and leadership in the cult, are necessary for the wider claim of the book of Kings: that it is the kings who lead the people either in covenant faithfulness or apostasy. The book of Kings only attributes sin to the people themselves on two occasions (1 Kgs 14.22; 2 Kgs 17.7).[81] In every other case, the king manages the success or failure of the entire kingdom. Jeroboam 'causes Israel to sin' (החטיא את־ישראל, 1 Kgs 14.16; 15.26, etc.). Manasseh 'causes' Judah to do the same (2 Kgs 21.11).[82] It is only the kings who lead people to obey that are judged good. As we saw above, this includes cult reform where necessary.

So the obedience that the book envisages of kings is something more than the obedience of individual Israelites, because the king is more than a figurehead. The obedience of a king, according to the deuteronomic ideal, is an obedience that includes the exercise of royal power to lead the nation as a whole into covenantal faithfulness,[83] as Gerbrandt comments:

> All of Josiah's acts would fit under [the description of 'covenant administrator']. Josiah's dismay upon reading the book of the law/covenant was due to his realisation that Judah had not been following the covenant, and he as king had not administered it as he should have. He then turned to the Lord and began to fulfil his responsibilities... As covenant administrator he

---

79. Sweeney, *King Josiah of Judah*, 162.
80. Gerbrandt, *Kingship*, 96–100, 189–90.
81. I discussed these instances in Chapter 3.
82. Lasine, 'Manasseh as Villain and Scapegoat', 167–73. On Manasseh as Davidic antitype, see Joseph, *Portrait of the Kings*, 187–224.
83. Goswell, 'King and Cultus', 184–5.

was expected to make sure that the covenant was maintained, and the cultic requirements [i.e. reformation] were thus clearly under his responsibility. Similarly Hezekiah fulfilled this aspect of his kingly role by also [reforming the cult].[84]

ii. *The Virtue of Faith*

We have already examined the narratives involving Hezekiah several times in this study,[85] so we need only summarise our relevant findings. Like Josiah, Hezekiah is also a covenant-keeping king in the historiography of the book. He is compared favourably to the Davidic ideal (2 Kgs 18.3) and explicitly said to have kept the commandments (2 Kgs 18.6). Our primary concern, though, is with what is entailed by Hezekiah's incomparable faith (בטח, 2 Kgs 18.5), which is the focus of the narrative.[86] We shall see that according to Kings, keeping the covenant entails more than right belief and orthodox worship. It also entails active faith in Yahweh's ongoing protection.

Like Josiah's obedience, Hezekiah's faith is unparalleled and a feature of the king's heart (2 Kgs 20.3). In Chapter 4 we examined this faith in relation to the deliverance of Jerusalem in 2 Kings 19. There we followed Bostock's argument that Jerusalem was not saved because of Hezekiah's faith, but rather because of Yahweh's promise to David.[87] Faith, which is an unusual concept in Dtr literature,[88] is incorporated into the narrative to show the possibility of trusting Yahweh over foreign gods and rival saviours. In Chapter 3 we argued that the Rab-Shakeh's offer to Israel was presented as a rival covenant to Yahweh's, entailing similar promises of blessing and prosperity to those found in the deuteronomic traditions (2 Kgs 18.31-35). Thus 2 Kings 18–19 is framed as a test of Hezekiah's faith in which he must choose whose promises to believe for salvation. In an unparalleled crisis, Hezekiah had placed his confidence in no rival saviour; neither Egypt nor Assyria (2 Kgs 18.19-25), but 'it was in Yahweh, God of Israel, that he trusted' (ביהוה אלהי־ישראל בטח, 2 Kgs 18.5). For this he earns the commendation of unparalleled faith (2 Kgs 18.5).

---

84. Gerbrandt, *Kingship*, 99–100.
85. See Chapter 3 on the portrayal of Assyria, Chapter 4 on the idea of a remnant, and Chapter 5 on Yahweh's sovereignty over Assyria.
86. The report of his reforms is more extensive in 2 Chron. 29–31, suggesting that the author of Kings is concerned with something other than obedience.
87. Bostock, *A Portrayal of Trust*, 167–204.
88. We noted that language of faith and deliverance (בטח and נצל) is clustered in 2 Kgs 18–20 and rare in the entire DtrH outside of this passage.

We also noted in Chapter 4 how salvation/victory (the same word in Hebrew, תשועה) is developed as a wider theme in relation to the remnant motif of the book. In the narrative, military victory is always something Yahweh does. In Outer Kings, monarchs who win military victories often have their accomplishments minimised by a narrative summary (e.g., 1 Kgs 14.19). Solomon, though he rules a vast empire with a standing army (e.g., 1 Kgs 4.21, 26 [5.1, 6, Heb.]), is never portrayed as fighting. Rather, Solomon's prayer of dedication implies that military victory is Yahweh's prerogative (1 Kgs 8.33-34).[89] In Inner Kings, Yahweh wields his own army (e.g., 2 Kgs 2.11-12; 6.17; 7.6), and bears the military title 'Yahweh of armies' יהוה/אלהי צבות, 1 Kgs 18.15; 19.10, 14; 2 Kgs 3.14). Hezekiah's remarkable trust is that Yahweh will fight and win.[90] Since the function of military security was provided in Israel by Yahweh directly, the implication is that national security was not mandated to Israel's kings (hence Deut. 17.16).

The virtue of faith, therefore, is related by the same theme to the covenant. In deuteronomic thought, Israel's longevity and security in the land coincides with their covenant fidelity (e.g., Deut. 5.33; 11.9; 30.18; 32.47), and not their military power (e.g., Deut. 7.7-8). So a faithful king should rely on Yahweh, rather than their own power. As Gebrandt comments:

> Since Israel's existence as a nation on the land was dependent upon her obeying the covenant, the king did not have direct responsibility for the defence of the nation. This was then the other side of his role. In times of military crisis his responsibility was to trust Yahweh; Yahweh was the one who had created Israel, and who would protect her from her enemies.[91]

iii. *The Virtue of Wisdom*

Solomon's incomparable wisdom is the third paradigmatic virtue in Kings (1 Kgs 3.12), but unlike obedience and faith, it is not portrayed as unambiguously positive.[92] We already examined the sub-textual critique of Solomon's kingdom, character, and wisdom in Chapter 3. There we discovered that although wisdom is portrayed as a divine gift, and although it is understood as a positive quality, the exercise of wisdom

---

89. Knoppers, 'Prayer and Propaganda', 247.
90. So Gerbrandt, *Kingship*, 180–2.
91. Gerbrandt, *Kingship*, 190.
92. Contrast Provan ('The Messiah in the Book of Kings', 80), who understands the messianic expectation of the book to embrace obedience, faith, and wisdom equally.

is also entwined with the logic of Solomon's downfall.[93] We concluded that Israel did not fail because Solomon stopped being wise, but rather failed through the exercise of his wisdom. In Chapter 3 we saw that this prevented an exilic yearning for a return to the golden age of Solomon.

What then are we to make of wisdom as a paradigmatic virtue of kingship in the book? Robert Gordon has suggested that wisdom is portrayed ambiguously in Hebrew narrative traditions other than Kings as well: 'not all manifestations of wisdom in (e.g.) the succession narrative are commendatory of the virtue'.[94] He observes that on several occasions not limited to Solomon, biblical narratives vacillate on the role of wisdom. He concludes that the Old Testament rarely makes the point that bad counsel is ineffective. It prefers to reflect that the effective wisdom of good counsel can run contrary to the divine purpose. Wisdom 'as a principle by which to determine human behaviour' is a house divided.[95]

One way of showing this point in relation to Solomon is to note the way wisdom is related to the heart language within the account of the dream at Gibeon (1 Kgs 3).[96] Solomon's gift of wisdom involves a change of heart. The incident begins when Solomon compares himself to his father (vv. 6-7) and comes away feeling inadequate for the burden of rule (v. 8).[97] So far in the narrative Solomon has been able to 'love Yahweh' and 'walk according to the customs of David' (1 Kgs 3.3). What then has he been missing? As Walsh observes, the narrative portrays a difference of heart.[98] Where David had walked before Yahweh 'in uprightness of heart' (בישרת לבב, v. 6), Solomon must request a heart (ונתת לעבדך לב..., v. 9): 'Unlike David, [Solomon] does not have the qualities of "heart" necessary to carry out what Yahweh expects of him: he asks, therefore, for such a heart'.[99]

---

93. See Brueggemann, *Solomon*, 153–9; Hays, 'Has the Narrator Come to Praise Solomon or to Bury Him?', 155; Davies, 'Discerning Between Good and Evil', 53–5; Pyper, 'Judging the Wisdom of Solomon', 35; Parker, 'Solomon as Philosopher King', 76; Leithart, *1&2 Kings*, 75–82; Weitzman, *Solomon*; Miller, 'Solomon the Trickster', 496–504; Walsh, 'Symmetry and the Sin of Solomon'; Kang, *The Persuasive Portrayal of Solomon*, 223–64; and Brettler, 'The Structure of 1 Kings 1–11'.

94. Robert P. Gordon, 'A House Divided: Wisdom in Old Testament Narrative Traditions', in Day, Gordon, and Williamson, eds., *Wisdom in Ancient Israel*, 97.

95. Gordon, 'A House Divided', 98–105.

96. See Walsh, *1 Kings*, 74–6.

97. Ironically, he is comparing himself to the Davidic exemplar of Kings, rather than the more human David of Samuel, who would have been more favourable (1 Sam. 21.12; 24.5; 27.1; 28.5; 2 Sam. 24.10).

98. See Walsh, *1 Kings*, 75.

99. Walsh, *1 Kings*, 76.

What does Solomon's heart lack? His request is for one that can 'listen' (לב שמע, v. 9). The combination of 'heart' (לב) with 'hear' (שמע) suggests two inter-textual connections, both recalling the covenant. The first is the nexus of references where Pharaoh's heart is hardened to not hear Moses (Exod. 7.13, 22; 8.15, 19; 9.12).[100] The second is the frequent deuteronomic language that enjoins Israel to keep the covenant (Deut. 6.4-5; 11.13; 13.3; 29.4; 30.2, 10, 17). This implies that Solomon, as he is presented here, understands the covenant to be necessary for the task he has in mind, discernment and administration of justice (לשפט את עמך and להבין בין טוב לרע,[101] v. 7).

Ironically, this is not what is granted. Solomon receives a 'wise and discerning heart' (לב חכם ונבון, v. 12), which is subtly different. Solomon's heart is defined in relation to wisdom (חכם, בין), but not in relation to obedience (שמע). This observation is reinforced by the narrative portrayal of Solomon in relation to the law of Moses. Solomon might claim to be the fulfilment of the Mosaic hope (1 Kgs 8.53), but he is never portrayed as relating to the law, let alone 'writing a copy of [it] approved by the Levitical priests' and 'reading it all the days of his life' (Deut. 17.18-19).[102]

Solomon's heart is therefore portrayed as more distant from the covenant than either Hezekiah's (2 Kgs 20.3) or Josiah's (2 Kgs 23.25). This invites a comparison with both, who succeed where Solomon fails. Solomon's wives 'turn his heart' (1 Kgs 11.3-4), but in contrast Josiah is the king who listens (שמע, 2 Kgs 22.11, 13, 18) with a soft heart (רך־לבב, 2 Kgs 22.19), and turns to Yahweh 'with all his heart, with all his soul, and with all his strength according to all the law of Moses' (בכל־לבבו ובכל־נפשו ובכל מאדו ככל תורת משה, 2 Kgs 23.25, see Deut. 6.4-5).

Hezekiah also succeeds where Solomon fails. Like Josiah, Hezekiah is a king who obeys the covenant (2 Kgs 18.3), and this is why he 'succeeds' (ישכיל, v. 7).[103] Although the semantic domain of שכל belongs alongside other Solomonic wisdom traits such as בין and חכם,[104] it is never applied

---

100. This is suggestive in light of the way Solomon's kingdom becomes like Egypt. We explored this in Chapter 3.

101. This phrase seems to be associated with mature (e.g., Deut. 1.39), capable (e.g., 2 Sam. 19.35), or exceptional discernment (e.g., 2 Sam. 14.17). I have previously suggested that it may also be an allusion to Gen. 3.5: Lovell, 'The Shape of Hope', 12. See also Davies, 'Discerning Between Good and Evil', 41–4; and Leithart, *1&2 Kings*, 42–7.

102. We discussed in Chapter 3 how Deut. 17 relates to the portrayal of Solomon in Kings.

103. Hezekiah succeeds 'בכל אשר יצא'. This is one thing Solomon claimed to have insufficient wisdom to do (1 Kgs 3.7). Note also Josh. 1.7-8.

104. *NIDOTTE*, s.v. '*Wisdom, knowledge, skill'.

to Solomon. The only other occurrence in Kings is David's injunction to Solomon that he keep everything written in the law of Moses 'so that he might succeed in everything he does' (למען תשכיל את כל־אשר תעשה, 1 Kgs 2.3, reiterating Deut. 29.9).

Solomon's wisdom is a good thing and should be regarded as a virtue. However, Kings understands the virtue as secondary because it does not automatically lead to covenant obedience. Later in this chapter I will argue that the portrayal of Solomon's wisdom in Kings is intended to orient him towards ANE kingship rather than the deuteronomic ideal. The ideology of the book of Kings does not overturn this model of kingship. Wisdom remains a desirable characteristic of a ruler. However, we shall see that it intends to moderate the ANE royal ideology by the deuteronomic ideal we have been exploring here.

The ideal deuteronomic ruler remains an ANE king, but he is a particular type of ANE king. He is one like David, with a heart oriented wholly towards Yahweh's covenant, full of the virtue of obedience, able to lead others in obedience, and possessing the courage of faith in times of trouble.

6.2.3. *Democratisation of Monarchy: Rehoboam and the Role of the 'People of the Land'*

We have been examining the disposition of the king's heart within the deuteronomic ideal found in Kings. The law of the king itself addresses this twice (Deut. 17.17, 20). The former, an injunction against marrying foreign wives, belongs to the category of covenant faithfulness (see also Deut. 7.3-4). The latter, however, orients the king's heart with respect to his subjects: 'to not exalt his heart above his brothers' (לבלתי רום־לבבו מאחיו). This is something we have not yet explored. We discovered above that the king should lead the people in covenant faithfulness. Other than this, what is the relationship between the king and the people in the ideology of Kings?

One avenue of discussion has been to observe the democratisation[105] of kingship in both Deuteronomy and DtrH.[106] In the context of scholarship on Kings the discussion emerges in relation to the role of the 'people of

---

105. In this context, 'democratisation' is either a process that redistributes monarchic benefits to the people, or a type of charismatic leadership where a king garners popular support. See Jamie A. Grant, *The King as Exemplar: The Function of Deuteronomy's Kingship Law in the Shaping of the Book of Psalms* (Atlanta, GA: SBL, 2004), 117–18.

106. E.g. McConville, *Deuteronomy*, 283–4; Nelson, *Deuteronomy*, 214; Lohfink, 'Distributions of the Functions of Power', 349.

the land' (עם־הארץ or, once, the עם־יהודה).¹⁰⁷ This group appears in the narrative of Kings on several occasions:¹⁰⁸

1. Seven years after Athaliah usurped the southern throne and nearly destroyed the Davidic line (2 Kgs 11.1), the people of the land were part of the popular movement that placed the only surviving Davidic descendent, Joash, back on the throne (2 Kgs 11.14, 19-20), and also removed Athaliah's Baalism from Judah (2 Kgs 11.18).
2. When Amaziah is the victim of a coup (2 Kgs 14.19), it is the people of Judah (עם־יהודה) who ensure the continuation of the Davidic dynasty (2 Kgs 14.21).
3. After Azariah contracts a skin disease and is forced to be separated from the rest of Judah, the people of the land are willingly subject to his son Jotham (2 Kgs 15.5).
4. Similar to Amaziah, Amnon is the victim of his servants (2 Kgs 21.23), but the people of the land ensure that the kingship passes to Josiah (2 Kgs 21.24).
5. After Josiah dies in battle, the people of the land ensure that his son Jehoahaz succeeds him (2 Kgs 23.30).

From this list, the people of the land function in the narrative to ensure the continuation of the Davidic dynasty. When contrasted with the Northern Kingdom, it is clear that it might have been otherwise. In the northern narratives, every attempted coup is successful and the people never act to ensure the future of their dynasties. In Judah, by contrast, the king and people support each other: David protects the people, and the people ensure Davidic succession.

107. Much of the scholarship on this group is dated. See J. Alberto Soggin, 'Der judäische 'am-ha' areṣ und das Königtum in Juda: Ein Beitrag zum Studium der deuteronomistischen Geschichtsschreibung', *VT* 13 (1963): 187–95; S. Talmon, 'The Judaean 'Am ha'Ares' in Historical Perspective', in *Fourth World Congress of Jewish Studies: Papers* (Jerusalem: Word Union of Jewish Studies, 1967), 71–6; Hayyim Tadmor, '"The People" and the Kingship in Ancient Israel: The Role of Political Institutions in the Biblical Period', *Cahiers d'histoire mondiale* 11 (1968): 3–23; T. Ishida, '"The People and the Land" and the Political Crises in Judah', *AJBI* 1 (1975): 23–38. More recent scholarship tends to accept and apply these earlier results; see, e.g., Laato, *A Star Is Rising*, 45; Sweeney, 'The Critique of Solomon', 620 n. 47.

108. Laato (*A Star Is Rising*, 45) adds to this list one example from Chronicles, as well as the observation that all except one of the kings of Judah who came to power this way were characterised as 'good'.

While both do what they should the kingdom is secure; however, beginning with Jehoiakim, the symbiosis weakens.[109] In Egyptian and Babylonian vassaldom, the people of the land can no longer ensure stability for the Davidic line, and they are portrayed as suffering the same tumult as the dynasty itself. It begins when the Davidic king allows a foreign monarch to exact a tax from the people of the land (2 Kgs 23.35). As we saw in Chapter 5, this action spirals to exile. These same people endure the Babylonian attacks (2 Kgs 25.3), and are removed to Babylon (2 Kgs 25.19). Thus the fate of the people of the land is entwined with the fate of David.

The only occasion in Kings when the people are divided against the Davidic king is the story of Rehoboam's succession: 'What portion do we have with the son of Jesse?' (מה לנו חלק בדוד ולא־נחלה בבן ישי, 1 Kgs 12.1-24). This narrative is of interest because the ideal relationship between king and people breaks down on this occasion, and so the royal attributes that the author believed would have supported it are explored.

To begin, there is disagreement concerning how the relationship between king and people is portrayed. Does the 'all Israel' (כל־ישראל) that gather at Shechem (v. 16) include Judah,[110] or does it indicate the northern tribes only?[111] As we saw in Chapter 4, the use of the term 'all Israel' will not settle the question. If it includes Judah, then Rehoboam is trying to inveigle the northern tribes by holding his coronation in their territory even though he is a southerner. Gathering Judah and going to Shechem, a northern town, to be crowned (להמליך) is a concession to the northern tribes. David and Solomon were both crowned by 'all Israel' in southern cities. This is a plausible reading. The allusion in 2 Kgs 12.16 (12.17, Heb.) to 2 Sam. 20.1 makes clear that some old tribal wounds that were plastered over during Solomon's monarchy have re-opened.[112] And this would show to the reader that political succession was not guaranteed through dynastic heritage.[113] Thus, if Rehoboam's coronation is being portrayed as a necessary attempt to garner popular support, then there is

---

109. See Chapter 5 on the way exile begins in 2 Kgs 23.31.

110. So Wray Beal, *1&2 Kings*, 180; Iain W. Provan, V. Philips Long, and Tremper Longman III, *A Biblical History of Israel*, 2nd ed. (Louisville, KY: Westminster John Knox, 2015), 344; Provan, *1 & 2 Kings*, 103, 105–6.

111. So J. Alberto Soggin, *An Introduction to the History of Israel and Judah* (London: SCM, 1999), 190–3; Cogan, *1 Kings*, 346.

112. See Chapter 4.

113. So Hayim Tadmor, 'Traditional Institutions and the Monarchy: Social and Political Tensions in the Time of David and Solomon', in Ishida, ed., *Studies in the Period of David and Solomon and Other Essays*, 253–4.

a strong democratic theme. Were the Davidic kings enthroned by popular acclaim?[114]

The alternative is that we are to understand Rehoboam as bargaining in Shechem from a position of strength. If 'all Israel' refers to the northern tribes then Judah is not present, either because Rehoboam was already sure of their support[115] or because he was already enthroned there.[116] In this case his agenda should be understood as re-exerting the influence his father once enjoyed over the northern tribes.

Both are possibilities and the narrative is not explicit, though the latter is the preferable reading. Rehoboam's brashness refers to his father's rule (1 Kgs 12.14), and comes across more as strong-arming than wooing. After the split he is confident to return to Judah (v. 18) and seems successful in raising an army there (v. 21). And the people themselves distinguish between Israel and Judah in their reply to Rehoboam (v. 16).

There is therefore no need to hypothesise that the book of Kings supports a model of kingship by popular acclaim rather than succession. As we saw in Chapter 3, the Davidic covenant guarantees dynastic succession in the covenantal logic of the book (2 Sam. 7.11-16). Kings does not doubt this promise. The motif of popular support should be understood to demonstrate the way Yahweh normally enacted the Davidic promise in the economy of Israel's history, through the loyalty of the people to David.

This does not mean the incident at Shechem reveals nothing concerning the deuteronomic ideal of kingship. The ideal king should garner popular support in the way Rehoboam failed to do. The people of the north make clear the conditions for this: they will serve (עבד) Rehoboam if he will be a king unlike his father (1 Kgs 12.4). The counsellors then present two alternative ideals of kingship: a kingdom like Solomon's, except greater in its excess (1 Kgs 12.10-11); or a different kingdom entirely: 'If today you will become a servant to this people, then they will serve you every day' (אם־היום תהיה־עבד לעם הזה ועבדתם...והיו לך עבדים כל־הימים). The wordplay exposes the ideology. Winning the fealty (עבד) of the northern tribes requires that Rehoboam serve (עבד) them.[117]

---

114. Soggin, 'Der judäische 'am-ha' ares und das Königtum in Juda', 191.

115. E.g. Cogan, *1 Kings*, 346; and Provan, *1 & 2 Kings*, 106.

116. Note that the *hifil* infinitive המליך can refer to the recognition of kingship as well as its initiation, e.g. 1 Chron. 29.22; and *HALOT*, s.v. 'I מלך'.

117. See also Moshe Weinfeld, 'The King as Servant of the People—The Source of the Idea', *JJS* 33 (1982): 189–94; Bodner, *Jeroboam's Royal Drama*, 64–5; and Berman, *Created Equal*, 15–50. I have suggested this previously; see my 'The Shape of Hope', 20–1, 27.

Behind this request is the deuteronomic law of the king, that he 'not exalt his heart above his brothers' (לבלתי רום לבבו מאחיו, Deut. 17.20). The critique of Rehoboam is that he was not willing to be a servant-king to his brothers.

6.3. *The Deuteronomic Moderation of Zion Kingship*

We have so far been investigating the deuteronomic ideal of kingship as presented in Kings, and discovered that the ideal king will not only keep the covenant himself, but lead the people of Israel to do this also. This means he will trust Yahweh's protection in moments of crisis and not exalt himself too far above his people to serve them. This is a positive ideal, and not simply a negative exilic reaction against an earlier, Zion ideology. How compatible is this deuteronomic ideal with the Zion model?

We noted above the conclusion that the Zion model of kingship had its origin in ANE culture more broadly even though it developed Israelite features. However, because there was variation amongst ANE ideals, so too there is variation in how well these ideals might fit with the deuteronomic one. It will be our argument here that some versions of it work, and some do not. We shall see that the deuteronomic ideal does not function in Kings as a simple anti-establishment critique, but rather as a call for Israel to positively moderate their Zion ideology, and to imagine their king in Zion to be a particular kind of ANE monarch.

Some generalisations of ANE royal ideology, from which Israel's Zion model may derive, are possible.[118] As we noted above, Kings were thought of primarily in a priestly capacity as mediators of divine rule, of divine origin, and responsible for the maintenance of divine order.[119] John Walton summarises:

> 'Kingship was the central institution of society and civilisation'. In the ancient world the king stood between the divine and human realms mediating the power of the deity in his city and beyond. He communed with the gods, was privy to their councils, and enjoyed their favour and protection. He was responsible for maintaining justice, for leading in battle, for initiating and accomplishing public building projects from canals to walls to temples, and

---

118. See nn. 3 and 4 in the present chapter.
119. Walton, *Ancient Near Eastern Thought and the Old Testament*, 256–68. Everything that follows describes the official rhetoric of kingship in ANE cultures. On this see Knapp, *Royal Apologetic*, 1–45, 359–66; Lambert, 'Kingship in Ancient Mesopotamia', 54.

had ultimate responsibility for the ongoing performance of the cult. Beyond that, every aspect of order and balance in the cosmos was associated with the king's execution of his role.[120]

Thus the king had a role to play in the maintenance of created order. Within his realm, the king administered social aspects of order: justice, protection of the vulnerable, and military security all fell under his purview.[121] He also was understood to participate in the maintenance of the natural order.[122] One Egyptian hymn to the sun-god Re, for example, articulates it this way:[123]

> Re has placed the king in the land of the living forever and ever, judging humankind and satisfying the gods, realising Ma'at [order] and destroying Izfet [chaos].

The king's first responsibility within this system was to build a temple which mirrored the house of the deity in the divine realm, and connected heaven to earth with a channel of divine blessing.[124] The king's ongoing responsibility as the chief patron of the cult ensured the maintenance of this connection.[125] The king could accomplish this because he was of a different kind of being than ordinary men.[126]

---

120. Walton, *Ancient Near Eastern Thought and the Old Testament*, 256; quoting Baines, 'Ancient Egyptian Kingship', 16.

121. On ANE kings and the execution of justice see Levinson, 'The Reconceptualisation of Kingship', 515–16. In Mesopotamian ideology, see Lambert, 'Kingship in Ancient Mesopotamia', 55, 69–70. For an example of this model, see the 'Instruction to Merikare' (*COS*, 1:61–6).

122. Brueggemann, *1 & 2 Kings*, 209.

123. See Jan Assmann, 'State and Religion in the New Kingdom', in *Religion and Philosophy in Ancient Egypt*, ed. William Kelly Simpson, Yale Egyptological Studies (New Haven, CT: Yale University Press, 1989), 59–66.

124. Wray Beal, *The Deuteronomist's Prophet*, 157–73. See also Baines, 'Ancient Egyptian Kingship', 17–18, 27–8, 42–3, 47, 50. On Kings as mediators in ANE generally, see Walton, *Ancient Near Eastern Thought and the Old Testament*, 259–61.

125. Hurowitz, *I Have Built You an Exalted House*, 330–7; Knoppers, *Two Nations Under God 2*, 35; John M. Lundquist, *The Legitimizing Role of the Temple in the Origin of the State* (London: Scholars Press, 1982).

126. Walton, *Ancient Near Eastern Thought and the Old Testament*, 256–58; Baines, 'Ancient Egyptian Kingship', 24, 26, 31.

Throughout the ANE, kings were not only elected by the gods (sometimes adopted),[127] they were imbued with special abilities: wisdom,[128] extraordinary strength,[129] and civic and military ability.[130] Only in Egypt is there evidence that kings were thought to participate in divinity,[131] but in other cultures they were still not mere humans.[132] Like modern superheroes, they were thought capable of extraordinary feats. Samuel Kramer comments of Sumerian kings:

> The Sumerian king was a idealised man in every facet of life and rule, including wisdom. In particular he was educated in the edubba [school of wisdom], literate and learned, an expert in poetry and music. He was the complete and perfect man: physically powerful and distinguished looking; brave and courageous in battle and in the chase; he was wise, understanding, astute, and psychologically penetrating; he was devoted to the cult, knew how to serve the gods, and saw to it that the temple rites and rituals were properly consummated.[133]

Two questions emerge from this summary. First, to what extent does the book of Kings portray Israel's Zion theology as taking part in this model? And second, to what extent is this compatible with the deuteronomic ideal we have been examining?

---

127. Walton, *Ancient Near Eastern Thought and the Old Testament*, 260–1. Language of 'adoption' is not universal, but election is implied. See Levinson, 'The Reconceptualisation of Kingship', 512–14; and Lambert, 'Kingship in Ancient Mesopotamia', 61.

128. Baines, 'Ancient Egyptian Kingship', 20–2; Ronald F. G. Sweet, 'The Sage in Akkadian Literature: A Philological Study', in *The Sage in Israel and the Ancient Near East*, ed. John G. Gammie and Leo G. Perdue (Winona Lake, IN: Eisenbrauns, 1990), 51–7.

129. Samuel Noah Kramer, 'The Sage in Sumerian Literature: A Composite Portrait', in Gammie and Perdue, eds., *The Sage in Israel and the Ancient Near East*, 42–3; Baines, 'Ancient Egyptian Kingship', 36; Lambert, 'Kingship in Ancient Mesopotamia', 58; and Parker, 'The Construction and Performance of Kingship', 359–62.

130. Extensively, see Part 1 of Hurowitz, *I Have Built You an Exalted House*, 32–128. Also Parker, 'The Construction and Performance of Kingship', 374–5; Lambert, 'Kingship in Ancient Mesopotamia', 60.

131. Baines, 'Ancient Egyptian Kingship', 19, 21–2, 33. There was a brief period in Mesopotamia where kings were thought divine; see Lambert, 'Kingship in Ancient Mesopotamia', 59.

132. Baines, 'Ancient Egyptian Kingship', 24, 26, 31, 36.

133. Kramer, 'The Sage in Sumerian Literature', 41.

6.3.1. *Solomon's Zion and the ANE Royal Ideal*

It is possible to discern different aspects of this ANE royal model in the portraits of various monarchs in the narrative of Kings.[134] Solomon, however, is instantly recognisable. The parallels are discussed in the literature,[135] so we can summarise them here:

1. Solomon is divinely elected and placed on the throne (e.g., 1 Kgs 8.20), and divinely gifted for rule (e.g., 1 Kgs 3.10-13). Although there is no indication of divine adoption in Kings, there is in 2 Sam. 7.14.
2. Solomon's exceedingly great wisdom, which is a divinely given gift to help him rule with justice (1 Kgs 3.7-9), has strong antecedents in other ANE material.[136] The dream account where Solomon is granted wisdom has near parallels in Egyptian literature.[137]
3. Solomon is portrayed as executing his kingship wisely, in such a way as to bring prosperity to his kingdom (e.g., 1 Kgs 10.21-27) and peace to his territory (e.g., 1 Kgs 4.24; 5.12 [5.4, 26, Heb.]).[138]
4. Solomon constructs the temple and acts as a patron to the cult (e.g., 1 Kgs 8.62-64; 9.25). His other building projects are equally impressive (1 Kgs 7.1-12; 9.15-19).[139]
5. Most of Solomon's royal trappings, such as his throne, have ANE parallels also.[140]

---

134. See, e.g., Leithart's comments (*1&2 Kings*, 132–7) concerning the priorities and economy of Ahab.

135. E.g. Millard, 'King Solomon in his Ancient Context'; Parker, 'Solomon as Philosopher King'; Whitelam, 'Symbols of Royal Power'; André Lemaire, 'Wisdom in Solomonic Historiography', in Day, Gordon, and Williamson, eds., *Wisdom in Ancient Israel*, 106–18; Currid, *Ancient Egypt and the Old Testament*; Heaton, *Solomon's New Men*; Lambert, 'Kingship in Ancient Mesopotamia'; Sweet, 'The Sage in Akkadian Literature'; McConville, 'King and Messiah', 283.

136. Lemaire, 'Wisdom in Solomonic Historiography'. See also Baines, 'Ancient Egyptian Kingship', 20, 22, 41–3.

137. Heaton, *Solomon's New Men*, 22–3.

138. On the theme of Solomon as a second Adam, see Davies, 'Discerning Between Good and Evil'; and Bodner, *The Theology of the Book of Kings*, 63, 79.

139. On Solomon's building projects in ANE context see Currid, *Ancient Egypt and the Old Testament*, 168–71; Heaton, *Solomon's New Men*, 61–100. On the temple in particular, see Hurowitz, *I Have Built You an Exalted House*, 131–259.

140. Whitelam, 'Symbols of Royal Power'; Marc Z. Brettler, *God Is King: Understanding an Israelite Metaphor* (New York: T&T Clark, 2009), 77–88.

Of the standard ANE attributes of kings, only extraordinary strength is missing.[141] Unlike the David portrayed in Samuel, Solomon is not characterised as a great warrior capable of killing lions and bears (e.g., 1 Sam. 17.36), or as a skilful general winning battles against all odds (e.g., 1 Sam. 18.27). This may be because his great wisdom suffices to bring submission without conflict (e.g., 1 Kgs 4.20-21 [4.20–5.1, Heb.]), or at least to have others do the fighting (e.g., 1 Kgs 9.16); or maybe the book of Kings is just uninterested in these characteristics. As we noted above, the book does not evaluate kings elsewhere by their accomplishments, either civil or military,[142] and seems content to relegate this kind of information to a cross-reference to the Annals of the Kings (e.g., 1 Kgs 16.27; 22.45 [22.46, Heb.]).

Solomon is also a patron of the cult. Israelite monotheism prevents the ascription of any measure of divinity, but this is not uniform in ANE royal ideology.[143] Like other ANE kings, Solomon is no mere mortal.[144] In Kings, Solomon enjoys unmediated access to Yahweh because the word of God comes directly to him (e.g., 1 Kgs 3.5; 6.11; 9.2; 11.11). Elsewhere in the narrative, this is a right normally reserved for prophets.[145] Note, however, that prophets play no part in the account of Solomon's kingdom. After Nathan conspires with Bathsheba to have Solomon enthroned (1 Kgs 1.11-14), prophets disappear from the narrative until Ahijah finds Jeroboam on the road out of Jerusalem (1 Kgs 11.29). Solomon's gesturing at the temple dedication in 1 Kings 8 presents him as a mediator – sometimes facing Israel, at other times Yahweh – offering sacrifices and prayers on behalf of the people.[146] And to some extent, he is also understood to be a channel of Yahweh's blessings, as the Queen of Sheba recognises (1 Kgs 10.9).

Although Solomon is a patron of the cult like other ANE kings, the relationship between him and the temple is nuanced. By devoting several, central chapters to the temple, the narrative recognises it as

---

141. See Whitelam, 'Israelite Kingship', 131.
142. E.g. Greenwood, 'Late Tenth and Ninth-Century Issues'.
143. Walton, *Ancient Near Eastern Thought and the Old Testament*, 260–1.
144. So Whitelam, 'Israelite Kingship', 135. See also the nuanced discussion of the relation between king and deity in Mark W. Hamilton, *The Body Royal: The Social Poetics of Kingship in Ancient Israel*, Biblical Interpretation Series (Leiden, Brill, 2005), 266–74.
145. The only exception is Jehu: 2 Kgs 10.30.
146. Musa Gotom, '1 & 2 Kings', in *Africa Bible Commentary*, ed. Tokunboh Adeyemo (Nairobi, Kenya: WordAlive Publishers, 2006), 425.

Solomon's greatest achievement. The narrator recounts four times that Solomon 'built' (בנה) and 'finished' (כלה) it (1 Kgs 6.9, 14, 38; 9.1). However, it also subtly distances Solomon from the temple. One way it does this is by giving structural prominence to the account of Solomon's palaces:[147]

A	1 Kgs 1–2	Succession
B	1 Kgs 3.1–5.14 [5.28, Heb.]	Wisdom, riches, and peace
C	1 Kgs 5.15-18 [5.29-32, Heb.]	Preparations to build the temple
D	1 Kgs 6.1-38	Building the temple
E	1 Kgs 7.1-12	Building the palaces
D'	1 Kgs 7.13–8.56	Temple furnishings and dedication
C'	1 Kgs 9.1-23	After building the temple
B'	1 Kgs 9.24–10.25	Wisdom, riches, and peace
A'	1 Kgs 11.1-43	Succession

The account of Solomon's palace begins with a fronted object (7.1), and like the temple Solomon 'builds' and 'finishes' the palace also, but it takes nearly twice as long. There is an intentional contrast here (1 Kgs 6.38–7.1):

6.38 ובשנה האחת עשרה ירח בול הוא החדש השמיני
כלה הבית לכל־דבריו ולכל־משפטו
ויבנהו שבע שנים:
7.1 ואת־ביתו בנה שלמה שלש עשרה שנה
ויכל את־כל־ביתו:

> 6:38In the eleventh year, in the month of Bul (it is the eighth month), the house was finished according to all its parts and designs. [Solomon] had been building it for seven years. 7:1But his own house, Solomon built for thirteen years, and he finished his whole house. (1 Kgs 6.38–7.1, my translation)

There are other distancing mechanisms. Solomon gathers the wealth and treasures of the natural world to his palaces (1 Kgs 10.14-25): gold, silver, ivory, apes, peacocks, garments, myrrh, spices, horses, and mules are

---

147. On the structure of 1 Kgs 3–11, see Williams, 'Once Again', 50–1; Brettler, 'The Structure of 1 Kings 1–11'; and Olley, 'Pharaoh's Daughter, Solomon's Palace, and the Temple', 364.

listed. In ANE thought such a menagerie would have been more usually associated with a temple, which was intended to represent a microcosm of creation.[148] Meyers comments of ANE temples that 'the whole creation was thus contained within the centre of creation',[149] but Solomon gathers the cosmos around himself.[150]

The narrative also subtly distances the construction of the temple from Solomon's wisdom. Everything else Solomon did and built, including gathering materials for the temple, resulted from his wisdom (1 Kgs 2.6, 9; 3.12, 28; 4.29-31, 34 [5.9-11, 14, Heb.]; 5.7, 9, 12 [5.21, 23, 26, Heb.]; 10.4, 6-8, 23-24), but the temple construction itself is the notable exception. Wisdom language is not used of Solomon in 1 Kings 6–9. Solomon contributes the wealth (6.14-37; 7.48-51; זהב 18 times), but it is Hiram of Tyre's 'skill' (חקמה, בינה, and ידעה, 1 Kgs 7.14) that ensures the temple cannot be listed as another of the accomplishments of Solomon's abilities.[151]

Solomon's wisdom, despite being a gift from Yahweh, seems to operate independently from the cult. After the deal with Hiram (1 Kgs 5.7 [5.21, Heb.]), he is not portrayed as using it for the benefit of the cult, and neither does he allow the cult (nor divine law) to influence his decisions of state. In his exercise of wisdom, Solomon is nearer to the Egyptian god-kings than to the Mesopotamian supermen.

Walton comments on the link between wisdom and divinity. He notes that in Egypt, where kings were regarded as divine, 'the almost total immersion of the persona of the king into the divine realm led inexorably to the conclusion that the acts of Pharaoh were the acts of deity'.[152] In

---

148. See Gregory K. Beale, *The Temple and the Church's Mission: A Biblical Theology of the Dwelling Place of God* (Downers Grove, IL: IVP, 2004), 66–70; Walton, *Ancient Near Eastern Thought and the Old Testament*, 165–70; Davies, 'Discerning Between Good and Evil', 41–2; and John H. Walton, 'Eden, Garden of', *DOTP*, 202–7.

149. Meyers, 'The Israelite Empire', 422.

150. Leithart, *1&2 Kings*, 77–82; and Bodner, *The Theology of the Book of Kings*, 68–9.

151. The narrative is careful not to attribute anything gold to Hiram (1 Kgs 7.13-47 has ten occurrences of 'bronze'), making clear that the grandeur of it exalts Solomon as well as Yahweh. However, much of the apparatus within the temple are crafted by Hiram, and Solomon seems to think little of these (7.47, see also 10.21).

152. Walton, *Ancient Near Eastern Thought and the Old Testament*, 259. Though, contrast Baines ('Ancient Egyptian Kingship', 28–46) who argues for nuance in understanding the relationship between King and deity in Egypt.

Egypt, the 'cosmic mission [of the king] means he can act in a peremptory way, beyond any normal...constraints, because so much is at stake'.[153] God-kings have no need of instruction and are above morality. Walton contrasts this with the Mesopotamian ideology where the king must put 'more effort...into the enterprise of learning the will of the gods'.[154] Since the king is not divine, instruction must be sought:

> The gravity of the concern and the angst that surrounded it are reflected in the prominence of divination in the court and in the reports of the king's advisors as they attempted to help him discern the will of the gods.[155]

Solomon's use of wisdom models him after the Egyptian pattern. Within the narrative – at least after 1 Kings 3 – he shows no concern for discerning the will of Yahweh: he never seeks Yahweh's counsel and seems at all times satisfied with the results of his wisdom. It is rather Yahweh who must interrupt Solomon, on four occasions, each to remind him that obedience to the law of Moses was the basic principle of kingdom construction (1 Kgs 3.14; 6.11-13; 9.2-9; 11.11-13).

In Chapter 3, I suggested that under Solomon, Israel had become Egypt-like and that the book did not yearn for a return to his golden age. Earlier in this chapter, we noticed the ambiguity of wisdom as a virtue in the book, for which Solomon is paradigmatic. Here we can draw these two thoughts together. The portrait of Solomon constructed by Kings, especially in his use of wisdom, aligns him to a particular ANE royal ideal of which the author of Kings did not approve. Although not god-like, Solomon is Pharaoh-like.

Just as the book does not opine for a return to Solomon's golden age, in the same way the narrative critiques the model of king that it finds Solomon to be. This demonstrates a kind of kingship that was prominent in the ANE royal *apologia*, but that the author of Kings could not endorse. Moreover, history had taught the author that Zion's kings were also inclined towards this ideal. So, with the benefit of exilic hindsight, the author of Kings argues that this was not a model of kingship towards which Zion's rulers should have striven. There was, however, an alternative model of ANE royal ideology that was more amenable to deuteronomic tastes.

---

153. Baines, 'Ancient Egyptian Kingship', 44.
154. Walton, *Ancient Near Eastern Thought and the Old Testament*, 259.
155. Walton, *Ancient Near Eastern Thought and the Old Testament*, 259.

6.3.2. *Zion and Ancient Near Eastern Shepherd Kings*

We have seen that Zion ideology was related to ANE royal ideology and that it could produce kings of a kind that the deuteronomic ideal could not endorse. However, this is not an argument that Zion ideology was always incompatible with the deuteronomic ideal. Hezekiah demonstrates the opposite: a scion of David who trusted in Yahweh's protection, kept the covenant, and is vindicated by divine protection of Zion (e.g., 2 Kgs 19.32-34). There is nothing in the Zion royal ideology that *prima facie* prevents the king from having a heart faithful to the covenant. Neither would the virtue of wisdom automatically disqualify a king (note שכל, 2 Kgs 18.7).

One example of the way Zion ideology borrows positively from ANE cultures is the metaphor of a shepherd-king, which is common in Israel's Zionist literature.[156] In the Old Testament, shepherding is a metaphor that is often associated with David's kingship in particular (e.g., 2 Sam. 5.2; Ps. 78.70-71).[157] It is used in the Davidic promise (2 Sam. 7.7-8) which draws on David's previous experience as a shepherd to show that he was an ideal ruler to guide Israel (e.g., 1 Sam. 16.11; 17.15, 34).[158] In Zion contexts the human shepherd-king mirrors the attributes of the divine king who is the true shepherd (e.g., Ps. 23; Isa. 40.10-11).[159]

This metaphor is not distinctively Israelite. Wilfred Lambert has argued that the shepherd-king metaphor originated in Mesopotamia,[160] and has traced its use across early (Sumerian and Akkadian), late southern (Babylonian), and late northern (Assyrian) literature. The metaphor was used to portray royal elements of guidance, protection, nurturing, and provision.[161] It was the role of the shepherd-king to lead his people in justice and to secure a world where their needs were met. Consider this example from second-millennium Mesopotamia:

---

156. See Timothy S. Laniak, *Shepherds After my own Heart: Pastoral Traditions and Leadership in the Bible* (Leicester: Apollos, 2006), 58–74, 94–114; Jack W. Vancil, 'Sheep, Shepherd', *AYBD*, 5:1187–90. With the exception of several texts in 2 Samuel, the metaphor is absent in Deuteronomy and DtrH, but common in Zion contexts (e.g., Ezek. 34.33; 37.24).

157. See also Hazony, *The Philosophy of Hebrew Scripture*, 103–39.

158. A. A. Anderson, *2 Samuel*, WBC 11 (Waco, TX: Word, 1989), 76, 120.

159. Laniak, *Shepherds After my own Heart*, 58–61, 67–9.

160. Lambert, 'Kingship in Ancient Mesopotamia'.

161. Laniak, *Shepherds After my own Heart*, 105–14; Vancil, 'Sheep, Shepherd', 1187–90; *DBI*, s.v. 'Sheep, Shepherd'.

> Under his rule may the people rest in grassy pastures with him as their herdsmen. May Ur-Ninurta [the king] make the numerous people follow the just path... As for sheep, may he search for food to eat, may he let them have water to drink!¹⁶²

Lambert observes that the shepherd-king metaphor is not used evenly throughout Mesopotamia's history. Rather, there is a correlation between the way different periods thought about the role of their king, and the use of the metaphor.¹⁶³

Lambert shows that the metaphor was first applied to kingship in its earliest Sumerian setting (in the third millennium BCE).¹⁶⁴ Kings emerged there as local rulers who managed the estate of the patron god of a city.¹⁶⁵ In this setting the metaphor encapsulated a local and managerial type of kingship. The god lived in his temple ('house'), attended to by courtiers who provided for the deity 'everything that wealthy humans would have expected', and the temple functioned as the major economic centre, 'something like large-scale mediaeval manors'.¹⁶⁶ The king was the manager of the estate, which was a role, and not an ontology:¹⁶⁷

> The Sumerian equivalents of 'king' do not really correspond to the English term. Notionally he was a subordinate in his one city to the chief deity, and was responsible for running the city...for that deity... The ideology stuck for a long time. 'Shepherd' was a royal title by metaphor...which persisted long after Sumerians had ceased to exist.¹⁶⁸

---

162. Cited in Laniak, *Shepherds After my own Heart*, 63.

163. Lambert marshals an impressive expertise in Assyriology and draws heavily on extant primary sources. A full evaluation of this idea falls beyond the scope of this study. For possible nuancing factors, see Laniak, *Shepherds After my own Heart*, 58–72.

164. Lambert, 'Kingship in Ancient Mesopotamia', 55–7.

165. Lambert, 'Kingship in Ancient Mesopotamia', 55. See also Seth Richardson, 'Before Things Worked: A "Low-Power" Model of Early Mesopotamia', in *Ancient States and Infrastructural Power: Europe, Asia, and America*, ed. Clifford Ando and Seth Richardson (Philadelphia, PA: University of Pennsylvania Press, 2017), 17–62.

166. Lambert, 'Kingship in Ancient Mesopotamia', 55–6.

167. See also Maria de Jong Ellis, 'Observations on Mesopotamian Oracles and Prophetic Texts: Literary and Historiographic Considerations', *JCS* 41 (1989): 144, 181, who shows that covenant type contracts which could be annulled existed between managerial kings and their deities.

168. Lambert, 'Kingship in Ancient Mesopotamia', 57.

Lambert then observes that this ideology changed in about 2350 BCE, when the Semitic king Sargon established Akkad as a regional and imperial power. Although Sargon still acknowledged his piety and dependence on the gods, the Akkadian system of kingship rejected the localised temple economy in favour of a palace economy. He established regional shipping routes, storehouses of goods, a standing army, and introduced 'might and power [as] a major part of the royal ethos'.[169] Lambert also credits the Akkadians with introducing divine kingship into the Mesopotamian context:

> Sumerian rulers generally did not experience apotheosis at death. Belief in an immortal soul resulted in lavish preparations for the next life...but this is not deification. The new concept arose only with Narām-Sin...[for whom the citizens of Akkad] built a temple.[170]

In this new ideological context the metaphor of shepherd-king fell out of frequent use, and according to Lambert and others,[171] this appears to be a general rule. Local, temple-based economies embraced the appellation 'shepherd' and thought of their rulers as humans doing a job. Empires with aspirations of grandeur and centralised palace-based economies tended not to.[172] The royal appellation of 'shepherd' re-emerged to an extent in Ur III, but only emerged to frequent use again in the context of the first Babylonian city-states where the concept of a divine ruler never re-emerged.[173]

The trend from these observations is that 'shepherd' was not a uniformly applied metaphor of kingship. Rather, it entailed a particular ideology. With respect to their gods, kings were shepherds if they were subordinate mortals who were divinely gifted for the role. With respect to their subjects, kings were shepherds if they were like them, rooted in a local economy, and able to lead and provide for the people.

---

169. Lambert, 'Kingship in Ancient Mesopotamia', 58.
170. Lambert, 'Kingship in Ancient Mesopotamia', 59.
171. Heim, 'Kings and Kingship'; and on Egypt, see Laniak, *Shepherds After my own Heart*, 69 n. 32.
172. The epithet is almost entirely absent in Egypt. It is rarely used of Egyptian gods, but not kings. There is an Israelite tradition that Egypt hated shepherds in any case; see, e.g., Gen. 46.33-34.
173. Babylon appears to have functioned as a de-centralised system of temple economies, ruled by a centralised system of justice and fealty. See Lambert, 'Kingship in Ancient Mesopotamia', 60–3.

Late Babylonian texts, in which the appellation is frequent, describe several ritual enactments intended to humiliate the king so he would remember this place of subordination:[174]

> Water is brought for the king's hands and he is taken into [Esag]il. The artisans depart to the gate… When Bel arrives the high priest goes out and picks up the sceptre, circlet, mace…and royal crown, takes them in [before] Bel and places them on a seat. Next he goes out and slaps the king's cheek. He…leads him into the presence of Bel…he drags him by the ears and makes him kneel down on the ground…and the king recites this once:
>
> I have [not] sinned, lord of the lands, I have not neglected your divinity,
>
> [I have not] destroyed Babylon, I have not ordered its dispersal,
>
> I have [not]…forgotten its rites,
>
> [I have not] slapped the face of any citizen, I have [not] humiliated them,
>
> [I have attended] to Babylon, I have not destroyed its walls.
>
> …
>
> When [the king] has spoken this, [the priest] will bring out the sceptre, circlet, mace and crown and [will give them] to the king. He will slap the cheek of the king, and if…tears flow, Bel is favourable. If tears do not flow, Bel is angry: an enemy will arise and will bring about his downfall.[175]

This ritual not only humiliates the king, but defines his relationship both to the deity and his subjects. The deity slaps the king on the face, but the same action is denied to the king with respect to his subjects. The logic is that the king is not a 'god' to the people. Bel owns Babylon and the people in it. He humiliates the king to remind the king that the people – including the king himself – are his. The people do not belong to the king. It also shows that these kings were monarchs by divine fiat that could be repealed.[176] Walton, for example, comments that 'if kings lost touch with deity, divine sponsorship could be forfeit and divine authority withdrawn'.[177]

---

174. On the semiotics of the royal body and physically enacted rituals like the one described here, see Hamilton, *The Body Royal*. Hamilton analyses royal ideology in light of the corporeal representation of the king in biblical texts. The theme of humiliation is a curious omission from his study given its development within the Book of the Twelve (e.g., Mic. 5.1 [Heb. 4.14]; Zeph. 1.8; Zech. 9.9).

175. Cited in Lambert, 'Kingship in Ancient Mesopotamia', 64–5.

176. Ellis, 'Observations on Mesopotamian Oracles and Prophetic Texts', 144, 181.

177. Walton, *Ancient Near Eastern Thought and the Old Testament*, 259.

Within the broad range of ANE royal ideologies, then, some offer a king that is amenable to the deuteronomic ideal. ANE shepherd-kings were thought of as managers of the patron god's estate who expected to be judged for their efforts. This kind of king should take care to please the deity, which would mean searching out and living by divine will and then protecting and leading the people. It was understood by such monarchs that the people did not belong to the king, but to the patron god. All of this sits well with the covenant traditions. Therefore, the deuteronomic ideal should be understood as a plea that Israel's Zion model be this kind of ANE king, rather than the other.

In the historiography of Kings this was rarely the case. Given its prominence elsewhere in the Old Testament, the metaphor of the shepherd-king is a striking omission from the book of Kings. Even though the author had the metaphor available to him, from the Davidic traditions and no doubt also from his wider literary culture, there are no shepherd-kings in the book of Kings.[178] Rather, the only reference to shepherd-kings in Kings comes from the prophet Micaiah, who laments their absence:

> [Micaiah] said, 'I saw all Israel scattered on the mountains, as sheep that have no shepherd'. And Yahweh said, 'These have no master; let each return to his home in peace'. (1 Kgs 22.17)

6.4. *The Future of the Monarchy*

We have seen that the narrative of Kings constructs a royal ideal to assess the character of Israel's monarchs. What purpose does a royal ideology serve in the exilic political historiography? The detailed way that the ideal has been constructed demands an explanation that goes beyond a justification of the exile, and scholarship has proposed two possibilities. The first is that, by showing the failure of Israel's kings, the book intends to replace royal power with prophetic power.[179] The second possibility is that the book intends to advocate messianic hope.[180]

---

178. In Samuel, the people of Israel recognise David as a shepherd-like ruler but this never happens again (2 Sam. 5.2).

179. See, e.g., Brueggemann and Hankins, 'The Affirmation of Prophetic Power'; Shemesh, 'The Elisha Stories as Saints' Legends', 4–7; Jonathan M. Robker, 'Satire and the King of Aram', *VT* 61 (2011): 646–56; and Paynter, *Reduced Laughter*, 158–82. I discuss some of these in detail below.

180. See Chapter 3 for a literature review, and my previous work: 'The Shape of Hope', 3–27.

The two possibilities seem mutually exclusive: one is pro-monarchic, and one anti-monarchic. Either would fit the broader theology of the book we have uncovered so far. The first would reinforce our findings from Chapter 5: that the book creates an exilic locus of identity around the ministries of the prophets in the absence of David and the temple. And the second would agree with the theology of promise we examined in Chapter 3: that Kings does not doubt the promise to David and so expects a future king.

In this final section I shall argue that the book is ultimately positive toward monarchic leadership and allows the prophets to replace it only temporarily. Prophetic leadership may form the locus of Israel's exilic identity, mediating a continued relationship with Yahweh and replacing the benefits of the temple. However, Kings does not expect to replace monarchic with prophetic leadership, because it hopes for the fulfilment of Yahweh's promise to David.

6.4.1. *Prophetic and Royal Power: Elisha and the Aramaean Wars*

Inner Kings has a sequence of narratives that explores the relationship between prophetic and military power, especially in military contexts against Aram. The Elijah and Elisha narratives intersperse these accounts with narratives focused on the miracles of the prophets for the 'sons of the prophets' (בני־הנביאים) which we examined in Chapter 4. The military narratives are as follows.[181]

Table 6.1. *Interactions between a Prophet and the King in Inner Kings*

The interactions can be confusing because the prophets do not consistently act either for or against Israel. Rather, they explore the proper limits of royal power.

		Interaction between Prophet and King in Inner Kings
A	I.18.1-19	Elijah confronts Ahab after the drought. Amid national crisis, Ahab has been personally (!) preoccupied with preserving his military and agricultural assets:[182] finding grass for his horses and mules (vv. 5–6), and has let Jezebel slaughter Yahweh's prophets. Elijah challenges him and the prophets of Baal to a confrontation on Carmel. Ahab, not Elijah, is the 'troubler of Israel'.

---

181. On this sequence of narratives, see Shemesh, 'The Elisha Stories as Saints' Legends', 5; Satterthwaite, 'The Elisha Narratives'; and Walsh, 'The Organization of 2 Kings 3–11'. Cohn ('The Literary Structure of Kings', 101–2) and Angel ('Hopping Between Two Opinions') both examine the way Stories A–D contribute to the portrayal of Ahab.

182. McConville, *God and Earthly Power*, 153; Leithart, *1&2 Kings*, 133.

		Interaction between Prophet and King in Inner Kings
B	I.20[183]	After negotiations between Aram and Israel break down, a prophet assures an acquiescent Ahab that Yahweh will bring salvation. Israel wins two victories with the help of prophetic intervention. Ben-Hadad surrenders and finds mercy from Ahab, who releases him in exchange for a considerable economic and military advantage (v. 34).[184] This action results in prophetic condemnation since Ahab has pre-empted Yahweh's holy war over Aram: the man was חרם (v. 42).[185] Yahweh's intention was to 'give Aram into your hand so that you will know that I am Yahweh' (v. 13); but Ahab's intention was a brotherhood (v. 32) and fidelity (v. 31) with Ben-Hadad.
C	I.21	Jezebel conspires to acquire Naboth's vineyard for Ahab, even though Naboth refused to sell it. She has Naboth executed on false charges, and Elijah condemns her. Elijah is the 'enemy' of Ahab (v. 20).
D	I.22.1-40	Ahab and Jehoshaphat form a military alliance against Aram, and Jehoshaphat convinces Ahab to consult Micaiah over the battle, even though all of Ahab's prophets already predict success. At first Micaiah also prophesies success but Ahab does not believe him. Michaiah then declares Ahab to be a false king, and Israel are likened to 'sheep that have no shepherd' (v. 17). He also explains that Yahweh has sent a lying spirit into Ahab's prophets to lure Ahab to his death.[186] Despite this revelation, Ahab and Jehoshaphat join the battle. As a precaution Ahab disguises himself and sends Jehoshaphat as his decoy. Nevertheless, Ahab is struck and killed by a stray arrow.
E	II.1	Ahaziah tries to have Elijah arrested after a prophetic condemnation that predicts his death. He sends 50 arresting officers to Elijah three times, but the first two times Elijah calls down fire from heaven and destroys them. On the third occasion he goes with them, and the king dies as predicted.

183. In the LXX, Naboth (Story C) precedes the battle against Aram (Story B). See Angel, 'Hopping Between Two Opinions', 7–10.

184. Cogan, *1 Kings*, 469; and Walsh, *1 Kings*, 243–4.

185. Since this is the only instance of (Israelite) holy war in the book of Kings, I take it that Kings does not intend to develop the concept of חרם which was no doubt present in the source behind this narrative. So Cogan and Tadmor, *2 Kings*, 470–1; and Wray Beal, *1&2 Kings*, 266–7.

186. See Wolfgang Roth, 'The Story of the Prophet Micaiah (1 Kings 22) in Historical Critical Interpretation', in Polzin and Rothman, eds., *The Biblical Mosaic*, 105–37.

		Interaction between Prophet and King in Inner Kings
F	II.3	A parallel story to Story D: Jehoram and Jehoshaphat form a military alliance against Moab, and Jehoshaphat convinces Jehoram to consult Elisha over the battle. Elisha predicts success, but only because Jehoshaphat is part of the alliance. At first Yahweh provides a miraculous victory,[187] but in the crisis of battle the king of Moab sacrifices his own son as a burned offering which causes Israel to withdraw (v. 27).[188]
G	II.5.1-14	An Aramean general, Naaman, hears a prophet in Israel can cure his leprosy. He appeals by letter, from the king of Aram, to the king of Israel. Since the king of Israel knows he cannot save him, he suspects an incitement to war, but Elisha steps in and heals Naaman.
H	II.6.8-23	The Aramaeans suspect an Israelite spy because their battle plans are leaked to the king of Israel. When it is revealed to them that Elisha is miraculously providing military information to Israel, they send troops to arrest him. Elisha's servant sees the military surrounding his house, but Elisha reveals to him the heavenly army which protects them. Elisha blinds the Aramean force then leads them into the middle of Samaria. In a reversal of Story B, the king offers to strike them down, but Elisha forces him to feed them and send them home again instead. By the end of this story, Elisha has effective command of the Aramean and Israelite forces, as well as an angelic army.
I	II.6.24–7.20	The Aramaeans besiege Samaria and the resulting famine is severe. In a macabre parody of Solomon's wisdom (1 Kgs 3.16-28), two women are arguing because they ate one of their babies yesterday, and the one with the remaining child refuses to let it be eaten today. They cry out to the king for salvation (הושיעה אדני המלך), but the king knows only Yahweh saves. He blames Elisha for the predicament and sends to have him arrested. Elisha predicts both the end of the famine and the death of the arresting officer, which both occur in unusual circumstances. The Aramaeans flee because they hear an army and fear Egypt has come. Some lepers discover that they have gone and lead the Samarians in plundering the loot, which ends the famine. The arresting officer dies in the rush.

---

187. Westbrook, 'Elisha's True Prophecy in 2 Kings 3', 530–2; Long, 'Elisha's Deceptive Prophecy', 168–71.
188. We discussed this difficult ending in Chapter 2. On the range of inferences that might be drawn concerning kingship, see Fretheim, *First and Second Kings*, 142–4; Brueggemann, *1 & 2 Kings*, 314–15; Sweeney, *I & II Kings*, 284.

There are many perplexing features of these stories when they are interpreted in isolation,[189] but our interest is to see whether they show a consistent pattern when they are interpreted together. In particular we are interested in the way prophetic and royal power are portrayed throughout.

One immediate question concerns the relationship between kings and prophets themselves, which is inconsistent. Why are the prophets sometimes portrayed as hostile to the king (*A, B, C, D, E, F, I*), but not always (*H*)? Why do they sometimes act for the benefit of Israelite forces (*B, F, I*), and at other times for Israel's enemies (*D, G*)? This even occurs within the same story (*H*). The problem is that the prophets do not seem loyal to a 'side'.

The narrative contract of Inner Kings has led the reader to expect the demise of Ahab's dynasty through the ministry of Elisha (1 Kgs 19.17). However, sometimes Elisha acts in the opposite way, as is the case when he functions as a spy for the Israelite king (2 Kgs 6.9-10). It would be easier if the prophets were consistently for or against the Israelite kings, but this is not the intended pattern. One interpretive possibility may be to challenge the assumption that the prophets ought to take a side. Elsewhere, Yahweh does not fight for Israel or their adversaries (e.g., Josh. 5.13-14).

If one asks different questions, the pattern is more consistent. For example, Brueggemann notices that throughout these narratives the kings are portrayed as ineffective, 'inept, and dysfunctional'.[190] The prophets, on the other hand, accomplish not only what the kings set out to do, but much more besides. Brueggemann parses this observation as the prophetic 'deconstruction' of royal power.[191]

Elisha, for example, has the 'capacity to traverse and disturb the royal landscape with uncontested power'.[192] He acts with authority over

---

189. Scholars have also struggled to piece together the redaction history of this section of the narrative. For an overview see Otto, 'The Composition of the Elijah–Elisha Stories', 487–508; McKenzie, *The Trouble with Kings*, 81–100; Hermann Joseph Stipp, *Elischa–Propheten–Gottesmänner: Die Kompositionsgeschichte des Elischazyklus und verwandter Texte, rekonstruiert auf der Basis von Text- und Literarkritik zu 1 Kön 20.22 und 2 Kön 2–7* (St. Ottilien: EOS, 1987). On the question of literary genre see Rofé, *The Prophetical Stories*.

190. Brueggemann and Hankins, 'The Affirmation of Prophetic Power', 72; see also Campbell and O'Brien, *Unfolding the Deuteronomistic History*, 415 n. 8.

191. Brueggemann and Hankins, 'The Affirmation of Prophetic Power'. See also Shemesh's brief notes on 'social satire against the royal house' ('The Elisha Stories as Saints' Legends', 5–6).

192. Brueggemann and Hankins, 'The Affirmation of Prophetic Power', 73.

sickness, disease, famine, foreign armies, the kings themselves, and even the angelic hosts, while Ahab is portrayed as a 'vexed and sullen' king, powerless to get what he wanted (e.g., 1 Kgs 20.43; 21.4-5).

For Brueggemann, this is not a deconstruction of Israelite kings in particular, but rather royal authority in general, which finds its historical context in the exilic and post-exilic prophetic movement:

> The deconstruction of sovereignty in the Books of Kings...would corrupt the entire enterprise of kingship and sovereign power. In the final form of the text in the sixth century, this sustained narrative of deconstruction and delegitimization must have mattered to the historian.[193]

Others have noted the same narrative pattern, but drawn the opposite conclusion from it. Wesley Bergen, for example, observes that the book cannot divest itself of royal power entirely. Commenting on the Jehu narratives:

> In the stories of Elisha and the kings, Elisha's power clearly surpasses that of the kings... This allows the prophet to be viewed as someone able to provide for Israel better than the king. The answer to Israel's plight in their request for a king (1 Sam 8:20) is a prophet, not a king... Yet as soon as the narrative allows this possibility, it closes it off by making the king a necessary part of the story... While the prophet provides advice, it is the king who acts. Finally, the removal of an evil king in Israel [Ahab] is naturally accomplished by someone who is to be a king [Jehu].[194]

Disagreement between Bergen and Brueggemann on the role of Jehu has led them to draw opposite conclusions about the role of prophets. Jehu occupies a critical place at the climax of the Elijah–Elisha narrative arc and the end of Ahab's dynasty, but how is his relationship to prophets conveyed? Brueggemann understands Jehu as a prophetic puppet king who, by usurping the throne, hands royal authority over to the prophetic guild:[195]

---

193. Brueggemann and Hankins, 'The Affirmation of Prophetic Power', 76.

194. Wesley J. Bergen, *Elijah and the End of Prophetism*, JSOTSup 286 (Sheffield: Sheffield Academic, 1999), 177.

195. Lamb (*Righteous Jehu and his Evil Heirs*, 256–8) argues similarly, that the Jehu demonstrates that dynastic succession has failed to produce righteous kings. He believes the narrative advances a prophetic agenda, but he does not see it as subverting royal ideology altogether.

> The steady dismissal of the king in the narrative, matched by the steady enhancement of the prophet, prepares the reader for this final act [i.e. Jehu]. Thus, the narrative deconstruction and brutal termination are of a piece. The outcome and the proclamation, 'Jehu is king', together yield a dynasty that has unmitigated 'zeal for the Lord' (10.16) and so is completely amenable to prophetic passion and authority.[196]

Bergen, on the other hand, thinks the prophets and not just the kings are critiqued by these narratives: the prophets fail as often as the kings,[197] and neither Elijah nor Elisha is competent all the time.[198]

Bergen's reading has better support. It is not obvious from 2 Kings 9–10 that Jehu is portrayed as a puppet ruler of the prophetic guild. At no point does Jehu appear to be 'completely amenable to prophetic passion and authority' unless it also suits his royal ambition.[199] It is true that he is anointed by the 'sons of the prophets' (בני־הנביאים) with a mandate that avenges them (ונקמתי דמי עבדי הנביאים, 2 Kgs 9.7-10). It is also true that Jehu claims to be motivated by self-proclaimed zeal for this task (2 Kgs 9.22; 10.16), but such a commission granted legitimacy to his coup and helped him to consolidate power. Jehu is a king who is anointed by a prophet and who, because of his actions, is prophetically promised a dynasty (2 Kgs 10.30). If the purpose of this sequence of stories was to undermine the institution of the monarchy in favour of prophetic leadership, then this is a strange climax.

The narratives of Inner Kings, therefore, whenever a prophet engages the king, do not undermine monarchy in favour of prophetic leadership. However, these narratives do delineate a boundary to royal authority and show that the kings overstep it when they act without prophetic endorsement. This is prominent in military contexts.[200]

---

196. Brueggemann and Hankins, 'The Affirmation of Prophetic Power', 75.

197. See also Paynter, *Reduced Laughter*, 128–32, 133–43; and John W. Olley, 'Yhwh and His Zealous Prophet: The Presentation of Elijah in 1 and 2 Kings', *JSOT* 80 (1998): 25–51.

198. Bergen's wider point (*Elijah and the End of Prophetism*, 104, 169–74) is that Elisha is portrayed as a lesser prophet than Elijah, and the last in the declining institution of charismatic prophetism.

199. On the ambiguity of Jehu's characterisation, see Roger Tomes, '"Come and See my Zeal for the Lord": Reading the Jehu Story', in Brooke and Kaestli, eds., *Narrativity in Biblical and Related Texts*, 64–7; Michael S. Moore, 'Jehu's Coronation and Purge of Israel', *VT* 53 (2003): 100; and, at monograph length, Wray Beal, *The Deuteronomist's Prophet*.

200. So Wray Beal, *1&2 Kings*, 261.

We saw the reason for this above when we examined Hezekiah's faith in the face of an invading army. Throughout Kings, salvation comes from Yahweh and it invariably involves the prophetic word. These narratives show that 'Yahweh of armies' (יהוה צבות) has his own army (2 Kgs 2.11-12; 6.17; 7.6), and that the prophets share counsel with Yahweh as to how he will wield it (1 Kgs 22.19-23).[201] Occasionally, they command it (2 Kgs 6.18).[202] Thus, for a king to engage in battle without prophetic endorsement is to overstep covenantal bounds.[203] As Leithart remarks:

> When Israel appeals to a king, there is no help; but the Israel that seeks help from Yahweh's prophet, or a king under the influence of a prophet, lives.[204]

The royal ideology in these narratives agrees, therefore, with what we discovered in other parts of this chapter. Inner Kings is not trying to undermine the monarchy as an institution, nor to deconstruct royal power in general. To the contrary, these chapters, where the prophets are portrayed as most active and characterised most richly, illustrate the limitations of what they can accomplish. The prophets may be king-makers (e.g., 1 Kgs 1.34; 19.16; 2 Kgs 9.3-12), and they may call people and king to covenant fidelity (e.g., 2 Kgs 17.13), but they do not lead the people in reformation or obedience. They do not reform the nation and they do not cause the people to sin. They are not kings and, despite their exilic role, they cannot replace the monarchy in the as yet unrealised ideal of Covenant-Israel.

6.4.2. *The Question of a Messiah*

Does, then, the book of Kings hope for a messiah? The question of messianic theology in the book of Kings has been a vexing one, partly because the study of messianic theology is fraught with methodological problems concerning prophetic eschatology.[205] However, since the book of Kings does not have an eschatological perspective, some of the issues

---

201. Simon J. de Vries, *Prophet Against Prophet* (Grand Rapids, MI: Eerdmans, 1978), 147–52; Cogan, *1 Kings*, 497–8.

202. Rachelle Gilmour, 'A Note on the Horses and Chariots of Fire at Dothan', *ZAW* 125 (2013): 308–13.

203. As Ahab demonstrates (Story D). See Angel, 'Hopping Between Two Opinions', 10.

204. Leithart, *1&2 Kings*, 208.

205. Daniel I. Block, 'My Servant David: Ancient Israel's Vision of the Messiah', in *Israel's Messiah in the Bible and the Dead Sea Scrolls*, ed. Richard S. Hess and M. Daniel Carroll R. (Grand Rapids, MI: Baker Academic, 2003), 17–18.

can be simplified. In our context, I use the term 'messianic' to mean hope that a future, righteous, Davidic king would arise within history. I take it that the book of Kings has already defined what royal righteousness would look like, which is what we have discovered in this chapter so far. It is also a different thing to ask whether the book of Kings on its own engenders such hope, or whether, once hope for a messiah already exists, readers might find support for it in Kings. The latter is almost certainly true but is not our question.[206]

The compiler of the book had messianic prophecies and traditions available to him had he wanted to use them, as the use of other Isaiah traditions demonstrates.[207] There are nevertheless no explicit messianic claims in the book of Kings. Josiah, the only prophesied Davidic king (1 Kgs 13.2), comes and goes with little fanfare. If he embodies messianic hope in some pre-exilic version of the book, his sudden death quashes it in the exilic version. Similarly, a study of the root משח in Kings yields very little insight. Certain kings are 'anointed' – Solomon (1 Kgs 1.39), Jehu (2 Kgs 9.6), Joash (2 Kgs 11.12), and Jehoiakim (2 Kgs 23.30) – but except for Joash these are not paradigms of virtue. In any case, Hazael of Syria is also anointed (1 Kgs 19.16). The term within Kings is used as a description of the historical ritual of inauguration,[208] without the eschatological significance common in prophetic texts.

The lack of any explicit promise of a coming messiah has left commentators to assess whether the book offers anything implicit.[209] Several avenues have been explored. One such path has been through the specific term נגיד,[210] which is not predicated of all of Israel's kings, but only Solomon (1 Kgs 1.35), Jeroboam (1 Kgs 14.7), Baasha (1 Kgs 16.2), and Hezekiah (2 Kgs 20.5). The significance of this word has been discussed with respect to Israel's early understanding of kingship.[211] What is the difference between a נגיד and a מלך? Early analysis linked the word נגיד

---

206. So, e.g., Laato, *A Star Is Rising*, 57–185; and Antti Laato, *Josiah and David Redivivus: The Historical Josiah and the Messianic Expectations of Exilic and Postexilic Times*, ConB (Stockholm: Almqvist & Wiksell, 1992).

207. Marvin Sweeney (*King Josiah of Judah*, 4, 19–20) explores this at length.

208. *NIDOTTE*, s.v. 'מָשַׁח'.

209. Note that it is typical of exilic literature to offer only muted messianic hope. Contrast, e.g., the pre-exilic messianic theology of Isa. 9 and 11 with the scant references to the messiah in Jer. 23.5-6 and 30.9.

210. Mettinger, *King and Messiah*, 64–79; Halpern, *The Constitution of the Monarchy in Israel*, 1–11.

211. E.g. Cross, *Canaanite Myth and Hebrew Epic*, 220. See also Laato, *A Star Is Rising*, 11–12, 237, on messianic hope in the early monarchy.

directly to messianic expectation. Tryggve Mettinger claimed it was a 'highly significant...new key word' with implications for Israel's royal ideology.[212]

More recently it has been observed that the word has a variety of uses in the Old Testament.[213] In later writings (such as Chronicles) it seems to designate a military commander of any sort, without even royal connotations. It is rare in other exilic literature but also used flexibly, for example, of the king of Tyre in Ezek. 28.2. Scholars have therefore focused on the way the term is used by Dtr. In addition to the four kings mentioned above, it is also used of Saul and David (1 Sam. 9.16; 10.1; 13.14; 25.30; 2 Sam. 5.2; 6.21; 7.8). Nine of these eleven uses are by Yahweh, designating a human as נגיד. On the basis of this evidence, and also noticing that נגיד seems etymologically related to the root נגד, Albrecht Alt proposed the meaning 'made known by Yahweh'.[214] The connection with divine election was picked up by Noth,[215] and from there many accepted that נגיד in DtrH meant something similar to 'messiah'.[216] This evidence explains the term's usage in Samuel better than Kings, where two of its four uses do not fit the pattern.[217]

In recent years, Linville has further developed the thought by expanding the criteria. Linville argues that in Samuel and Kings the title is used in relation to people who are divinely selected as kings, founders of dynasties, or raised up specifically during moments of historical transition (especially within the monarchy) to deal with threats to Israel:[218]

> To sum up, נגיד represents the solution Yahweh proposes to a leadership crisis: Israel's problems with foreign powers, Samuel's corrupt sons, the wayward Saul, the severe taskmasters who were David's successors, and the threat against Jerusalem in the wake of the fall of Samaria.[219]

---

212. Mettinger, *King and Messiah*, 61.
213. Note also Ps. 76.12 [Heb. 13]. See *NIDOTTE*, s.v. 'נָגִיד'; *HALOT*, s.v. 'נָגִיד'.
214. Albrecht Alt, 'The Formation of the Israelite State in Palestine', in *Essays on Old Testament History and Religion*, trans. R. A. Wilson (New York: Doubleday, 1968), 254 n. 54.
215. Martin Noth, *The History of Israel*, 2nd English ed. (London: A. & C. Black, 1960), 169 n. 1.
216. See Halpern, *The Constitution of the Monarchy in Israel*, 1–3, 257–58 (nn. 1, 2, 7); and Mettinger, *King and Messiah*, 69–70.
217. Alt ('The Formation of the Israelite State in Palestine', 233) argued that David overstepped his authority in appointing Solomon as נגיד.
218. Linville, *Israel in the Book of Kings*, 143–9.
219. Linville, *Israel in the Book of Kings*, 149.

However, there are weaknesses in Linville's argument. Not everyone agrees with such a theologically laden analysis of a single word[220] and, more critically, there are instances in Kings when one might expect a נגיד but the word is not used: J(eh)oash would be one such candidate (2 Kgs 11) and Josiah would be another (2 Kgs 22–23). Linville's conclusion is part of his wider argument, which we examined and rejected in Chapter 3, that after Solomon the Southern Kingdom 'lost' the kingship of Israel to the north, only to be regained later under Hezekiah.[221] The usage of נגיד in Kings is insufficient to bear the weight of this thesis, but it seems difficult to maintain a messianic reading of the word without it.

There are other pathways to messianic theology in Kings that seem more promising. Janzen argued that part of the purpose of the book may well have been to shape future Davidic rulers towards a messianic ideal.[222] By its persistent critique of the royals, the book shows to the Davidides in exile what kind of king they should be when Yahweh restores the monarchy.[223] Janzen concludes this of Jehoiachin:

> ...since the narrative never annuls the eternal promise to David...a hopeful future is still a possibility if Jehoiachin can become an ideal king. If Jehoiachin leads repentance like Josiah and trusts in YHWH to deliver in the context of this repentance like Hezekiah, then his sins...can be overwritten.[224]

Janzen thus argues that the book of Kings functions in two ways with respect to exilic royalty like Jehoiachin: first to instruct them as to what a righteous king might look like, and second to assure them that Yahweh might yet find a way to overlook their previous sins so that they might become one. This argument has much to commend it. We have already seen in this chapter how carefully the book of Kings constructs a royal ideal and, given that the narrative concludes with the release of Jehoiachin (2 Kgs 25.27-30), it seems reasonable to conclude that the book intends to shape future kings.

We can develop this observation further. In Chapter 3 we noted the likelihood that the release of Jehoiachin in 2 Kgs 25.27-30 should be interpreted in light of the Davidic promise.[225] When read this way, Jehoiachin's

---

220. E.g. Cross, *Canaanite Myth and Hebrew Epic*, 220; Halpern, *The Constitution of the Monarchy in Israel*, 9–11.
221. Linville, *Israel in the Book of Kings*, 146–50.
222. Janzen, 'The Sins of Josiah and Hezekiah'.
223. See also Knoppers, 'There Was None Like Him'.
224. Janzen, 'The Sins of Josiah and Hezekiah', 369.
225. So von Rad, *Old Testament Theology*, 1:334–47.

release engenders hope that Yahweh might yet do what he promised for David, even from the context of exile. Critics of this position, like Wolff, argue that even if this promise does imply restoration, it only guarantees the possibility of the continuation of the dynasty, without necessarily implying the coming of a righteous king.[226] However, Wolff is too negative. We saw in Chapter 3 that the logic of covenant and promise within the book entwines hope with fidelity. A king is hoped for because of the promise to David, and must be righteous because only in that case can Yahweh bless him. In the logic of fulfilment in Kings, therefore, we saw that a righteous king was inevitable.[227]

This is not a messianic hope in the full, prophetic and eschatological sense. Yet even so, the book generates a powerful expectation that God will yet do what he promised for David, and constructs a royal ideal to show what this fulfilment will look like when it occurs.

6.4.3. *Conclusions*

For the exilic readers who, the book argues, should one day reconstitute their nation according to the covenant, the ideology of Kings shows what went wrong with Israel's former monarchy and reveals what kind of regime they should implement when it becomes possible.

The book of Kings contains a much more coherent royal ideology than has often been assumed. The deuteronomic ideal does more than offer a critique of Israel's existing royal institutions. By comparing to an idealised Davidic exemplar, and by exploring the paradigms of the incomparable kings (obedience, faith, and wisdom), an ideal monarch is constructed. Such a king ought to be, above all, a covenant-keeping king. His heart must be inclined to Yahweh like David. He should embody obedience like Josiah and, in moments of crisis, trust like Hezekiah. Although he would also be wise, the book of Kings is concerned to show how wisdom does not necessarily lead to obedience and faith, and so gives a qualified endorsement of this virtue. It also explores the ideal relationship between a king and his subjects, showing that the king should be a servant to his people.

None of this overturns existing models of kingship in ANE cultures, including Israel's Davidic–Zion synthesis. ANE kings were chosen by divine election and imbued with characteristics necessary to rule well: wisdom, strength, and justice. The book of Kings endorses this model, but

---

226. Wolff, 'Kerygma'.
227. So Provan, 'The Messiah in the Book of Kings', 71–6, 80, 84–5; and McConville, 'King and Messiah', 293–5.

only to a point. Where, in some ANE cultures, the king could be thought superhuman, and at times divine, Kings reminds us of the deuteronomic ideal which prevents such exaltation. Deuteronomic kingship, then, serves to moderate, not deconstruct, the ANE ideal. This more moderate form of kingship can also be found outside Israel, for example, in Mesopotamia's shepherd-king model.

Hope for a future, idealised Covenant-Israel is created through the logic of covenant and promise in the book. In the same way, expectation generated for an ideal future king. Unlike the temple, which the book has argued can be embodied by prophetic ministry, the monarchy is not replaceable by the prophets. If Israel's institutions are functioning well, then monarchic power, especially military power, is curtailed by prophetic oversight. Even so, the prophets are not covenant administrators. They do not lead the people to sin or obedience, and neither are they held accountable for this in the way kings are.

The book of Kings, therefore, encourages the belief in a future king who will embody ANE kingship at its best, and live up to the deuteronomic ideal as well. He will be elected by Yahweh, be the son of God, have a heart for Yahweh, be obedient to the covenant, be faithful in crisis, be wise without becoming self-reliant, and be a servant to his people.

7

CONCLUSIONS:
ISRAEL AMONG THE NATIONS

In this final chapter I shall attempt to draw together the various threads of this study, and to summarise the political identity that the narrative of Kings attempts to produce for its exilic readers. As I progress, rather than repeating footnotes or arguments, I will reference the sections (§) of the study where I discuss each idea more fully.

We began this study with Smith's observation that 'exile is the nursery of nationalism' (§1.1). This is because moments of severe national crisis strip away so many of the symbols, stories, myths, legends, laws, customs, and dreams that bind communities together. As these national fingerprints dissolve, communities are forced to re-imagine themselves: to tell themselves new stories about what it means to belong, to incorporate the recent crises into their historical narratives, and to find something new to hope from the future – a new destiny.

For Israel, there were many particular losses associated with the exile, which we have analysed under the headings of *covenant*, *nationhood*, *land*, and *rule* (§1.1). If Israel had thought of themselves as a people in covenant with Yahweh, then the exile would seem to threaten that relationship. Is it possible any longer to be a covenant people if the covenant has been broken? In what sense does Israel in exile claim continuity with those who came before? What of the land, which Israel understood to have been a blessing for covenant obedience – was it any longer possible to be Israel from outside of it? What of all the stories attached to it, the territorialised memories of the patriarchs, judges, and kings as they wandered through it? Were all of these cultural memories suddenly invalid? Much of Israel's identity in the monarchic era revolved around a Davidic king and the temple that Solomon constructed. In Israel's understanding, the Davidic line was guaranteed by Yahweh, and the holy mountain on which the temple sat was inviolable because of Yahweh's presence. The exile questions all of this, and so the exiles are forced to imagine their national identity in new ways.

I have proposed, then, that the book of Kings might be read not only as a source for political reflection – which it came to be as Scripture to both Jews and Christians – but as the product of it. It is the attempt to construct, through the genre of historiography, a new national identity (§1.2). Even though the book of Kings presents the history of Israel's monarchic period in Canaan, it is also the story of Israel amongst the nations. It is the story of a people, united by covenant, divided by conflict, conquered, and then transported to Babylon. In telling this story, the book attempts to imagine an Israel that maintains continuity with their previous existence, gives meaning to their current situation, and provides a vision for their future.

Recalling the narrative structure of the book as a literary intercalation (§2.3.2), we will examine this theme in two mutually interpretive stages. Outer Kings best helps us to reflect on what it means to be Israel amongst the nations. Through the narration of its history, it connects the exilic community to both their past and future, and provides meaning to their present experience. Inner Kings complements this through concrete examples. It portrays the exploits of a people who were a little like the exiles. Claiming to be Israel, these people were alienated from David and the temple, and they existed as strangers in their own land, ruled by a foreign god and queen.

7.1. *The Political Vision of Outer Kings*

The primary narrative arc of Outer Kings, the most prominent of the book's plotlines, recounts how Israel ended up in Babylon (§2.3.3). It opens with an image of a powerful and distinctly Israelite polity, Covenant-Israel (§3.1). They are a people united through a covenant, gathered at a sacred place (§3.2.1), and governed by a promised king (§3.2.2). Solomon's dedication is a glorious occasion, but Outer Kings strips everything away. First the northern tribes break away and are eventually conquered. The temple is plundered to pay off the nations, then taken apart and transported.

The book ends with all three, the temple, the king, and the people, on Babylonian soil, but this ending is pregnant with possibility. As a polity, Israel has been dismantled and transported, but not destroyed. In exile they are the remnant (§4.3.3). Solomon's united monarchy, most richly expressed at the temple dedication, was divided into two administrations, but not two peoples (§4.1.3). Even after the division they remained one garment torn into two pieces. When the Northern Kingdom was destroyed, the book presents the south as the remnant of all Israel (§4.3.2). This remnant is itself plundered by Egypt until only Jerusalem is left (§5.3.2). The empire of Solomon is thus peeled, layer by layer, as if an onion, until by the final chapters only Jerusalem and the temple remain. This is in some ways a return to the beginning, to the full expression of Israel gathered at the temple in Jerusalem during Solomon's dedication (§3.2.1). When this remnant is finally transported, all Israel is in Babylon (§5.3.3), and they have all they need, in incipient form, to reconstitute what was lost. Israel is not destroyed by Babylon; they are preserved within it (§4.3.3).

The logic of covenant and promise in the book (§2.3.1) encourages a desired future amongst the exiles, a destiny (§3.2.4), which is to become a reconstituted nation. This time they will live in fidelity to the covenant (§3.2.4), and the sin that led to exile will be purged (§4.4). They will be returned to their land, which Yahweh never left (§§5.3.1, 5.3.3), because Yahweh promised to hear their prayers from there even if they could only pray from exile (§5.4.2). The temple will be rebuilt as the ideal place for all Israel to worship (§5.2.3).

There will be a new Davidic ruler (§6.4.2). Because of its special focus on the failure of Israel's and Judah's kings, the narrative of Outer Kings builds a robust picture of what kind of king the exiles should hope for. He should be a Davidic descendent, so that the promise to David will be fulfilled, and faithful to the covenant for the same reason (§3.2.2). In Kings, this is another way of saying he should be 'like David' (§6.2.1). This king should be faithful in moments of crisis, like Hezekiah who trusted Yahweh to deliver Jerusalem, and obedient like Josiah who fulfilled the *Shema* (§6.2.2). He should also be wise, but not entirely after the pattern set by Solomon, whose wisdom did not lead to covenant fidelity (§6.3.1). The hoped-for king is an ANE king, but after the pattern of shepherd-kings who understand themselves to be managers of their deity's estate, rather than the god-like kings who build empires for their own glory (§6.3.2). The king should enjoy the popular support of his people, who are the normal means that Yahweh uses to ensure proper dynastic succession (§6.2.3), and the king should be a servant to his people (§6.5). In summary, the king that the narrative hopes for is not a saviour, nor an empire builder, but a covenant administrator who will lead Israel in fidelity to Yahweh.

Since the king is not a saviour, Israel's reconstitution relies on Yahweh's intervention. There is nothing they can do to hasten it. According to the pattern that the book established with Jehu's and Assyria's invasions, restoration never follows judgment immediately (§4.3). Israel should repent of their previous failures (§3.2.3), but this will not precipitate the blessing. Restoration will only come when Yahweh sends a saviour (§4.4). Because of this, Israel in exile enters a time of waiting.

How should they wait? The last four verses of Kings, cryptic as they have seemed to many interpreters, propose an answer. We have already noticed how they excite messianic hope when read in the context of the promise to David (§6.4.2). They also give the exiles a clue as to how they should live in their immediate situation. Israel's journey into exile was Jehoiachin's journey first. Jehoiachin was a pre-exilic Israelite (2 Kgs 24.8), taken to Babylon because of unfaithfulness to the covenant (vv. 9-10), but who ultimately moves from captivity (בית כלא, 2 Kgs 25.27) to honour (נשא...ראש). He is divested of his prison garments (בגדי כלאו, v. 29), he is seated above other kings (ויתן את כסאו מעל כסא המלכים, v. 28), and lives a comfortable life. However, these comforts are 'given' by the Babylonian king who speaks 'kind words' to him (וידבר אתו טבות ויתן..., v. 28). Jehoiachin therefore demonstrates the possibility of fruitful, even comfortable existence in Babylon, and in doing so shows that – during the period of waiting at least – submission to Babylonian rule is acceptable. These four verses therefore function akin to Jeremiah's letter to the exiles, which was sent immediately after Jehoiachin was taken captive (Jer. 29.1). For the author of Kings, as for Jeremiah (Jer. 29.5-7), Israel must settle down, live their lives, and prosper through the prosperity of their captors, for a time.

Submitting to Babylonian rule in this way does not place the exiles outside of the rule of Yahweh. This is because the exiles would understand Yahweh to be in control of Babylon. The God who once put his bridle on Sennacherib and turned him back the way that he came can do the same again with Evil-merodach (§5.4.1). Yahweh's sovereignty, then, opens the possibility for Israel to live life in Babylon. Since the exile was Yahweh's doing (§3.3.4), it must be acceptable for Israel to be ruled by the Babylonian king. However, this is a fine line for the exiles to walk because we already know the book engenders hope in a different destiny. Acquiescence to Babylonian rule may be acceptable, even desirable for a time, but there is ultimately no hope for Israel in Babylon. Assyria is presented in Kings as an alternative to Yahweh, a covenant-making saviour, with catastrophic results for every king who accepts this definition (§3.3.3). Empires do not make good gods, and emperors cannot save nations. Yahweh, not Babylon, must save (§4.4), and so the exiles submit to the Babylonians without hoping in them.

7. Conclusions

This situation must have seemed intolerable to those used to thinking of Israelite identity in terms of what had been lost: king, temple, and land (§1.1), but the narrative of Outer Kings refocuses Israelite identity during this period of waiting. This is primarily done through the concept of the remnant (§4.3.3), but this is not the only way. Outer Kings also explores the possibility of a faithful form of Yahwism apart from David and the temple, through the narrative of the separation of the Northern Kingdom (§4.1.1). Jeroboam was prophetically promised a kingdom like David's if he would keep the covenant. Even though this did not eventuate, the promise implies the possibility. Even after their sin and separation, the north was never excluded from 'Israel' (§4.1.2). The fact that, for most of the book, there are two administrative polities who both share a partial claim to Israelite identity, demonstrates that political administration is tangential to the ideal of Covenant-Israel. Israel's unity lies in the covenant, and not political administration (§4.1.3). The covenant is the core of Israelite identity (§3.1).

Since the covenant is central to the political definition of Israel, the greatest challenge to the exiles lies in keeping it. They cannot embody Israel unless they do. Outer Kings has shown that political contingencies have never been the cause of Israel's failure (§3.3). Israel have proven themselves as likely to fail in a time of national ascendency (§3.3.1) as in a time of crisis (§3.3.3). So, if they do fail in exile, it will not be because Babylon 'won'. Rather, it will be because they have become like Babylon. Solomon's neglect of the covenant reshaped Israel into a new Egypt (§§3.3.1, 6.2.2, 6.3.1), and Ahaz's transformed Judah into a clone of Damascus (§3.3.3). The pattern throughout the book of Kings is that abandoning the covenant results in the loss of political identity, the loss of Israel. A faithful expression of Israel is not threatened by submission to the Babylonian king, but it will be quickly undone if they worship Babylonian gods or marry Babylonian women (§3.4).

This does not imply that the exiles should attempt to isolate themselves from all contact with Babylonian culture. We will see this more explicitly below, but even in Outer Kings there are strong indications that Israel should be open towards outsiders. According to Solomon's dedication, foreigners as well as Israelites could find Yahweh at the temple (§5.4.2). Those who were resettled into the northern territories after the Assyrian invasion learned to some extent what it meant to become fearers of Yahweh, and also to some extent adopted the norms of the covenant as their own (§4.2). This implies that the exiles should also be open to the possibility that Babylonians might learn to fear Yahweh. This must happen through proximity to the exiles themselves. No outsiders come to Yahweh in Kings except through Israel or an Israelite (§5.4.2). So, Israel's presence in Babylon brings surprising hope for Babylon, but only so long as Israel continue to express a covenant-shaped polity (§4.4).

7.2. *The Political Vision of Inner Kings*

The primary narrative arc of Inner Kings centres on the destruction of Ahab's house, which was prophetically announced to Elijah and fulfilled through Jehu and Hazael during the ministry of Elisha (§2.3.3). Like Outer Kings, Inner Kings is also concerned with the preservation of a remnant of Israel through this judgment (§4.3.1), and so shares some of the same mechanisms used to redefine political Israel (§4.4). The particular political logic of the Inner Kings narrative is developed through subtext. Elijah and Ahab have different political visions when each accuses the other of being the 'troubler of Israel' (§3.3.2). Elijah is the prophet of the covenant who wants Israel to be a people of the covenant. Ahab is portrayed as introducing Baal through his marriage to Jezebel and then, influenced by her, embarking on an intentional process of re-Canaanising the Northern Kingdom (§3.3.2). As this happens the conquest is reversed, and it becomes clear that Ahab's Israel is not Israel. Initially, Elijah believes himself to be all that is left of the true Israel and, although the reader is aware this is untrue, the narrative still portrays those who are faithful to the covenant as a dwindling number in a land in which they have become unwelcome (§4.3.1).

This portrait is not coincidental. As we have explored, Outer Kings has raised the possibility of being faithful under the influence of foreign rule. Inner Kings develops this idea into a rich tapestry of narratives that explore what this may look like (§2.4). It does this through its complex portrayal of Elijah, Elisha, and a broad array of supporting characters, who all live under the hostile rule of Ahab and Jezebel and their successors (§2.3.4). Already set in the Northern Kingdom (§2.3.4), most characters of Inner Kings find themselves, like the exiles, separated from both the temple and Davidic rule (§2.4). The regular detours of the narrative outside of Canaan take the reader, with the characters, outside of the promised land as well. All of this is fruitful theological territory for an exploration of exilic identity.

Despite the absence of the temple, the king and the land, the possibility of a faithful and covenantal Yahwism is never doubted throughout this narrative. The prophets are key to this because they incorporate the dynamics of all three. With respect to the land, the prophets perform miracles as frequently outside Israel as inside, showing that Yahweh's domain of action is larger than Israel's territory (§5.4.1). Elijah performs miracles associated with Baal in Baal's territory (§3.3.2), and ascends to heaven on the east of the Jordan (§5.4). Elisha can tell the Israelite king what the king of Syria is thinking. The prophets lead Israel to victory (and defeat) as easily in Moab as in Samaria, and as easily in the plains of Syria as in the hills of Ephraim. And people come to learn that Yahweh is the only God both within and outside of Israel, through contact with a prophet (§5.4).

The prophets also assist the reader to rethink the role of the temple. First, the prophets demonstrate that faithful worship of Yahweh, even sacrifice, does not depend on the presence of the temple. Kings has a theology of centralisation, but it is not as strongly expressed as is often supposed. Israel are supposed to worship at the temple when it is available, but this should not prevent worship in other situations (§5.2.3). According to Elijah, the removal of (non-centralised) altars is a sign of covenant violation (§5.2.2), and Elijah makes his own altar on Mount Carmel and sacrifices there in the name of Yahweh (§5.2.1). Namaan also, with permission from Elisha, returns to Syria to offer sacrifice to Yahweh there (§5.2.2). Second, the prophets function in the Inner Kings narrative to provide what the reader has learned to expect from the temple in Outer Kings (§5.2.2). Solomon's dedication established the reader's expectation of the way the temple should function in the contingencies of Israel's life. It was the place where the prayers of Israelites and foreigners could be heard and answered. This is something the prophets do in Inner Kings (§5.4.2). It was also the place where Yahweh's blessings would be channelled when requested with faith: forgiveness, healing, life, justice, rain, and victory. All of these are supplied by the prophets in Inner Kings (§5.4.2). As the prophets fulfil the role of the temple, they also become the focal point of the community: an alternative to the temple in its absence. Elisha gathers and leads a band of followers who are invariably portrayed as faithful to the covenant and who are the beneficiary of most of his miracles (§5.4.2).

Except for Jehoshaphat, upon whom the narrative does not linger (§2.3.4), the kings of Inner Kings are not faithful, and most are understood to persecute those Israelites who are (§4.3.1). The prophets, then, by their leadership of the community take on some of the role of the kings. However, the narrative is careful that they are not portrayed to have eclipsed the role of the king entirely (§6.4.1). Just as Inner Kings continues to assert a role for the temple in Jerusalem (§5.2.2), so also it continues to hope for a Davidic king – even in the Northern Kingdom

– who will be faithful to the covenant (§6.4.2). The crisis of the main plot of Inner Kings concerns the future of the Davidic monarchy. The threat posed by Athaliah to the Davidic line in Inner Kings is at least as grave as that confronted in Sennacherib's military action in Outer Kings (§2.3.3). Yet, at the same moment that the reader is informed that the Judean king has married into Jezebel's family, Inner Kings reminds us that Yahweh acts for the sake of David and will keep a lamp burning in Jerusalem for him (§2.3.1). Resolution to the Jezebel–Athaliah threat is the only scene in Inner Kings set in the Southern Kingdom and, not coincidentally, it is a priest of the temple that saves the Davidic line. The prophets may be king-makers, but it is the king Jehu and not the prophet Elisha who rids Israel of Baal (§6.4.1). And kings, not prophets, for better or worse, lead the people to fidelity or cause all Israel to sin. Elijah's popular reform fails; only Joash's succeeds.

The prophets, through their interaction with the kings, demonstrate the proper limits of royal power. Throughout the entire book of Kings, Yahweh, and not the king, is responsible for the military security of Israel. Salvation in Kings is always from Yahweh (§§4.4, 6.2.2, 6.4.1). Outer Kings demonstrated this through the angel who rescued Hezekiah (§4.3.2). Inner Kings shows the same principle in a variety of ways (§6.4.1). Sometimes it is through explicit control of military forces. In the account of the captured soldiers, Elisha begins the narrative surrounded by Syrian forces and about to be arrested. Just a few verses later Elisha is in control of the Syrian armies, the Israelite armies, and the fiery chariots of Yahweh also. Sometimes it is through a miraculous defeat of power as when Elijah calls fire from heaven down on Ahaziah's soldiers. Sometimes the means are much more subtle. It is the lepers outside the gates who end the siege of Samaria when they realise the enemy has broken ranks, and it is an optical illusion that causes the Moabite forces to flee. In each case, whether through providence or direct intervention, the prophets show that Yahweh is willing and able to fight for Israel (§6.4.1). Faithful kings realise this, and do not rely on their own military capabilities (§§6.2.2, 6.3.1).

If, as we saw above, the account of Jehoiachin's release, which concludes Outer Kings, is the narrative equivalent of Jeremiah's letter to the exiles, then the ending of Inner Kings is the narrative equivalent of Ezekiel's vision of dry bones (Ezek. 37.1-14). 2 Kings 13 is the final chapter before the narrative transitions back to Outer Kings (§2.3). By the end of the chapter the characters of Inner Kings have died, the various prophetic words have all been fulfilled, Baal has been removed, and Israel has won back territory that was lost. The Northern Kingdom has been returned approximately to the state it was in when Inner Kings opened (§2.3.3). The reader's attention is drawn particularly to vv. 14-25 which, along with Elijah's ascension (2 Kgs 2), are the only events in the entire book reported outside of narrative time (§2.3.4). The events in these verses are structured in the following sequence:

A   14-19   Prediction of Elisha's death and Israel's deliverance from Hazael
B   20-21   Elisha's death
C   22-25   Israel's deliverance from Hazael

The first story (A) is the prediction of deliverance from Hazael, the fulfilment of which (C) will bring important closure to Elijah's commissioning on Mount Horeb (§2.3.1). It also opens with a note that Elisha had fallen ill (v. 14) which links the two otherwise unrelated events. Stories B and C are also linked by an unusual use of the word 'throw' or 'cast away' (*hifil* of שלך). In Story B the bones of Elisha revive the man who is 'thrown' onto them (וישליכו, v. 21). For the third and final time in Kings, Yahweh uses a prophet to raise the dead (see 1 Kgs 17.17-24; 2 Kgs 4.8-37). In Story C, the same word is used to describe the exiles. The narrative remarks that Yahweh had not 'cast them away from his presence until this time' (ולא השליכם מעל פניו עד עתה, v. 23), but the exilic reader knows this no longer to be the case (see, e.g., 1 Kgs 9.7; 2 Kgs 17.20; 24.20, all of which use the *hifil* of שלך). What will Yahweh now do with the exiles, who *have* been 'cast away' from his presence?

The juxtaposition holds a clue (§2.2). Yahweh would not 'cast away' Israel in the days of Elisha's death, because of the promise he made to Abraham, Isaac, and Jacob (v. 23). This is the only direct reference to the patriarchal covenant in Kings, but by the same logic that we applied to the Davidic promise, the readers of Kings would have understood this promise to stand as well (§2.3.1). The reference to the Abrahamic promise creates hope that Yahweh has not abandoned Israel. The juxtaposition with the resurrection of the 'cast away' man reinforces this hope. Yahweh can restore Israel from exile because Yahweh can raise the dead.

Appendix:
Promise and Fulfilment Narrative Arcs in Kings

This table compiles prophecies in Kings with their fulfilments. Similar tables that have been compiled for a different purpose can be found in von Rad[1] and in Wray Beal.[2] As with elsewhere in this study, this table uses abbreviated notation. 1 Kings 16.34, for example, is denoted I.16.34. The final column indicates whether the prophecy is explicitly mentioned when it is fulfilled, for example, '…in accordance with the word of the Yahweh spoken by Joshua son of Nun' (1 Kgs 16.34). The prophecies are arranged by when they were given, not when they are fulfilled.

Prophecy		Fulfilment		Explicit?
Josh. 6.26	Jericho will be rebuilt at the cost of the firstborn.	I.16.34	Hiel loses two of his children rebuilding Jericho.	yes
1 Sam. 2.27-36	Eli's priestly line will come to an end, even though parallel language to Davidic promise – unconditional and forever.	I.2.27	Solomon exiles Abiathar, who was priest in support of Adonijah.	yes
2 Sam. 7.13	Establish throne of David forever, build house.	I.8.20	House built, throne established.	yes
2 Sam. 7.14-15	Father/son, discipline for sin but not forsake.	I.11.39	The offspring of David is afflicted but not forever.	no

1. Von Rad, 'The Deuteronomic Theology of History in 1 and 2 Kings', 159.
2. Wray Beal, *The Deuteronomist's Prophet*, 184–5.

Appendix

Prophecy		Fulfilment		Explicit?
2 Sam. 7.16	House and Kingdom sure forever.			no
I.9.6-8	Temple will be destroyed, Israel exiled, if sinful	II.25.9-11	Sinful, so exile, temple destroyed.	no
I.11.29-36	Ten tribes taken from Solomon, but kingdom to survive.	I.12.15	Rehoboam ends the united kingdom, ten tribes revolt.	yes
I.13.2	Jeroboam's altar will be destroyed by a scion of David.	II.23.15-20	Josiah destroys Jeroboam's altar.	yes
I.13.3	Jeroboam's altar will be torn down and ashes poured on it as a sign.	I.13.5	It was.	yes
I.13.21	Unnamed prophet's body will not go back to the south.	I.13.24-26	A lion kills him.	yes
I.14.6-11, 14	Jeroboam's dynasty will end.	I.15.29	Baasha usurps the throne from Jeroboam's son.	yes
I.14.12-13	Jeroboam's sick child will die.	I.14.17-18	The child dies.	yes
I.14.15-16	The Northern Kingdom will perish.	II.17.21-23	It happens because of Jeroboam's sin.	yes
I.16.1-4	Baasha's dynasty will end.	I.16.12	Zimri usurps the throne from Baasha.	yes
I.17.1	No rain except by Elijah's word.	I.18.45	It rains after Elijah's victory (cf. 18.1)	no
I.17.14	Jar and jug will not run out.	I.17.16	It happened.	yes

Prophecy		Fulfilment		Explicit?
I.19.17	Hazael and Jehu will destroy the house of Ahab.	Hazael: II.8.28-29; 9.14-15; 10.32; 12.17 [12.18, Heb.]; 13.3, 22. Jehu: II.9.24-26; II.10.1-11	It happens.	no
I.21.21-23	Ahab's dynasty will end.	I.21.27-29 II.10.17	Punishment delayed because of repentance. Jehu destroys Ahab's dynasty.	yes
I.21.24	Dogs will eat anyone belonging to Ahab who dies in the city.	I.22.38	Dogs licked up Ahab's blood.	yes
I.21.23	Dogs will eat Jezebel within the walls of Jezreel.	II.9.26, 36-37	It happens.	yes
I.22.17	Israel will be like sheep without shepherd, everyone should go home.	I.22.35	Ahab is mortally wounded and everyone goes home.	no
II.1.6	Ahaziah will not recover from his illness.	II.1.17	Ahaziah dies from his illness.	yes
II.2.21	God will make water clean.	II.2.22	Water is clean.	yes
II.4.43	God will provide food with left overs.	II.4.44	Food is provided.	yes
II.5.10	Naaman will be cleansed if he washes in the Jordan.	II.5.14	Naaman is cleansed in the Jordan.	yes
II.7.1-2	The siege will end against all odds, economy restored within one day.	II.7.16	Lepers go and pillage stores of other camp, and economy is restored.	yes

Appendix

Prophecy		Fulfilment		Explicit?
II.8.11	Ben Hadad will die.	II.8.15	Ben Hadad dies.	no
II.9.7	Jehu will strike down the house of Ahab.	II.9.24-26; II.10.1-11	Jehu does.	yes
II.10.30	Jehu's sons will reign to fourth generation.	II.15.10-12	Zechariah dies to conspiracy in fifth generation.	yes
		II.14.25	An unknown prophecy from Jonah son of Amittai is fulfilled.	yes
II.19.6-7	Sennacherib will hear a rumour, and die in his own land.	II.19.9, 37	Sennacherib hears a rumour and dies in Nineveh.	no
II.19.32-33	Assyria will not defeat Jerusalem.	II.19.35-36	The Assyrian army is destroyed and they leave.	no
II.20.5, 9-10	Hezekiah will be healed, and the shadow go back ten steps.	II.20.11, 12	Hezekiah is healed, and the shadow went back ten steps.	no
II.20.16-18	Babylon will plunder Hezekiah's house and sons.	II.25.8-21	The temple is plundered by Babylon, and the Davidic line taken to Babylon.	no
II.21.10-15	Jerusalem will be destroyed because of Manasseh.	II.24.2-3	Jerusalem is destroyed according to prophets, because of Manasseh.	yes
II.21.15-17	Jerusalem will be destroyed.	II.24.2-3	Jerusalem is destroyed according to prophets, because of Manasseh.	yes
II.21.18-20	Josiah will be gathered to his fathers and not see disaster of Jerusalem.	II.23.30	Josiah is gathered to his fathers after being killed in battle.	no

BIBLIOGRAPHY

Ackroyd, Peter R. *Exile and Restoration: A Study of Hebrew Thought of the Sixth Century BC*. Louisville, KY: Westminster John Knox, 1968.
Ahituv, Shmuel. *Echoes from the Past: Hebrew and Cognate Inscriptions from the Biblical Period*. Jerusalem: Carta, 2008.
Albright, William F. *Yahweh and the Gods of Canaan*. Bristol: Athlone, 1968.
Alt, Albrecht. 'The Formation of the Israelite State in Palestine'. Pages 224–309 in *Essays on Old Testament History and Religion*. Translated by R. A. Wilson. New York: Doubleday, 1968.
Alter, Robert. *The Art of Biblical Narrative*. New York: Basic, 1981.
Alter, Robert. 'Imagining History in the Bible'. Pages 53–72 in *History and...: Histories within the Human Sciences*. Edited by Ralph Cohen and Michael S. Roth. Charlottesville, VA: University of Virginia Press, 1995.
Amit, Yairah. *History and Ideology: Introduction to Historiography in the Hebrew Bible*. Sheffield: Sheffield Academic, 1999.
Amit, Yairah. *Hidden Polemics in Biblical Narrative*. Biblical Interpretation Series. Leiden: Brill, 2000.
Amit, Yairah. *Reading Biblical Narratives: Literary Criticism and the Hebrew Bible*. Minneapolis, MN: Fortress, 2001.
Anderson, A. A. *2 Samuel*. WBC 11. Waco, TX: Word, 1989.
Anderson, Benedict. *Imagined Communities: Reflections on the Origin and Spread of Nationalism*. 2nd ed. London: Verso, 1991.
Anderson, John A. *Nations Before Nationalism*. Chapel Hill, VA: University of North Carolina Press, 1982.
Anderson, John A. 'Nationalist Ideology and Territory'. Pages 18–39 in *Nationalism, Self-Determination and Political Geography*. Edited by R. J. Johnston, D. Knight and E. Kofman. London: Croom Helm, 1988.
Angel, Hayyim. 'Hopping Between Two Opinions: Understanding the Biblical Portrait of Ahab'. *JBQ* 35 (2007): 3–10.
Ansburry, Christopher B., and Jerry Hwang. 'No Covenant Before the Exile? The Deuteronomic Torah and Israel's Covenant Theology'. Pages 74–94 in *Evangelical Faith and the Challenge of Historical Criticism*. Edited by Christopher M. Hays and Christopher B. Ansburry. London: SPCK, 2013.
Arnold, Bill T. 'The Weidner Chronicle and the Idea of History in Israel and Mesopotamia'. Pages 129–48 in *Faith, Tradition, and History: Old Testament Historiography in its Near Eastern Context*. Edited by Alan R. Millard, James K. Hoffmeier and David W. Baker. Winona Lake, IN: Eisenbrauns, 1994.
Arnold, Bill T., and Richard S. Hess, eds. *Ancient Israel's History: An Introduction to Issues and Sources*. Grand Rapids, MI: Baker Academic, 2014.

Arnold, Bill T., and H. G. M. Williamson, eds. *Dictionary of the Old Testament: Historical Books*. Downers Grove, IL: IVP, 2005.

Assmann, Jan. 'State and Religion in the New Kingdom'. Pages 55–88 in *Religion and Philosophy in Ancient Egypt*. Edited by William Kelly Simpson. Yale Egyptological Studies. New Haven, CT: Yale University Press, 1989.

Aster, Shawn Z. *Reflections of Empire in Isaiah 1–39: Responses to Assyrian Ideology*. ANE Monographs. Atlanta, GA: SBL, 2017.

Athas, George. 'A Man after God's Own Heart: David and the Rhetoric of Election to Kingship'. *JESOT* 2 (2012): 191–8.

Auld, A. Graeme. *Kings Without Privilege: David and Moses in the Story of the Bible's Kings*. Edinburgh: T&T Clark, 1994.

Auld, A. Graeme. *I & II Samuel: A Commentary*. OTL. Louisville, KY: Westminster John Knox, 2011.

Auld, A. Graeme. *Life in Kings: Reshaping the Royal Story in the Hebrew Bible*. Atlanta, GA: SBL, 2017.

Avioz, Michael. *Nathan's Oracle (2 Samuel 7) and its Interpreters*. Bible in History. Bern: Peter Lang, 2005.

Avioz, Michael. 'The Book of Kings in Recent Research (Part 2)'. *CBR* 5 (2006): 11–57.

Avioz, Michael. 'Josiah's Death in the Book of Kings: A New Solution to an Old Theological Conundrum'. *ETL* 83 (2007): 359–66.

Baines, John. 'Ancient Egyptian Kingship: Official Forms, Rhetoric, Context'. Pages 16–53 in *King and Messiah in Israel and the Ancient Near East: Proceedings of the Oxford Old Testament Seminar*. Edited by John Day. London: T&T Clark, 2013.

Bakhtin, Mikhail. *Problems of Dostoevsky's Poetics*. Translated by Caryl Emerson. Minneapolis, MN: University of Minnesota Press, 1984.

Balentine, Samuel E. *Prayer in the Hebrew Bible: The Drama of Divine–Human Dialogue*. Minneapolis, MN: Fortress, 1993.

Bar-Efrat, Shimeon. *Narrative Art in the Bible*. London: T&T Clark, 2004.

Barker, Paul A. *The Triumph of Grace in Deuteronomy: Faithless Israel, Faithful Yahweh in Deuteronomy*. Eugene, OR: Wipf & Stock, 2004.

Barstad, H. M. *A Way in the Wilderness: The 'Second Exodus' in the Message of Second Isaiah*. Manchester: University of Manchester Press, 1989.

Bartholomew, Craig G. *Where Mortals Dwell*. Grand Rapids, MI: Baker Academic, 2011.

Beale, Gregory K. *The Temple and the Church's Mission: A Biblical Theology of the Dwelling Place of God*. Downers Grove, IL: IVP, 2004.

Ben Zvi, Ehud. 'Once the Lamp Has Been Kindled: A Reconsideration of the Meaning of the MT nîr in 1 Kgs 11:36; 15:4; 2 Kgs 8:19 and 2 Chr 21:7'. *ABR* 39 (1991): 19–30.

Ben Zvi, Ehud. 'The Secession of the Northern Kingdom in Chronicles: Accepted "Facts" and new Meanings'. Pages 61–88 in *The Chronicler as Theologian: Essays in Honour of Ralph W. Klein*. Edited by M. Patrick Graham, Steven L. McKenzie and Gary N. Knoppers. JSOTSup 371. London: T&T Clark, 2003.

Ben Zvi, Ehud. 'Prophetic Memories in the Deuteronomistic Historical and the Prophetic Collections of Books'. Pages 75–102 in *Israelite Prophecy and the Deuteronomistic History: Portrait, Reality, and the Formation of a History*. Edited by Mignon R. Jacobs and Raymond F. Person Jr. Atlanta, GA: SBL, 2013.

Bergen, Robert D. 'Text as a Guide to Authorial Intention: An Introduction to Discourse Criticism'. *JETS* 30 (1987-9): 327–36.

Bergen, Wesley J. *Elijah and the End of Prophetism*. JSOTSup 286. Sheffield: Sheffield Academic, 1999.

Berlin, Adele. *Poetics and Interpretation of Biblical Narrative*. Sheffield: Almond Press, 1983.
Berlin, Adele, Marc Zvi Brettler and Michael A. Fishbane, eds. *The Jewish Study Bible*. Oxford: Oxford University Press, 2004.
Berlyn, Patricia J. 'Elijah's Battle for the Soul of Israel'. *JBQ* 40 (2012): 52–62.
Berman, Joshua. *Created Equal: How the Bible Broke with Ancient Political Thought*. Oxford: Oxford University Press, 2008.
Berner, Christoph. 'Literary Connections Between Exodus 1–15 and 1 Kings 1–12?' Pages 211–40 in *Pentateuch, Hexateuch, or Enneatuech? Identifying Literary Works in Genesis through Kings.* Edited by Thomas B. Dozeman, Thomas Römer and Konrad Schmid. AIL. Atlanta, GA: SBL, 2011.
Berrigan, Daniel. *The Kings and their Gods: The Pathology of Power*. Grand Rapids, MI: Eerdmans, 2008.
Bess, Herbert S. 'Systems of Land Tenure in Ancient Israel'. Ph.D. diss., University of Michigan, 1963.
Blenkinsopp, J. 'Another Contribution to the Succession Narrative Debate (2 Samuel 11–20; 1 Kings 1–2)'. *JSOT* 38 (2013): 35–58.
Blenkinsopp, Joseph. *David Remembered: Kingship and National Identity in Ancient Israel*. Grand Rapids, MI: Eerdmans, 2013.
Block, Daniel I. *The Gods of the Nations: Studies in Ancient Near Eastern National Theology*. Grand Rapids, MI: Baker Academic, 2000.
Block, Daniel I. 'My Servant David: Ancient Israel's Vision of the Messiah'. Pages 17–56 in *Israel's Messiah in the Bible and the Dead Sea Scrolls.* Edited by Richard S. Hess and M. Daniel Carroll R. Grand Rapids, MI: Baker Academic, 2003.
Block, Daniel I. 'How Many Is God? An Investigation into the Meaning of Deuteronomy 6:4–5'. *JETS* 47 (2004): 193–212.
Block, Daniel I. 'The Burden of Leadership: The Mosaic Paradigm of Kingship (Deut 17:14-20)'. *BSac* 162 (2005): 259–78.
Block, Daniel I. 'The Grace of Torah: The Mosaic Prescription for Life (Deut 4:1-8; 6:20–25)'. *BSac* 162 (2005): 3–22.
Block, Daniel I. 'The Joy of Worship: The Mosaic Invitation to the Presence of God (Deut 12:1-14)'. *BSac* 162 (2005): 131–49.
Block, Daniel I. '"You Shall not Covet Your Neighbour's Wife": A Study in Deuteronomic Domestic Ideology'. *JETS* 53 (2010): 449–74.
Bodner, Keith. *1 Samuel: A Narrative Commentary*. Hebrew Bible Monographs 19. Sheffield: Sheffield Phoenix, 2009.
Bodner, Keith. *Jeroboam's Royal Drama*. Oxford: Oxford University Press, 2012.
Bodner, Keith. *Elisha's Profile in the Book of Kings: The Double Agent*. Oxford: Oxford University Press, 2013.
Bodner, Keith. *The Theology of the Book of Kings*. Cambridge: Cambridge University Press, 2019.
Bostock, David. *A Portrayal of Trust: The Theme of Faith in the Hezekiah Narratives*. Biblical Monographs. Colorado Springs, CO: Paternoster, 2006.
Bosworth, David A. 'Revisiting Karl Barth's Exegesis of 1 Kings 13'. *BibInt* 10 (2002): 360–83.
Botha, Phil J. '"No King Like Him…": Royal Etiquette According to the Deuteronomistic Historian'. Pages 36–49 in *Past, Present, Future: The Deuteronomistic History and the Prophets.* Edited by Harry F. van Rooy. Leiden: Brill, 2000.

Brettler, Marc Z. 'Ideology, History and Theology in 2 Kings XVII 7-23'. *VT* 39 (1989): 268–82.

Brettler, Marc Z. 'The Structure of 1 Kings 1–11'. *JSOT* 49 (1991): 87–97.

Brettler, Marc Z. *The Creation of History in Ancient Israel*. London: Routledge, 1995.

Brettler, Marc Z. *God Is King: Understanding an Israelite Metaphor*. New York: T&T Clark, 2009.

Brodie, Thomas L. *The Crucial Bridge: The Elijah–Elisha Narrative as an Interpretive Synthesis of Genesis-Kings and a Literary Model for the Gospels*. Collegeville, MA: Liturgical, 2000.

Bronner, Leah. *The Stories of Elijah and Elisha as Polemics against Baal Worship*. Pretoria Oriental. Leiden: Brill, 1968.

Brown, Arthur Mason. 'The Concept of Inheritance in the Old Testament'. Ph.D. diss., Columbia University, 1965.

Brueggemann, Walter A. *The Land: Place as Gift, Promise, and Challenge in Biblical Faith*. OBT. London: SPCK, 1978.

Brueggemann, Walter A. *1 & 2 Kings*. Smyth & Helwys Bible Commentary. Macon, GA: Smyth & Helwys, 2000.

Brueggemann, Walter A. *Solomon: Israel's Ironic Icon of Human Achievement*. Columbia, MO: University of South Carolina, 2005.

Brueggemann, Walter A., and Davis Hankins. 'The Affirmation of Prophetic Power and Deconstruction of Royal Authority in the Elisha Narratives'. *CBQ* 76 (2014): 58–76.

Brunner, H. 'Gerechtigkeit als Fundament des Thrones'. *VT* 8 (1958): 426–8.

Burney, Charles F. *Notes on the Hebrew Text of the Books of Kings*. Oxford: Clarendon, 1903.

Campbell, Antony F. *Of Prophets and Kings: A Late Ninth-Century Document (1 Samuel 1–2 Kings 10)*. CBQMS. Washington: Catholic Bible Association, 1986.

Campbell, Antony F., and Mark A. O'Brien. *Unfolding the Deuteronomistic History: Origins, Upgrades, Present Text*. Minneapolis, MN: Fortress, 2000.

Canciani, F., and G. Pettinato. 'Salomos Thron: Philologische und archäologische Erwägungen'. *ZPDV* 81 (1965): 88–108.

Carr, David M. *The Formation of the Hebrew Bible: A New Reconstruction*. New York: Oxford University Press, 2011.

Carroll, Robert P. 'The Myth of the Empty Land'. *Semeia* 59 (1992): 79–93.

Cazelles, Henri. 'Sacral Kingship'. *AYBD*, 5:863–6.

Childs, Brevard S. *Isaiah and the Assyrian Crisis*. SBT. London: SCM, 1967.

Childs, Brevard S. *Old Testament Theology in a Canonical Context*. Philadelphia, PA: Fortress, 1989.

Clark, W. Malcolm. 'The Origin and Development of the Land Promise Theme in the Old Testament'. Ph.D. diss., Yale, 1964.

Clements, Ronald Ernest. *Isaiah and the Deliverance of Jerusalem: A Study in the Interpretation of Prophecy in the Old Testament*. Sheffield: JSOT, 1984.

Clifford, Richard J. 'The Temple in the Ugaritic Myth of Baal'. Pages 137–47 in *Symposia Celebrating the Seventy-Fifth Anniversary of the Founding of the American Schools of Oriental Research (1900–1975)*. Edited by Frank M. Cross. Zion Research Foundation Occasional Publications. Cambridge: American Schools of Oriental Research, 1979.

Coakley, John. 'Mobilizing the Past: Nationalist Images of History'. *Nationalism and Ethnic Politics* 10 (2004): 531–60.

Cogan, Mordechai. 'Israel in Exile: The View of a Josianic Historian'. *JBL* 97 (1978): 40–4.

Cogan, Mordechai. '"Ripping Open Pregnant Women" in Light of an Assyrian Analogue'. *JAOS* 103 (1983): 755–7.
Cogan, Mordechai. 'For We, Like You, Worship your God: Three Biblical Portrayals of Samaritan Origins'. *VT* 38 (1988): 286–92.
Cogan, Mordechai. *1 Kings: A New Translation with Introduction and Commentary*. AB 10. New Haven, CT: Yale University Press, 2008.
Cogan, Mordechai, and Hayim Tadmor. *2 Kings: A New Translation with Introduction and Commentary*. AB 11. New Haven, CT: Yale University Press, 2008.
Cogan, Morton (Mordechai). *Imperialism and Religion: Assyria, Judah, and Israel in the Eighth and Seventh Centuries B.C.* SBL Monographs. Missoula, MT: Scholars Press, 1974.
Cohn, Robert L. 'The Literary Logic of 1 Kings 17–19'. *JBL* 101 (1982): 333–50.
Cohn, Robert L. *2 Kings*. Berit Olam: Studies in Hebrew Narrative & Poetry. Collegeville, MN: Liturgical, 2000.
Cohn, Robert L. 'Characterisation in Kings'. Pages 89–105 in *The Books of Kings: Sources, Composition, Historiography and Reception*. Edited by Baruch Halpern and André Lemaire. VTSup 129. Leiden: Brill, 2010.
Cohn, Robert L. 'The Literary Structure of Kings'. Pages 107–22 in *The Books of Kings: Sources, Composition, Historiography and Reception*. Edited by Baruch Halpern and André Lemaire. VTSup 129. Leiden: Brill, 2010.
Cortese, E. 'Lo schema deuteronomistico per i re di Giuda e d'Israel'. *Bib* 56 (1975): 37–52.
Cross, Frank Moore. *Canaanite Myth and Hebrew Epic: Essays in the History of the Religion of Israel*. OTL. Cambridge, MA: Harvard University Press, 1973.
Crüsemann, Frank. *Der Widerstand gegen das Königtum: die antiköniglichen Texte des Alten Testamentes und der Kampf um den frühen israelitischen Staat*. WMANT. Neukirchen-Vluyn: Neukirchener Verlag, 1978.
Cudworth, Troy D. 'Yahweh's Promise to David in the Books of Kings'. *VT* 66 (2016): 194–216.
Currid, John D. *Ancient Egypt and the Old Testament*. Grand Rapids, MI: Baker Academic, 1997.
Davies, Eryl W. 'Land: Its Rights and Privileges'. Pages 349–69 in *The World of Ancient Israel: Sociological, Anthropological and Political Perspectives*. Edited by R. E. Clements. Cambridge: Cambridge University Press, 1989.
Davies, John A. '"Discerning Between Good and Evil": Solomon as a New Adam in 1 Kings'. *WTJ* 73 (2011): 39–57.
Davies, Philip R. *In Search of Ancient Israel: A Study in Biblical Origins*. JSOTSup 148. Sheffield: Sheffield Academic, 1992.
Day, John, ed. *King and Messiah in Israel and the Ancient Near East: Proceedings of the Oxford Old Testament Seminar*. London: T&T Clark, 2013.
Day, John. 'The Canaanite Inheritance of the Israelite Monarchy'. Pages 72–90 in *King and Messiah in Israel and the Ancient Near East: Proceedings of the Oxford Old Testament Seminar*. Edited by John Day. London: T&T Clark, 2013.
de Vries, Simon J. *Prophet Against Prophet*. Grand Rapids, MI: Eerdmans, 1978.
de Vries, Simon J. *1 Kings*. WBC 12. Waco, TX: Word, 2003.
Delaney, David. *Territory: A Short Introduction*. London: Blackwell, 2005.
Dever, William G. 'Archeology and the Question of Sources in Kings'. Pages 517–40 in *The Books of Kings: Sources, Composition, Historiography and Reception*. Edited by Baruch Halpern and André Lemaire. VTSup 129. Leiden: Brill, 2010.

Dietrich, Walter. *Prophetie und Geschichte: Ein Redaktionsgeschichtliche Untersuchung zum deuteronomistischen Geschichtswerk*. FRLANT. Göttingen: Vandenhoeck & Ruprecht, 1972.

Dietrich, Walter. 'Martin Noth and the Future of the Deuteronomistic History'. Pages 153–75 in *The History of Israel's Traditions: The Heritage of Martin Noth*. Edited by Steven L. McKenzie and M. Patrick Graham. JSOTSup 182. Sheffield: Sheffield Academic, 1994.

Dittmann, Herbert. 'Der heilige Rest im Alten Testament'. *TSK* 87 (1914): 603–18.

Downing, F. G. 'Markan Intercalation in Cultural Context'. Pages 105–18 in *Narrativity in Biblical and Related Texts: La narrativité dans la bible et les textes apparentés*. Edited by G. J. Brooke and J. D. Kaestli. Belgium: Leuven University, 2000.

Droge, A. J. 'The Lying Pens of the Scribes: Of Holy Books and Pious Frauds'. *Method and Theory in the Study of Religion* 15 (2003): 117–47.

Dubovský, Peter. 'Tiglath-Pileser III's Campaigns in 734–732 BC: Historical Background of Isa 7; 2 Kgs 15–16 and 2 Chr 27–28'. *Bib* 87 (2006): 153–70.

Dubovský, Peter. 'Assyrian Downfall Through Isaiah's Eyes (2 Kings 15–23): The Historiography of Representation'. *Bib* 89 (2008): 1–16.

Dubovský, Peter. 'Why did the Northern Kingdom Fall According to 2 Kings 15?' *Bib* 95 (2014): 321–46.

Dumbrell, William J. 'The Prospect of Unconditionality in the Siniatic Covenant'. Pages 141–55 in *Israel's Apostasy and Restoration: Essays in Honor of Roland K. Harrison*. Edited by Avraham Gileadi. Grand Rapids, MI: Baker, 1988.

Dus, Jan. 'Gibbon – eine Kultstätte des SMS und die Stadt des benjaminitischen Schicksals'. *VT* 10 (1960): 353–74.

Dutcher-Walls, Patricia. *Jezebel: Portraits of a Queen*. Collegeville, MA: Liturgical Press, 2004.

Effa, Allan. 'Prophet, Kings, Servants, and Lepers: A Missiological Reading of an Ancient Drama'. *Missiology* 35 (2007): 305–13.

Elazar, Daniel. *Covenant and Polity in Biblical Israel*. New Brunswick, NJ: Transaction, 1995.

Ellis, Maria deJong. 'Observations on Mesopotamian Oracles and Prophetic Texts: Literary and Historiographic Considerations'. *JCS* 41 (1989): 127–86.

Engnell, Ivan. *Studies in Divine Kingship in the Ancient Near East*. Oxford: Blackwell, 1967.

Eriksen, Thomas Hylland. 'The Problem of African Nationhood'. *Nations and Nationalism* 22 (2016): 222–31.

Esler, Philip F., and Anselm C. Hagedorn. 'Social-Scientific Analysis of the Old Testament: A Brief History and Overview'. Pages 15–34 in *Ancient Israel: The Old Testament in its Social Context*. Edited by Philip F. Esler. Minneapolis, MN: Fortress, 2006.

Evans, Carl D. 'Naram–Sin and Jeroboam: The Archetypal *Unheilsherrscher* in Mesopotamia and Biblical Historiography'. Pages 97–127 in *Scripture in Context II: More Essays on the Comparative Method*. Edited by William W. Hallo, James C. Moyer and Leo G. Perdue. Winona Lake, IN: Eisenbrauns, 1983.

Evans, Paul S. 'The Hezekiah–Sennacherib Narrative as Polyphonic Text'. *JSOT* 33 (2009): 335–58.

Fokkelman, J. P. *Reading Biblical Narrative: An Introductory Guide*. Louisville, KY: Westminster John Knox, 1999.

Frankel, David. *The Land of Canaan and the Destiny of Israel: Theologies of Territory in the Hebrew Bible*. Winona Lake, IN: Eisenbrauns, 2011.

Frankfort, Henri. *Kingship and the Gods: A Study of Ancient Near Eastern Kingship as the Integration of Society and Nature*. Chicago, IL: University of Chicago Press, 1948.

Freedman, David N. 'Divine Commitment and Human Obligation: The Covenant Theme'. *Interpretation* 18 (1964).

Frei, H. W. *The Eclipse of Biblical Narrative: A Study in Eighteenth and Nineteenth Century Hermeneutics*. New Haven, CT: Yale University Press, 1974.

Fretheim, Terence E. *The Suffering of God: An Old Testament Perspective*. Philadelphia, PA: Fortress, 1984.

Fretheim, Terence E. *First and Second Kings*. Louisville, KY: Westminster John Knox, 1999.

Friedman, Richard E. *The Exile and Biblical Narrative: The Formation of the Deuteronomistic and Priestly Works*. Chico, CA: Scholars Press, 1981.

Frisch, Amos. 'Structure and its Significance: The Narrative of Solomon's Reign (1 Kings 1–12:24)'. *JSOT* 51 (1991): 3–14.

Fritz, Volkmar. *1 & 2 Kings*. Translated by Anselm Hagedorn. ICC. Minneapolis, MN: Fortress, 2003.

Galil, Gershon. 'The Message of the Book of Kings in Relation to Deuteronomy and Jeremiah'. *BSac* 158 (2001): 406–14.

Garsiel, Moshe. 'The Book of Samuel: Its Composition, Structure and Significance as a Historiographical Source'. *JHebS* 10 (2010): 2–42.

Garsiel, Moshe. *From Earth to Heaven: A Literary Study of Elijah Stories in the Book of Kings*. Bethesda, MD: CDL, 2014.

Gerbrandt, Gerald E. *Kingship According to the Deuteronomistic History*. SBLDS 87. Atlanta, GA: Scholars Press, 1986.

Gibson, John C. L. *Davidson's Introductory Hebrew Grammar: Syntax*. Edinburgh: T&T Clark, 1994.

Gileadi, Avraham. 'The Davidic Covenant: A Theological Basis for Corporate Protection'. Pages 157–63 in *Israel's Apostasy and Restoration: Essays in Honor of Roland K. Harrison*. Edited by Avraham Gileadi. Grand Rapids, MI: Baker, 1988.

Gilmour, Rachelle. *Representing the Past: A Literary Analysis of Narrative Historiography in the Book of Samuel*. VTSup 143. Leiden: Brill, 2011.

Gilmour, Rachelle. 'A Note on the Horses and Chariots of Fire at Dothan'. *ZAW* 125 (2013): 308–13.

Gilmour, Rachelle. *Juxtaposition and the Elisha Cycle*. London: T&T Clark, 2014.

Gnuse, Robert Karl. *No Tolerance for Tyrants: The Biblical Assault on Kings and Kingship*. Collegeville, MN: Liturgical Press, 2011.

Goldingay, John. *Israel's Gospel*. Downers Grove, IL: IVP, 2003.

Goldstein, Ronnie. 'A Suggestion Regarding the Meaning of 2 Kings 17:9 and the Composition of 2 Kings 17:7-23'. *VT* 63 (2013): 393–407.

Goldsworthy, Graeme. *The Goldsworthy Trilogy*. Exeter: Paternoster, 2000.

Goldsworthy, Graeme. *According to Plan: The Unfolding Revelation of God in the Bible*. Grand Rapids, MI: IVP, 2002.

Gordon, Robert P. *1&2 Samuel*. London: Paternoster, 1986.

Gordon, Robert P. 'A House Divided: Wisdom in Old Testament Narrative Traditions'. Pages 94–105 in *Wisdom in Ancient Israel*. Edited by John Day, Robert P. Gordon and H. G. M. Williamson. Cambridge: Cambridge University Press, 1995.

Goswell, Greg. 'King and Cultus: The Image of David in the Book of Kings'. *JESOT* 5 (2017): 167–86.

Gotom, Musa. '1 & 2 Kings'. Pages 409–66 in *Africa Bible Commentary*. Edited by Tokunboh Adeyemo. Nairobi, Kenya: WordAlive, 2006.
Gottwald, Norman K. *The Politics of Ancient Israel*. Louisville, KY: Westminster John Knox, 2001.
Grant, Jamie A. *The King as Exemplar: The Function of Deuteronomy's Kingship Law in the Shaping of the Book of Psalms*. Atlanta, GA: SBL, 2004.
Gray, John. *I and II Kings*. OTL. Philadelphia, PA: Westminster John Knox, 1970.
Gray, John. *Near Eastern Mythology*. Rev. ed. New York: Peter Bedrick, 1985.
Green, Alberto R. 'Israelite Influence at Shishak's Court'. *BASOR* 233 (1979): 59–62.
Green, Barbara. *Mikhail Bakhtin and Biblical Scholarship: An Introduction*. Atlanta, GA: SBL, 2000.
Greenberg, Moshe. 'Biblical Attitudes Toward Power: Ideal and Reality in Law and Prophets'. Pages 101–12 in *Religion and Law: Biblical-Judaic and Islamic Perspectives*. Edited by Edwin B. Firmage, Bernard G. Weiss and John W. Welch. Winona Lake, IN: Eisenbrauns, 1990.
Greenberg, Moshe. *Studies in the Bible and Jewish Thought*. Philadelphia, PA: Jewish Publication Society, 1995.
Greenwood, Kyle. 'Late Tenth and Ninth-Century Issues: Ahab Underplayed? Jehoshaphat Over-played?' Pages 286–318 in *Ancient Israel's History: An Introduction to Issues and Sources*. Edited by Bill T. Arnold and Richard S. Hess. Grand Rapids, MI: Baker Academic, 2014.
Gressmann, H. *Der Ursprung der israelitisch-jüdischen Eschatologie*. Göttingen: Vandenhoeck & Ruprecht, 1905.
Grosby, Steven Elliott. *Biblical Ideas of Nationality: Ancient and Modern*. Winona Lake, IN: Eisenbrauns, 2002.
Gunkel, Hermann. *Elijah, Yahweh, and Baal*. Translated by K. C. Hanson. Eugene, OR: Cascade, 2014.
Gutman, Israel, 'Manesseh – Was he Judah's Worst King?' Pages 49–66 in *Homage to Shmuel: Studies in the World of the Bible*. Edited by Zipora Talshir, Shamir Yona and Daniel Sivan. Jerusalem: Ben-Gurion University Press, 2001.
Habel, Norman C. *The Land Is Mine: Six Biblical Land Ideologies*. OBT. Minneapolis, MN: Fortress, 1995.
Halbertal, Moshe, and Stephen Holmes. *The Beginning of Politics: Power in the Biblical Book of Samuel*. Princeton, NJ: Princeton University Press, 2017.
Halpern, Baruch. *The Constitution of the Monarchy in Israel*. HSM. Chico, CA: Scholars Press, 1981.
Halpern, Baruch. *The First Historians: The Hebrew Bible and History*. New York: Harper & Row, 1988.
Halpern, Baruch. 'Why Manasseh Is Blamed for the Babylonian Exile: The Evolution of Biblical Tradition'. *VT* 48 (1998): 473–514.
Halpern, Baruch, and André Lemaire, 'The Composition of Kings'. Pages 123–53 in *The Books of Kings: Sources, Composition, Historiography and Reception*. Edited by Baruch Halpern and André Lemaire. VTSup 129. Leiden: Brill, 2010.
Halpern, Baruch, and David S. Vanderhooft. 'The Editions of Kings in the 7th–6th Centuries BCE'. *HUCA* 62 (1991): 179–244.
Hamilton, Mark W. 'The Past as Destiny: Historical Visions in Sam'al and Judah under Assyrian Hegemony'. *HTR* 91 (1998): 215–50.

Hamilton, Mark W. 'Critiquing the Sovereign: Perspectives from Deuteronomy and Job'. *Römische Quartalschrist für christliche Altertumskunde und Kirchengeschichte* 47 (2005): 237–49
Hamilton, Mark W. *The Body Royal: The Social Poetics of Kingship in Ancient Israel.* Biblical Interpretation. Leiden: Brill. 2005.
Hamilton, Mark W. 'Isaiah 32 as Literature and Political Meditation'. *JBL* 131 (2012): 663–84.
Hamilton, Mark W. *A Kingdom for a Stage: Political and Theological Reflection in the Hebrew Bible.* FAT 116. Tübingen: Mohr Siebeck, 2018.
Hamilton Jr., James M. *God's Glory in Salvation Through Judgment: A Biblical Theology.* Wheaton, IL: Crossway, 2010.
Hardmeier, Christof. 'King Josiah in the Climax of the Deuteronomic History (2 Kings 22–23) and the Pre-Deuteronomic Document of a Cult Reform at the Place of Residence (23.4-15): Criticism of Sources, Reconstruction of Literary Pre-Stages and the Theology of History in 2 Kings 22–23'. Pages 123–63 in *Good Kings and Bad Kings.* LHBOTS 393. Edited by Lester L. Grabbe. New York: T&T Clark, 2007.
Hardy II, Humphrey H., and Benjamin D. Thomas. 'Another Look at Biblical Hebrew bəmə "High Place"'. *VT* 62 (2012): 175–88.
Hasel, Gerhard F. *The Remnant: The History and Theology of the Remnant Idea from Genesis to Isaiah.* Berrien Springs, MI: Andrews University, 1972.
Hasel, Gerhard F. 'Semantic Values of Derivatives of the Hebrew Root šāʾar'. *AUSS* 11 (1973): 152–69.
Hasel, Gerhard F. 'Review of *Die Vorstellung vom Rest im Alten Testament.* By Werner E. Muller. Edited by Horst Dietrich Preuss'. *AUSS* 13 (1975): 90–1.
Hastings, Adrian. *The Construction of Nationhood: Ethnicity, Religion and Nationalism.* Cambridge: Cambridge University Press, 1997.
Hauser, Alan J., and Russell Gregory. *From Carmel to Horeb: Elijah in Crisis.* Sheffield: Sheffield Academic, 1990.
Hayes, John H. 'Tradition of Zion's Inviolability'. *JBL* 82 (1963–12): 419–26.
Hays, J. Daniel. 'Has the Narrator Come to Praise Solomon or to Bury Him? Narrative Subtlety in 1 Kings 1–11'. *JSOT* 28 (2003): 149–74.
Hazony, Yoram. *The Philosophy of Hebrew Scripture.* Cambridge: Cambridge University Press, 2012.
Heaton, Eric W. 'The Root שאר and the Doctrine of the Remnant'. *JTS* 3 (1952): 28.
Heaton, Eric W. *Solomon's New Men: The Emergence of Ancient Israel as a Nation State.* London: Thames & Hudson, 1974.
Heim, K. M. 'Kings and Kingship'. *DOTH*, 610–23.
Henige, David. 'Found But Not Lost: A Skeptical Note on the Document Discovered in the Temple under Josiah'. *JHebS* 7 (2007): 2–17.
Hens-Piazza, Gina. *1–2 Kings.* AOTC. Nashville, TN: Abingdon, 2006.
Hess, Richard S. 'The Form and Structure of the Solomonic District List in 1 Kings 4:7-19'. Pages 279–92 in *Crossing Boundaries and Linking Horizons: Studies in Honour of Michael C. Astour on His 80th Birthday.* Edited by G. D. Young, Mark W. Chavalas and R. E. Averbeck. Bethesda, MD: CDL, 1997.
Hess, Richard S. 'Hezekiah and Sennacherib in 2 Kings 18–20'. Pages 23–41 in *Zion, City of our God.* Edited by Richard S. Hess and Gordon J. Wenham. Grand Rapids, MI: Eerdmans, 1999.

Hess, Richard S. 'Introduction: Foundations for a History of Israel'. Pages 1–22 in *Ancient Israel's History: An Introduction to Issues and Sources*. Edited by Bill T. Arnold and Richard S. Hess. Grand Rapids, MI: Baker Academic, 2014.
Hobbs, Thomas R. *2 Kings*. WBC 13. Waco, TX: Word, 1985.
Hooke, S. H., ed. *Myth, Ritual, and Kingship: Essays on the Theory and Practice of Kingship in the Ancient Near East and in Israel*. London: Clarendon, 1960.
Hoppe, Leslie J. 'The Death of Josiah and the Meaning of Deuteronomy'. *LASBF* 48 (1998): 31–47.
Howard-Brook, Wes. *Come Out My People! God's Call Out of Empire in the Bible and Beyond*. New York: Orbis, 2010.
Huizinga, Johan. 'A Definition of the Concept of History'. Pages 1–10 in *Philosophy and History: Essays Presented to Ernst Cassierrer*. Edited by Raymond Klibansky and Herbert James Paton. New York: Harper & Row, 1963.
Hunt, Alice Wells. 'Bringing Dialogue from Cacophony: Can Bakhtin Speak to Biblical Historiography?' *PRSt* 32 (2005): 325–37.
Hurowitz, Victor A. *I Have Built You an Exalted House: Temple Building in the Bible in Light of Mesopotamian and Northwest Semitic Writings*. JSOTSup 115. Sheffield: Sheffield Academic, 1992.
Hutton, Jeremy M. *The Transjordanian Palimpsest: The Overwritten Texts of Personal Exile and Transformation in the Deuteronomistic History*. BZAW 396. Berlin: de Gruyter, 2009.
Hweio, Haala. 'Tribes in Libya: From Social Organization to Political Power'. *African Conflict and Peacebuilding Review* 2 (2012): 111–21.
Hyman, Ronald T. 'The Rabshakeh's Speech (II Kg. 18–25): A Study of Rhetorical Intimidation'. *JBQ* 23 (1995): 213–20.
Irvine, Stuart A. *Isaiah, Ahaz, and the Syro-Ephraimitic Crisis*. SBLDS. Atlanta, GA: Scholars Press, 1990.
Ishida, T. '"The People and the Land" and the Political Crises in Judah'. *AJBI* 1 (1975): 23–38.
Janowski, Bernd. *Arguing with God: A Theological Anthropology of the Psalms*. Louisville, KY: Westminster John Knox, 2013.
Janzen, David. 'An Ambiguous Ending: Dynastic Punishment in Kings and the Fate of the Davidides in 2 Kings 25.27-30'. *JSOT* 33 (2008): 39–58.
Janzen, David. 'The Sins of Josiah and Hezekiah: A Synchronic Reading of the Final Chapters of Kings'. *JSOT* 37 (2013): 349–70.
Japhet, Sara. *The Ideology of the Book of Chronicles and its Place in Biblical Thought*. Beiträge zur Erforschung des Alten Testaments und des antiken Judentums. Frankfurt: Peter Lang, 1997.
Jensen, Hans Jørgen Lundager. 'Desire, Rivalry and Collective Violence in the "Succession Narrative"'. *JSOT* 55 (1992): 39–59.
Jeon, Yong Ho. *Impeccable Solomon? A Study of Solomons Faults in Chronicles*. Eugene, OR: Wipf & Stock, 2013.
Jonker, Louis C. *Historiography and Identity (Re)formulation in Second Temple Historiographical Literature*. New York: T&T Clark, 2010.
Joosten, Jan. *People and Land in the Holiness Code: An Exegetical Study of the Ideational Framework of the Law in Leviticus 17–26*. VTSup 67. Leiden: Brill, 1996.
Joseph, Alison L. *Portrait of the Kings: the Davidic Prototype in Deuteronomistic Poetics*. Minneapolis, MN: Fortress, 2015.

Joüon, Paul, and T. Muraoka. *A Grammar of Biblical Hebrew*. SubBi. Rome: Pontificio Istituto Biblico, 2006.
Kang, Jung Ju. *The Persuasive Portrayal of Solomon in 1 Kings 1–11*. New York: Peter Lang, 2003.
Kartveit, Magnar. 'The Date of II Reg 17,24–41'. *ZAW* 126 (2014): 31–44.
Kass, Leon R. *The Beginning of Wisdom: Reading Genesis*. Chicago, IL: University of Chicago Press, 2006.
Kaufman, Peter I. *Redeeming Politics*. Princeton, NJ: Princeton University Press, 1992.
Kaufmann, Y. *The Religion of Israel from Its Beginnings to the Babylonian Exile*. Chicago, IL: University of Chicago Press, 1960.
Keil, Carl Friedrich, and Franz Delitzsch. *Commentary on the Old Testament*. Translated by James Martin. Grand Rapids, MI: Eerdmans, 1988.
Keys, Gillian. *The Wages of Sin: A Reappraisal of the 'Succession Narrative'*. JSOTSup 221. Sheffield: JSOT, 1996.
Knapp, Andrew. *Royal Apologetic in the Ancient Near East*. WAWSup. Atlanta, GA: SBL, 2015.
Knauf, Ernst Axel. 'Does a "Deuteronomistic Historiography" (DtrH) Exist?' Pages 388–98 in *Israel Constructs its History. Deuteronomistic Historiography in Recent Research*. Edited by A. de Pury, Thomas Römer and J. D. Macchi. JSOTSup 306. London: T&T Clark, 2000.
Knoppers, Gary N. 'There Was None Like Him: Incomparability in the Books of Kings'. *CBQ* 54 (1992): 411–31.
Knoppers, Gary N. *Two Nations Under God: The Deuteronomistic History of Solomon and the Dual Monarchies. The Reign of Solomon and the Rise of Jeroboam*. HSM. Atlanta, GA: Scholars Press, 1993.
Knoppers, Gary N. *Two Nations Under God: The Deuteronomistic History of Solomon and the Dual Monarchies: The Reign of Jeroboam, the Fall of Israel, and the Reign of Josiah*. HSM. Atlanta, GA: Scholars Press, 1994.
Knoppers, Gary N. 'Aaron's Calf and Jeroboam's Calves'. Pages 92–104 in *Fortunate the Eyes that See: Essays in Honour of David Noel Freedman in Celebration of his Seventieth Birthday*. Edited by A. B. Beck et al. Grand Rapids, MI: Eerdmans, 1995.
Knoppers, Gary N. 'Prayer and Propaganda: Solomon's Dedication of the Temple and the Deuteronomist's Program'. *CBQ* 57 (1995): 229–54.
Knoppers, Gary N. 'The Deuteronomist and the Deuteronomic Law of the King: A Re-examination of a Relationship'. *ZAW* 108 (1996): 329–46.
Knoppers, Gary N. 'Is There a Future for the Deuteronomistic History?' Pages 119–34 in *The Future of the Deuteronomistic History*. Edited by Thomas Römer. BETL. Leuven: Leuven University Press, 2000.
Knoppers, Gary N. 'Rethinking the Relationship Between Deuteronomy and the Deuteronomistic History: The Case of Kings'. *CBQ* 63 (2001): 393–415.
Knoppers, Gary N. 'Cutheans or Children of Jacob? The Issue of Samaritan Origins in 2 Kings 17'. Pages 223–40 in *Reflection and Refraction: Studies in Biblical Historiography in Honour of A. Graeme Auld*. Edited by Robert Rezetko, Timothy Henry Lim and W. Brian Aucker. VTSup 113. Leiden: Brill, 2007.
Knoppers, Gary N. 'Theories of the Redaction(s) of Kings'. Pages 69–88 in *The Books of Kings: Sources, Composition, Historiography and Reception*. Edited by Baruch Halpern and André Lemaire. VTSup 129. Leiden: Brill, 2010.

Knoppers, Gary N. 'David's Relation to Moses: The Contexts, Content and Conditions of the Davidic Promises'. Pages 91–118 in *King and Messiah in Israel and the Ancient Near East: Proceedings of the Oxford Old Testament Seminar.* Edited by John Day. London: T&T Clark, 2013.

Konkel, August H. 'The Sources of the Story of Hezekiah in the Book of Isaiah'. *VT* 43 (1993): 462–82.

Köstenberger, Andreas J., and Peter Thomas O'Brien. *Salvation to the Ends of the Earth.* Grand Rapids, MI: IVP, 2001.

Kramer, Samuel Noah. 'The Sage in Sumerian Literature: A Composite Portrait'. Pages 31–44 in *The Sage in Israel and the Ancient Near East.* Edited by John G. Gammie and Leo G. Perdue. Winona Lake, IN: Eisenbrauns, 1990.

Kratz, Reinhard G. *The Composition of the Narrative Books of the Old Testament.* London: T&T Clark, 2005.

Laato, Antti. *Josiah and David Redivivus: The Historical Josiah and the Messianic Expectations of Exilic and Postexilic Times.* ConB. Stockholm: Almqvist & Wiksell, 1992.

Laato, Antti. 'Assyrian Propaganda and the Falsification of History in the Royal Inscriptions of Sennacherib'. *VT* 45 (1995): 198–226.

Laato, Antti. *A Star Is Rising: The Historical Development of the Old Testament Royal Ideology and the Rise of the Jewish Messianic Expectations.* Atlanta, GA: Scholars Press, 1997.

Lamb, David T. *Righteous Jehu and his Evil Heirs: The Deuteronomist's Negative Perspective on Dynastic Succession.* Oxford Theology and Religion Monographs. Oxford: Oxford University Press, 2008.

Lambert, Wilfred G. 'The God Assur'. *Iraq* 45 (1983): 82–6.

Lambert, Wilfred G. 'Kingship in Ancient Mesopotamia'. Pages 54–71 in *King and Messiah in Israel and the Ancient Near East: Proceedings of the Oxford Old Testament Seminar.* Edited by John Day. London: T&T Clark, 2013.

Laniak, Timothy S. *Shepherds After my own Heart: Pastoral Traditions and Leadership in the Bible.* Leicester: Apollos, 2006.

Lasine, Stuart. 'Reading Jeroboam's Intentions: Intertextuality, Rhetoric and History in 1 Kings 12'. Pages 133–52 in *Reading Between Texts: Intertextuality and the Hebrew Bible.* Edited by Danna N. Fewell. Louisville, Ky: Westminster John Knox, 1992.

Lasine, Stuart. 'Manasseh as Villain and Scapegoat'. Pages 163–83 in *The New Literary Criticism and the Hebrew Bible.* Edited by J. Cheryl Exum and David J. A. Clines. JSOTSup 143. Sheffield: JSOT, 1993.

Lasine, Stuart. '"Go in peace" or "Go to hell"? Elisha, Naaman and the Meaning of Monotheism in 2 Kings 5'. *JSOT* 25 (2011): 3–28.

Lee, Sang-Won. 'Die Königsbeurteilungen und die Literargeschichte des Deuteronomistischen Geschichtswerks Anmerkungen zu einer kontroversen Diskussion'. *VT* 68 (2018): 581–605.

Leeman, Jonathan. *Political Church: The Local Assembly as Embassy of Christ's Rule.* Grand Rapids, MI: IVP Academic, 2016.

Leithart, Peter J. 'Counterfeit Davids: Davidic Restoration and the Architecture of 1–2 Kings'. *TynB* 56 (2005): 19–34.

Leithart, Peter J. *1&2 Kings.* BTCB. Grand Rapids, MI: Brazos, 2006.

Lemaire, André. 'Wisdom in Solomonic Historiography'. Pages 106–18 in *Wisdom in Ancient Israel.* Edited by John Day, Robert P. Gordon and H. G. M. Williamson. Cambridge: Cambridge University Press, 1995.

Lemaire, André. 'Toward a Redactional History of the Book of Kings'. Pages 446–61 in *Reconsidering Israel and Judah: Recent Studies on the Deuteronomistic History*. Edited by Gary N. Knoppers and J. Gordon McConville. SBTS. Winona Lake, IN: Eisenbrauns, 2000.

Leuchter, Mark, 'Samuel: A Prophet like Moses or a Priest like Moses?' Pages 147–68 in *Israelite Prophecy and the Deuteronomistic History: Portrait, Reality, and the Formation of a History (4)*. Edited by Mignon R. Jacobs and Raymond F. Person Jr. Atlanta, GA: SBL, 2013.

Levenson, Jon D. 'Who Inserted the Book of the Torah?' *HTR* 68 (1975): 203–33.

Levenson, Jon D. 'The Last Four Verses in Kings'. *JBL* 103 (1984): 353–61.

Levenson, Jon D. *Sinai and Zion: An Entry into the Jewish Bible*. New York: Harper, 1987.

Levin, Christoph. *Die Verheißung des neuen Bundes in ihrem theologie geschichtlichen Zusammenhang ausgelegt*. FRLANT 29. Göttingen: Vandenhoeck & Ruprecht, 1985.

Levin, Christoph. 'The Empty Land in Kings'. Pages 61–90 in *The Concept of Exile in Ancient Israel and its Historical Contexts*. Edited by Ehud Ben Zvi and Christoph Levin. New York: de Gruyter, 2010.

Levin, Christoph. 'On the Cohesion and Separation of Books within the Enneateuch'. Pages 127–54 in *Pentateuch, Hexateuch, or Enneatuech? Identifying Literary Works in Genesis through Kings*. Edited by Thomas B. Dozeman, Thomas Römer and Konrad Schmid. AIL. Atlanta, GA: SBL, 2011.

Levine, Baruch A. 'Assyrian Ideology and Israelite Monotheism'. *Iraq* 67 (2005): 411–27.

Levinson, Bernard M. 'The Reconceptualisation of Kingship in Deuteronomy and the Deuteronomistic History's Transformation of Torah'. *VT* 51 (2001): 511–34.

Levinson, Bernard M. 'The First Constitution: Rethinking the Origins of Rule of Law and Separation of Powers in Light of Deuteronomy'. *Cardozo Law Review* 27 (2006): 1853–88.

Lewis, Rebecca. 'Insider Movements: Retaining Identity and Preserving Community'. Pages 673–6 in *Perspectives on the World Christian Movement: A Reader*. Edited by Ralph D. Winter and Steven C. Hawthorne. Pasadena, CA: William Carey, 2009.

Lindblom, Johannes. *Prophecy in Ancient Israel*. Philadelphia, PA: Fortress, 1962.

Linville, James R. 'Rethinking the 'Exilic' Book of Kings'. *JSOT* 22 (1997): 21–42.

Linville, James R. *Israel in the Book of Kings: The Past as a Project of Social Identity*. Sheffield: Sheffield Academic, 1998.

Linville, James R. 'On the Authority of Dead Kings'. Pages 203–22 in *Deuteronomy-Kings as Emerging Authoritative Books: A Conversation*. Edited by Diana V. Edelman. Ancient Near East Monographs. Atlanta, GA: SBL, 2014.

Liverani, Mario. *Assyria: The Imperial Mission*. Winona Lake, IN: Eisenbrauns, 2017.

Lohfink, Norbert. 'The Cult Reform of Josiah of Judah: 2 Kings 22–23 as a Source for the History of Israelite Religion'. Pages 459–75 in *Ancient Israelite Religion: Essays in Honor of Frank Moore Cross*. Edited by J. M. Miller, P. D. Hanson and S. D. McBride. Philadelphia, PA: Fortress, 1987.

Lohfink, Norbert. 'Distributions of the Functions of Power: The Laws Concerning Public Offices in Deuteronomy 16:18–18:22'. Pages 336–52 in *A Song of Power and the Power of Song*. Edited by Duane L. Christensen. Winona Lake, IN: Eisenbrauns, 1993.

Long, Burke O. *1 Kings: With an Introduction to Historical Literature*. FOTL. Grand Rapids, MI: Eerdmans, 1984.

Long, Burke O. *2 Kings*. FOTL. Grand Rapids, MI: Eerdmans, 1991.

Long, Jesse C. 'Elisha's Deceptive Prophecy in 2 Kings 3: A Response to Raymond Westbrook'. *JBL* 126 (2007): 168–71.

Lovell, Nathan H. 'The Shape of Hope in the Book of Kings: The Resolution of Davidic Blessing and Mosaic Curse'. *JESOT* 3 (2014): 3–27.
Lovell, Nathan H. 'A Text-Linguistics Approach to the Literary Structure and Coherence of 2 Kings 17:7-23'. *VT* 68 (2018): 220–31.
Lundquist, John M. *The Legitimizing Role of the Temple in the Origin of the State*. London: Scholars Press, 1982.
Lunn, Nicholas P. 'Prophetic Representations of the Divine Presence: The Theological Interpretation of the Elijah–Elisha Cycles'. *JTI* 9 (2015): 49–63.
MacDonald, John. 'The Structure of II Kings XVII'. *Glasgow University Oriental Society* 23 (1970): 29–41.
MacDonald, Neil B. '1 Kings 8:23 – A Case of Repunctuation?' *VT* 53 (2003): 115–17.
Machinist, Peter. 'Literature as Politics: The Tukulti-Ninurta Epic and the Bible'. *CBQ* 38 (1976): 455–82.
Machinist, Peter. 'Assyria and its Image in the First Isaiah'. *JAOS* 103 (1983): 719–37.
McBride, S. Dean. 'Polity of the Covenant People: The Book of Deuteronomy'. *Int* 41 (1987): 229–44.
McCarthy, Dennis J. 'II Samuel 7 and the Structure of the Deuteronomic History'. *JBL* 84 (1965): 131–8.
McConville, J. Gordon. 'God's "Name" and God's "Glory"'. *TynB* 30 (1979): 149–63.
McConville, J. Gordon. 'Narrative and Meaning in the Books of Kings'. *Bib* 70 (1989): 31–49.
McConville, J. Gordon. '1 Kings VIII 46-53 and the Deuteronomic Hope'. *VT* 42 (1992): 67–79.
McConville, J. Gordon. *Grace in the End: A Study in Deuteronomic Theology*. Grand Rapids, MI: Zondervan, 1993.
McConville, J. Gordon. 'The Old Testament Historical Books in Modern Scholarship'. *Them* 22 (1997): 3–13.
McConville, J. Gordon. *Deuteronomy*. Leicester: Apollos, 2002.
McConville, J. Gordon. 'Law and Monarchy in the Old Testament'. Pages 69–88 in *A Royal Priesthood? The Use of the Bible Ethically and Politically: A Dialogue with Oliver O'Donovan*. Edited by Craig G. Bartholomew. Grand Rapids, MI: Paternoster Press, 2002.
McConville, J. Gordon. *God and Earthly Power: An Old Testament Political Theology, Genesis–Kings*. London: T&T Clark, 2008.
McConville, J. Gordon. 'King and Messiah in Deuteronomy and the Deuteronomistic History'. Pages 271–95 in *King and Messiah in Israel and the Ancient Near East: Proceedings of the Oxford Old Testament Seminar*. Edited by John Day. London: T&T Clark, 2013.
McKay, John W. *Religion in Judah Under the Assyrians, 732–609 BC*. SBT. Naperville, IL: A. R. Allenson, 1973.
McKenzie, Steven L. *The Trouble with Kings: The Composition of the Book of Kings in the Deuteronomistic History*. Leiden: Brill, 1991.
McKenzie, Steven L. 'The Books of Kings in the Deuteronomistic History'. Pages 281–307 in *The History of Israel's Traditions: The Heritage of Martin Noth*. Edited by Steven L. McKenzie and M. P. Graham. JSOTSup 182. Sheffield: Sheffield Academic, 1994.
Mead, James K. 'Kings and Prophets, Donkeys and Lions: Dramatic Shape and Deuteronomistic Rhetoric in 1 Kings XIII'. *VT* 49 (1999): 191–205.

Mendelsohn, I. 'Samuel's Denunciation of Kingship in the Light of Akkadian Documents from Ugarit'. *BASOR* 143 (1956): 17–32.
Mendenhall, G. E. 'The Monarchy'. *Int* 29 (1975): 155–70.
Mendenhall, George E. 'Ancient Oriental and Biblical Law'. *BA* 172 (1954): 26–46.
Mendenhall, George E. 'Covenant Forms in Israelite Tradition'. *BA* 17 (1954): 50–76.
Mettinger, Tryggve N. D. *King and Messiah: The Civil and Sacral Legitimation of the Israelite Kings*. ConB. London: Coronet, 1976.
Mettinger, Tryggve N. D. *The Dethronement of Sabaoth: Studies in the Shem and Kabod Theologies*. ConB. Lund: C. W. K. Gleerup, 1982.
Meyer, Lester V. 'Remnant'. *AYBD*, 5:669–71.
Meyers, Carol. 'The Israelite Empire: In Defense of King Solomon'. *Michigan Quarterly* 22 (1983): 412–28.
Meyers, Carol. 'Kinship and Kingship'. Pages 221–71 in *The Oxford History of the Biblical World*. Edited by M. D. Coogan. Oxford: Oxford University Press, 1998.
Millard, Alan R. 'King Solomon in his Ancient Context'. Pages 30–56 in *The Age of Solomon: Scholarship at the Turn of the Millennium*. Edited by Lowell K. Handy. SHANE. Leiden: Brill, 1997.
Miller, Robert D. 'Solomon the Trickster'. *BibInt* 19 (2011): 496–504.
Millgram, Hillel I. *The Elijah Enigma: The Prophet, King Ahab and the Rebirth of Monotheism in the Book of Kings*. Jefferson, MO: McFarland, 2014.
Montgomery, James A. *A Critical and Exegetical Commentary on the Books of Kings*. ICC. Edinburgh: T&T Clark, 1951.
Moore, Michael S. 'Jehu's Coronation and Purge of Israel'. *VT* 53 (2003): 97–114.
Morgenstern, Mira. *Conceiving a Nation: The Development of Political Discourse in the Hebrew Bible*. University Park, PA: Pennsylvania State University Press, 2009.
Mtshiselwa, Ndikhokele. 'Reconstructing a Deuteronomistic Athaliah in the (South) African Context: A Critique of the Patriarchal Perception of Women'. *VE* 36 (2015): 1–8.
Mtshiselwa, Ndikhokele. 'A Re-Reading of 1 Kings 21:1-29 and Jehu's Revolution in Dialogue with Farisani and Nzimande: Negotiating Socio-economic Redress in South Africa'. *OTE* 27 (2014): 205–30.
Mullen, E. Theodore. *Narrative History and Ethnic Boundaries: The Deuteronomistic Historian and the Creation of Israelite National Identity*. Atlanta, GA: Scholars Press, 1993.
Müller, W. E. L. and Horst Dietrich Preuss. *Die Vorstellung vom Rest im Alten Testament*. 2nd ed. Neukirchen-Vluyn: Neukirchener Verlag, 1973.
Murray, Donald F. 'Of All the Years the Hopes—or Fears? Jehoiachin in Babylon (2 Kings 25:27-30)'. *JBL* 120 (2001-7): 245–65.
Na'aman, Nadav. 'The Deuteronomist and Voluntary Servitude to Foreign Powers'. *JSOT* 65 (1995): 37–53.
Na'aman, Nadav. 'Sources and Composition in the History of Solomon'. Pages 57–80 in *The Age of Solomon: Scholarship at the Turn of the Millennium*. Edited by Lowell K. Handy. SHANE. Leiden: Brill, 1997.
Na'aman, Nadav. 'The 'Discovered Book' and the Legitimation of Josiah's Reform'. *JBL* 130 (2011): 47–62.
Na'aman, Nadav. 'A ניר for David in Jerusalem'. *JNSL* 39 (2013): 29–38.
Nam, Roger S. '"The Poorest of the Land": Perception and Identity of the Remnant in 2 Kings and Jeremiah'. *JRS* 10 (2014): 61–9.

Nelson, Richard D. *The Double Redaction of the Deuteronomistic History*. JSOTSup 18. Sheffield: Sheffield Academic, 1981.
Nelson, Richard D. 'The Anatomy of the Book of Kings'. *JSOT* 40 (1988): 39–48.
Nelson, Richard D. *Deuteronomy: A Commentary*. OTL. Louisville, KY: Westminster John Knox, 2002.
Newsom, Carol A. 'Bakhtin, the Bible, and Dialogic Truth'. *JR* 76 (1996): 290–306.
Nicholson, Ernest W. 'Josiah and the Priests of the High Places (II Reg 23,8a.9)'. *ZAW* 119 (2007): 499–513.
Nicholson, Ernest W. 'Once Again Josiah and the Priests of the High Places (II Reg 23,8a.9)'. *ZAW* 124 (2012): 356–68.
Niemann, Hermann. 'The Socio-Political Shadow Cast by the Biblical Solomon'. Pages 252–99 in *The Age of Solomon: Scholarship at the Turn of the Millennium*. Edited by Lowell K. Handy. SHANE. Leiden: Brill, 1997.
Nihan, Christophe. 'Rewriting Kingship in Samuel: 1 Samuel 8 and 12 and the Law of the King (Deuteronomy 17)'. *HBAI* 2 (2013): 315–50.
Nissinen, Martti. 'Prophets and Prophecy in Joshua–Kings: A Near Eastern Perspective'. Pages 103–28 in *Israelite Prophecy and the Deuteronomistic History: Portrait, Reality, and the Formation of a History (4)*. Edited by Mignon R. Jacobs and Raymond F. Person Jr. Atlanta, GA: SBL, 2013.
Noble, John T. 'Cultic Prophecy and Levitical Inheritance in the Elijah–Elisha Cycle'. *JSOT* 41 (2016): 45–60.
Noll, Kurt L. 'Deuteronomistic History or Deuteronomic Debate? (A Thought Experiment)'. *JSOT* 31 (2007): 311–45.
Noth, Martin. *The History of Israel*. 2nd English ed. London: A. & C. Black, 1960.
Noth, Martin. *Könige*. Biblischer Kommentar: Altes Testament. Neukirchener Verlag des Erziehungsvereins, 1968.
Noth, Martin. *The Deuteronomistic History*. 2nd ed. Translated by David J. A. Clines. JSOTSup 15. Sheffield: JSOT, 1981.
O'Brien, Mark. 'Prophetic Stories Making a Story of Prophecy'. Pages 169–86 in *Israelite Prophecy and the Deuteronomistic History: Portrait, Reality, and the Formation of a History*. Edited by Mignon R. Jacobs and Raymond F. Person Jr. Atlanta, GA: SBL, 2013.
O'Donovan, Oliver. *The Desire of the Nations: Rediscovering the Roots of Political Theology*. Cambridge, MA: Cambridge University Press, 1996.
O'Kennedy, D. F. 'The Prayer of Solomon (1 Ki 8:22-53): Paradigm for the Understanding of Forgiveness in the Old Testament'. *OTE* 13 (2000): 72–88.
Ollenburger, Ben C. *Zion: The City of the Great King*. JSOTSup 41. Sheffield: JSOT, 1987.
Olley, John W. 'Yhwh and His Zealous Prophet: The Presentation of Elijah in 1 and 2 Kings'. *JSOT* 80 (1998): 25–51.
Olley, John W. '"Trust in the Lord": Hezekiah, Kings and Isaiah'. *TynB* 50 (1999): 59–77.
Olley, John W. 'Pharaoh's Daughter, Solomon's Palace, and the Temple: Another Look at the Structure of 1 Kings 1–11'. *JSOT* 27 (2003): 355–69.
Olley, John W. '2 Kings 13: A Cluster of Hope in God'. *JSOT* 36 (2011): 199–218.
Olmstead, A. T. *History of Assyria*. Chicago, IL: University of Chicago Press, 1968.
Olson, Dennis T. 'Biblical Theology as Provisional Monologization: A Dialogue with Childs, Brueggemann and Bakhtin'. *BibInt* 6 (1998): 162–80.
Omanson, Roger L., and John E. Ellington. *A Handbook on 1&2 Kings*. UBS Handbook Series. Münster: UBS, 2008.

Oritz, Steven M. 'The United Monarchy: Archeology and Literary Sources'. Pages 227–61 in *Ancient Israel's History: An Introduction to Issues and Sources*. Edited by Bill T. Arnold and Richard S. Hess. Grand Rapids, IL: Baker, 2014.

Östborn, Gunnar. *Yahweh and Baal*. Lund: Gleerup, 1956.

Oswalt, John N. *The Book of Isaiah, Chapters 1–39*. NICOT. Grand Rapids, IL: Eerdmans, 1986.

Otto, Susanne. 'The Composition of the Elijah–Elisha Stories and the Deuteronomistic History'. *JSOT* 27 (2003): 487–508.

Oz, Amos. *The Story Begins: Essays on Literature*. Translated by M. Bar-Tura. New York: Harcourt Brace, 1996.

Pakkala, Juha. 'Jeroboam Without Bulls'. *ZAW* 120 (2008): 501–25.

Pangle, Thomas L. 'The Hebrew Bible's Challenge to Political Philosophy: Some Reflections'. Pages 67–82 in *Political Philosophy and the Human Soul: Essays in Memory of Allan Bloom*. Edited by Michael Palmer and Thomas L. Pangle. Lanham, MD: Roman & Littlefield, 1995.

Parker, Bradley J. 'The Construction and Performance of Kingship in the Neo-Assyrian Empire'. *JAR* 67 (2011): 357–86.

Parker, Kim I. 'Repetition as a Structuring Device in 1 Kings 1–11'. *JSOT* 42 (1988): 19–27.

Parker, Kim I. 'Solomon as Philosopher King: The Nexus of Law and Wisdom in 1 Kings 1-11'. *JSOT* 53 (1992): 75–91.

Parshall, Phil. 'Danger! New Direction in Contextualisation'. *Evangelical Missions Quarterly* 34 (1998): 404–10.

Pat-El, Naama. 'Israelian Hebrew: A Re-Evaluation'. *VT* 67 (2017): 227–63.

Paynter, Helen. *Reduced Laughter: Seriocomic Features and their Functions in the Book of Kings*. Biblical Interpretation Series. Leiden: Brill, 2016.

Perlitt, Lothar. 'Der Staatsgedanke im Deuteronomium'. Pages 182–98 in *Language, Theology and the Bible: Essays in Honour of James Barr*. Edited by S. E. Balentine and J. Barton. Oxford: Clarendon, 1994.

Person, Raymond F. *The Deuteronomic School: History, Social Setting, and Literature*. Studies in Biblical Literature. Atlanta, GA: SBL, 2002.

Person, Raymond F. 'In Conversation with Thomas Römer, The So-Called Deuteronomistic History: A Sociological, Historical and Literary Introduction'. *JHebS* 9 (2009): Article 17.

Pietsch, Michael. 'Prophetess of Doom: Hermeneutical Reflections on the Huldah Oracle (2 Kings 22)'. Pages 71–80 in *Soundings in Kings: Perspectives and Methods in Contemporary Scholarship*. Edited by Mark Leuchter and Klaus-Peter Adam. Minneapolis: Fortress, 2010.

Pohlmann, Karl-Friedrich. *Studien zum Jeremiabuch: Ein Beitrag zur Frage nach der Entstehung des Jeremiabuches*. FRLANT 118. Göttingen: Vandenhoeck & Ruprecht, 1978.

Pohlmann, Karl-Friedrich. *Ezechielstudien: Zur Redaktionsgeschichte des Buches und zur Frage nach den ältesten Texten*. BZAW 478. Berlin: de Gruyter, 1992.

Polzin, Robert M. *Biblical Structuralism: Method and Subjectivity in the Study of Ancient Texts*. Philadelphia, PA: Fortress, 1977.

Polzin, Robert M. 'Literary Unity in Old Testament Narrative: A Response'. *Semeia* 15 (1979): 45–50.

Polzin, Robert M. *Moses and the Deuteronomist: A Literary Study of the Deuteronomic History, Part One: Deuteronomy, Joshua, Judges*. New York: Seabury, 1980.

Polzin, Robert M. *Samuel and the Deuteronomist: A Literary Study of the Deuteronomic History, Part Two: 1 Samuel.* San Francisco, CA: Harper & Row, 1989.

Polzin, Robert M. *David and the Deuteronomist: A Literary Study of the Deuteronomic History, Part 3: 2 Samuel.* Bloomington, IN: Indiana University Press, 1993.

Polzin, Robert M., and Eugene Rothman, eds. *The Biblical Mosaic: Changing Perspective.* Atlanta, GA: SBL, 1982.

Porten, Bezalel. 'The Structure and Theme of the Solomon Narrative (I Kings 3–11)'. *HUCA* 1 (1967): 93–128.

Porter, J. R. 'בני־הנביאים'. *JTS* 32 (1981): 423–9.

Provan, Iain W. *Hezekiah and the Books of Kings: A Contribution to the Debate About the Composition of the Deuteronomistic History.* New York: de Gruyter, 1988.

Provan, Iain W. *1 & 2 Kings.* New International Biblical Commentary. Grand Rapids, MI: Baker Academic, 1995.

Provan, Iain W. 'Solomon'. *NDBT*, 788–9.

Provan, Iain W. 'The Messiah in the Book of Kings'. Pages 67–85 in *The Lord's Anointed: Interpretation of Old Testament Messianic Texts.* Edited by Philip E. Satterthwaite, Richard S. Hess and Gordon J. Wenham. Eugene, OR: Wipf & Stock, 2012.

Provan, Iain W., V. Philips Long and Tremper Longman III. *A Biblical History of Israel.* 2nd ed. Louisville, KY: Westminster John Knox, 2015.

Pyper, Hugh S. 'Judging the Wisdom of Solomon: The Two-Way Effect of Intertextuality'. *JSOT* 59 (1993): 25–36.

Rainey, Anson F., and R. Steven Notley, eds. *The Sacred Bridge: Carta's Atlas of the Biblical World.* Jerusalem: Carta, 2006.

Rasmussen, Carl G. *Zondervan Atlas of the Bible.* Rev. ed. Grand Rapids, MI: Zondervan, 2009.

Ray, John D. 'Egyptian Wisdom Literature'. Pages 17–29 in *Wisdom in Ancient Israel.* Edited by John Day, Robert P. Gordon and H. G. M. Williamson. Cambridge: Cambridge University Press, 1995.

Redford, Donald B., 'Studies in the Relations Between Palestine and Egypt During the First Millennium B.C.: 1. The Taxation System of Solomon'. Pages 141–56 in *Studies on the Ancient Palestinian World: Presented to Professor F. V. Winnett on the Occasion of his Retirement 1 July 1971.* Edited by John W. Wevers and Donald B. Redford. Toronto: University of Toronto Press, 1972.

Reed, Walter L. *Dialogues of the Word: The Bible as Literature According to Bakhtin.* Oxford: Oxford University Press, 1993.

Reimer, David J. 'Isaiah and Politics'. Pages 84–103 in *Interpreting Isaiah.* Edited by David G. Firth and H. G. M. Williamson. Grand Rapids, MI: IVP Academic, 2009.

Rendsburg, Gary A. 'Morphological Evidence for Regional Dialects in Ancient Hebrew'. Pages 65–88 in *Linguistics and Biblical Hebrew.* Edited by Walter Ray Bodine. Winona Lake, IN: Eisenbrauns, 1992.

Rendsburg, Gary A. *Israelian Hebrew in the Book of Kings.* Winona Lake, IN: Eisenbrauns, 2002.

Richardson, Seth. 'Before Things Worked: A 'Low-Power' Model of Early Mesopotamia'. Pages 17–62 in *Ancient States and Infrastructural Power: Europe, Asia, and America.* Edited by Clifford Ando and Seth Richardson. Philadelphia, PA: University of Pennsylvania Press, 2017.

Richter, Sandra L. *The Deuteronomistic History and the Name Theology: lᵉšakkēn šᵉmôšām in the Bible and the Ancient Near East.* New York: de Gruyter, 2002.

Richter, Sandra L. 'Deuteronomistic History'. *DOTH*, 219–30.

Richter, Sandra L. 'Eighth-Century Issues: The World of Jeroboam II, the Fall of Samaria, and the Reign of Hezekiah'. Pages 319–49 in *Ancient Israel's History: An Introduction to Issues and Sources*. Edited by Bill T. Arnold and Richard S. Hess. Grand Rapids, MI: Baker, 2014.

Roberts, J. J. M. 'Davidic Origin of the Zion Tradition'. *JBL* 92 (1973): 329–44.

Roberts, J. J. M. 'Zion in the Theology of the Davidic-Solomonic Empire'. Pages 93–108 in *Studies in the Period of David and Solomon and Other Essays*. Edited by Tomoo Ishida. Winona Lake, IN: Eisenbrauns, 1982.

Roberts, J. J. M. 'In Defense of the Monarchy: The Contribution of Israelite Kingship to Biblical Theology'. Pages 377–96 in *Ancient Israelite Religion: Essays in Honor of Frank Moore Cross*. Edited by Patrick D. Miller, Paul D. Hanson and Sean D. McBride. Repr., Minneapolis, MN: Fortress, 2009.

Roberts, J. J. M. 'Public Opinion, Royal Apologetics, and Imperial Ideology: A Political Analysis of the Portrait of David, "A Man after God's Own Heart"'. *Theology Today* 69 (2012): 116–32.

Roberts, J. J. M. *First Isaiah*. Hermeneia. Minneapolis, MN: Fortress, 2015.

Robker, Jonathan M. 'Satire and the King of Aram'. *VT* 61 (2011): 646–56.

Rofé, Alexander. *The Prophetical Stories: The Narratives about the Prophets in the Hebrew Bible; Their Literary Types and History*. Jerusalem: Magnes, 1988.

Römer, Thomas C. 'Transformations in Deuteronomistic and Biblical Historiography: On "Book-Finding" and Other Literary Strategies'. *ZAW* 109 (1997): 1–11.

Römer, Thomas C. *So-Called Deuteronomistic History: A Sociological, Historical and Literary Introduction*. London: T&T Clark, 2007.

Römer, Thomas C. 'How Many Books (teuchs): Pentateuch, Hexateuch, Deuteronomistic History, or Enneateuch?' Pages 241–60 in *Pentateuch, Hexateuch, or Enneateuch? Identifying Literary Works in Genesis through Kings*. Edited by Thomas B. Dozeman, Thomas Römer and Konrad Schmid. AIL. Atlanta, GA: SBL, 2011.

Römer, Thomas C. 'The Case of the Book of Kings'. Pages 187–202 in *Deuteronomy-Kings as Emerging Authoritative Books: A Conversation*. Edited by Diana V. Edelman. Ancient Near East Monographs. Atlanta, GA: SBL, 2014.

Römer, Thomas C. 'The Current Discussion on the So-Called Deuteronomistic History: Literary Criticism and Theological Consequences'. *Christianity and Culture* 46 (2015): 43–66.

Rösel, Hartmut N. 'Why 2 Kings 17 Does Not Constitute a Chapter of Reflection in the "Deuteronomistic History"'. *JBL* 128 (2009): 85–90.

Roth, Wolfgang. 'The Story of the Prophet Micaiah (1 Kings 22) in Historical Critical Interpretation'. Pages 105–37 in *The Biblical Mosaic: Changing Perspectives*. Edited by Robert M. Polzin and Eugene Rothman. SemeiaSt. Philadelphia, PA: Fortress, 1982.

Rudman, Dominic. 'Is the Rabshakeh also Among the Prophets? A Rhetorical Study of 2 Kings XVIII 17-35'. *VT* 50 (2000): 100–110.

Rutersworden, U. *Von der politischen Gemeinshaft zur Gemeinde: Studien zu Dt 16,18–18,22*. BBB. Frankfurt: Athenaum, 1987.

Said, Edward W. *Culture and Imperialism*. New York: Random House, 1993.

Satterthwaite, Philip E. 'The Elisha Narratives and the Coherence of 2 Kgs 2–8'. *TynB* 49 (1998): 1–28.

Savran, George. '1 & 2 Kings'. Pages 146–65 in *The Literary Guide to the Bible*. Edited by Robert Alter and Frank Kermode. Cambridge, MA: Belknap, 1990.

Schenker, Adrian. 'Jeroboam and the Division of the Kingdom in the Ancient Septuagint: LXX 3 Kingdoms 12:24a-z, MT 1 Kings 11–12; 14 and the Deuteronomistic History'. Pages 214–57 in *Israel Constructs its History: Deuteronomistic History in Recent Research.* Edited by A. de Pury, Thomas Römer and J. D. Macchi. JSOTSup 306. Sheffield: Sheffield Academic, 2000.

Schenker, Adrian. 'The Septuagint in the Text History of 1–2 Kings'. Pages 3–17 in *The Books of Kings: Sources, Composition, Historiography and Reception.* Edited by Baruch Halpern and André Lemaire. VTSup 129. Leiden: Brill, 2010.

Schilling, O. '"Rest" in der Prophetie des Alten Testaments'. Ph.D. diss., Universität Münster, 1942.

Schmid, Konrad. 'Manasse und der Untergang Judas: "Golaorientierte" Theologie in den Königsbüchern?' *Bib* 78 (1997): 87–99.

Schniedewind, William M. 'History and Interpretation: The Religion of Ahab and Manasseh in the Book of Kings'. *CBQ* 55 (1993): 649–61.

Schniedewind, William M., and D. Sivan. 'The Elijah–Elisha Narratives: A Test-Case for the Northern Dialect of Hebrew'. *JQR* 87 (1997): 303–37.

Schwartz, Matthew B., and Kalman J. Kaplan. *Politics in the Hebrew Bible: God, Man, and Government.* Lanham, MD: Jason Aronson, 2013.

Scott, R. B. Y. 'Weights and Measures of the Bible'. *BA* 22 (1959): 22–40.

Seibert, Eric A. *Subversive Scribes and the Solomonic Narrative: A Rereading of 1 Kings 1–11.* New York: T&T Clark, 2006.

Shanks, Herschel et al., eds. *The Rise of Ancient Israel: Symposium at the Smithsonian Institution, October 26, 1991.* Washington: Biblical Archeology Society, 1992.

Shemesh, Yael. 'The Elisha Stories as Saints' Legends'. *JHebS* 8 (2008): 5.

Shepherd, Tom. 'The Narrative Function of Markan Intercalation'. *NTS* 41 (1995–10): 522–40.

Smelik, Klaas A. D. 'The New Altar of King Ahaz (2 Kings 16): Deuteronomistic Re-Interpretation of a Cult Reform'. Pages 263–78 in *Deuteronomy and Deuteronomic Literature: Festschrift for C. H. W. Brekelmans.* Edited by Marc Vervenne and Johan Lust. Leuven: Leuven University Press, 1997.

Smend, Rudolf. 'Das Gesetz und die Völker. Ein Beitrag zur deuteronomistischen Redaktionsgeschichte'. Pages 494–509 in *Probleme biblischer Theologie: Festschrift Gerhard von Rad.* Edited by Hans W. Wolff. Munich: Kaiser, 1971.

Smend, Rudolf. 'The Law and the Nations. A Contribution to Deuteronomistic Tradition History'. Pages 95–110 in *Reconsidering Israel and Judah: Recent Studies on the Deuteronomistic History.* Edited by Gary N. Knoppers and J. Gordon McConville. SBTS. Winona Lake, IN: Eisenbrauns, 2000.

Smith, Anthony D. *The Ethnic Origins of Nations.* Hoboken, NJ: Blackwell, 1986.

Smith, Anthony D. *Chosen Peoples: Sacred Sources of National Identity.* Oxford: Oxford University Press, 2003.

Soggin, J. Alberto. 'Der judäische 'am-ha' areṣ und das Königtum in Juda: Ein Beitrag zum Studium der deuteronomistischen Geschichtsschreibung'. *VT* 13 (1963): 187–95.

Soggin, J. Alberto. *An Introduction to the History of Israel and Judah.* London: SCM, 1999.

Span, John. 'God Saves. Go in Peace: Wholeness Affirmed or Promotion Piece (2 Parts)'. *Biblical Missiology* (2013).

Sternberg, Meir. *Poetics of Biblical Narrative: Ideological Literature and the Drama of Reading.* Bloomington, IN: Indiana University Press, 1987.

Sternberg, Meir. 'Time and Space in Biblical (Hi)story Telling: The Grand Chronology'. Pages 81–145 in *The Book and the Text: The Bible and Literary Theory*. Edited by Regina M. Schwartz. Oxford: Blackwell, 1990.

Stipp, Hermann Joseph. *Elischa–Propheten–Gottesmänner: Die Kompositionsgeschichte des Elischazyklus und verwandter Texte, rekonstruiert auf der Basis von Text- und Literarkritik zu 1 Kön 20.22 und 2 Kön 2–7*. St. Ottilien: EOS, 1987.

Stipp, Hermann Joseph. *Jeremia im Parteienstreit: Studien zur Textentwicklung von Jer 26:36-43 und 45 als Beitrag zur Geschichte Jeremias, seines Buches und judäischer Pareien im 6. Jahrhundert*. BBB 82. Frankfurt: Anton Hain, 1992.

Storey, David. 'Land, Territory and Identity'. Pages 11–22 in *Making Sense of Place: Multidisciplinary Perspectives*. Edited by Ian Convery, Gerard Corsane and Peter Davis. Suffolk: Boydell, 2012.

Swagman, Charles F. 'Tribe and Politics: An Example from Highland Yemen'. *JAR* 44 (1988): 251–61.

Sweeney, Marvin A. 'The Critique of Solomon in the Josianic Edition of the Deuteronomistic History'. *JBL* 114 (1995): 607–22.

Sweeney, Marvin A. *King Josiah of Judah: The Last Messiah of Israel*. Oxford: Oxford University Press, 2001.

Sweeney, Marvin A. 'A Reassessment of the Masoretic and Septuagint Versions of the Jeroboam Narratives in 1 Kings/3 Kingdoms 11–14'. *JSJ* 38 (2007): 165–95.

Sweeney, Marvin A. *I & II Kings*. OTL. Louisville, KY: Westminster John Knox, 2007.

Sweeney, Marvin A. 'Prophets and Priests in the Deuteronomistic History: Elijah and Elisha'. Pages 35–50 in *Israelite Prophecy and the Deuteronomistic History: Portrait, Reality, and the Formation of a History (4)*. Edited by Mignon R. Jacobs and Raymond F. Person Jr. Atlanta, GA: SBL, 2013.

Sweet, Ronald F. G. 'The Sage in Akkadian Literature: A Philological Study'. Pages 45–68 in *The Sage in Israel and the Ancient Near East*. Edited by John G. Gammie and Leo G. Perdue. Winona Lake, IN: Eisenbrauns, 1990.

Tadmor, Hayim. '"The People" and the Kingship in Ancient Israel: The Role of Political Institutions in the Biblical Period'. *Cahiers d'histoire mondiale* 11 (1968): 3–23.

Tadmor, Hayim. 'Traditional Institutions and the Monarchy: Social and Political Tensions in the Time of David and Solomon'. Pages 239–57 in *Studies in the Period of David and Solomon and Other Essays*. Edited by T. Ishida. Winona Lake, IN: Eisenbrauns, 1982.

Tadmor, Hayim, and Mordechai Cogan. 'Ahaz and Tiglath-Pileser in the Book of Kings: Historiographic Considerations'. *Bib* 60 (1979): 499–508.

Talmon, S. 'The Judaean 'Am ha'Ares' in Historical Perspective'. Pages 71–6 in *Fourth World Congress of Jewish Studies: Papers*. Jerusalem: Word Union of Jewish Studies, 1967.

Talshir, David. 'The Habitat and History of Hebrew During the Second Temple Period'. Pages 251–75 in *Biblical Hebrew: Studies in Chronology and Typology*. Edited by Ian Young. London: T&T Clark, 2003.

Talshir, Zipora. *The Alternative Story of the Division of the Kingdom: 3 Kingdoms 12:24a-z*. Jerusalem: Simor, 1993.

Talshir, Zipora. 'Towards the Structure of the Book of Kings: Formulaic Synchronism and Story Synchronism (1 Kings 12–2 Kings 17)'. Pages 73–88 in *Texts, Temples, and Traditions: A Tribute to Menahem Haran*. Edited by Michael V. Fox et al. Winona Lake, IN: Eisenbrauns, 1996.

Tamarkin, M. 'Tribal Associations, Tribal Solidarity, and Tribal Chauvinism in a Kenya Town'. *The Journal of African History* 14 (1973): 257–74.

Tanska, Juha. 'Changing Paradigms in Biblical Criticism: 2 Kings 22:1–23:30 in the Flux of Discourses'. PhD diss., University of Helsinki, 2011.

Thomas, H. A. 'Zion'. *DOTP*, 907–14.

Throntveit, Mark A. 'The Relationship of Hezekiah to David and Solomon in the Books of Chronicles'. Pages 105–21 in *The Chronicler as Theologian: Essays in Honour of Ralph W. Klein.* Edited by M. Patrick Graham, Steven L. McKenzie and Gary N. Knoppers. JSOTSup 371. London: T&T Clark, 2003.

Tomes, Roger. '"Come and See my Zeal for the Lord': Reading the Jehu story'. Pages 53–68 in *Narrativity in Biblical and Related Texts: La narrativité dans la bible et les textes apparentés.* Edited by G. J. Brooke and J. D. Kaestli. Leuven: Leuven University Press, 2000.

Tov, Emanuel. 'Some Thoughts about the Diffusion of Biblical Manuscripts in Antiquity'. Pages 151–69 in *The Dead Sea Scrolls: Transmission of Traditions and Production of Texts.* Edited by Sarianna Metso, Hindy Najman and Eileen Schuller. STDJ 92. Leiden: Brill, 2010.

Tov, Emanuel. *Textual Criticism of the Hebrew Bible*. 3rd ed. Philadelphia, PA: Fortress, 2011.

Travis, John J. 'The C-Spectrum: A Practical Tool for Defining Six Types of "Christ Centred Communities" Found in Muslim Contexts'. Pages 664–7 in *Perspectives on the World Christian Movement: A Reader.* Edited by Ralph D. Winter and Steven C. Hawthorne. Pasadena, CA: William Carey, 2009.

Trebolle Barrera, Julio C. 'Old Latin, Old Greek, and Old Hebrew in the Books of Kings (1 Ki 18:25 and 2 Ki 20:11)'. *Textus* 13 (1986): 85–94.

Trebolle Barrera, Julio C. 'The Text-Critical Use of the Septuagint in the Books of Kings'. Pages 285–99 in *VII Congress of the International Organisation for Septuagint and Cognate Studies, Leuven 1989.* Edited by C. E. Cox. SBLSCS. Atlanta, GA: Scholars Press, 1991.

Trebolle Barrera, Julio C. 'Redaction, Recension, and Midrash in the Books of Kings'. Pages 475–92 in *Reconsidering Israel and Judah: Recent Studies on the Deuteronomistic History.* Edited by Gary N. Knoppers and J. Gordan McConville. Winona Lake, IN: Eisenbrauns, 2000.

Trebolle Barrera, Julio C. 'Qumran Fragments of the Books of Kings'. Pages 3–19 in *The Books of Kings: Sources, Composition, Historiography and Reception.* Edited by Baruch Halpern and André Lemaire. VTSup 129. Leiden: Brill, 2010.

Trebolle Barrera, Julio C. 'Textual Criticism and the Literary Structure and Composition of 1–2 Kings/3–4 Reigns: The Different Sequence of Literary Units in MT and LXX'. *Septuaginta* (2012): 55–78.

Turkanik, Andrzej S. *Of Kings and Reigns: A Study in the Translation Technique in the Gamma/Gamma Section of 3 Reigns (1 Kings)*. FAT 2/30. Tübingen: Mohr Siebeck, 2008.

Uehlinger, Christoph. 'Was there a Cult Reform under King Josiah? The Case for a Well-Grounded Minimum'. Pages 279–318 in *Good Kings and Bad Kings.* Edited by Lester L. Grabbe. LHBOTS 393. London: T&T Clark, 2005.

Unterman, Jeremiah. *Justice for All: How the Jewish Bible Revolutionized Ethics*. JPS Essential Judaism. Lincoln, NE: University of Nebraska Press, 2017.

Van der Kooij, Arie. 'Standardization or Preservation? Some Comments on the Textual History of the Hebrew Bible in the Light of Josephus and Rabbinic Literature'. Pages 63–78 in *The Text of the Hebrew Bible: From the Rabbis to the Masoretes*. Edited by Elvira Martín-Contreras and Lorena Miralles-Maciá. JAJS 13. Göttingen: Vandenhoeck & Ruprecht, 2014.

Van Drunen, David. *A Biblical Case for Natural Law*. Grand Rapids, MI: Acton Institute, 2006.

Van Keulen, Percy S. F. *Manasseh Through the Eyes of the Deuteronomists: The Manasseh Account (2 Kings 21:1-18) and the Final Chapters of the Deuteronomistic History*. Leiden: Brill, 1996.

Van Seters, John. *In Search of History: Historiography in the Ancient World and the Origins of Bible History*. New Haven, CT: Yale University Press, 1983.

Van Seters, John. *The Life of Moses: The Yahwist as Historian in Exodus–Numbers*. Netherlands: Kok Pharos, 1994.

Van Winkle, D. W. '1 Kings XII 25–XIII 34: Jeroboam's Cultic Innovations and the Man of God from Judah'. *VT* 46 (1996): 101–14.

Vancil, Jack W. 'Sheep, Shepherd'. *AYBD*, 5:1187–90.

Veijola, Timo. *Die ewige Dynastie: David und die Entstehung seiner Dynastie nach der deuteronomistischen Historiographie*. Annales Academiæ Scientiarum Fennicae, Series B. Helsinki: Suomalainen Akatemia, 1975.

Veijola, Timo. *Das Königtum in der Beurteilung der deuteronomistischen Historiographie: Eine redaktionsgeschichtliche Untersuchung*. Annales Academiæ Scientiarum Fennicae, Series B. Helsinki: Suomalainen Akatemia, 1977.

Veijola, Timo. 'Martin Noth's *Überlieferungsgeschichtilche Studien* and Old Testament Theology'. Pages 101–28 in *The History of Israel's Traditions: The Heritage of Martin Noth*. Edited by Steven L. McKenzie and M. P. Graham. JSOTSup 182. Sheffield: Sheffield Academic, 1994.

Veijola, Timo. *Das fünfte Buch Mose: Kapitel 1,1–16,17*. ATD 8/1. Göttingen: Vandenhoeck & Ruprecht, 2004.

Viviano, Pauline A. '2 Kings 17: A Rhetorical and Form-Critical Analysis'. *CBQ* 49 (1987): 548–59.

Von Rad, Gerhard. *Studies in Deuteronomy*. Translated by David M. G. Stalker. SBT. London: SCM, 1953.

Von Rad, Gerhard. *Old Testament Theology*, vol. 1. Translated by David M. G. Stalker. New York: Harper & Row, 1962.

Von Rad, Gerhard. *Deuteronomy*. OTL. London: SCM, 1966.

Von Rad, Gerhard. 'The Promised Land and Yahweh's Land in the Hexateuch'. Pages 79–93 in *The Problem of the Hexateuch and Other Essays*. London: SCM, 1984.

Von Rad, Gerhard. *Old Testament Theology*. Peabody, MA: Prince, 2005.

Von Rad, Gerhard. 'The Deuteronomic Theology of History in 1 and 2 Kings'. Pages 154–66 in *From Genesis to Chronicles: Explorations in Old Testament Theology*. Minneapolis, MN: Fortress, 2005.

Walsh, Jerome T. *Ahab: The Construction of a King*. Interfaces. New York: Liturgical, 2006.

Walsh, Jerome T. 'The Contexts of 1 Kings 13'. *VT* 39 (1989): 355–70.

Walsh, Jerome T. 'Symmetry and the Sin of Solomon'. *Shofar* 12 (1993): 11–27.

Walsh, Jerome T. *1 Kings*. Berit Olam: Studies in Hebrew Narrative & Poetry. Collegeville, MA: Liturgical, 1996.

Walsh, Jerome T. 'The Organization of 2 Kings 3–11'. *CBQ* 72 (2010): 238–54.

Walsh, Jerome T. 'The Rab Šāqēh Between Rhetoric and Redaction'. *JBL* 130 (2011): 263–79.
Waltke, Bruce K. 'The Phenomenon of Conditionality within Unconditional Covenants'. Pages 123–39 in *Israel's Apostasy and Restoration: Essays in Honor of Roland K. Harrison*. Edited by Avraham Gileadi. Grand Rapids, MI: Baker, 1988.
Waltke, Bruce K. and Michael P. O'Connor. *An Introduction to Biblical Hebrew Syntax*. Winona Lake, IN: Eisenbrauns, 1990.
Walton, John H. *Ancient Israelite Literature in its Cultural Context: A Survey of Parallels Between Biblical and Ancient Near Eastern Texts*. Grand Rapids, MI: Zondervan, 1990.
Walton, John H. 'Eden, Garden of'. *DOTP*, 202–7.
Walton, John H. *Ancient Near Eastern Thought and the Old Testament: Introducing the Conceptual World of the Hebrew Bible*. 2nd ed. Grand Rapids, MI: Baker Academic, 2018.
Walzer, Michael. *Exodus and Revolution*. New York: Basic, 1986.
Walzer, Michael. *In God's Shadow: Politics in the Hebrew Bible*. New Haven, CT: Yale University Press, 2012.
Watts, John D. W. 'Deuteronomic Theology'. *Review & Expositor* 74 (1977): 321–36.
Webb, Barry G. *The Book of Judges: An Integrated Reading*. JSOTSup 46. Sheffield: JSOT, 1987.
Webb, Barry G. *The Book of Judges*. Grand Rapids, MI: Eerdmans, 2012.
Weinfeld, Moshe. *Deuteronomy and the Deuteronomic School*. Ann Arbor, MI: Clarendon, 1972.
Weinfeld, Moshe. 'The King as Servant of the People—The Source of the Idea'. *Journal of Jewish Studies* 33 (1982): 189–94.
Weinfeld, Moshe. 'Deuteronomy's Theological Revolution'. *Biblical Research* 12 (1996): 38–41, 44.
Weippert, Helga. 'Die "deuteronomistischen" Beurteilungen der Könige von Israel und Juda und das Problem der Redaktion der Königsbücher'. *Biblia* 53 (1972): 301–39.
Weitzman, Steven. *Solomon: The Lure of Wisdom*. New Haven, CT: Yale University Press, 2011.
Wellhausen, Julius. *Prolegomena to the History of Israel*. Eugene, OR: Wipf & Stock, 2003.
Westbrook, Raymond. 'Elisha's True Prophecy in 2 Kings 3'. *JBL* 124 (2005): 530–2.
Westermann, Claus. *Die Geschichtsbücher des Alten Testaments: Gab es ein deuteronomistisches Geschichtswerk?* Theologische Bücherei Altes Testament. Gütersloh: Kaiser, 1994.
White, Marsha. 'The Elohistic Depiction of Aaron: A Study in the Levite–Zadokite Controversy'. Pages 149–59 in *Studies in the Pentateuch*. Edited by John A. Emerton. VTSup 41. Leiden: Brill, 1990.
Whitelam, Keith W. *The Just King: Monarchical Judicial Authority in Ancient Israel*. Sheffield: JSOT, 1979.
Whitelam, Keith W. 'The Symbols of Royal Power: Aspects of Royal Propaganda in the United Monarchy'. *BA* 49 (1986): 166–73.
Whitelam, Keith W. 'Israelite Kingship: The Royal Ideology and its Opponents'. Pages 119–39 in *The World of Ancient Israel: Sociological, Anthropological and Political Perspectives*. Edited by Ronald E. Clements. Cambridge: Cambridge University, 1989.
Whitney, J. T. '"Bamoth" in the Old Testament'. *TynB* 30 (1979): 125–47.
Whybray, Roger N. *The Succession Narrative: A Study of II Samuel 9-20; I Kings 1 and 2*. London: SCM, 1968.

Wildavsky, Aaron. *Moses as Political Leader*. Jerusalem: Shalem, 2005.
Williams, David S. 'Once Again: The Structure of the Narrative of Solomon's Reign'. *JSOT* 86 (1999): 49–66.
Williams, J. G. 'The Prophetic "Father"'. *JBL* 85 (1966): 344–8.
Williamson, H. G. M. *Israel in the Book of Chronicles*. Cambridge: Cambridge University Press, 1977.
Willis, John T. 'David and Zion in the Theology of the Deuteronomistic History: Theological Ideas in 2 Samuel 5–7'. Pages 125–40 in *David and Zion: Biblical Studies in Honor of J. J. M. Roberts*. Edited by Bernard F. Batto and Katheryn L. Roberts. Winona Lake, IN: Eisenbrauns, 2004.
Wilson, Ian D. *Kingship and Memory in Ancient Judah*. Oxford: Oxford University Press, 2017.
Wilson, Robert R. 'Unity and Diversity in the Book of Kings'. Pages 293–310 in *A Wise and Discerning Mind: Essays in Honor of Burke O. Long*. Edited by Saul M. Olyan and Robert C. Culley. Providence, RI: Brown Judaic Studies, 2000.
Wimsatt, William K., and Monroe C. Beardsley. 'The Intentional Fallacy'. Pages 3–18 in *The Verbal Icon: Studies in the Meaning of Poetry*. Edited by William K. Wimsatt. Lexington, KY: University of Kentucky Press, 1954.
Wissmann, Felipe Blanco. '"He Did What Was Right": Criteria of Judgment and Deuteronomism in the Books of Kings'. Pages 241–60 in *Pentateuch, Hexateuch, or Enneateuch? Identifying Literary Works in Genesis through Kings*. Edited by Thomas B. Dozeman, Thomas Römer and Konrad Schmid. AIL. Atlanta, GA: SBL, 2011.
Wöhrle, Jakob, 'The Un-Empty Land: The Concept of Exile and Land in P'. Pages 189–206 in *The Concept of Exile in Ancient Israel and its Historical Contexts*. Edited by Ehud Ben Zvi and Christoph Levin. New York: de Gruyter, 2010.
Wolff, Hans W. 'The Kerygma of the Deuteronomic Historical Work'. Pages 83–100 in *The Vitality of Old Testament Traditions*. Atlanta, GA: John Knox, 1982.
Wray Beal, Lissa M. *The Deuteronomist's Prophet: Narrative Control of Approval and Disapproval in the Story of Jehu (2 Kings 9 and 10)*. New York: T&T Clark International, 2007.
Wray Beal, Lissa M. *1&2 Kings*. AOTC. Grand Rapids, MI: IVP, 2014.
Wright, Christopher J. H. *God's People in God's Land: Family, Land, and Property in the Old Testament*. Carlisle: Paternoster, 1997.
Würthwein, Ernst. *Die Bücher der Könige: 1 Könige 1–16*. ATD 11/1. Göttingen: Vandenhoeck & Ruprecht, 1977.
Würthwein, Ernst, and Alexander A. Fischer. *The Text of the Old Testament: An Introduction to the Biblia Hebraica*. 3rd ed. Translated by Errol F. Rhodes. Grand Rapids, MI: Eerdmans, 2014.
Yadin, Y. 'Solomon's City Wall and Gate at Gezer'. *Israel Exploration Journal* 8 (1958): 80–6.
Young, Ian. 'The "Northernisms" of the Israelite Narratives in Kings'. *ZA* 8 (1995): 63–70.
Young, Ian. 'Evidence of Diversity in Pre-Exilic Judahite Hebrew'. *Hebrew Studies* 38 (1997): 7–20.
Young, Ian, Robert Rezetko and Martin Ehrensvärd. *Linguistic Dating of Biblical Texts: An Introduction to Approaches and Problems*. London: Equinox, 2008.
Young, Robb A. *Hezekiah in History and Tradition*. VTSup 155. Leiden: Brill, 2017.

Younger Jr., K. Lawson. 'The Figurative Aspect and the Contextual Method in the Evaluation of the Solomonic Empire (1 Kgs 1–11)'. Pages 157–75 in *The Bible in Three Dimensions: Essays in Celebration of Forty Years of Biblical Studies in the University of Sheffield*. Edited by David J. A. Clines, Stanley E. Porter and Stephen E. Fowl. Sheffield: JSOT, 1990.

Zucker, David J. 'Elijah and Elisha: Part 1 – Moses and Joshua'. *JBQ* 40 (2012): 225–30.

Index of References

Hebrew Bible/ Old Testament

Genesis
3.5	219
6.17	105
12.7	196
14	202
15.5	81
15.18	49
22.17	49, 81
32.28	133
37.7-11	116
46.33-34	234
49.8-12	116
49.22-36	116

Exodus
1.11	96
1.14	27, 97
2.24	26, 27
7.13	219
7.22	219
8.15	219
8.19	219
9.12	219
12.28	27
19.20	196
22.11	165
23.14-17	214
24.17	196
25.1	196
25.4	196
25.7	196
25.17	196
25.23	196
25.31	196
32.11	144
34.18	214
34.21-23	214
40.3	196
40.5	196
40.19	196

Leviticus
4.2	150
6–7	109
18.3	150
18.30	150
20.23	150
24.15	150
25.10-54	174
26.34	174
26.42	27

Numbers
14.9	110
15	109
17.8-10	196
18.22	150
20.6	196

Deuteronomy
1.7-8	160
1.8	160
1.28	210
1.33	82
1.39	219
2.9	160
3.10	188
4	187
4.9	210
4.10	77, 81, 196
4.11	82
4.20	84
4.21	100
4.25-31	161
4.25-28	27
4.28	187
4.29-31	155
4.29	210
4.32-35	110
4.34	162, 187
4.35	187
4.36	187
4.38	100
4.39	187, 210
5.3	77
5.6-10	27
5.7	150
5.22	77, 81, 82
5.29	210
5.33	217
6.4-5	212, 219
6.4	86, 210
6.5	210
6.6	210
6.10	160
6.13	150
6.18	209
6.20-25	76
6.24	150
7	82
7.1-8	76
7.3-4	27, 94, 95, 115, 220
7.3	101
7.6	84
7.9-12	83
7.9	83
7.12	83

7.17	210	15.10	210	30.1-10	85, 88, 120, 155, 161
8.2	210	16.1-16	76		
8.5	210	16.1-8	27, 214		
8.7-10	110	16.1-2	214	30.1-2	210
8.8	81	16.2	160	30.2	219
8.10-14	95	16.3	214	30.5	174
8.14	210	16.6	160	30.6	88, 135, 157, 210
8.17	210	16.11	160		
9.4	210	16.18	213	30.10	210, 219
9.5	210	17	94, 119, 213, 214, 219	30.14	210
9.10	77			30.15	210
9.12	122			30.17	210, 219
10.4	77	17.2-7	213	30.18	217
10.8	166, 196	17.8-13	213	31.2	185
10.12	150, 210	17.14-20	19, 27, 204, 213	31.9	166
10.16	210			31.15	82
10.19	161	17.16-17	94	31.25-26	166
11.9	217	17.16	96, 217	32.8	160
11.13	210, 219	17.17	94, 210, 220	32.46	210
11.16	210			32.47	217
11.18	210	17.18-19	219	34.4	160
11.24	160	17.19	86	34.10-12	212
11.31-32	160	17.20	210, 212, 220, 224		
12	21, 27, 162–5, 168–70, 189, 198		213, 214	*Joshua*	
		18.1-8		1.7-8	219
		18.6-8	170	2.1	59
		18.15-22	213	2.11	186
12.1-5	168	18.22	160	2.25	102
12.5-14	214	20.3	210	5.10-11	102
12.5	160, 164	21.9	209	5.13-14	240
12.7	165	24.16	27	6.26	102, 258
12.8-11	160	26.1-11	161	8.8	50
12.8	210	26.2	160	8.27	50
12.9	100	26.16	210	10.14	102
12.10	84	26.17	150	13.16	188
12.11	160, 164	27–28	27	14.11	185
12.18	165	28–29	111	21.45	48
12.21	160, 164	28.1-14	59	22.16-19	110
12.25	209	28.4-6	174	23.14	48
12.28	209	28.6	185	24.15	174
12.29	164	28.19	185		
13.3	219	29.4	219	*Judges*	
13.18	209	29.9	220	2	85
14.23-24	160	29.18	210	2.11-13	137
15.4	100	29.24-28	60	2.14	137
15.7	210			2.16	137
15.9	210			2.18	102

3.9	102	*2 Samuel*			1.1–16.28	51, 56, 66
3.15	102	1.25	167		1.1–14.20	56
6.31-32	70	2.10	116		1.1	56
6.36	102	5.2	232, 236,		1.11-14	228
6.37	102		245		1.29	108, 158
8.22-23	204	6.2	166		1.34	243
9.7-20	204	6.21	245		1.35	116, 125,
10.10	150	7	19, 23, 27,			244
10.15	150		59, 61, 70,		1.39	244
17–21	25		166, 204		2	181, 204
17.6	210	7.1-17	19		2.3	220
21.25	210	7.2	166		2.4	19, 78, 79,
		7.4-11	209			81, 210,
1 Samuel		7.4	49			211
2	61	7.7-8	232		2.6	230
2.10	139	7.8	245		2.8-9	36, 95
2.27-36	60, 258	7.8-16	78, 121		2.9	230
2.30	61	7.10	84		2.12	81
7.6	150	7.11-16	223		2.24	211
8.1-22	19, 204	7.11	84		2.27	49, 60,
8.5	201	7.12-16	8			258
8.20	201, 241	7.12	84		2.32	116
9.11-26	167	7.13-15	59		3–11	229
9.12-25	167	7.13	60, 166,		3–10	23, 91, 93,
9.12-13	167		258			94, 175,
9.16	245	7.14-16	78			203
10.1	245	7.14-15	258		3	181, 218,
10.5-13	167	7.14	227			231
12	85	7.16	61, 84,		3.1–5.14	229
12.20	211		259		3.1	36, 92,
12.24	211	8	143			94–6
13.4	211	11–20	91, 211		3.2	160, 166–
13.14	245	11.1–12.25	51			70, 212
15.10	49	12.11	80		3.3-15	93
16.11	232	14.17	219		3.3	95, 113,
17.15	232	19.35	219			218
17.34	232	20.1	116, 222		3.4	168
17.36	228	20.15	107		3.5	228
21.12	211, 218	23.5	59		3.6-7	218
22.34	167	24.10	211, 218		3.6	82, 84,
23.8	107	24.11	49			211, 212
24.5	211, 218				3.7-9	227
25.22	141	*1 Kings*			3.7	185, 211,
27.1	211, 218	1–11	42			219
28.5	211, 218	1–2	91, 203,		3.8	218
35.30	245		211,		3.9	213, 218,
			229			219

3.10-13	92, 227	5.9-11 Heb.	230	7.47	230
3.12	217, 219, 230	5.9-10 Heb.	96	7.48-51	230
		5.9	230	8	41, 79-81, 92, 95, 165, 166, 175, 187, 204. 228
3.13	97	5.11-14 Heb.	96		
3.14	82, 231	5.12	59, 227, 230		
3.16-28	239				
3.28	92, 95, 230	5.13-18	95, 97		
		5.14 Heb.	230	8.1-11	215
4	175	5.15-18	229	8.1-9	81, 166
4.1-19	96	5.15	36	8.1-5	165
4.1	175	5.16	36	8.1	81
4.7-19	117	5.17-19 Heb.	166	8.3-11	194
4.7	175	5.19 Heb.	160	8.4-11	27
4.20–5.5 Heb.	81	5.21 Heb.	81, 92, 128, 230	8.5	81
4.20–5.1 Heb.	49, 92, 228			8.6	186, 187
		5.23 Heb.	230	8.7-15	181
4.20-25	81	5.26 Heb.	59, 227, 230	8.9	117, 150
4.20-21	49, 92, 228			8.10-13	82
		5.27-32 Heb.	95, 97	8.10-11	179
4.20	116	5.28 Heb.	229	8.12-53	41, 166
4.21	160, 177, 217	5.29-32 Heb.	229	8.14	81
		6–9	230	8.15-21	81, 166
4.22-24	96	6–8	62	8.15-18	211
4.24-25	97	6–7	97	8.15	49, 59, 81
4.24	175, 227	6.1-38	229	8.16	79, 166, 178
4.25	110, 116	6.1-7	181		
4.26	92, 217	6.1	81, 117	8.17	166
4.27-28	96	6.8-23	181	8.18	166
4.29-34	92	6.9	229	8.19	166
4.29-31	230	6.11-13	93, 231	8.20	59, 60, 81, 166, 211, 227, 258
4.29-30	36, 96	6.11	49, 228		
4.31-34	96	6.12	211		
4.34	230	6.14-37	230	8.21	81
5	181	6.14	229	8.22-53	85
5.1 Heb.	160, 177, 217	6.23-35	187	8.22	81
		6.23-25	186	8.23-26	82
5.2-4 Heb.	96	6.38–7.1	229	8.23-24	82, 84
5.3-5	166	6.38	229	8.23	82, 83, 186, 187
5.4 Heb.	175, 227	7	156		
5.4-5 Heb.	97	7.1-12	227, 229	8.24-26	211
5.5	160	7.1	229	8.24	49, 59, 82, 84, 92
5.5 Heb.	110, 116	7.8	92, 96		
5.6 Heb.	92, 217	7.13–8.56	229	8.25-26	82, 84, 153
5.7-8 Heb.	96	7.13-47	230		
5.7	81, 92, 128, 230	7.14	230	8.25	59, 78, 79
		7.23	36	8.26	59
5.9-14 Heb.	92	7.29-36	186, 187	8.27-53	82

292

Index of References

8.27	186–8	8.63	117	10.22	97
8.29	113, 160, 166, 186, 187	8.65 9 9.1-23	81, 143 62, 181 229	10.23-24 10.26-29 11–14	230 94 11
8.30	165	9.1-9	93	11–13	41
8.31-51	192, 193	9.1	229	11	36, 61, 93, 111, 121, 124
8.31-32	192	9.2-9	231		
8.31	165	9.2	228		
8.33-34	192, 217	9.3	180, 193	11.1-43	229
8.33	165	9.4-5	60, 78, 79	11.1-13	41
8.35-36	192	9.4	212	11.1-8	94, 155
8.35	160, 165	9.5	211	11.1-6	94
8.36	100, 175, 186, 187	9.6-9	60, 88, 94, 111, 136, 155, 175, 180, 193	11.1-3 11.1-2 11.2-4 11.2	101 92, 96 88 95, 115
8.37-40	131, 192				
8.38	192				
8.39	128	9.6-8	60–2, 259	11.3-4	219
8.41-43	131, 192	9.6	180	11.4	95, 212
8.43	128, 160, 166, 186, 187	9.7-8 9.7	178 60, 155, 156, 180, 257	11.5 11.6 11.7	98, 113 60 98, 113, 167, 168
8.44-45	192				
8.44	165, 178	9.8	60	11.9	88
8.46-53	155, 156, 161	9.9 9.15-28	180 95	11.11-13	93, 124, 231
8.46-51	120, 175, 192	9.15-19 9.15	227 97	11.11 11.12-13	228 211
8.46-49	86, 87	9.16	92, 95–7, 228	11.13	125
8.48	165, 178, 180	9.19	96	11.14 11.23	93 93
8.50	86	9.20-22	150	11.25-26	36
8.51	175	9.22-23	97	11.25	93
8.52	186, 187	9.22	117	11.26	36
8.53	115, 175, 219	9.23 9.24–10.25	36 229	11.29-40 11.29-39	121 37, 41, 79
8.54-61	126	9.24-25	36	11.29-36	259
8.55	81	9.24	92, 96	11.29	228
8.56-61	84	9.25	165, 227	11.30-31	124
8.56	49, 84, 92	10.3-10	92	11.31-39	61
8.57	88	10.4	230	11.32-39	211
8.58	84, 88, 212	10.6-8 10.9	230 128, 228	11.32-36 11.32	204 198
8.60	186, 187	10.14-25	229	11.33	209
8.61	84, 210, 212	10.18-20 10.21-27	97 227	11.34 11.36	125 19, 61, 78, 125, 166, 198
8.62-66	165, 215	10.21	92, 97, 230		
8.62-64	227				

11.38	61, 164, 209	13.24	71	15.14	167, 209, 212
11.39	37, 61, 258	13.26	50	15.23-24	66
		13.28	71	15.23	212
		14–16	53	15.25-26	66
11.40	36	14	36, 37	15.25	215
11.41	92	14.1-18	37, 61	15.27-28	61
12–14	121	14.6-11	259	15.29	50, 141, 259
12	22, 36, 42, 97, 98, 126, 148	14.6	113		
		14.7-16	136, 147		
		14.7	125, 244	15.31-32	66
12.1–16.27	65	14.8-9	122	15.33-34	66
12.1-24	222	14.8	124, 209	16.1-4	259
12.4	27, 97, 117, 223	14.9	37, 113	16.1	49, 72
		14.10-11	141	16.2	125, 244
12.10-11	223	14.12-13	61, 259	16.3	149
12.14-16	117	14.14	61, 259	16.4	72, 141
12.14	223	14.15-16	61, 259	16.5-7	66
12.15	259	14.16	150, 215	16.8	66
12.16-19	125	14.17-18	259	16.9-20	72
12.16	27, 116, 222, 223	14.18	50	16.11-13	63, 72
		14.19-20	66	16.11	141
12.17	117, 126, 149	14.19	212, 217	16.12	50, 259
		14.21–16.28	56	16.14	66
12.18	223	14.21-31	55	16.15	66
12.19	126	14.21-24	66	16.20	66
12.20	66	14.21	55, 166, 204	16.21-22	66
12.21	124, 223			16.23-26	66
12.24	122, 126	14.22-24	150	16.23	38
12.26-28	121	14.22	215	16.24	98
12.26	124	14.23-24	168	16.27-28	66
12.28-33	122	14.23	168	16.27	228
12.28	27	14.24	113, 175	16.28	67
12.31	113, 167, 168	14.29-31	66	16.29–22.40	65
		15–16	55	16.29-33	68
13–16	42	15.1-5	66	16.29	51, 55, 56
13	45, 49	15.4-5	211	16.31-33	136
13.2-3	61	15.4	61, 78, 125, 198, 204	16.31-32	70
13.2	61, 123, 164, 244, 259			16.31	98, 100, 101
		15.5	209, 211, 212	16.32	98, 113, 150
13.3	61, 259				
13.4	71	15.7-8	66	16.33	113
13.5	61, 259	15.9-14	66	16.34	27, 50, 102, 258
13.6	71, 144	15.11	208, 209		
13.20	49	15.12-14	209	17–19	99
13.21	259	15.13	150	17	21, 42, 128, 181
13.24-26	259				

17.1	194, 259	18.36-37	123, 193,	20.32	238
17.2-7	99		194	20.34	238
17.2	49	18.39	86, 101,	20.29-30	188
17.5	50		188	20.35	123, 143,
17.6-23	66	18.40	99		188, 194
17.8-16	99, 194	18.41-46	99, 194	20.38-43	194
17.8	49, 149	18.45	259	20.43	241
17.9	99	19	65, 141,	21	100, 238
17.12	128		145, 181	21.3	100, 175
17.14	182, 259	19.1	62, 86	21.4-5	241
17.15	100	19.3	69, 100	21.4	175
17.16	50, 259	19.10	98, 101,	21.5	100
17.17-24	99, 194,		123, 139,	21.7	100
	257		142, 169,	21.8	100
17.20	193		217	21.10	100
17.22	102, 193	19.14	98, 101,	21.13	100
17.24	128, 194		123, 139,	21.15	100, 175
18–19	134		142, 169,	21.16	175
18	46, 62, 70,		217	21.17-19	100
	133	19.15-18	55, 137,	21.17	49
18.1-19	237		139–41	21.18	175
18.1	49, 196,	19.15-16	139	21.19	175
	259	19.15	55, 140,	21.20-26	100
18.3	131		182	21.20-21	196
18.4	99, 139	19.16-18	62	21.20	98, 238
18.7-16	98	19.16	140, 243,	21.21-24	140
18.7	196		244	21.21-23	260
18.12	131	19.17-18	23, 140,	21.23	260
18.13	99, 139		141	21.24	72, 260
18.15	196, 217	19.17	63, 139,	21.25-29	86
18.17-20	99		140, 240,	21.25	99-101
18.17-18	98, 102		260	21.26	101, 113
18.18	98, 101	19.18	63, 139,	21.27-29	63, 137,
18.19	99		140, 142		260
18.21	99, 101,	19.19	99	21.28	49
	123	19.34	198	21.29	144
18.22	139, 142	20–22	21	22	46, 47,
18.24	166, 169,	20	181, 188,		181
	188, 194		189,	22.1-40	67, 238
18.26-29	99		238	22.4	63
18.27	99	20.1-22	188	22.5	47
18.29	169	20.13	194, 238	22.7	47
18.31-38	21, 165	20.15	149	22.16	194
18.31	49, 123,	20.23-25	188	22.17	236, 238,
	133	20.23	188		260
18.32	123	20.28	188, 194	22.19-23	243
		20.31	238	22.19	113

22.35	260	3.1	47	5.18	189, 190
22.38	50, 260	3.7	47, 63	5.22	123, 143,
22.39-40	68	3.11	47		194
22.39	212	3.14	47, 217	6	155
22.41-52 Heb.	67	3.17	194	6.1-6	195
22.41-51 Heb.	67	3.26-27	43	6.1-4	194
22.41-51	67	3.27	239	6.1	123, 143,
22.41-50	67	4.1-7	194, 195		194
22.41-43	68	4.1	123, 131,	6.5	196
22.42	208		143, 194	6.8-23	239
22.43	167, 209	4.8-37	257	6.9-10	240
22.44 Heb.	167	4.9-10	196	6.12	155
22.45-50	68	4.10	196	6.17	196, 217,
22.45	228	4.12	196		243
22.46 Heb.	228	4.16	196	6.18	243
22.51-53	68	4.18-37	194	6.24–7.20	194, 239
22.51	46	4.28	196	6.26-27	108, 158
22.52 Heb.	46	4.37	196	7.1-2	260
		4.38-44	194	7.6	217, 243
2 Kings		4.38-41	195	7.16	50, 260
1–3	46	4.38	123, 143,	8–11	21, 136
1	46, 238		194	8–10	141
1.3	189	4.40	102	8–9	137
1.6	189, 260	4.42-44	195	8	63
1.9-15	196	4.43	260	8.1-6	175, 194
1.9-10	196	4.44	50, 260	8.7-15	63, 141
1.13	196	5	7, 190	8.9	211
1.17-18	68	5.1-14	194, 239	8.11	261
1.17	50, 63,	5.1	108, 158,	8.13	182
	260		182, 189,	8.15	261
2–3	43		190	8.16-24	67
2	46, 68,	5.3	191	8.16-19	141
	102, 143,	5.5	191	8.16-18	68
	194, 257	5.6-7	108, 158	8.16	63
2.3-15	123	5.6	189	8.18	47, 63
2.11-12	217, 243	5.7-8	191	8.19	61, 63, 78,
2.11	196	5.7	189		125, 153,
2.15	195, 196	5.8	189		204
2.19-22	195	5.10-12	189	8.23-24	68
2.19	102, 196	5.10	260	8.24	63
2.21	260	5.11	194	8.25-27	68
2.22	260	5.12-14	191	8.26-29	141
2.23-25	43	5.14	260	8.26	67
2.24	194	5.15	128, 188–	8.28-29	260
3	46, 47, 63,		90, 194,	9–10	63, 72,
	67, 239		196		134, 141,
3.1-3	68	5.17	189, 190		242

9.1-13	63, 141	11.1-3	63	13.4-5	144	
9.1	68, 123, 143, 194	11.1	68, 221	13.4	102, 144	
		11.3	178	13.5	50, 102, 136, 137, 143, 144, 156	
9.3-12	243	11.4-20	64			
9.5	106	11.4	86			
9.6	244	11.9-20	194			
9.7-10	141, 242	11.11	106	13.6	144	
9.7	261	11.12	244	13.7	102, 142, 144	
9.14-28	141	11.14	221			
9.14-15	141, 260	11.18	221	13.8-9	68	
9.15	141	11.19-20	221	13.9	50	
9.22	242	11.20	68, 178	13.10-13	55	
9.24-26	260, 261	11.21–12.3	68	13.10-11	68	
9.24	68	12–16	42	13.11	142	
9.26	50, 260	12	55	13.12-13	68	
9.27-29	63, 68	12.2	86, 194, 208	13.14-25	257	
9.29	68			13.14-24	68	
9.30-37	141	12.3	86, 167	13.14-19	55, 64, 143, 257	
9.30-31	68	12.3 Heb.	86, 208			
9.31	63, 72	12.4 Heb.	86	13.14	257	
9.34-36	68	12.4-16	194	13.17	50, 144	
9.36-37	260	12.16	222	13.18	50	
10	141	12.17-18	55, 64, 136, 143	13.20-21	55, 257	
10.1-11	141, 260, 261			13.21	257	
		12.17	260	13.22-25	64, 257	
10.11	141	12.17 Heb.	222	13.22-24	55	
10.12-17	141	12.18-19 Heb.	55, 64, 143	13.22	102, 142, 260	
10.12-14	63					
10.14	141	12.18 Heb.	260	13.23	59, 77, 123, 144, 145, 257	
10.16	242	12.19-21	68			
10.17	50, 72, 141, 142, 260	12.24	50			
		13–15	53	13.24-25	144	
		13–14	102, 143, 145	13.25	55, 56	
10.18-28	70			13.32	50	
10.18-27	141	13	21, 42, 50, 55, 143, 144, 256	14	55, 143	
10.19	99			14.1–25.30	66	
10.21	141			14.1–17.40	65	
10.28	137, 141	13.1-9	55	14.1–15.38	56	
10.29	61, 142	13.1-6	137	14.1-4	66	
10.30	64, 142, 228, 242, 261	13.1-3	68	14.1	55	
		13.1	50	14.3	208	
		13.2-3	144	14.4	167	
10.31	142	13.2	26, 50, 142	14.11	69	
10.32-33	137, 141			14.15-16	68	
10.32	63, 260	13.3-4	143	14.18-22	66	
11	42, 47, 55, 246	13.3	102, 142, 260	14.19	221	
				14.21	221	

14.23-24	66	16.3-4	168	17.17	113, 149,
14.24	142	16.3	108, 113,		150
14.25	27, 50,		150, 175	17.18-19	149, 151
	143, 261	16.4	113	17.18	149, 151
14.26	102, 142	16.5	107, 108	17.19-20	111
14.27	102, 108,	16.7	108	17.19	151, 153
	135, 144,	16.8	105, 108	17.20	89, 137,
	145, 158	16.9	108, 109		149, 151,
14.28-29	66	16.10	108, 109		257
15–19	103, 104	16.12-15	109	17.21-24	147
15	55, 104,	16.19-20	66	17.21-23	259
	106	17–19	136	17.21	117, 124
15.1-4	66	17	22, 41, 42,	17.22	149
15.4	167		62, 104,	17.23	130, 177,
15.5	221		120, 127,		180, 199
15.6-7	66		131, 133,	17.24-51	131
15.8-9	66		147, 151	17.24-41	7
15.10-12	66, 261	17.1-6	103	17.24-28	103, 128
15.12	64	17.1-5	147	17.24	129, 133
15.13	66	17.1-2	66	17.25-41	128, 147
15.14-15	66	17.5-6	177	17.25-33	129
15.16-22	103	17.5	66	17.25	131
15.16-18	66	17.6-20	113	17.26	179
15.16	106, 108	17.6-7	148	17.28	62, 131,
15.19-21	105	17.6	147, 148		132, 180
15.19	103, 105,	17.7-24	175	17.29-34	128
	106, 177	17.7-23	41	17.30-31	133
15.20	105	17.7-20	136, 147,	17.32-33	131, 168
15.21-22	66		149	17.33-34	129, 132
15.23-24	66	17.7-8	27, 149,	17.33	129, 132
15.25-26	66		150	17.34-40	120, 129,
15.27-31	103	17.7	114, 148,		130
15.27-28	66		150, 215	17.34-35	130
15.29	106	17.8	113, 150,	17.34	129–33
15.30-31	66		175	17.35-39	131
15.32-35	66	17.9-12	149, 150	17.35	129-31
15.35	167	17.9	113	17.36	131, 133
15.36-38	66	17.10-12	137, 168	17.37-38	150
15.37	177	17.11	113	17.37	129, 130
15.38	38, 51, 55,	17.13-17	150	17.39	131
	56	17.13-16	149, 150	17.41	128, 129
16	55, 106,	17.13-14	23	17.43	131
	108, 194	17.13	150, 243	18–25	42
16.1–25.30	51, 56	17.15	89, 91,	18–20	27, 103,
16.1-20	65, 103,		113, 115		152, 203,
	106	17.16	70, 113,		216
16.1-4	66		150		

18–19	104, 110, 151, 155, 216	19.19	186, 187	21.4	112, 113, 166
		19.20	186, 187		
		19.21-28	104	21.5	113
18	110	19.21-22	183	21.6	150
18.3-6	86	19.21	182	21.7-8	211
18.3	208, 216, 219	19.22	196	21.7	112, 113
		19.23-24	183	21.8	112, 175
18.4	168	19.23	182, 183	21.9	113, 114
18.5	151, 216	19.24	183	21.10-15	112, 261
18.6	216	19.25-28	183	21.11	113, 114, 215
18.7	110, 232	19.25	184, 185		
18.9-12	151	19.26	184	21.12-15	155
18.13	151	19.27	184, 185	21.12	113
18.17-35	182	19.28	184, 185	21.13	113
18.19-25	110, 152, 216	19.29-31	134, 153, 158	21.14	112, 114, 151, 155
18.19	111	19.30-31	156	21.15-17	261
18.20	110, 111	19.31	151	21.15	112, 114
18.21	110, 111	19.32-34	232	21.16	112, 113, 150
18.22	110, 111, 152	19.32-33	261		
		19.34	61, 151, 153, 211	21.18-20	261
18.24	110, 111			21.23	221
18.28-35	110, 152	19.35-37	112	21.24	221
18.30	111	19.35-36	111, 261	22–23	176, 246
18.31-35	216	19.35	71, 108, 136, 158	22.2	86, 208
18.31-32	110			22.8-14	194
18.33-35	110, 152	19.37	111, 261	22.8	163
18.33	182	20	155	22.10	86
18.34	133	20.1-11	71	22.11	86, 219
18.35	152	20.3	213, 216, 219	22.13	86, 219
19	182, 216			22.15-20	49
19.2-4	194	20.4	49	22.16-20	86, 155
19.4	134, 151	20.5	125, 244, 261	22.16	86
19.6-7	261			22.18-19	86
19.9-13	185	20.6	103, 153, 211	22.18	219
19.9	261			22.19	86, 219
19.10-13	110, 152	20.9-10	261	23.2-4	194
19.10	111	20.11	261	23.2	86
19.11-12	110	20.12	261	23.3	86
19.15-19	185	20.16-18	86, 155, 261	23.4-20	179
19.15	165, 185–7			23.4-7	169, 179
		21.2-9	112	23.4-5	70
19.16	186, 187	21.2	113, 114, 175	23.5	169
19.17-18	185			23.8-12	179
19.17	185	21.3	70, 86, 113	23.8-9	170
19.18	143, 187, 188			23.9	170
		21.4-7	166, 204	23.13-20	179

23.13	169	25.1-7	177	17.9	209
23.15-20	62, 119, 259	25.3	222	19.2-3	123
		25.8-21	261	21.12-15	123
23.15	123, 169	25.8	177	25.7-11	123
23.16	50	25.9-12	177	28.23	108
23.19-20	167	25.9-11	259	29–31	216
23.19	169	25.11-12	177	30.1-12	123
23.20	169	25.11	155, 156	30.11	123
23.21	86	25.12	155	33.10-13	112
23.24	194	25.13-17	62, 156, 177	33.11	103
23.25-26	86	25.18-20	177		
23.25	86, 212, 213, 219	25.19	222	*Ezra*	
		25.21	177	4.2	129
23.26-27	87, 112	25.22-26	179		
23.27	166, 178	25.22	155, 179	*Nehemiah*	
23.29	49, 103	25.26	155, 179	1.5	83
23.30	56, 221, 244, 261	25.27-30	62, 156, 176, 249	9.32	83
23.31–25.30	56	25.27	252	*Psalms*	
23.31–24.7	176	25.28	252	2	203
23.31	222	25.29	252	2.7	108
23.33	177			2.8	173
23.35	177, 222	*3 Kingdoms (LXX)*		18	203
24–25	19, 78, 103, 136, 155, 172, 175–7	2.22	35	22.23	151
		2.23–21.43	35	23	232
		2.35	35-37	68.17	196
		3.1–21.43	35	72	203
24.2-4	89	11.26	36	76.12	245
24.2-3	261	11.29-39	37	76.13 Heb.	245
24.2	50	12.24	35-37	77.16	133
24.3	112, 177, 178	22.1	35	78.70-71	232
				89	203
24.7	177			89.29	83
24.8–25.7	176	*4 Kingdoms (LXX)*		93.2	196
24.8-17	172	25.30	35	105.6	133
24.8	252			106.45	83
24.9-10	252	*1 Chronicles*		110	202, 203
24.10-17	177	16.13	133	137.4	161
24.12	156	29.22	223		
24.13	156			*Isaiah*	
24.14-16	156	*2 Chronicles*		6.1	196
24.14	155, 156	6.14	83	7	106
24.18-20	111	8.11	92	7.1	106, 107
24.20	199	11.13-17	123	7.2	107
25	27, 62, 177	15.9-10	123	7.3	107
		17–20	67	7.6	106
25.1-21	172	17.3	209	9	244

11	244	11.23	179
29.6	196	20.29	168
36–39	27, 152	28.2	245
36.2	107	34.33	232
37.4	134	36.26	135, 157
37.16	186	37.1-14	256
37.30-32	134	37.24	232
40–55	161	47.13–48.29	77
40.10-11	232		
44.6	34	*Daniel*	
44.28–45.1	156	9.4	83
45.25	151		
66.15	196	*Micah*	
		4.14 Heb.	235
Jeremiah		5.1	235
2.5	89		
2.7	174, 175	*Habakkuk*	
3.18	105	3.8	196
3.19	175		
7.31	168	*Zephaniah*	
9.26	135, 157	1.8	235
16.18	174		
19.5	168	*Zechariah*	
23.5-6	244	9.9	235
24.7	135, 157		
25.9	105	*Malachi*	
29.1	252	3.6	133
29.5-7	252		
30.9	244	NEW TESTAMENT	
31.31-34	87	*Matthew*	
31.33	135, 157	1.1	119
31.37	151	12.23	119
32.8	174		
32.35	163, 168	*James*	
32.39-41	135, 157	5.16-17	193
39	27		
48.35	168	INSCRIPTIONS	
52	27	*Ketef Hinnom Amulet*	
		1	82
Ezekiel			
1.4	196		
1.13	196		
1.15	196		
2.3	110		
3.7	135, 157		
6.3-6	168		
11.19	135, 157		

Index of Authors

Ackroyd, P. R. 3, 85
Ahituv, S. 83
Albright, W. F. 121
Alt, A. 245
Alter, R. 4, 9, 15
Amit, Y. 3, 4, 48, 53, 93, 100
Anderson, A. A. 232
Anderson, B. 5, 6, 8, 76, 159, 179
Anderson, J. A. 5
Angel, H. 98–100, 188, 237, 238, 243
Ansburry, C. B. 30
Arnold, B. T. 29, 121, 134
Assmann, J. 225
Aster, S. Z. 5, 152, 183
Athas, G. 211
Auld, A. G. 24, 25, 61, 211
Avioz, M. 23, 26, 112, 204

Baines, J. 202, 225–7, 230, 231
Bakhtin, M. 45
Balentine, S. E. 192
Bar-Efrat, S. 9, 53
Barker, P. A. 210
Barstad, H. M. 161
Bartholomew, C. G. 8, 10, 159
Beale, G. K. 230
Beardsley, M. C. 13
Ben Zvi, E. 4, 34, 123, 125
Bergen, R. D. 13, 15
Bergen, W. J. 241, 242
Berlin, A. 9, 15, 83
Berlyn, P. J. 98
Berman, J. 10, 76, 223
Berner, C. 26
Berrigan, D. 10
Bess, H. S. 173
Blenkinsopp, J. 10, 91, 211
Block, D. I. 8, 76, 161, 162, 165, 174, 180, 210, 243

Bodner, K. 7, 10, 11, 43, 46, 50, 64, 93, 101, 102, 122, 128, 139, 142, 175, 181, 194, 223, 227, 230
Bostock, D. 110, 151, 152, 216
Bosworth, D. A. 45
Botha, P. J. 104
Brettler, M. Z. 13, 43, 83, 93, 122, 147–50, 218, 227, 229
Brodie, T. L. 64
Bronner, L. 99
Brown, A. M. 173
Brueggemann, W. A. 11, 41, 44, 47, 64, 81, 95, 202, 207, 218, 225, 236, 239–42
Brunner, H. 97
Burney, C. F. 40, 69, 148, 149

Campbell, A. F. 22, 141, 142, 164, 240
Canciano, F. 97
Carr, D. M. 32
Carroll, R. P. 172
Cazelles, H. 202
Childs, B. S. 9, 186
Clark, W. M. 173
Clements, R. E. 185, 203
Clifford, R. J. 121
Coakley, J. 3, 4, 8, 74, 88–92, 159
Cogan, M. 31, 83, 95, 98, 99, 101, 102, 104–9, 112, 126, 128–30, 137, 139, 141, 143, 147, 149, 150, 152, 162, 165, 167–70, 173, 177, 179, 180, 182, 185, 186, 188–91, 193, 194, 223, 238, 243
Cohn, R. L. 41–3, 48, 50, 55, 64, 65, 68, 70, 98, 110, 112, 113, 142, 143, 147, 151, 176, 179, 189, 190, 237
Cortese, E. 208
Cross, F. M. 9, 20, 40, 41, 78, 120, 121, 147, 176, 204, 212, 213, 244, 246
Crüsemann, F. 206
Cudworth, T. D. 80
Currid, J. D. 92, 97, 227

Davies, E. W. 173
Davies, J. A. 93, 94, 218, 219, 227, 230
Davies, P. R. 14, 29
Day, J. 202, 203, 212
de Vries, S. J. 60, 139, 168, 243
Delaney, D. 159
Delitzsch, F. 118
Dever, W. G. 30, 96
Dietrich, W. 21, 23, 30, 147
Dittmann, H. 134
Downing, F. G. 51
Droge, A. J. 163
Dubovský, P. 103–6, 110, 112, 182
Dumbrell, W. J. 80
Dus, J. 107
Dutcher-Walls, P. 11, 100

Effa, A. 190
Ehrensvärd, M. 69
Elazar, D. 10, 75–7
Ellington, J. E. 83, 148
Ellis, M. deJ. 233, 235
Engnell, I. 202
Eriksen, T. H. 127
Esler, P. F. 11
Evans, C. D. 90, 122
Evans, P. S. 45, 104, 110, 182

Fischer, A. A. 35
Fishbane, M. A. 83
Fokkelman, J. P. 15
Frankel, D. 8, 129, 130, 160, 180, 186, 187, 200
Frankfort, H. 121
Freedman, D. N. 79
Frei, H. W. 15
Fretheim, T. E. 41, 48, 141, 143, 176, 190–2, 211, 239
Friedman, R. E. 79, 213
Frisch, A. 43
Fritz, V. 64, 190

Galil, G. 29
Garsiel, M. 99, 211
Gerbrandt, G. E. 202, 204, 207, 215–17
Gibson, J. C. L. 107, 132, 140
Gileadi, A. 79
Gilmour, R. 4, 10, 17, 43–6, 51, 72, 194, 243

Gnuse, R. K. 10
Goldingay, J. 119, 211
Goldstein, J. 147, 150
Goldsworthy, G. 6, 118
Gordon, R. P. 26, 218
Goswell, G. 208, 209, 211, 215
Gotom, M. 228
Gottwald, N. K. 5, 8, 202, 203
Grant, J. A. 220
Gray, J. 121, 129, 141, 147, 168
Green, A. R. 97
Green, B. 45
Greenberg, M. 31, 75
Greenwood, K. 67, 98, 228
Gregory, R. 99, 139, 196
Gressmann, H. 134
Grosby, S. E. 10
Gunkel, H. 99
Gutman, I. 112

Habel, N. C. 8, 77, 94, 101, 173–5, 204
Hagedorn, A. C. 11
Halbertal, M. 7, 10
Halpern, B. 13, 15, 19, 20, 78–80, 96, 111, 112, 176, 206, 208, 244–6
Hamilton Jr., J. M. 118
Hamilton, M. W. 4, 5, 17, 205, 207, 228, 235
Hankins, D. 11, 44, 47, 202, 236, 240–2
Hardmeier, C. 163
Hardy II, H. H. 163
Hasel, G. F. 134, 135, 139, 143, 145
Hastings, A. 2, 75
Hauser, A. J. 99, 139, 196
Hayes, J. H. 203
Hays, J. D. 93, 94, 218
Hazony, Y. 11, 232
Heaton, E. W. 92, 97, 135, 227
Heim, K. M. 201, 234
Henige, D. 163
Hens-Piazza, G. 48, 64
Hess, R. S. 1, 29, 43, 103, 110
Hobbs, T. R. 3, 143, 144, 148, 152, 156, 170, 177, 180, 182, 185, 191, 193
Holmes, S. 7, 10
Hooke, S. H. 202
Hoppe, L. J. 85–7
Howard-Brook, W. 10
Huizinga, J. 12

Hunt, A. W. 45
Hurowitz, V. A. 121, 225, 226
Hutton, J. M. 181
Hwang, J. 30
Hweio, H. 127
Hyman, R. T. 104, 110, 152

Irvine, S. A. 108
Ishida, T. 221

Janowski, B. 44
Janzen, D. 3, 85, 87, 104, 111, 153, 155, 246
Japhet, S. 123
Jensen, H. J. L. 211
Jeon, Y. H. 93, 97
Jonker, L. C. 10
Joosten, J. 10
Joseph, A. L. 4, 13, 16, 69, 122, 208–10, 212, 213, 215
Joüon, P. 88, 183

Kang, J. J. 81, 93, 218
Kaplan, K. J. 10
Kartveit, M. 128, 129, 147
Kass, L. R. 11
Kaufman, P. I. 3, 89, 90
Kaufmann, Y. 165
Keil, C. F. 118
Keys, G. 26
Knapp, A. 203, 211, 224
Knauf, E. A. 24
Knoppers, G. N. 20, 22–4, 30, 32, 64, 78, 80, 81, 94, 95, 119, 121, 122, 126, 129, 133, 162, 164–6, 169, 191, 192, 206, 207, 210, 212–14, 217, 225, 246
Konkel, A. H. 103
Köstenberger, A. J. 118
Kramer, S. N. 226
Kratz, R. G. 20, 30

Laato, A. 78, 103, 202, 205, 206, 221, 244
Lamb, D. T. 141, 142, 241
Lambert, W. G. 5, 201, 202, 224–7, 232–5
Laniak, T. S. 232–4
Lasine, S. 112, 113, 122, 190, 215
Lee, S.-W. 205

Leeman, J. 8, 159
Leithart, P. J. 42, 86, 93–7, 99, 101, 102, 111, 122, 156, 176, 189, 191, 193, 194, 211, 218, 219, 227, 230, 237, 243
Lemaire, A. 96, 129, 176, 227
Leuchter, M. 194
Levenson, J. D. 78, 155, 206
Levin, C. 3, 24–6, 171–3, 179
Levine, B. A. 5
Levinson, B. M. 10, 75, 205, 207, 225, 226
Lewis, R. 190
Lindblom, J. 194
Linville, J. R. 2, 14–16, 19, 25, 29, 79, 86, 116, 122, 124–8, 131, 245, 246
Liverani, M. 5, 183
Lohfink, N. 76, 167, 170, 213, 220
Long, B. O. 41, 43, 147, 152, 181, 189, 190, 208
Long, J. C. 44, 239
Long, V. P. 222
Longman III, T. 222
Lovell, N. H. 1, 28, 59–61, 78, 85–7, 97, 143, 145, 147–51, 155, 219, 236
Lundquist, J. M. 225
Lunn, N. P. 169, 195–7

MacDonald, J. 147
MacDonald, N. B. 82, 83
Machinist, P. 4, 5
McBride, S. D. 7, 75, 76, 213
McCarthy, D. J. 206
McConville, J. G. 2, 3, 7, 10, 17, 25, 41, 75–7, 79, 80, 87, 88, 94, 97, 116, 119, 127, 153, 161, 162, 164, 175, 186, 206, 210, 213, 214, 220, 227, 237, 247
McKay, J. W. 108, 109
McKenzie, S. L. 20–2, 33, 64, 69, 147, 169, 176, 240
Mead, J. K. 49
Mendelsohn, I. 206
Mendenhall, G. E. 76, 207
Mettinger, T. N. D. 164, 207, 244, 245
Meyer, L. V. 135
Meyers, C. 94, 202, 230
Millard, A. R. 97, 227
Miller, R. D. 93, 218
Millgram, H. I. 3
Montgomery, J. A. 128, 129, 148, 168

Moore, M. S. 242
Morgenstern, M. 10
Mtshiselwa, N. 11
Mullen, E. T. 2, 6, 10, 14, 92, 93, 119
Müller, W. E. L. 134, 135, 139
Muraoka, T. 88, 183
Murray, D. F. 3, 155

Na'aman, N. 87, 92, 106–8, 126
Nam, R. S. 155
Nelson, R. D. 3, 4, 20, 79, 85, 94, 112, 147, 151–3, 186, 204, 212–14, 220
Newsom, C. A. 45
Nicholson, E. W. 170
Niemann, H. 96
Nihan, C. 205
Nissinen, M. 160, 179, 204
Noble, J. T. 194
Noll, K. L. 25
Noth, M. 1, 22, 28, 40, 41, 44, 85, 88, 147, 148, 165, 205, 245
Notley, R. S. 103

O'Brien, M. A. 49, 164, 240
O'Brien, P. T. 118
O'Connor, M. P. 107, 132, 140, 183
O'Donovan, O. 6, 10, 89, 160
O'Kennedy, D. F. 30, 192, 193
Ollenburger, B. C. 185, 203
Olley, J. W. 43, 55, 59, 104, 110, 111, 143, 152, 153, 229, 242
Olmstead, A. T. 108
Olson, D. T. 45
Omanson, R. L. 83, 148
Oritz, S. M. 96
Östborn, G. 99
Oswalt, J. N. 107
Otto, S. 22, 43, 64, 240
Oz, A. 48

Pakkala, J. 121
Pangle, T. L. 10
Parker, B. J. 8, 226, 227
Parker, K. I. 42, 93, 218
Parshall, P. 190
Pat-El, N. 69
Paynter, H. 43, 45, 62, 64, 236, 242
Perlitt, L. 75
Person, R. F. 24, 27, 29, 31, 32, 34
Pettinato, G. 97

Pietsch, M. 49, 87
Pohlmann, K.-F. 171, 172
Polzin, R. M. 24, 26, 45
Porten, B. 42, 50
Porter, J. R. 194
Preuss, H. D. 134, 139
Provan, I. W. 3, 19–21, 23, 30, 41, 56, 78, 97, 102, 119, 122, 126, 147, 151, 163, 167, 176, 189, 208, 211–13, 217, 222, 223, 247
Pyper, H. S. 93, 218

Rad, G. von 2, 3, 48–50, 75, 78, 85, 87, 94, 101, 134, 135, 137, 139, 145, 164, 173, 174, 190, 191, 206, 210, 211, 246, 258
Rainey, A. F. 103
Rasmussen, C. G. 188
Ray, J. D. 96
Redford, D. B. 96, 97
Reed, W. L. 45
Reimer, D. J. 10
Rendsburg, G. A. 22, 29, 69
Rezetko, R. 69
Richardson, S. 233
Richter, S. L. 21, 25, 28, 30, 103, 164–6, 178
Roberts, J. J. M. 202–4, 207
Robker, J. M. 236
Rofé, T. C. 190
Römer, T. C. 21, 24, 26, 30, 34, 64, 163, 214
Rösel, H. N. 147, 150
Roth, W. 238
Rothman, E. 45
Rudman, D. 104, 110, 152
Rutersworden, U. 76, 213

Said, E. W. 3, 4
Satterthwaite, P. E. 43, 46, 194, 237
Savran, G. 42, 55, 62, 64
Schenker, A. 35, 36
Schilling, A. 134
Schmid, K. 112
Schniedewind, W. M. 69, 113
Schwartz, M. B. 10
Scott, R. B. Y. 97
Seibert, E. A. 91
Shanks, H. 29
Shemesh, Y. 46, 236, 237, 240

Shepherd, T. 51
Sivan, D. 69
Smelik, K. A. D. 109
Smend, R. 20
Smith, A. D. 2, 5–8, 74, 76, 77, 88–90, 116, 127, 159, 160
Soggin, J. A. 221–3
Span, J. 190
Sternberg, M. 9, 11, 15, 56
Stipp, H. J. 172, 240
Storey, D. 159
Swagman, C. F. 127
Sweeney, M. A. 1, 2, 20, 22, 35, 36, 41, 43, 60, 64, 79, 81, 82, 107, 109, 112, 117, 119–21, 128, 130, 137, 141, 143, 144, 147, 149, 151, 152, 163, 166, 168, 180, 185, 186, 193, 194, 204, 205, 212, 215, 221, 239, 244
Sweet, R. F. G. 226, 227

Tadmor, H. 101, 102, 104, 108, 129, 130, 143, 149, 150, 152, 165, 170, 173, 177, 179, 182, 185, 186, 188–91, 194, 221, 222, 238
Talmon, S. 221
Talshir, D. 36, 43, 64, 69
Tamarkin, M. 127
Tanska, J. 19
Thomas, B. D. 163
Thomas, H. A. 203
Throntveit, M. A. 119
Tomes, R. 242
Tov, E. 31, 35
Travis, J. J. 190
Trebolle Barrera, J. C. 31, 32, 35
Turkanik, A. S. 35

Uehlinger, C. 170
Unterman, J. 10

Van Drunen, D. 10
Van Keulen, P. S. F. 113
Van Seters, J. 4, 12, 17, 40, 44
Van Winkle, D. W. 49
Van der Kooij, A. 31
Vancil, J. W. 232

Vanderhooft, D. S. 19, 79, 80, 96, 208
Veijola, T. 21, 23, 137, 163, 201, 204
Viviano, P. A. 147

Walsh, J. T. 10, 41–3, 49, 55, 64, 81, 93, 99, 100, 102, 104, 110, 117, 128, 139, 152, 164, 218, 237, 238
Waltke, B. K. 79, 80, 107, 132, 140, 183
Walton, J. H. 201–3, 224–6, 228, 230, 231, 235
Walzer, M. 10
Watts, J. D. 117
Webb, B. G. 25, 137
Weinfeld, M. 18, 147, 164, 165, 186, 223
Weippert, H. 24, 129, 208
Weitzman, S. 93, 218
Wellhausen, J. 121, 204, 206
Westbrook, R. 44, 239
Westermann, C. 25
White, M. 121
Whitelam, K. W. 202–4, 227, 228
Whitney, J. T. 168, 169
Whybray, R. N. 91, 211
Wildavsky, A. 10
Williams, D. S. 43, 194, 229
Williamson, H. G. M. 13, 16, 119, 123, 134
Willis, J. T. 204
Wilson, I. D. 205, 211
Wilson, R. R. 18, 19
Wimsatt, W. K. 13
Wissmann, F. B. 30, 167, 187
Wöhrle, J. 172
Wolff, H. W. 3, 85, 86, 155, 247
Wray Beal, L. M. 49, 79, 82, 97, 99–102, 109, 114, 133, 141, 143, 177, 179, 189–91, 210, 222, 225, 238, 242, 258
Wright, C. J. H. 80, 173
Würthwein, E. 30, 35, 112, 121

Yadin, Y. 97
Young, I. 69
Young, R. A. 152
Younger Jr., K. L. 92

Zucker, D. J. 196

Index of Names and Places

Abiathar 60, 258
Adonijah 60, 61, 258
Ahab 3, 10, 38, 46, 47, 55, 56, 62, 63, 65, 67, 68, 70, 72, 73, 98–103, 108, 113, 115, 131, 136–44, 146, 150, 154, 156, 157, 169, 175, 197, 208, 227, 237, 238, 240, 241, 243, 254, 260, 261
Ahaz 55, 56, 65, 66, 103, 104, 106–10, 113, 115, 168, 208, 253
Ahaziah 63, 67, 68, 141, 238, 256, 260
Ahijah 36, 37, 61, 121, 125, 136, 228
Amaziah 56, 66, 167, 208, 209, 221
Amnon 221
Amorite 101, 113
Angel of Yahweh 136, 151
Aphek 188
Aram 46, 47, 189, 236–9
Asa 66, 150, 167, 208, 209
Asherah 113, 149, 150, 168
Assyria 5, 70, 89, 103–12, 115, 129, 136, 148, 150–2, 155, 157, 182–5, 216, 251, 252, 261
Athaliah 11, 47, 63, 67, 68, 72, 86, 221, 256
Azariah 66, 167, 209, 221

Baal 46, 70, 98, 99, 101, 110, 113, 115, 121, 137–42, 145, 149, 150, 156, 169, 237, 254–6
Baasha 66, 72, 125, 141, 244, 259
Babylon 3, 8, 70, 94, 96, 98, 104, 111, 133, 136, 155, 156, 161, 172, 173, 176, 177, 179, 197, 199, 200, 222, 234, 235, 250–4, 261
Bathsheba 228
Beth-Shemesh 69
Bethel 61, 62, 123, 179

Canaan 8, 89, 101, 108, 121, 129, 130, 160, 180, 186, 187, 200, 250, 254

Damascus 103, 108, 109, 115, 140, 181, 189, 191, 253

Egypt 29, 37, 70, 89, 92, 94–8, 101, 108, 110, 114, 115, 148, 155, 157, 162, 176, 177, 179, 183, 202, 213, 214, 216, 219, 225–7, 230, 231, 234, 239, 251, 253
Elijah 3, 10, 21–3, 38, 42, 43, 55, 62–4, 68, 69, 72, 86, 91, 98–100, 102, 123, 128, 133, 134, 136, 139, 140, 142, 150, 169, 171, 181, 182, 188, 190, 193–7, 237, 238, 241, 242, 254–7, 259
Elisha 11, 17, 21–3, 38, 42–6, 51, 55, 62, 64, 68, 69, 72, 99, 101, 102, 123, 128, 134, 139, 140, 142, 143, 150, 169, 181, 182, 189, 190, 193–7, 236, 237, 239–42, 254–7
Evil-merodach 252

Geba 169, 170
Gedaliah 173, 179
Gibeah 168, 169
Gibeon 60, 218

Hazael 38, 55, 62–4, 103, 136, 137, 139–44, 157, 181, 244, 254, 257, 260
Hezekiah 3, 19–21, 23, 30, 41, 45, 56, 71, 73, 78, 85–7, 103, 104, 107, 110, 111, 119, 123, 125, 126, 128, 147, 151–3, 155, 156, 165, 167, 168, 176, 182, 185–9, 193, 201, 206, 208, 209, 211–13, 216, 217, 219, 232, 243, 244, 246, 247, 251, 256, 261
Hiram of Tyre 81, 230
Horeb 62, 77, 99, 136, 139, 181, 187, 196, 257
Hoshea 66, 103, 147, 148
Huldah 49, 86

Index of Names and Places

Isaiah 5, 10, 31, 86, 103, 104, 106–108, 112, 134, 151, 152, 161, 182, 183, 185, 186, 193, 203, 205, 244

J(eh)oram 67, 68, 141
Je(ho)ash 55, 208
Jehoahaz 55, 56, 68, 136, 137, 142–4, 176, 208, 221
Jehoiachin 3, 28, 62, 85, 172, 173, 176, 246, 252, 256
Jehoiada 86
Jehoiakim (Eliakim) 176, 177, 208, 222, 224
Jehoshaphat 46, 47, 63, 67, 68, 167, 208, 209, 238, 239, 255
Jehu 11, 38, 49, 62–4, 67, 68, 70, 72, 102, 136, 137, 139–44, 151, 157, 181, 228, 241, 242, 244, 251, 254, 256, 260, 261
Jericho 27, 102, 195, 258
Jeroboam I (son of Nebat) 136, 208
Jeroboam II 103, 136, 142–4
Jerusalem 10, 19, 36, 61, 63, 68, 71, 83, 86, 103, 107–13, 120–3, 125, 126, 134, 137, 151–3, 156, 157, 163, 166, 167, 169–71, 176–80, 182, 185, 190, 198, 201–4, 206, 216, 221, 228, 245, 251, 255, 256, 261
Jezebel 11, 63, 70, 99–102, 139, 141–3, 157, 175, 237, 238, 254, 256, 260
Jezreel 181, 260
Joash 221, 244, 256
Jordan River 189
Josiah 3, 19, 20, 22, 27, 49, 56, 61–2, 64, 73, 79, 85–8, 103, 104, 111, 112, 114, 117, 119–21, 147, 151, 153, 155, 162–5, 167, 169–71, 176, 178–80, 201, 208, 209, 212–16, 219, 221, 244, 246, 247, 251, 259, 261
Jotham 56, 66, 167, 209, 221

Manasseh 78, 86, 87, 103, 111–14, 155, 166, 208, 215, 261
Menahem 43, 66, 103, 105–8, 110, 115
Mesha 46
Micaiah 236, 238
Moab 43, 44, 67, 181, 239, 255

Naaman 7, 133, 181, 188–91, 239, 260
Naboth 100, 175, 238

Nathan 1, 23, 26, 51, 60, 61, 204, 209, 228
Nebuchadnezzar 111, 176, 177

Pekah 66, 103, 105–7

Pharaoh 27, 36, 43, 92, 96, 97, 148, 176, 177, 219, 229–31

Queen of Sheba 128, 228

Rab-Shakeh 110, 152, 182, 216
Ramoth Gilead 181
Rehoboam 37, 55, 56, 66, 98, 117, 122, 150, 208, 220, 222–4, 259
Rezin 106, 107

Samaria 72, 103, 132, 148, 172, 179, 181, 189, 191, 239, 245, 255, 256
Sennacherib 45, 103, 104, 110, 111, 132, 137, 152, 182, 185, 252, 256, 261
Shechem 37, 222, 223
Sidon 72, 99, 181
Sinai 81, 160, 196, 200, 206
Solomon 22, 23, 30, 32, 34–7, 39, 41–3, 49, 50, 56, 60–2, 73, 80–2, 84, 86, 88, 91–8, 101, 108, 111, 115, 117–20, 125, 128, 131, 136, 137, 155, 156, 160, 164–9, 175, 177, 178, 180, 186–9, 191–3, 202–6, 211–13, 215, 217–23, 227–31, 239, 244–6, 249–51, 253, 255, 258, 259
Syria 55, 72, 140, 141, 144, 181, 188–90, 244, 255

Tiglath Pileser III (Pul) 105, 106, 109
Tyre 70, 81, 230, 245

Uriah 27, 194, 209

Widow of Zarephath 128, 133

Zedekiah (Mattaniah) 111, 173, 176
Zimri 63, 66, 72, 259
Zion 70, 81, 103, 121, 151, 153, 156, 182, 185, 186, 201–4, 206, 207, 211, 212, 214, 224, 226, 227, 231, 232, 236, 247

www.ingramcontent.com/pod-product-compliance
Lightning Source LLC
Chambersburg PA
CBHW072122290426
44111CB00012B/1748